Fun Q

A Functional Introduction to Machine Learning in Q

Nick Psaris

$\vec{\sigma}$

Vector Sigma
New York

Copyright © 2020 Nick Psaris

All Rights Reserved. No part of this publication may be reproduced, stored in a retrieval system, or transmitted, in any form, or by any means, electronic, mechanical, photocopying, recording, or otherwise, without the prior consent of the publisher.

Kx and kdb+ are registered trademarks of Kx Systems, Inc.

Books may be purchased in quantity and/or special sales by contacting the publisher, Vector Sigma at sales@vector-sigma.com.

Published by: Vector Sigma, New York USA

ISBN: 978-1-7344675-0-5

10 9 8 7 6 5 4 3 2 1

In loving memory of Jasmine, who insisted on the title and challenged me to be prolific.

Contents

Preface   **xix**

1 Introduction   **1**
    1.1 Who is This Book For?   2
    1.2 How to Read This Book   2
    1.3 Getting Started   3
    1.4 What is in This Book?   5
    1.5 Naming Conventions   9

2 K-Nearest Neighbors   **11**
    2.1 K-Nearest Neighbors Example   12
    2.2 Iris Data Set   13
    2.3 Downloading Data Sets   14
    2.4 Loading Data Sets   16
    2.5 Partitioning Data   17
    2.6 Distance Metrics   20
    2.7 Norm Metrics   24
    2.8 Minimize Flipping   28

2.9	Finding K Neighbors	31
2.10	Weighted Average or Mode	32
2.11	Weighting Schemes	37
2.12	Euclidean Distance Squared	39
2.13	Pairwise Euclidean Distance Squared	40
2.14	K-Fold Cross Validation	41

3 K-Means — 45

3.1	K-Means Example	46
3.2	Centroid Initialization	50
3.3	K-Means++ Initialization	52
3.4	Lloyd's Algorithm	58
3.5	Ungrouping Clusters	60
3.6	The Elbow Method	61
3.7	Partitional Clustering	62

4 Hierarchical Agglomerative Clustering — 67

4.1	Hierarchical Agglomerative Clustering Example	68
4.2	Cluster Benchmark Data Sets	70
4.3	Dissimilarity Matrix	70
4.4	Lance-Williams Algorithm	71
4.5	Linkage Functions	73
4.6	Building Clusters	76
4.7	The Silhouette Method	78

5 Expectation-Maximization — 83

5.1	Bernoulli Distribution	84
5.2	Expectation-Maximization Algorithm	85
5.3	Binomial Distribution	86
5.4	Multinomial Distribution	92
5.5	Bernoulli Mixture Models	98
5.6	Gaussian Mixture Model	103

6 Naive Bayes — 109

- 6.1 Fit Naive Bayes 110
- 6.2 Gaussian Naive Bayes 111
- 6.3 Multinomial Naive Bayes 113
- 6.4 Binary Classification 121
- 6.5 Text Classification 125

7 Decision Trees — 131

- 7.1 Impurity Functions 132
- 7.2 Iterative Dichotomizer 3 137
- 7.3 Visualizing Decision Trees 138
- 7.4 Decision Tree Classification 141
- 7.5 Building the Decision Tree 143
- 7.6 Gain Functions 147
- 7.7 Cost Complexity Pruning 152
- 7.8 K-Fold Cross Validation 156
- 7.9 Regression Trees 159
- 7.10 One Hot 162

8 Decision Tree Ensembles — 165

- 8.1 Ensemble Example 165
- 8.2 Wisconsin Diagnosis Breast Cancer Data Set 166
- 8.3 Bootstrap Aggregation 167
- 8.4 Random Forest 169
- 8.5 Adaptive Boosting 173
- 8.6 Discrete Adaboost 174
- 8.7 AdaBoost Cross Validation 178

9 Linear Regression — 181

- 9.1 Matrices — 182
- 9.2 Matrix Operators — 183
- 9.3 Least Squares Regression — 184
- 9.4 Multi-Dimensional Least Squares — 184
- 9.5 Custom Matrix Operators — 187
- 9.6 Normal Equations — 189
- 9.7 Gradient Descent — 190
- 9.8 Linear Regression Cost — 192
- 9.9 Linear Regression Gradient — 194
- 9.10 Feature Scaling — 195
- 9.11 FMINCG — 199
- 9.12 Stopping Conditions — 201
- 9.13 Stochastic Gradient Descent — 204
- 9.14 Regularization — 208
- 9.15 Optimal Regularization — 213

10 Logistic Regression — 217

- 10.1 Logistic Regression Example — 217
- 10.2 Wisconsin Diagnosis Breast Cancer Data Set — 218
- 10.3 Sigmoid — 220
- 10.4 Log-Loss Cost — 221
- 10.5 Logistic Regression Cost — 222
- 10.6 Logistic Regression Gradient — 223
- 10.7 Optimal Regularization — 224
- 10.8 Receiver Operating Characteristic — 226
- 10.9 Area Under the Curve — 230
- 10.10 Multi-Class Classification — 231
- 10.11 One-vs.-All Classifier — 231
- 10.12 Fitting One vs. All — 232
- 10.13 Predicting One vs. All — 234

11 Neural Networks **237**

- 11.1 Perceptron 237
- 11.2 Neural Network 239
- 11.3 Neural Network Example 240
- 11.4 Neural Network Matrices Initialization 241
- 11.5 Neural Network Topology 243
- 11.6 Neural Network Weight Initialization 244
- 11.7 Neural Network Cost 245
- 11.8 Neural Network Gradient 247
- 11.9 Neural Network Activation Functions 249
- 11.10 Neural Network Cost and Gradient 252
- 11.11 Neural Network Multinomial Classification 254
- 11.12 Neural Network Regression 257

12 Recommender Systems **261**

- 12.1 MovieLens Data Set 262
- 12.2 Content-Based Filtering 265
- 12.3 Rating Data Summary 269
- 12.4 Null-Aware Aggregations 271
- 12.5 User-User Collaborative Filtering 273
- 12.6 Item-Item Collaborative Filtering 279
- 12.7 Collaborative Filtering 281
- 12.8 Collaborative Filtering Cost 282
- 12.9 Collaborative Filtering Gradient 284
- 12.10 Stochastic Gradient Descent 287
- 12.11 Alternating Least Squares 290

13 PageRank — 295

- 13.1 Adjacency Matrix — 297
- 13.2 Markov Matrix — 298
- 13.3 Google Matrix — 299
- 13.4 Power Method — 300
- 13.5 Algebraic PageRank — 301
- 13.6 Iterative PageRank — 302
- 13.7 Sparse Matrices — 303
- 13.8 Sparse Matrix Iterative PageRank — 308

14 Graphics — 313

- 14.1 ASCII plots — 314
- 14.2 Mandelbrot Set — 323
- 14.3 Portable Image Formats — 327
- 14.4 Sparklines — 334
- 14.5 Charting Stock Prices — 336

A Source Code — 339

- A.1 Utilities — 339
- A.2 Machine-Learning Algorithms — 345
- A.3 External Libraries Ported to Q — 372
- A.4 Data Libraries — 379

Index — 385

Acknowledgments — 393

About the Author — 395

List of Figures

7.1 Weather Decision Tree 141

11.1 Perceptron with Heaviside Activation 238
11.2 Neural Network with Two Hidden Layers 240

13.1 Example Web Page Links 297

14.1 Black and White Mandelbrot Set 330
14.2 Grayscale Mandelbrot Set 332

List of Equations

2.1	Manhattan Distance	22
2.2	Euclidean Distance	22
2.3	Minkowski Distance	22
2.4	Manhattan Norm	24
2.5	Euclidean Norm	25
2.6	Parameterized Norm	25
2.7	Cosine Similarity	26
2.8	Pairwise Euclidean Distance Squared	40
4.1	Lance-Williams Recursive Update	74
5.1	Binomial Likelihood	88
5.2	Binomial Maximum Likelihood Estimator	89
5.3	Multinomial Likelihood	95
5.4	Multinomial Mixture Model Maximum Likelihood Estimator	95
5.5	Bernoulli Mixture Model Likelihood	101
5.6	Binomial Mixture Model Maximum Likelihood Estimator	102
5.7	Multivariate Gaussian Likelihood	105
5.8	Multivariate Gaussian Maximum Likelihood Estimator	106
7.1	Decision Tree Cost Complexity	153
8.1	AdaBoost Strong Classifier	174
8.2	Exponential Loss	175
9.1	Normal Equations	189
9.2	Regularized Linear Regression Cost	192
9.3	Regularized Linear Regression Gradient	194
9.4	Ridge Regression	211
10.1	Sigmoid	220
10.2	Log-Loss	221

10.3	Regularized Logistic Regression Cost	222
10.4	Regularized Logistic Regression Gradient	223
11.1	Heaviside Step	238
11.2	Neural Network Cost	246
11.3	Sigmoid	249
11.4	Sigmoid Gradient	249
11.5	Hyperbolic Tangent	250
11.6	Hyperbolic Tangent Gradient	250
11.7	ReLU	251
11.8	ReLU Gradient	251
11.9	LReLU	251
11.10	LReLU Gradient	252
11.11	Softmax	254
11.12	Cross Entropy	256
12.1	Collaborative Filtering Cost	283
12.2	Collaborative Filtering Gradient	284
12.3	Matrix-Factorization Optimization	287
12.4	Matrix-Factorization Updates	288
14.1	Complex Multiplication	323

List of Examples

2.1	Distance Metrics	21
3.1	K-Means	46
3.2	K-Means Initial Clusters	47
3.3	K-Means Centroids After One Round	48
3.4	K-Means Clusters After One Round	48
3.5	K-Means Centroids After Two Rounds	48
3.6	K-Means Centroids After Three Rounds	49
3.7	K-Means Clusters After Convergence	49
3.8	Contrived K-Means	54
3.9	Sum of Squared Errors Within	61
3.10	Percentage of Total Variance	62
4.1	Large HAC Clusters	69
4.2	Silhouette I	69
4.3	Small HAS Clusters	78
4.4	Silhouette II	81
5.1	Binomial EM Confusion Matrix	91
5.2	Multinomial EM Confusion Matrix	98
5.3	MNIST Digits	99
5.4	Prototypical Digits with Random Noise	101
5.5	Prototypical Digits	103
5.6	Bernoulli Mixture Model EM Confusion Matrix	104
5.7	Gaussian Mixture Model EM Confusion Matrix	106
6.1	Naive Bayes Mistakes	113
6.2	Binary Classification Confusion Matrix	121
7.1	Mean Squared Errors	133
7.2	Misclassification	135

7.3	Entropy	136
7.4	Gini	136
8.1	Bootstrap Aggregation Accuracy	169
8.2	Random Forest Regression Training Error	170
8.3	Random Forest Regression Test Error	171
8.4	Random Forest Classification Training Error	171
8.5	Random Forest Classification Test Error	172
8.6	AdaBoost Training Accuracy	178
8.7	AdaBoost Test Accuracy	179
9.1	Sine	191
9.2	Linear Regression Cost Convergence	195
9.3	Optimal Linear Regression Regularization	214
10.1	Sigmoid	220
10.2	Log-Loss	222
10.3	Optimal Logistic Regression Regularization	225
10.4	Logistic Regression Binary Classification Confusion Matrix	226
10.5	Low Threshold Binary Classification Confusion Matrix	228
10.6	High Threshold Binary Classification Confusion Matrix	228
10.7	Discriminating Receiver Operating Characteristic	229
10.8	Non-discriminating Receiver Operating Characteristic	229
10.9	Negative Discriminating Receiver Operating Characteristic	230
10.10	MNIST Digits	232
10.11	Logistic Regression One-vs.-All Confusion Matrix	235
10.12	Incorrectly Classified MNIST Digits	236
11.1	Neural Network Multinomial Classification Confusion Matrix	242
11.2	Row-Normalized Confusion Matrix	257
11.3	Column-Normalized Confusion Matrix	258
14.1	Heat Map	317
14.2	Axis Labels	322
14.3	Black and White Mandelbrot Set	326
14.4	Gray Scale Mandelbrot Set	328

Preface

I love data. Let me clarify that. I love structured data. My first job was to administer a Sybase database and the Perl scripts that loaded client positions. I then transitioned to a trading desk where we used Visual Basic for Applications (VBA) to enter trades into a Microsoft Access database. From there, I moved to an automated trading team that stored all data in proprietary self-describing text messages.

Lucky for me, I switched to a team that used kdb+ as the data warehouse and therefore q as the programming language. Over the ensuing years, I continued to use q as my development language of choice, and spent many days—if not weeks—writing functions and C-bindings to import data from (and export data to) different formats including fixed-width binary files and proprietary middleware APIs. The goal in each case was to bring more data to the q ecosystem.

Convinced that q was the language of choice for big data analysis, I turned my attention to bringing analytics to the language as well. Data scientists often treat kdb+ as nothing more than a source of data. To accommodate the limited capacity for large data sets in languages such as R and Python, they are required to aggregate the data and, in the process, lose information. Instead of bringing summary statistics into languages that were not designed for scale, wouldn't it be better to perform the analysis directly on the data stored in kdb+?

I was first introduced to machine-learning algorithms in 2015 when a friend suggested I take the Coursera Machine Learning course[1] taught by Coursera's co-founder, Andrew Ng. After completing all the homework assignments in Octave (an open source alternative to Matlab), I decided to re-implement the whole course in q.

My goal was to push q to its limits, find its Achilles heel and keep pushing until it begged for mercy. In the process, I found the functional vector implementation of

---

[1] "Machine Learning," Coursera. [Online]. Available: https://www.coursera.org/learn/machine-learning. [Accessed: 12-Mar-2020].

many algorithms quite elegant. Others, however, were down-right embarrassing. I found that q's internal data structures were not designed for fast matrix multiplication. With carefully factored code, however, and the use of an open-source math library, the performance could be improved dramatically. I found the lack of complex data types frustrating and wished q had native sparse matrix operators. I found that transposing large matrices severely impacts performance and algorithms must be designed to prevent this. And finally, I found that q's limits on function, argument and branch length make translating code from other languages very difficult without refactoring.[2]

I became addicted to implementing machine-learning algorithms and continued to read the original papers for algorithms such as decision trees, adaptive boosting and recommender systems. As I added each new algorithm, I refactored the library to maximize code performance and reuse. I wrote each algorithm on the free 32-bit version of kdb+ and limited all interaction (including visualization) to the q terminal. To make the code suitable for inclusion in this book, all functions and comments were required to be less than 77 characters wide. I believe this constraint improved the code clarity by forcing algorithms to be refactored into functions with descriptive names.

I learned that there exists a problem domain where q implementations of machine-learning algorithms, such as k-means, perform well. Others, such as support vector machines, are best delegated to the canonical implementation written in C/C++. This book is dedicated to machine-learning algorithms implemented in pure q.

I enjoy coding in q. In fact, I truly believe coding in q is *fun*. My goal is to share this passion with you while simultaneously teaching you machine-learning algorithms and concepts as well as many q coding paradigms. Along the way, I hope you have fun too.

---

[2] Some of these limits have been relaxed with the release of kdb+ 3.6. Instructions embedded within if, do, and while branching control structures were previously limited to 255 bytecodes. This has now been extended to 65,025 bytecodes. The number of permitted constants, as well as the number local and global variables, has also been increased. The limit of 8 function arguments, however, still remains.

Chapter 1

Introduction

Data comes in many shapes: bytes, text, integral and floating. Data comes in many sizes: boolean flags, text config files, binary images and partitioned databases. Stored and ignored, data is expensive to maintain and backup. The quality of the data is only revealed once it is analyzed. And the value of the data is only determined once it is used to make and test predictions.

Analysis can take the form of visual inspection or statistical summary. Predictions are routinely performed and tested in academia and business. The goal of accurate predicting varies slightly between these two fields, however. While academia strives for truth, business searches for profit. And where there is incentive in academia to share data and analysis, business has historically held it captive.

Recent advances in computational analysis and computing power, and the reduction in storage costs, have ignited a data revolution. Whether we call it "data science", "machine learning", "deep learning" or "artificial intelligence", the combined power of data and computational analysis reconfirms that we live in the "information age".

Data is worthless if you can't extract information from it. As Clifford Stoll and Gary Schubert are quoted with saying:

> Data is not information, information is not knowledge, knowledge is not understanding, understanding is not wisdom.
>
> — Clifford Stoll and Gary Schubert

Each step along the path from data to wisdom requires the expenditure of effort and results in an increase in organization and structure. Recent developments in machine-learning techniques have enabled computers to automate the first step from data to information. The success of these algorithms can be attributed to 10 to 100-fold improvement in algorithm design, an increase in computer speeds by at least 100-fold and an explosion in the amount of data (up to 1,000-fold).[1]

Given the universal availability of algorithms and hardware, a remaining problem is accessing the volumes of data. Kdb+ is known not only for its database performance, but also for its flexible programming language q. Would it not make sense, therefore, to bring the machine-learning algorithms *to* the data stored in a kdb+ database?

1.1 Who is This Book For?

This book assumes an introductory knowledge of kdb+. It also assumes you have q installed (or know how to install it). Most q developers use the language to build tickerplants, databases or CEP engine. Few use q as an analytics platform, however. This is beginning to change. This book is for the community of developers who, like me, have fallen in love with programming in q and want to extend their computing knowledge into the world of big data and machine-learning algorithms while simultaneously learning how to write better q. It is also for the data scientists who find that the data they need—or want—to analyze is increasingly being stored in a kdb+ database. Using their existing machine-learning knowledge, they will be able to learn q programming idioms that will improve their ability to write efficient code.

1.2 How to Read This Book

This book was written to be read linearly from beginning to end. All code required to run the examples in these chapters is explained when first introduced. You may, of course, jump to future chapters if you are comfortable using functions without understanding their implementation. The last chapter, Chapter 14 [313], is an exception and can be read at any time you are looking for some fun.

---

[1] E. Brynjolfsson and A. McAfee, "What's Driving the Machine Learning Explosion?," *Harvard Business Review*, 18 Jul 2017.

I am excited that you purchased this book and are interested in both machine learning and q. Having the book on your desk is a great first step, but the knowledge embedded within won't magically jump to your brain. I suggest that you run each of the examples yourself. Play with the inputs, examine the outputs and perhaps step through the algorithms by declaring variables with the same name as the function parameters. This is made easier by the consistent naming conventions used in the funq project and listed in Section 1.5 [9]. I wrote this book for you and hope you make it through each chapter.

1.3 Getting Started

The source code for this book is included in Appendix A [339] for reference, but can—and should—be downloaded from https://www.fun-q.net. To ensure compatibility with the examples in this book, download release v1.0.0. Once downloaded, you should start your q process from the funq project folder. In this example, I've downloaded the 32-bit version of kdb+ 4.0. I always use the -s <n> command line option to start q with multiple secondary threads to enable parallel code execution.

```
bash-3.2$ cd funq
bash-3.2$ q -s 4
KDB+ 4.0 2020.06.18 Copyright (C) 1993-2020 Kx Systems
m32/ 4(4)core 8192MB nick nicks-macbookpro.local 192.168.1.3 NONEXPIRE

q)
```

There are four main libraries that include the utilities and machine-learning algorithms: ut.q [339], ml.q [345], fmincg.q [372] and porter.q [376]. The funq.q [339] library loads each of these files.[2]

```
q)\l funq.q
q)
```

In addition to the directories distributed with q, the ut, ml, fmincg and porter directories should now be visible.

```
q)key `
`q`Q`h`j`o`ut`ml`fmincg`porter
```

---
[2]The funq.q library also attempts to load a few other libraries, but these require extra packages to be installed are not used in this book.

The `funq` project also includes many other libraries dedicated to downloading data from the internet and loading them into memory. We can, for example, load the full text of *Pride and Prejudice* by Jane Austen.

```
q)\l pandp.q
[down]loading pride and prejudice text
"http://www.gutenberg.org/files/1342/1342_0.txt"
```

The text, with each chapter represented by a vector of characters, can then be found in `pandp.s`.

```
q)pandp.s
"It is a truth universally acknowledged, that a single man in\npossession..
"Mr. Bennet was among the earliest of those who waited on Mr.\nBingley. H..
"Not all that Mrs. Bennet, however, with the assistance of her\nfive daug..
"When Jane and Elizabeth were alone, the former, who had been\ncautious i..
"Within a short walk of Longbourn lived a family with whom the\nBennets w..
"The ladies of Longbourn soon waited on those of Netherfield. The\nvisit ..
"Mr. Bennet's property consisted almost entirely in an estate of\ntwo tho..
..
```

Other data sets automatically load their contents as tables, matrices and vectors—depending on the appropriate abstraction.

Writing a book that requires data is a brittle process. The examples will break if the data sets move location or change format. All data sets are, therefore, loaded from a dedicated q source file. If future modifications are required, the `funq` project will be updated to ensure the examples remain valid. Also, if you find that a data set required in the examples below has changed location, please raise an issue in the `funq` repository.

Installing 7-Zip

The `funq` project was written with the expectation that it can be run on any platform that kdb+ is supported: Windows, Linux, Solaris and Mac operating systems. Although Linux, Solaris, and Mac come with utilities to uncompress data files in various formats such as `.zip`, `.gz` and `.tar.gz`, Windows does not. To uncompress files on a machine running the Windows operating system, the `ut.q` [339] library uses the 7-Zip utility (`7z.exe`). This utility can be downloaded from https://www.7-zip.org.

1.4 What is in This Book?

We begin our journey through machine-learning algorithms in Chapter 2 [11] with the most intuitive supervised learning algorithm: k-nearest neighbors (k-NN). The chapter starts by introducing the funq project, which includes all the code required to run the examples in this book. It then demonstrates the project's ability to download external data sets by loading, and performing k-NN analysis on, the ever-popular Iris data set. It then takes a step back to explain different distance metrics that are used in machine learning and their relationship with norm metrics. The k-NN implementation is then discussed and examples of using it with different distance metrics are presented. A few common optimizations are then reviewed and the chapter concludes with a presentation of the confusion matrix and a discussion on using cross validation to pick the best value for k (the number of neighbors).

We next turn to a simple, yet elegant, unsupervised clustering algorithm in Chapter 3 [45] called k-means. To explain the k-means algorithm, we discuss the implementation of the "Lloyd" method of iterative assignment and update steps, which results in the convergence of k distinct clusters. Three different initialization techniques are covered including random cluster selection, random cluster assignment and an algorithm specifically designed to produce distant clusters: k-means++. The elbow method is then used to pick the optimal number of neighbors. To demonstrate the flexibility of the algorithm, different distance metrics are used to implement k-medians and k-harmonic means. The chapter ends with a discussion of k-medoids, which requires the centroids—the center of each cluster—be actual points within the data set.

We continue our discussion on clustering techniques in Chapter 4 [67] by presenting hierarchical agglomerative clustering. The chapter begins by downloading and describing the University of Eastern Finland's clustering benchmark data set. After first building a dissimilarity matrix, the iterative Lance-Williams algorithm is dissected and its efficiency and flexibility are demonstrated. Different linkage functions are defined and Ward's method is explained. Methods for generating and ungrouping clusters are reviewed before the chapter concludes by demonstrating how the silhouette cluster quality method can be used to determine the optimal number of clusters.

The final clustering algorithm, expectation-maximization (EM), is described in Chapter 5 [83]. The expectation-maximization algorithm, which is used to estimate distribution parameters, can be used as a generalization of the k-means clustering algorithm. Where the k-means algorithm assigns each observation to a single cluster, the expectation-maximization algorithm assigns each observation a probability of belonging to each of the specified clusters. Probabilities require distributions and the chapter introduces the binomial, multinomial, Bernoulli mixture model and Gaussian mixture model distributions using coin flips, dice rolls, the MNIST handwritten-digit data set and the Iris data set respectively. The concepts of likelihood and log likelihood estimators are also introduced.

Chapter 6 [109] returns to supervised learning algorithms and the use of probability distributions with the naive Bayes algorithm. The Iris data set is used again to demonstrate the implementation of Gaussian naive Bayes while the SMS spam data set is analyzed with multinomial naive Bayes. The SMS spam data set is our first introduction to text processing—also referred to as natural language processing (NLP). We then introduce a q implementation of the Porter stemmer--which allows us to combine English words with the same meaning: transformer and transformers for example. We then review binary classification statistics that allow us to quantify how good our binary predictions are. The chapter concludes by introducing the term-frequency inverse document frequency (TF-IDF) statistic and uses it to predict which Jane Austen book a randomly selected chapter comes from.

Chapter 7 [131] describes a powerful (and perhaps my favorite) machine-learning algorithm—decision trees. By continuously splitting a data set based on the values of each feature, we build a tree that, most importantly, creates an intuitive model of the underlying data. Decision trees have a long history and many competing designs. The funq project provides a general-purpose tree-building algorithm that is parameterized to allow the generation of multiple implementations. After the chapter introduces the impurity functions, which are used to determine how much *information* is in each of the data set features, the ID3 classification-tree algorithm is examined and applied to the famous weather data set. Before proceeding to review more complex classification and regression trees (CART), the chapter demonstrates two visualization tools: the first produces a terminal-appropriate text tree while the second generates output that can be used to produce an image with the Graphviz tool. Digging into the algorithm, the chapter continues to discuss different information-gain calculations, which are used to identify which feature should be split at each branch in the tree. The Iris data set is once again used to demonstrate the power of decision trees. To prevent overly *bushy* trees and their tendency to over fit, a pruning technique and cross validation are used to pick the appropriate tree complexity. Regression trees that can be used to predict numeric values are then introduced and the chapter concludes by explaining how one-hot encoding can be used to transform categorical features into multiple features with binary values.

If one decision tree is good, multiple decision trees must be great. Chapter 8 [165]

1.4. WHAT IS IN THIS BOOK?

introduces the concept of ensemble learning to distinguish between benign and malignant tumors in the Wisconsin Diagnosis Breast Cancer data set. By combining multiple fully grown trees, we can reduce the tendency of single trees to overfit. This is explained in the section about random forests. The second ensemble method combines multiple decision stumps—decision trees with a single branch—in an algorithm called AdaBoost. By expertly combining multiple weak classifiers, we build a powerful strong classifier. The chapter concludes by using cross validation to determine the optimal number of decision stumps to combine.

We next take our first step towards the magic of deep learning. The journey starts in Chapter 9 [181] with linear regression. Matrices and matrix operators are reviewed and used with the wine-quality data set to predict the quality of red wine. We then review abstractions built into the funq project that enable faster matrix operations. After presenting the normal equations, gradient descent is introduced so optimization problems without closed-form solutions can be solved. After describing the concept of feature scaling, we present functions to perform conjugate gradient and stochastic gradient descent. L1 and L2 regularization functions are reviewed before their relationship with LASSO, ridge regression and elastic net is explained. The chapter ends with a review of the cross-validation technique used to determine the best regularization parameters.

A popular binary classification algorithm called logistic regression is used with the Wisconsin Diagnosis Breast Cancer data set in Chapter 10 [217] to model tumor malignancy. The chapter begins by introducing the sigmoid function and the log-loss cost function. In order to find optimal model parameters with gradient descent, the logistic regression cost and gradient functions are defined. Multi-class classification then explained and a one-vs.-all classifier is implemented. The chapter concludes by testing the accuracy of the algorithm on the MNIST handwritten-digit data set.

Having warmed up with a lap through logistic regression, Chapter 11 [237] sprints through the neural network finish line. The chapter begins with a brief history of the perceptron before describing a fully-connected neural network with a single hidden layer. To prevent the common vanishing-gradient problem, two different parameter-initialization techniques are reviewed. The cost and gradient functions for a neural network with a sigmoid activation function and log-loss cost function are introduced along with the concepts of feed-forward loss calculation and backward propagation. To demonstrate the flexibility of the functional neural network implementation, different activation functions—such as the hyperbolic tangent and rectified linear unit relu—and cost functions—such as the cross entropy and softmax functions—are used to analyze the MNIST handwritten-digit data set. The chapter concludes by demonstrating how, in addition to classification problems, neural networks can be used to model regression problems as well.

With the concepts of linear regression, k-nearest neighbors, gradient descent and regularization firmly in our tool belt, Chapter 12 [261] leverages these techniques to implement movie recommender systems. The chapter begins by reviewing the MovieLens data set and uses linear regularization to create a content-based recommender system. By using genre labels such as "Romance" and "Comedy", the model is able to recommend movies that match the genres that we have ranked the highest. We then implement a user-user collaborative filtering recommender system that uses k-nearest neighbors to recommend movies other people with similar tastes also liked. We then introduce two matrix-factorization techniques that decompose the rating matrix into user and item matrices that reflect the user's interest in, and the movie's exposure to, hidden features. The first technique uses gradient descent and the second uses a method called alternating least squares.

We finish our discussion of machine learning with an algorithm that made it to the top 10 machine-learning algorithms in 2006. It has since dropped off the list but remains a powerful algorithm that affects our everyday lives. Chapter 13 [295] explains the PageRank algorithm, which was developed by Larry Page and Sergei Brin to rank search results. The chapter begins with the construction of an adjacency matrix to model the links between web pages. This is transformed into a transition matrix also called a stochastic or Markov matrix. By adding random *surfing*, a Google matrix is created. Three implementations of the PageRank algorithm are then introduced. The power method, which iteratively produces better rankings, is explained first. This is followed by an algebraic solution that uses matrix inversion. The final algorithm uses another iterative approach that allows new observations to adjust a previously stored page rank vector. The chapter concludes with the introduction of sparse matrices and a sparse matrix implementation of the iterative PageRank algorithm.

Admittedly, implementing this many machine-learning algorithms in q may be more fun than you can handle. But if you are ready for more, the last chapter is for you. Chapter 14 [313] is dedicated to using q to visualize data. The chapter begins by reviewing the ASCII plotting tool used throughout the book. The next section uses complex numbers to generate a black and white, as well as grayscale, image of the Mandelbrot set. We then use utility functions to store the Mandelbrot matrices in each of the three Netpbm portable bitmap file formats: black and white, grayscale and color. This allows us to view the images in their full glory with most standard graphics programs. The chapter, book and fun comes to an end when we use q to implement an algorithm to generate sparklines and plot financial time-series data.

1.5 Naming Conventions

The `funq` project uses single-letter variables, where possible, for function parameters and local variables. In an attempt at consistency, I list the most common variables and their meanings below. Atoms, vectors, tables and functions use lowercase letters. Matrices, however, are represented with uppercase letters.

Table 1.1: Naming Conventions

Variable	Description
a	gradient descent learning rate (a)lpha
A	pagerank (A)djacency matrix
b	(b)aseline URL to be downloaded
c	(c)luster index list
	(c)orpus
C	cluster (C)entroid matrix
cf	(c)entroid (f)unction
	(c)lassification (f)unction
	(c)ost (f)unction
cgf	decision tree (c)ategorical (g)ain (f)unction
d	generic (d)ictionary
df	(d)istance (f)unction
D	(D)issimilarity matrix
ef	(e)rror (f)unction
f	(f)ile
	(f)unction
ff	(f)itting (f)unction
gf	(g)radient (f)unction
h	file (h)andle
i	(i)ndices used to index a vector
ipf	decision tree (i)m(p)urity (f)unction
I	nested list of cluster (I)ndices
l[12]	l1 and l2 regularization (l)ambda coefficients
L	hierarchical agglomerative clustering (L)inkage statistics
k	(k) for k-means or k-nearest neighbors or k-fold cross validation
lf	hierarchical agglomerative clustering (l)inkage (f)unction
	expectation-maximization (l)ikelihood (f)unction
ogf	decision tree (o)rdered (g)ain (f)unction
p	(p)robability vector

Table 1.1: (continued)

Variable	Description
pf	(p)rediction (f)unction
M	cluster (M)edoid matrix
mn	(m)i(n)
mx	(m)a(x)
n	integer (n)umber
r	pagerank (r)anking vector
rf	(r)egularization (f)unction
s	(s)tring
sf	(s)ampling (f)unction
t	generic (t)able
tf	(t)rain (f)unction
tr	decision (tr)ee
v	(v)ocabulary
w	vector of (w)eights
wf	(w)eighting (f)unction
x	vector of independent data
X	matrix of independent (training) data
Xt	matrix of independent (testing) data
y	vector of dependent (training) data
yt	vector of dependent (testing) data
Y	matrix of dependent (training) data
Yt	matrix of dependent (testing) data
theta	vector of unrolled regression weights
THETA	matrix of regression weights

Chapter 2

K-Nearest Neighbors

A man is known by the company he keeps.

— Aesop

Machine-learning algorithms can be divided into two types: supervised and unsupervised. Supervised learning algorithms are trained by giving them a set of inputs and told explicitly what the output should be. Unsupervised learning algorithms, however, are only given input data sets and are expected to find models that describe the relationship between data points. Where unsupervised learning algorithms only model the provided data, supervised learning algorithms build models on training data sets so the models can then be used to make predictions on as-yet unseen test data sets.

Building a model to describe the training data has two benefits:

- The costly process of building a model can be performed *offline*, while classification and regression can be quickly performed *online*.

- Large amounts of training data can be used to build the model and then left behind during prediction.

These algorithms are known as *eager learning* algorithms because they consume their training data immediately. While the remainder of this book will focus on *eager learning* examples, this chapter is about the *lazy learning* algorithm called k-nearest neighbors. It is *lazy* because all computations on the training data are deferred until the predictions are required. The k-nearest neighbors algorithm is also known as an *instance-based* algorithm because the training instances are kept with the model and used to make predictions for new observations. Algorithms that build models, and leave the training data behind, are intuitively called *model-based* algorithms.

The k-nearest neighbors algorithm is the simplest and most intuitive supervised learning algorithm. It begins by building a matrix of distances between the training and test data set. The algorithm then attempts to make a classification (regression) prediction by using the labels (values) of the *k* nearest training data points to classify (predict) the label (value) of the new observations.

2.1 K-Nearest Neighbors Example

Let's start with a quick demonstration of how the funq project can use the k-NN algorithm to model the iris data set. This may seem like a cursory treatment of the material. Have no fear, we will dissect every line of code as the chapter progresses.

The following code loads the funq.q [339] library and the iris data set from the iris.q [380] library.[1] It then splits the data into training and test partitions and extracts the data into matrices X and Xt, representing the training and test observations, and vectors y and yt representing the training and test species labels.

```
q)\l funq.q
q)\l iris.q
[down]loading iris data set
q)d:.ut.part[`train`test!7 3;0N?] iris.t
q)y:first get first `Y`X set' 0 1 cut value flip d`train
q)yt:first get first `Yt`Xt set' 0 1 cut value flip d`test
```

Using the training partition to classify each unseen Iris observation in the test partition with the k-nearest neighbors algorithm obtains an accuracy of 98% when only the nearest neighbor is used.

```
q)avg yt=.ml.knn[1f%;1;y] .ml.edist[X] each flip Xt
0.9777778
```

Using three neighbors manages to make a perfect prediction.

---

[1] If you are running these examples on a Windows machine, remember to install the 7-Zip utility mentioned in the section called "Installing 7-Zip" [4]

```
q)avg yt=.ml.knn[1f%;3;y] .ml.edist[X] each flip Xt
1f
```

And finally, the performance degrades when we start using more distant neighbors.

```
q)avg yt=.ml.knn[1f%;7;y] .ml.edist[X] each flip Xt
0.9555556
```

This is just one example of how k-nearest neighbors can be parameterized. The algorithm requires us to make three choices:

- Which distance metric should we use?

- How many neighbors should we include?

- How much weight should we give each neighbor?

Before addressing each of these questions, we introduce the Iris data set and .ut.download utility.

2.2 Iris Data Set

Our example started by downloading the famous Iris data set, which was collected by Dr. E Anderson and first published 1936 by Ronald Fisher.[2] The data set contains measurements of three species of genus Iris: Iris setosa, Iris versicolor and Iris virginica. With 50 measurements of each species, there are 150 records in total.

Confusingly, academic papers have been written on two different versions of the Iris data. Additionally, the original electronic version stored on the University of California at Irvine's server was also different from Fisher's original publication for two records.[3] This was identified by James C. Bezdek and a second—corrected—file can be found on the site. We must therefore pick between the two data sets: iris.data, which differs from Fisher's publication in the 35th and 38th instance of Iris Setosa, and bezdekIris.data, which matches Fisher's publication.

---

[2] R. A. Fisher, "The Use of Multiple Measurements in Taxonomic Problems," *Annals of Eugenics*, vol. 7, no. 2, pp. 179-188, 1936, doi: 10.1111/j.1469-1809.1936.tb02137.x.

[3] Dua, D. and Graff, C. (2019). UCI Machine Learning Repository [http://archive.ics.uci.edu/ml]. Irvine, CA: University of California, School of Information and Computer Science.

By default, the iris.q [380] library loads the bezdekIris.data file because it matches Fisher's article. You can change the library to use the iris.data file by modifying the index used to pick the file name on the first line of the file from 1 to 0. Once loaded, we can access the complete data set within the iris namespace.

```
q)iris.t
species      slength swidth plength pwidth
------------------------------------------
Iris-setosa 5.1     3.5    1.4     0.2
Iris-setosa 4.9     3      1.4     0.2
Iris-setosa 4.7     3.2    1.3     0.2
Iris-setosa 4.6     3.1    1.5     0.2
Iris-setosa 5       3.6    1.4     0.2
..
```

The data includes the Iris species, followed by the sepal and petal lengths and widths.

2.3 Downloading Data Sets

To download the Iris data set (like all other data sets in the funq project) the iris.q [380] library uses the .ut.download utility function.

.ut.download

```
/ (b)ase url, (f)ile, (e)xtension, (u)ncompress (f)unction
download:{[b;f;e;uf]
 if[0h=type f;:.z.s[b;;e;uf] each f];
 if[l~key l:`$":",f;:l];                              / local file exists
 if[()~key z:`$":",f,e;z 1: .Q.hg`$":",0N!b,f,e];     / download
 if[count uf;system 0N!uf," ",f,e];                   / uncompress
 l}
```

The function expects four parameters: the base URL (without the file name), the file name (which will also appear on disk), the compressed file's extension and an uncompress function used to extract the data.

Machine-learning data sets can be quite large and are often stored in a compressed format. To distinguish the URL of the compressed file name with the uncompressed file name, we must pass them as separate arguments. Since the function also uncompresses the file, the compressed file extension must be specified separately.

2.3. DOWNLOADING DATA SETS

Common extensions for compressed files are .zip for zip-ed files, .gz for gzip-ed files and .tar.gz for tar-ed and zip-ed files.

The final argument to the function is the actual uncompress command to run. Since compression types vary between files (and operating systems), the command used to uncompress the downloaded file is left to the function's caller. If the file does not need to be uncompressed, both the extension and uncompress command can be passed as empty strings.

The .ut.download function begins by checking to see if a list of files has been supplied. It then uses a common technique within the funq project to call itself recursively using the .z.s operator. The function then checks for the existence of the local (uncompressed) file using the key operator and exits early if found. The third line downloads the compressed file with the .Q.hg builtin if it does not already exist. Finally, the function uncompresses the file if an uncompress function has been supplied. The Iris data set is small enough that compression is not needed and the call to .ut.download leaves both the extension and the uncompress function empty.

To provide feedback, the .ut.download function prefixes the full data URL with the 0N! operator. This causes the URL to be displayed before the function attempts the download the data. The function also displays the uncompress function if it is executed. You can tell, therefore, when the function is attempting to download and uncompress the file. If there is an error running the command, you can copy and paste the command in a terminal to further debug the problem.

We can, for example, download the iris.data file.

```
q)b:"http://archive.ics.uci.edu/ml/machine-learning-databases/iris/"
q)f:"iris.data"
q).ut.download[b;;"";""] f;
"http://archive.ics.uci.edu/ml/machine-learning-databases/iris/iris.data"
```

Running the command a second time will recognize that the files exists and will not attempt to download the file.

```
q).ut.download[b;;"";""] f;
```

> **SSL_VERIFY_SERVER**
>
> Many websites are moving their pages (and data) from the HTTP protocol to the more secure HTTPS protocol. To configure the .Q.hg builtin to work for these domains, you can either point q to a certificate file (or path) with the SSL_CA_CERT_FILE (or SSL_CA_CERT_PATH) environment variables, or disable verification altogether with:
>
> ```
> $ export SSL_VERIFY_SERVER=NO
> ```
>
> For security purposes, it is not possible to change q's behavior by setting these variables from within the process. They must be set in the environment before the process is started.

2.4 Loading Data Sets

Downloading, parsing and storing a data set into familiar variables is a common task. The different data sets within the funq project are therefore available by loading their eponymous files. Loading the iris.q [380] library, for example, performs 5 steps:

1. Downloads the Iris data set.
2. Stores the complete data set (petal and sepal measurements as well as species labels) into the iris.XY matrix.
3. Stores the independent features (petal and sepal measurements) into the iris.X matrix.
4. Stores the dependent feature (species labels) into the iris.Y matrix and the iris.y vector.
5. Stores the complete data set (this time with column headers) into the iris.t table.

These steps are common among all data sets with the only difference being the namespace.

Once the iris.q [380] library is loaded, we have access to the independent (petal and sepal measurements) and dependent (species labels) variables.

2.5. PARTITIONING DATA

```
q)iris.y
`Iris-setosa`Iris-setosa`Iris-setosa`Iris-setosa`Iris-setosa`Iris-setosa`..
q)iris.X
5.1 4.9 4.7 4.6 5   5.4 4.6 5   4.4 4.9 5.4 4.8 4.8 4.3 5.8 5.7 5.4 5.1 5..
3.5 3   3.2 3.1 3.6 3.9 3.4 3.4 2.9 3.1 3.7 3.4 3   3   4   4.4 3.9 3.5 3..
1.4 1.4 1.3 1.5 1.4 1.7 1.4 1.5 1.4 1.5 1.5 1.6 1.4 1.1 1.2 1.5 1.3 1.4 1..
0.2 0.2 0.2 0.2 0.2 0.4 0.3 0.2 0.2 0.1 0.2 0.2 0.1 0.1 0.2 0.4 0.4 0.3 0..
```

2.5 Partitioning Data

Some data sets provide separate training and testing partitions. The Iris data set does not. It provides 150 observations in three sections of 50—one section per species. We can, however, cut the observations into training and testing sets ourselves by using the .ut.part utility.

.ut.part

```
/ use (w)eight vector or dictionary to partition (x). (s)ampling (f)unction:
/ til = no shuffle, 0N? = shuffle, list or table = stratify
part:{[w;sf;x]
  if[99h=type w;:key[w]!.z.s[value w;sf;x]];
  if[99h<type sf;:x (floor sums n*prev[0f;w%sum w]) _ sf n:count x];
  x@:raze each flip value .z.s[w;0N?] each group sf; / stratify
  x}
```

The .ut.part utility accepts a vector (or dictionary) of weights as the first parameter, a sampling function as the second parameter and a vector—or table in our case—as the third parameter. A vector (or dictionary) of partitions whose size corresponds to the proportions provided in the weight parameter is returned. The first line of the function handles cases where a dictionary is provided as an argument. In this case, the key of the dictionary is removed and the function is recursively called on the remaining vector of weights. Once the resulting partitions are obtained, the key is replaced and a dictionary of partitions is returned. The second line of the function checks for cases where the sampling function is indeed a function. This function should accept the length of the x parameter as its only argument and return a vector of integers—one for each index of the x parameter.

To randomly shuffle the data, we can supply the 0N? projection, which generates a vector of unique random values from 0 to n-1[4].

```
q)0N?10
7 1 4 2 3 6 5 8 0 9
```

If we do not want to randomly shuffle the data, perhaps because the table represents a time-series data set, we can supply the til operator as the sampling function. This creates a vector of indices that will return the original data set unaltered.

```
q)til 10
0 1 2 3 4 5 6 7 8 9
```

Instead of immediately indexing the x parameter with the results of the sf sampling function, the indices themselves are partitioned first. Only then are the partitioned indices used to index back into the x parameter. For simple data structures such as vectors, this has no benefit. But for more complicated structure such as a table, the process of shuffling the data must reorder the elements of every column of the table before reshaping the table during the partition step. By shuffling the indices instead of x directly, the function only rearranges the data in x a single time.

Once the indices are generated—shuffled or not—the function then partitions them into the requested sizes with the _ cut operator.

```
q)0 3 5 _ til 10
0 1 2
3 4
5 6 7 8 9
```

The second line of the .ut.part utility finishes by indexing back into the x parameter to partition the data and then returns the result.

A common train/test ratio is 70% training data and 30% test data. We supply this as a dictionary with "train" and "test" keys. We also provide the 0N? shuffle sampling function. The result is a dictionary mapping the keys we specified to the partitioned tables.

```
q)\S -314159
q)count each d:.ut.part[`train`test!7 3;0N?] iris.t
train| 105
test | 45
```

---

[4]The ability to generate a random permutation by passing the null integer 0N as the left operand of the ? operator requires a minimum kdb+ version of 3.3 with a release date of 2016.05.12 or later.

2.5. PARTITIONING DATA

> **Random Number Generator Seed**
>
> Every q process generates random numbers in the same order. This demonstrates that although we refer to the values as random numbers, they are in fact pseudorandom numbers. The generated numbers are controlled by the random number generator seed. When a q process starts, this value is initialized to a negative integer representing the first six digits of π. We can see this by using the \S system command.
>
> ```
> q)\S
> -314159i
> ```
>
> To achieve reproducibility in our examples, we can also reset the random number generator seed with the \S N system command. The value can be any nonzero integer, but using the first six digits of π resets q back to its original state.
>
> ```
> q)\S -314159i
> ```

Creating partitions by randomly sampling the data opens up the possibility that the train and test sets have unrepresentative frequencies of the target classes. In this example, we ended up with a few more Iris virginica samples than Iris versicolor samples.

```
q)count each group d[`test]`species
Iris-versicolor| 13
Iris-virginica | 17
Iris-setosa    | 15
```

To address this situation, the .ut.part utility has special handling for cases when the sf sampling function is not a function. In this case, the sf parameter is assumed to be a vector or table and the .ut.part utility performs a stratified sampling of the data. The third line of the function groups the elements in the sf variable and recursively partitions each group. The resulting vector of partitions is then flipped into a partition of vectors. To complete the stratified partitioning, each partition is razed and the resulting indices are used to partition the x parameter.

If we partition the Iris data set again, but this time provide the species as the sampling function, we obtain train and test partitions that have species frequencies the same as the original data set.

```
q)d:.ut.part[`train`test!7 3;iris.t.species] iris.t
q)count each group d[`test]`species
```

```
Iris-setosa     | 15
Iris-versicolor | 15
Iris-virginica  | 15
```

The k-nearest neighbors algorithm requires a matrix of data, not a table. Our next step is to extract the training matrix X and species-label vector y—noting that the species column appears first in the table.

```
q)y:first get first `Y`X set' 0 1 cut value flip d`train
```

The test matrix Xt and species-label vector yt is then extracted.

```
q)yt:first get first `Yt`Xt set' 0 1 cut value flip d`test
```

Q uses *copy on write* semantics to minimize memory allocations. Data is passed by reference and is only copied when elements are modified. Even though it looks like we copied the data from the dictionary into global variables, only references to the data were created. The -16! internal function allows us to see that there are in-fact three references to the training species labels: y, Y and d.train.species.

```
q)-16!y
3i
```

We can also see that the original species data stored in iris.XY, iris.X, iris.Y and iris.T all reference the same memory.

```
q)-16!iris.y
4i
```

We are now ready to attack the first decision we must make—choosing a distance metric. We begin by reviewing a few different distance metrics that often appear in machine-learning algorithms.

2.6 Distance Metrics

There are, interestingly, many possible metrics to use when computing the distance between two multidimensional points. Consider three points: A, B and C, which are located at (1,1), (1,2) and (2,2) respectively.

2.6. DISTANCE METRICS

```
q)flip xy:(1 1 2;1 2 2)
1 1
1 2
2 2
```

Example 2.1 [21] visualizes these points using the .ut.plot utility, which is described in full detailed in Chapter 14 [313]. The plotting utility dynamically adjusts the axes to fit the data, so we add point (0,0) to force the inclusion of the origin.

Example 2.1 Distance Metrics
```
q).ut.plot[19;10;"  ABC";avg] (0,'xy),enlist 0 1 2 3
2.5| "                    "
2  | "         B          C"
   | "                    "
1.5| "                    "
   | "                    "
1  | "         A          "
   | "                    "
0.5| "                    "
   | "                    "
0  | "                    "
```

The distance between A and C, for example, might be considered 2 if we travel along the y-axis one unit from A to B and then another unit on the x-axis from B to C. Alternatively, the distance might be considered 1.414214 ($\sqrt{2}$) if we traveled on a diagonal line directly from A to C. These two distance metrics are called the Manhattan distance and the Euclidean distance respectively.

Manhattan Distance

The Manhattan distance (Equation 2.1 [22]) is also called the Taxicab distance after its similarity to hailing a taxi to travel between addresses in New York City. It is computed by summing the absolute distances of every dimension.

```
q){sum abs x-y} . (1 1;2 2)
2
```

$$\text{Manhattan distance} = \sum_{i=1}^{n} |x_i - y_i|$$

Equation 2.1: Manhattan Distance

Euclidean Distance

The second distance metric is called the Euclidean distance (Equation 2.2 [22]) and is computed by summing the squared distances of every dimension and then taking the square root.

$$\text{Euclidean distance} = \sqrt{\sum_{i=1}^{n} |x_i - y_i|^2}$$

Equation 2.2: Euclidean Distance

```
q){sqrt sum x*x-:y} . (1 1;2 2)
1.414214
```

Minkowski Distance

These two metrics are, in fact, special cases of a more general distance metric—the Minkowski distance (Equation 2.3 [22]). The Minkowski distance is computed by summing the p-th power of the absolute distance between each dimension and then taking the p-th root.

$$\text{Minkowski distance} = \sqrt[p]{\sum_{i=1}^{n} |x_i - y_i|^p}$$

Equation 2.3: Minkowski Distance

In this formulation, the Manhattan distance corresponds to a p-value of 1 and the Euclidean distance corresponds to a p-value of 2.

```
q){sum[abs[y-z] xexp x] xexp 1f%x}[1] . (1 1;2 2)
2f
q){sum[abs[y-z] xexp x] xexp 1f%x}[2] . (1 1;2 2)
```

2.6. DISTANCE METRICS 23

```
1.414214
```

Functions for the Manhattan, Euclidean and Minkowski distance are available as `.ml.mdist`, `.ml.edist` and `.ml.mkdist` respectively. They are not implemented as demonstrated above, but are instead implemented in terms of their respective norm functions. Functions in the funq project are relentlessly factored into smaller composable utilities. This provides three benefits. Firstly, each function is shorter and easier to understand. The second benefit is that we can focus on optimizing core functions and all callers of the function will automatically get a performance boost. Finally, the third benefit of decomposing functions into their smallest pieces is that they each get a name, thus making the code more literate.

.ml.mdist

```
mdist:mnorm (-)::            / Manhattan (taxicab) distance
```

.ml.edist

```
edist:enorm (-)::            / Euclidean distance
```

.ml.mkdist

```
mkdist:{[p;x;y]pnorm[p] x-y}              / Minkowski distance
```

Notice how `.ml.mdist` and `.ml.edist` end with a trailing `::`. This creates a function composition that indicates everything before the operator will be applied once the missing parameters are supplied. The `.ml.mdist` function, for example, is waiting for two parameters, which it will subtract from each other before passing the result to `.ml.mnorm`. We can use the `get` operator to see its definition—noting, however, that q does not have an explicit composition display format and therefore merely concatenates the definitions.

```
q)get .ml.mdist
sumabs
-
```

It is a composition of two operators: a composition of the `sum` and `abs` operators and the k - negate operator. We can see how the first element is composed as well.

```
q)get first get .ml.mdist
sum
abs
```

An alternate (and inferior) approach to building compositions is to use the @ operator instead of the :: operator. We can see how using the @ operator adds an extra operator to the function train—thus adding a little overhead to each invocation.

```
q)sqrt sum abs::
sqrtsumabs
q)sqrt sum abs@
sqrtsum@[abs]
```

In addition to adding the extra operator, using the @ operator only creates a composition that can accept a single parameter. Building the composition with :: does not have this limitation.

To understand the implementation of these distance functions, we now turn to the norm metrics.

2.7 Norm Metrics

Computing the distance between two points in a multi-dimensional vector space is equivalent to computing the norm of the subtracted vectors. For clarity and generality, the *distance* functions have been implemented in terms of their respective *norm* functions: .ml.mnorm (Equation 2.4 [24]), .ml.enorm (Equation 2.5 [25]) and .ml.pnorm (Equation 2.6 [25]).

.ml.mnorm

```
mnorm:sum abs::                          / Manhattan (taxicab) norm
```

.ml.enorm

```
enorm:sqrt enorm2::                      / Euclidean norm
```

.ml.pnorm

```
pnorm:{[p;x]sum[abs[x] xexp p] xexp 1f%p} / parameterized norm
```

$$\|\vec{x}\|_1 = \sum_{i=1}^{n} |x_i|$$

Equation 2.4: Manhattan Norm

2.7. NORM METRICS

$$\|\vec{x}\|_2 = \sqrt{\sum_{i=1}^{n}|x_i|^2}$$

Equation 2.5: Euclidean Norm

$$\|\vec{x}\|_p = \sqrt[p]{\sum_{i=1}^{n}|x_i|^p}$$

Equation 2.6: Parameterized Norm

Although the .ml.mnorm and .ml.enorm functions have custom implementations designed for performance, they could have, in principle, been implemented in terms of the parameterized-norm function .ml.pnorm. We can see that the using p values of 1 and 2 produce the Manhattan and Euclidean norms respectively.

```
q).ml.pnorm[1] 3 4
7f
q).ml.pnorm[2] 3 4
5f
```

Interestingly, the norm values decrease as we increase p until finally, at infinity, the norm is equal to the maximum value of the vector. Using infinity results in numeric overflow and is therefore not numerically stable. We can obtain the same results with a large—but not too large—value for p.

```
q).ml.pnorm[100] 3 4
4f
```

The .ml.enorm function is simply the square root of the .ml.enorm2 function. At first glance, this may seem like we've taken a good idea too far and overly factored the code. It turns out, however, that we will use .ml.enorm2 many more times because the act of summing squared values is ubiquitous. The implementation uses the wsum weighted sum operator to multiply the argument by itself and sum the result.

.ml.enorm2

```
enorm2:{x wsum x}                        / Euclidean norm squared
```

It is common to use the Euclidean distance squared as a distance metric because it preserves relative ordering between distances without having to perform the expensive `sqrt` operation.

We return now to the last of our distance metrics: cosine distance.

Cosine Distance

Sometimes it is the angular distance between two points that matters more than the linear distance. The typical example for this distance metric is word frequencies. When comparing books—or perhaps chapters within a book—we don't care how many words are in the book—or chapters. What matters is the relative frequencies. In this case we want to compute the angle between the word count vectors. This distance metric is based on the cosine similarity measurement. If a line drawn from the origin to one of the points also passes through the other point (regardless of its distance from the origin), the angle between the two points is 0. Since the cosine of 0 is 1, the two points have maximum similarity.

Let's return to the three points plotted in Example 2.1 [21]. Although point C is further from the origin than point A, they are perfectly similar because there is no angle between a line drawn from the origin directly to point C and another line drawn to point A. Following that line of thought, point B is the same distance from point C as it is from point A.

The cosine similarity (Equation 2.7 [26]) can be calculated by taking the dot product of the two vectors and normalizing the value by dividing by the length (Euclidean norm) of each vector.

.ml.cossim

```
cossim:{sum[x*y]%enorm[x i]*enorm y i:wnan(x;y)} / cosine similarity
```

$$\cos(\theta) = \frac{\sum_{i=1}^{n} x_i y_i}{\sqrt{\sum_{i=1}^{n} x_i^2} \sqrt{\sum_{i=1}^{n} y_i^2}}$$

Equation 2.7: Cosine Similarity

Native functions like `avg`, `var` and `dev` handle null values by removing them from calculations. Though it makes the implementation more complicated, handling null values is an important consideration when designing robust algorithms. The

2.7. NORM METRICS

cosine-similarity function .ml.cossim handles nulls by using the where-not-any-null function .ml.wnan so that it only includes dimensions that are not missing values.

.ml.wnan

```
/ where not any null
wnan:{$[all type each x;where not any null x;::]}
```

Instead of returning null values, it uses the available data.

```
q).ml.cossim[1 2 3;10 20 30]
1f
q).ml.cossim[1 2 3;-10 -20 0N]
-1f
```

Mirroring the behavior of the distance functions, the .ml.cossim cosine-similarity function also permits passing matrices for either, or both, of the arguments.

```
q).ml.cossim[(-1 200 3;-10 -20 30);1 10]
-1 0 1f
q).ml.cossim[1 10;(-1 200 3;-10 -20 30)]
-1 0 1f
q).ml.cossim[(1 2 3;2 -2 4);(10 -20 -30;20 -20 -40)]
1 0 -1f
```

When used for matrices, however, the logic for excluding dimensions with null values, would no longer make sense. The .ml.wnan function handles this by returning the null value :: that, when used to index a list, returns the full list.

```
q)1 2 3[::]
1 2 3
```

The cosine similarity metric ranges from a minimum value of -1 (which represents perfect dissimilarity) through 0 (which represents no similarity) to a maximum value of 1 (which represents perfect similarity). To convert this to a distance metric we can subtract its value from 1.

.ml.cosdist

```
cosdist:1f-cossim::                              / cosine distance
```

We will focus on the Euclidean distance in this chapter, discuss the Manhattan distance a bit more in Chapter 3 [45] and review the cosine distance in Chapter 12 [261].

2.8 Minimize Flipping

Once a distance metric is chosen, the first step of implementing the k-nearest neighbors algorithm is to compute the distance from the test data to each point in the training data. This is the most computationally intense step of the algorithm. It also requires the most memory.

If there are M training vectors and N test vectors, the result will be an M x N matrix. Given the size of M and N, the memory requirements of the resulting matrix can be quite substantial. Machine-learning data sets can be quite large. It is important to be vigilant about how memory is allocated. Although we will show how to save memory by running the algorithm a few times on subsets of the N test vectors, we now turn our attention to a memory-saving trick that can prevent us from doubling the memory needed for a single machine-learning data set.

In our initial example, we used the Euclidean distance operator .ml.edist to generate a vector of distances between each observation in the test data set and those in the training data set.

```
q).ml.edist[X] each flip Xt
0.4123106 0.6403124 0.4898979 0.2236068 0.509902  0.244949  0.4690416 0.3..
0.9486833 1.067708  0.4795832 0.9486833 0.5       0.591608  0.4123106 0.8..
0.5744563 0.9433981 0.5477226 0.7549834 0.7071068 0.6       0.6164414 0.4..
0.9539392 0.9539392 0.7071068 0.591608  0.3464102 0.4242641 0.5291503 0.8..
1.122497  1.122497  0.6082763 0.969536  0.3605551 0.591608  0.4123106 1.0..
0.3       0.7       0.9273618 0.6403124 1.157584  0.8717798 1.029563  0.5..
1.090871  0.9327379 0.8124038 0.9746794 0.4242641 0.6480741 0.509902   1.0..
..
```

Algorithm efficiency is a guiding principle in the funq project. To that end, all algorithms were written and tested on the 32-bit version of kdb+. During the initial stages of development, it became obvious that using the flip operator to transpose large matrices resulted in the q process terminating with a wsfull exception due to insufficient memory. For small data sets, flipping a matrix before operating on each of the rows is, in fact, the most efficient approach. Once the data sets increase in size, however, we no longer have this choice. Instead, we need to run the function over each of the columns. The .ml.f2nd function was created to apply a supplied function f over the second dimension of a matrix X.

.ml.f2nd

```
/ apply (f)unction (in parallel) to the 2nd dimension of (X)
f2nd:{[f;X]$[noflip[];(f value::) peach flip (count[X]#`)!X;f peach flip X]}
```

2.8. MINIMIZE FLIPPING

The function has two modes of operation depending on what the .ml.noflip function returns.

.ml.noflip

```
/ returns boolean indicating preference not to flip matrices
noflip:{system"g"}            / redefine to customize behavior
```

If the .ml.noflip function returns false, the .ml.f2nd function will transpose the matrix and apply the function f across each of the resulting rows. If, on the other hand, the .ml.noflip function returns true, the .ml.f2nd function takes advantage of the fact that a q table is a flipped dictionary of lists and efficiently converts the matrix into a table so the function can be applied across each row of the table. The peach adverb is used in both cases to request parallel code execution.

The default implementation of the .ml.noflip function returns the global garbage collection setting. If garbage collection has been enabled, the assumption is that you are running in a memory-constrained environment and would like to reduce memory allocations at the expense of some execution efficiency. This behavior can be changed by overriding the .ml.noflip function.

Let's take a step back and see how this memory-saving trick is implemented. Since our goal is to convert the matrix X into a table, we first transform it into a dictionary of lists with a symbol-vector key. The actual key values do not matter because we will never refer to them.

```
q)(count[X]#`)!X
| 5.1 5.2 4.9 5.1 4.6 4.6 4.6 4.4 5.1 5   4.9 5.1 4.6 5   4.4 4.8 4.5 5.4..
| 3.3 3.4 3.1 3.7 3.1 3.6 3.4 3.2 3.8 3.3 3   3.4 3.2 3   3   3   2.3 3.4..
| 1.7 1.4 1.5 1.5 1.5 1   1.4 1.3 1.6 1.4 1.4 1.5 1.4 1.6 1.3 1.4 1.3 1.5..
| 0.5 0.2 0.2 0.4 0.2 0.2 0.3 0.2 0.2 0.2 0.2 0.2 0.2 0.2 0.2 0.3 0.3 0.4..
```

We can now flip this dictionary of lists to obtain a table.

```
q)flip (count[X]#`)!X

---------------
5.1 3.3 1.7 0.5
5.2 3.4 1.4 0.2
4.9 3.1 1.5 0.2
5.1 3.7 1.5 0.4
4.6 3.1 1.5 0.2
..
```

Kdb+ tables are column-oriented—each column is stored in contiguous memory. Unlike flipping a matrix, the process of flipping a dictionary of lists, does not rearrange memory. The rows of the original matrix become columns of the table. If we apply a function across each row of the table, q will pass the function a dictionary whose key is the table's column names and whose value is the row elements. Let's use the `0N!` display operator on the first two rows of the table to see the dictionaries.

```
q)(0N!) peach 2#flip (count[X]#`)!X;
````!5.2 3.4 1.4 0.2
````!5.1 3.3 1.7 0.5
```

The function passed to `.ml.f2nd` will be expecting a vector, however, not a dictionary. To match the behavior when garbage collection is not enabled, we need to throw away the key before applying the function.

```
q)(0N!value::) peach 2#flip (count[X]#`)!X;
5.2 3.4 1.4 0.2
5.1 3.3 1.7 0.5
```

Because each column of a table is stored in contiguous memory, iterating across rows, requires the row elements to be copied into a temporary vector before being passed to the iterating function. But since this is only done for one row at a time (and our data sets usually have fewer table columns than rows), the process does not allocate a considerable amount of extra memory. The algorithm is, however, less efficient.

Both garbage collection and parallel execution can be set on the q command line and changed from within the code. If both have been initially set using the `-g 1` and `-s <n>` command line options respectively, the system commands `\g 0` and `\s 0` can be used to turn them off. This allows the behavior of the `.ml.f2nd` function, as well as many other functions in the funq project to be adjusted at runtime.

Setting the number of secondary threads to 0 helps debug errors that occur within a peached function. The q debugger cannot be invoked from secondary threads, so the only way to debug an error within a peached function is to disable all secondary threads. It is even possible to increase the number of active secondary threads up to the value specified with the `-s <n>` command line parameter.[5]

Many q operators also have the ability to execute in parallel across secondary threads.[6] However, since only one level of parallel execution is performed, nested

---

[5]The ability to increase secondary threads was added in kdb+ 3.5.
[6]A hallmark feature of kdb+ 4.0 was the ability to use secondary threads within native operators.

uses of peach and calls to q operators will not distribute their calculations across threads again.

We can now use `.ml.f2nd` in place of `each flip` and benefit from the fact that it uses the `peach` adverb, even if we forget.

```
q).ml.f2nd[.ml.edist X] Xt
1.118034  1.034408  0.7348469 1.174734  0.5196152 0.6855655 0.6164414 0.3..
0.6557439 0.5744563 0.2       0.8246211 0.2645751 0.7549834 0.4898979 0.4..
1.272792  1.140175  1.53948   0.9219544 1.714643  1.462874  1.493318  1.7..
0.4795832 0.6403124 0.509902  0.6164414 0.5385165 0.9433981 0.5477226 0.7..
0.678233  0.6480741 0.9848858 0.4123106 1.16619   1.122497  0.9949874 1.3..
0.5744563 0.4358899 0.7348469 0.1414214 0.8660254 0.7416198 0.6480741 0.9..
0.6164414 0.3741657 0.781025  0.3605551 1         0.9486833 0.8660254 1.1..
..
```

## 2.9 Finding K Neighbors

With this matrix of distances, we can compute the k-nearest neighbors by performing the following algorithm for each vector.

- Find the index of the k nearest neighbors.
- Determine the value (or label) of these k neighbors.
- Compute the weighted `avg` (or `mode`) of these k values (or labels).

**.ml.knn**

```
/ find (k) smallest values from (d)istance vector (or matrix) and use
/ (w)eighting (f)unction to return the best estimate of y
knn:{[wf;k;y;d]
 if[not type d;:.z.s[wf;k;y] peach d];    / recurse for matrix d
 if[any n:null d;d@:i:where not n; y@:i]; / filter null distances
 p:(waom . (wf d:::;y)@\:#[;iasc d]::) peach k&count d; / make predictions
 p}
```

The first line of the function detects if a matrix of distances has been supplied. If so, the function recursively calls itself for each row of the matrix. In fact, it uses the `peach` adverb to run each computation in parallel.

The second line checks for null values in the distance vector and removes those entries from both d and y. And finally, the last line of .ml.knn performs the k-NN algorithm for each of the supplied values in k. The line begins by ensuring that we don't request more neighbors than exist. By using the & minimum operator, all k values are capped to the length of the d vector. We don't need to differentiate between a singular k value and a list of k values because the each and peach adverbs seamlessly handle this difference—they modify the iterating function to return a single value if passed an atom, and a list if passed a list.

Instead of writing another function, which would require us to pass the wf, d, y and k variables, the implementation of k-NN has been written as a composition of functions, ending with the :: operator and surrounded with parentheses. The composition first computes the index of the sorted distances with iasc operator and then takes the indices corresponding to the neighbors with the k smallest distances. The weighted-average-or-mode function .ml.waom is then called with the results of applying the weighting function to the k closest distances and their associated labels.

## 2.10 Weighted Average or Mode

Many supervised learning algorithms can be implemented as either classification or regression functions. If the estimated value is a categorical variable, the final value is computed by taking the weighted mode of the values. Alternatively, if the estimated value is an ordered numeric variable, the final value should be computed by taking the weighted average of the values. This decision is handled by the .ml.waom function.

**.ml.waom**

```
waom:{[w;x]$[isord x;nwavg;wmode][w;x]}      / weighted average or mode
```

The .ml.waom function uses the .ml.isord function, which returns a boolean indicating if the given vector contains numerically ordered values.

**.ml.isord**

```
isord:{type[x] in 0 8 9h}                    / is ordered
```

The funq project defines ordered data as being single and double floating-point numbers (types 8h and 9h) and matrices (type 0h) whose values are themselves

## 2.10. WEIGHTED AVERAGE OR MODE

double floating-point numbers. For these types of data, an average will be computed. Everything else is assumed to be a precise value that is not meant to be aggregated. Assuming an equal weight for each observation, we can see that passing integer numbers returns the value matching the mode of the list, while passing floating-point numbers returns the average.

```
q).ml.waom[1 1 1 1;1 2 3 3]
3
q).ml.waom[1 1 1 1;1 2 3 3f]
2.25
```

The only change required to switch between a k-nearest neighbors classification problem and a regression problem is to change the data type of the y-vector. We will see the same distinction is made for classification and regression decision trees in Chapter 7 [131].

## Weighted Mode

The .ml.waom function uses the .ml.nwavg and .ml.wmode functions to compute the weighted average and weighted mode respectively. Permit me to delay the discussion of .ml.nwavg, which is a null-aware variant of q's wavg weighted-average operator, until Section 12.4 [271] when we discuss all of funq's null-aware functions in detail. The .ml.wmode function, however, should be discussed immediately.

### .ml.wmode

```
/ given a (w)eight atom or vector and data (x), return x with maximum
/ weighted frequency
wmode:imax wfreq::           / weighted mode
```

It is implemented as a composition of the weighted-frequency function .ml.wfreq, which returns a sorted dictionary of all unique values mapped to their frequency, and the .ml.imax function which returns the index of the maximum element.

### .ml.wfreq

```
/ given a (w)eight atom or vector and data (x), return a dictionary (sorted
/ by key) mapping the distinct items to their weighted count
wfreq:{[w;x]@[x!count[x:asc distinct x]#0*first w;x;+;w]}
```

### .ml.imax

```
imax:{find[x;max x]}            / index of max element
```

The .ml.freq and .ml.mode functions are special cases of the .ml.wfreq and .ml.wmode functions where all weights are the same (and in this case equal to one).

**.ml.freq**

```
freq:wfreq[1]
```

**.ml.mode**

```
mode:wmode[1]                   / standard mode
```

Though we skipped examples for the weighted variants of .ml.freq and .ml.mode, it is instructive to demonstrate an example for these equal-weighted projections. The .ml.mode projection is similar to, but more efficient and accurate than, a common implementation.

A naive implementation of the mode function groups the data, counts each of the groups, compares each count to the maximum count and then picks the first one.

```
q)mode:{first where x=max x:count each group x}
q)mode 2 2 2 1 1 1 1 3 3
2
```

One problem with this implementation is that the result depends on the order of the supplied data. By rearranging the values, we obtain a different result. This is not a desirable behavior for numerical calculations.

```
q)mode 1 1 1 1 2 2 2 2 3 3
1
```

In addition to being numerically inconsistent, this implementation pays a penalty for grouping the data and then scanning the whole dictionary of boolean values that indicate whether the count is equal to the maximum count. The numeric inconsistency and computational inefficiency can be overcome.

To prevent the allocation of large transient vectors, the .ml.wfreq function, and therefore its .ml.freq projection, creates a dictionary and increments the frequency for each record. And to ensure numeric consistency, it returns a dictionary with sorted keys.

## 2.10. WEIGHTED AVERAGE OR MODE

```
q).ml.freq 2 2 1 1 3
1| 2
2| 2
3| 1
```

Instead of sorting all the data, however, the .ml.wfreq function efficiently sorts the unique values when building the dictionary's key. The group operator, in contrast, is ordered based on the order in which the values are first encountered.

```
q)group 2 2 1 1 3
2| 0 1
1| 2 3
3| ,4
```

This means any statistic derived from this function depends on the order of the data. The .ml.wmode and, by projection, the .ml.mode functions are implemented in terms of the .ml.wfreq function and therefore benefit from the numerical consistency of having the dictionary sorted.

The mode (or weighted mode) is calculated by searching for the maximum value within the frequency distribution. Instead of comparing each of the frequencies to the maximum frequency, the .ml.wmode function uses the .ml.imax function, which employs the ? find operator to scan the dictionary. The ? operator returns immediately after finding the first occurrence of the requested value.

The .ml.imax and sibling .ml.imin functions are used frequently throughout the funq project.

**.ml.imin**

```
imin:{find[x;min x]}          / index of min element
```

They are both implemented in terms of the .ml.find function.

## Find

The .ml.find function extends the functionality of the ? operator. Not only does it accept vectors and dictionaries, but the .ml.find function can also find the indices of the first occurrence of a value over the second dimension of matrices and flipped tables.

**.ml.find**

```
/ return first index of atom/vec y in vec/dict/matrix/flipped table x
find:{$[0h>type first x;?;type x;key[x]mfind::;mfind][x;y]}
```

To match the signature of the ? find operator, the .ml.find function accepts the object to be searched as its first argument and the value to be searched for as the second argument. The behavior is controlled by the type of the first element of first argument x. This may seem a bit odd at first glance, but it is a nice trick to differentiate lists and simple dictionaries from structures such as matrices and flipped tables which are aggregations of lists.

If the x argument is a list (or simple dictionary), the native ? operator is used to find the index (or key) of the first occurrence of the y argument. For example, using .ml.imin on a vector returns the index of the minimum value, while using it on a dictionary returns the key corresponding to the minimum value.

```
q).ml.imin 1 2 3 10 8 0
5
q).ml.imin `a`b`c`d`e`f!1 2 3 10 8 0
`f
```

Without complicating things, we can also find the index of the minimum element of each *row* of a matrix by using the each adverb.

```
q).ml.imin each (2 4 6;7 6 5)
0 2
```

There are cases, however, when we need to find the index of the minimum (or maximum) element of each *column* of a matrix (.ml.cgroup introduced in Chapter 3 [45]) or *row* of a table (.ml.pnb introduced in Chapter 6 [109]). The .ml.mfind matrix-find function is used for these cases. If the type of the first element of the x argument is not an atom, the .ml.find function uses the .ml.mfind function to find the indices of the first occurrence over the second dimension of the matrix or flipped table.

```
q).ml.imin (2 4 6;7 6 5)
0 0 1
q).ml.imax (2 4 6;7 6 5)
1 1 0
```

The only difference between the handling of a matrix and a flipped table is that although the indices of a matrix are returned directly, the indices are mapped back to the dictionary keys (column names) of the flipped table.

```
q).ml.imin `a`b!(2 4 6;7 6 5)
`a`a`b
q).ml.imax `a`b!(2 4 6;7 6 5)
`b`b`a
```

## Matrix Find

We've taken a long detour on our way to understanding the implementation of the .ml.mode function. Though we're almost finished, we need to review the implementation of .ml.mfind before we continue.

**.ml.mfind**

```
/ find row indices of each atom/vec y in matrix/flipped table x
mfind:{{[x;i;j;y]?[y=x;i&j;i]}[y]/[count[first x]#n;til n:count x;x]}
```

The .ml.mfind matrix-find function scans *every* row of a matrix and keeps track of the location of the first occurrence of the requested value. Unlike the ? operator which can stop as soon as the value is found, the .ml.mfind function must iterate across all rows of the matrix because every column is independent. The saving grace is that the matrices we tend to work with have far fewer rows, which correspond to features, than columns, which correspond to samples. The performance boost we obtain by using the ?[;;] vector conditional operator far outweighs the overhead of iterating over rows.

To handle the case where values are not found, the row indices are initialized to the length of the matrix. This ensures they are assigned an index of one past the last row. If a match is found during the iteration, the minimum of the current row and the previously recorded row is returned. Otherwise, the previously recorded row is kept. As an implementation side effect, the value to be searched for can be either an atom or a vector whose length matches the number of elements in each row of the matrix.

## 2.11 Weighting Schemes

It is common practice to weight each observation by the reciprocal of its distance. This allows the closest training point to have the most influence on the prediction.

For the following example, we pass the 1f% projection as the weighting function and 5 for the number of points k. Comparing each element to the correct classification and taking the average gives us the algorithm's accuracy.

```
q)avg yt=.ml.knn[1f%;5;y] .ml.f2nd[.ml.edist X] Xt
0.9777778
```

Using the reciprocal of the distance is intuitive—the smaller the distance, the higher the weight. It does, however, break down when the distance is exactly zero. In this case, the reciprocal is infinite, and the resulting weighted average will be null. This may seem unlikely, but consider the case where our X values are limited to a small set of fixed values. The chances of repeat observations become more likely. One way of preventing the value from zero from destroying our weighted average calculation is to add a very small number to each of the values. This prevents the number zero from appearing anywhere in our data set. This won't have a large impact on our iris data set, but the technique will come in handy in Section 12.5 [273].

```
q)avg yt=.ml.knn[1f%1e-8+;5;y] .ml.f2nd[.ml.edist X] Xt
1f
```

Another method of weighting that naturally handles zero distances is to use a decaying exponential of the form $e^{-ax}$. When the distance x is zero, the weight becomes 1, and when the distance is infinite, the weight becomes 0. The speed at which this decay occurs depends on our choice of $a$. If we set $a$ to zero, the points will be equally weighted. If, on the other hand, we use a very large value for $a$, the weights of the points will decay very fast—even for small differences in distances. Sadly, this extra variable $a$ introduces another parameter to tune—making the technique less popular.

```
q)avg yt=.ml.knn[exp neg 1f*;5;y] .ml.f2nd[.ml.edist X] Xt
1f
```

Although we can achieve equal weighting by using an exponential decay with $a$ set to 0, there is a more efficient method that does not require the exp operator. We can compare the values to 0n and pass the resulting boolean vector as the weights.

```
q)avg yt=.ml.knn[0n<;5;y] .ml.f2nd[.ml.edist X] Xt
1f
```

Finally, we can remove the actual distance values out of consideration and rely only on the ranking of the values based on their distance. In this case, the furthest

neighbor receives a weight of 1 and the closest neighbor obtains a weight of k—
equal to the number of neighbors chosen.

```
q)avg yt=.ml.knn[1+rank neg::;5;y] .ml.f2nd[.ml.edist X] Xt
1f
```

The iris species have pretty tight clusters. Our choice of weighting scheme did
not change our results at all. The .ml.knn k-nearest-neighbors function was built
with flexibility in mind, and therefore allows the user to supply any of the popular
weighting functions.[7]

## 2.12 Euclidean Distance Squared

A popular alternative to using the Euclidean distance metric is to use the Euclidean
distance squared. This is allowed because the sqrt operator is monotonic and
merely scales all the results without affecting the relative ordering of the values.
We can, therefore, use .ml.edist2 instead of .ml.edist when a distance function
is required.

**.ml.edist2**

```
edist2:enorm2 (-)::                / Euclidean distance squared
```

Using the .ml.edist2 operator produces a different (but compatible) distance matrix.

```
q).ml.f2nd[.ml.edist2 X] Xt
0.46 1.85 0.34 1.02 0.57 0.28 0.62 0.27 1.18 0.38 0.97 1.02 0.91 0.5  1.1..
0.33 1.32 0.13 0.39 0.26 0.09 0.19 0.26 0.77 1.17 0.38 0.69 0.74 0.21 0.5..
0.14 2.01 0.42 1.02 0.65 0.28 0.46 0.11 1.26 0.38 0.97 1.18 0.99 0.42 1.1..
0.42 0.63 0.14 0.26 0.11 0.12 0.38 0.81 0.26 1.38 0.27 0.22 0.17 0.18 0.3..
0.94 0.09 0.46 0.1  0.21 0.52 0.42 1.75 0.02 2.94 0.09 0.06 0.11 0.3  0.1..
0.25 1.34 0.11 0.53 0.26 0.05 0.33 0.22 0.75 0.69 0.52 0.65 0.6  0.23 0.6..
0.38 0.75 0.02 0.22 0.05 0.02 0.22 0.55 0.34 1.22 0.21 0.26 0.27 0.1  0.2..
..
```

We should remember to add the sqrt operator back when computing the weighted
average. Since the .ml.knn function accepts the weighting function, we can easily
add it there.

---

[7]Z. Geler, V. Kurbalija, M. Radovanović, and M. Ivanović, "Comparison of different weighting schemes for the kNN classifier on time-series data," *Knowl Inf Syst*, vol. 48, no. 2, pp. 331–378, Aug. 2016, doi: 10.1007/s10115-015-0881-0.

```
q)avg yt=.ml.knn[sqrt 1f%;5;y] .ml.f2nd[.ml.edist2 X] Xt
0.9777778
```

## 2.13 Pairwise Euclidean Distance Squared

Starting with Equation 2.2 [22] for a vector of data points, we can expand the squared difference into a sum of squares and a cross-term to arrive at Equation 2.8 [40].

$$D_{ij} = \|\vec{x}_i - \vec{x}_j\|^2 = \|\vec{x}_i\|^2 - 2\vec{x}_i^T \vec{x}_j + \|\vec{x}_j\|^2$$

Equation 2.8: Pairwise Euclidean Distance Squared

This expansion does not offer savings when computed over a single pair of data points. When a vector of points is considered, however, it allows us to implement the algorithm using vectorized operators and matrix multiplication instead of eaching within the .ml.edist2 function. This is implemented in the pairwise-Euclidean-distance-squared function .ml.pedist2.

**.ml.pedist2**

```
pedist2:{enorm2[x]+/:enorm2[y]+-2f*mtm["f"$y;"f"$x]} / pairwise edist2
```

> **Matrix Multiplication only Works with Floats**
>
> Q will only apply matrix multiplication on vectors of floating-point values. The .ml.pedist2 function must, therefore, cast the input arguments to ensure proper behavior. Even if we try to save memory by storing data as 4-byte integers, 4-byte reals, 2-byte shorts or even a single byte, the data must be expanded into 8-byte floats before performing the matrix multiplication. Note that this function uses the mtm operator, which is an abstraction of matrix multiplication. We will review this decision in Section 9.5 [187].

Instead of applying the .ml.edist2[X] projection over the second dimension of the Xt matrix, we can use the more efficient .ml.pedist2 operator directly on the X and Xt matrices.

```
q)avg yt=.ml.knn[sqrt 1f%;5;y] .ml.pedist2[X;Xt]
1f
```

There are other approaches to improving the performance of the k-nearest neighbors algorithm such as using k-d trees and ball-trees, which speed up the distance computation at the expense of using more memory (and some upfront processing time), to create data structures that organize the data based on proximity. Their implementations require nested loops and are not well-suited for q. In addition, their performance depends critically on the number and dimension of the data.

## 2.14 K-Fold Cross Validation

As we saw in the initial example, the performance of k-nearest neighbors depends on the number of neighbors we include. Comparing the accuracy across a few different values for k allows us to pick a k that maximizes the accuracy. By combining the creation of the distance matrix with the k-NN algorithm, we can create a function that encapsulates the fitting data and produces a function that is ready to be used for predicting new samples. The .ml.fknn fit-k-nearest-neighbors function returns this composition. Functions that accept functions as arguments or return functions as results are called higher-order functions.

**.ml.fknn**

```
/ given (w)eighting (f)unction, (d)istance (f)unction, atom or vector of (k)
/ values, a (y) vector and matri(X), 'fit' a knn 'model'
fknn:{[wf;df;k;y;X] knn[wf;k;y] df[X]::}
```

We can create a fitting function ff that has the weighting function and the distance function specified, but leaves the remaining parameters unspecified. By passing a list of k values, and finding the one with maximum accuracy, we can see that using three clusters is optimal.

```
q)ff:.ml.fknn[sqrt 1f%;.ml.f2nd .ml.edist2@]
q)ks .ml.imax avg e:yt=ff[ks:1+til 10;y;X] Xt
3
```

I hope you felt bad about using the test data to pick the best k parameter. Using the test data to train the model is an extremely poor practice. Doing so uses all the data to build the model, and we have nothing left to evaluate it out of sample. We may have seriously over-fit the data. A better solution is to use an algorithm called k-fold cross validation to split our training data into k folds and create k different models. The final parameter will be the average (or mode) of the k models. We will use the .ut.part function to generate the k folds and the .ml.xv function to perform the cross validation.

**.ml.xv**

```
/ use all (f)old(s) (except the (i)th) to fit a model using the (f)itting
/ (f)unction and then use (p)rediction (f)unction on fs[i]. fs can be a list
/ of tables or (y;X) pairs -- corresponding to ff arguments.
xv:{[ff;pf;fs;i]                / cross validate
 v:fs i;fs _ : i;               / split training and validation sets
 a:$[type v;enlist raze fs;[v@:1;(raze;,'/)@'flip fs]]; / build ff arguments
 m:ff . a;                      / fit model on training set
 p:pf[m] v;                     / make predictions on validation set
 p}
```

The .ml.xv cross-validation function accepts a fitting function, prediction function, the folds which will be tables, or y vector and X matrix pairs, and finally the index, which we will iterate over ourselves. The first line of the algorithm stores the i-th fold into v so it can be used for validation. That fold is then dropped from fs. The second line of the algorithm handles differences between cross validation for functions that accept a table and functions that accept a y vector and X matrix. If the validation fold is a table, it is merely razed. If, however, it is a y vector and X matrix pair, the handling is a bit more complicated. The first step is to throw the validation y vector away and store the validation X matrix in v. The y vectors can be merged across folds with the raze operator, but we do not want to raze the X matrices themselves. We need to raze the rows of each matrix across folds. To achieve this, the ,'/ composition is used. In either case, the result is a list of arguments which are passed on the third line to ff with the . apply operator. The resulting model is then used on the last line with the prediction function pf to generate a prediction.

To implement k-fold cross validation, we first generate a list of indices i and partition our X matrix and y vector into 5 folds.

```
q)n:5
q)i:.ut.part[n#1;0N?] til count X 0
q)Xs:flip X[;i]
q)ys:y i
```

## 2.14. K-FOLD CROSS VALIDATION

The k-nearest neighbors algorithm performs the fitting and predicting in one shot, so although the .ml.xv function requires us to supply both, the .ml.pknn predict-k-nearest-neighbors function is simply defined as the @ apply operator.

**.ml.pknn**

```
pknn:@                    / predict knn by applying model returned from fknn to X
```

We can now test different values for k by passing the fitting function ff and the prediction function pf to .ml.xv with the first parameter of ff bound to our list of k values in ks.

```
q)pf:.ml.pknn
q)e:ys=p:(.ml.xv[ff[ks];pf;flip (ys;Xs)]) each til n
```

Flipping the ys and Xs pair generates a list of pairs corresponding to each fold. After we run the cross validation across all folds, the predicted values are stored in p and the errors in e. We now have an error for each observation, fold and k combination.

```
q)e
1111111000b 1111111111b 1111111111b 1111111111b 1111111111b 1111111111b 1..
1111111111b 0011111111b 1111111111b 1111111111b 1111111111b 1111111111b 1..
1111111111b 1111111111b 1111111111b 1111111111b 1111111111b 1111111111b 1..
1111111111b 0000000000b 1111111111b 1101010000b 1111111111b 1111111111b 1..
1111111111b 1111111111b 1111111111b 1111111111b 1111111111b 1111111111b 1..
```

The next step is to compute the accuracy of the observations within a fold and then average the accuracies across folds to obtain an accuracy for each choice of k. We can then use the .ml.imax function to find the value of k which maximizes the algorithm's accuracy.

```
q)ks .ml.imax avg avg each e
4
```

The k-nearest neighbors algorithm is intuitive, but forces us to lug around all the training data. In the next chapter, we discuss the k-means algorithm, which summarizes the training data into k clusters—each of which are defined by a single point called a centroid.

# Chapter 3

# K-Means

> A city, far from being a cluster of buildings, is actually a sequence of spaces enclosed and defined by buildings.
>
> — I. M. Pei

While the k-means algorithm sounds similar to k-nearest neighbors because of the leading *k*, it is a completely independent algorithm. Whereas k-nearest neighbors is a supervised pattern recognition algorithm, k-means is an unsupervised clustering algorithm and is not used for prediction. There is, therefore, no need to split the data into training and testing partitions. Like k-nearest neighbors, the algorithm uses different distance metrics. But unlike k-nearest neighbors, labels are not used to determine accuracy.

The k-means algorithm is an example of a partitional clustering algorithm where each cluster is defined by the data points' proximity to the cluster's center. By specifying the number of clusters and the distance metric, the data scientist uses the algorithm to define clusters which minimize the intra-cluster distance while maximizing the intra-cluster distances.

An example where clustering algorithms could be used is for a T-shirt manufacturer. Assume the manufacturer has determined to build 5 shirt-sizes: XS, S, M, L, XL. Given a sampling of people's measurements, a clustering algorithm could tell the manufacturer what dimensions each of those sizes should be in order to minimize the distance from each person's measurements to the nearest shirt size.

A new shopper would then buy the shirt whose size most closely reflects their measurements. The object of clustering is to find latent structure in data where labels are not provided.

We start by demonstrating the k-means algorithm before detailing the implementation.

## 3.1 K-Means Example

Example 3.1 [46] begins by loading the funq project and then the iris data set. It then defines a cplt function composition, which can be reused to plot the centroids alongside the petal length and width data. The last line generates and plots three centroids from the iris data set.

**Example 3.1** K-Means
```
q)\l funq.q
q)\l iris.q
q)X:iris.X
q)cplt:.ut.plt .ml.append[0N;-2#X],'.ml.append[1] -2#
q)cplt C:.ml.forgy[3] X
3| "                              "
 | "                              "
 | "                 ....         "
 | "                 .... .       "
2| "                 .......      "
 | "         @... .              "
 | "         ..@..@.             "
1| "         ....                 "
 | " .                            "
 | "...                           "
0| "...                           "
```

Using these centroids, we can group the iris data into clusters corresponding to each data point's closest centroid. In this case, we define "closeness" using the Euclidean distance squared (which produces results equivalent to the Euclidean distance but is faster).

```
q).ml.cgroup[.ml.edist2;X] C
0 1 2 3 4 5 6 7 8 9 10 11 12 13 14 15 16 17 18 19 20 21 22 23 24 25 26 27..
50 51 52 54 56 58 65 71 74 75 76 85 86 91 97
63 68 72 73 77 83 87 100 101 102 103 104 105 107 108 109 110 111 112 115 ..
```

## 3.1. K-MEANS EXAMPLE

Passing these results to the `.ut.ugrp` ungroup utility generates a vector with unique values per cluster. Example 3.2 [47] shows how we can use these values to visualize the clusters.

**Example 3.2** K-Means Initial Clusters

```
q)mplt:.ut.plot[19;10;.ut.c10;.ml.mode] (-2#X),enlist .ut.ugrp ::
q)mplt .ml.cgroup[.ml.edist2;X] C
3| "                             "
 | "              .@@@           "
 | "             @@@@ @"
2| "            .@@@@@@"
 | "          .+@@ @    "
 | "        ...++ @     "
1| "         ....        "
 | " .                   "
 | "...                  "
0| "...                  "
```

Note how we used the underlying `.ut.plot` function instead of the `.ut.plt` projection so that we could redefine how overlapping values within each "pixel" are treated. Instead of using the default `avg`, we use `.ml.mode` to ensure each pixel belongs to one of the three clusters. Again, we stored this plotting projection into a variable `mplt` so we can reuse it.

Using the initial centroids C, we can run one round of the k-means algorithm and the centroids redistribute themselves more evenly throughout the data. The move to the center of each cluster is displayed in Example 3.3 [48]. One centroid, however, seems to have gone awry and positioned itself where there is no data.

Example 3.4 [48] shows an enlargement of the middle cluster.

Another round of k-means and Example 3.5 [48] shows how the rogue centroid has jumped to the cluster of data in the lower left.

This last round of k-means, shown in Example 3.6 [49], sees the centroids make minor adjustments to their position.

We can use the / adverb to iterate a fixed number of times,

```
q)show C:2 .ml.kmeans[X]/ .ml.forgy[3] X
5.20303    6.84878  5.867442
3.269697   3.070732 2.718605
2.056061   5.668293 4.548837
0.4787879  2.02439  1.518605
```

**Example 3.3** K-Means Centroids After One Round

```
q)cplt C:.ml.kmeans[X] C
3| "                          "
 | "              ....        "
 | "              .... .      "
2| "             ..@....      "
 | "              .... .      "
 | "             ...@. .      "
1| "              ....        "
 | " .    @                   "
 | "...                       "
0| "...                       "
```

**Example 3.4** K-Means Clusters After One Round

```
q)mplt .ml.cgroup[.ml.edist2;X] C
3| "                          "
 | "              @@@@        "
 | "              @@@@ @      "
2| "             +@@@@@@      "
 | "              ++++ @      "
 | "             +++++ @      "
1| "              ...+        "
 | " .                        "
 | "...                       "
0| "...                       "
```

**Example 3.5** K-Means Centroids After Two Rounds

```
q)cplt C:.ml.kmeans[X] C
3| "                          "
 | "              ....        "
 | "              .... .      "
2| "             ...@...      "
 | "              .... .      "
 | "             ...@. .      "
1| "              ....        "
 | " .                        "
 | "..@                       "
0| "...                       "
```

## 3.1. K-MEANS EXAMPLE

---

**Example 3.6** K-Means Centroids After Three Rounds

```
q)cplt C:.ml.kmeans[X] C
3|  "                          "
 |  "            ....          "
 |  "            .... .        "
2|  "            ...@...       "
 |  "            .... .        "
 |  "           ..@.. .        "
1|  "            ....          "
 |  " .                        "
 |  "...                       "
0|  ".@.                       "
```

---

or use the over adverb to run the k-means algorithm until convergence,

```
q)show C:.ml.kmeans[X] over C
5.006 5.901613 6.85
3.428 2.748387 3.073684
1.462 4.393548 5.742105
0.246 1.433871 2.071053
```

and see the final state of the clusters in Example 3.7 [49].

---

**Example 3.7** K-Means Clusters After Convergence

```
q)mplt .ml.cgroup[.ml.edist2;X] C
3|  "                          "
 |  "          +@@@            "
 |  "          @@@@ @"
2|  "          ++@@@@@"
 |  "          ++++ @          "
 |  "          +++++ @         "
1|  "         ++++              "
 |  " .                        "
 |  "...                       "
0|  "...                       "
```

---

The centroids can then be mapped back to their labels for inspection.

```
q)flip (4#iris.c)!C
slength  swidth  plength  pwidth
```

```
----------------------------------
5.006    3.428    1.462    0.246
5.901613 2.748387 4.393548 1.433871
6.85     3.073684 5.742105 2.071053
```

You may be left with a few questions. Was the random selection of initial centroid optimal? What guided the centroids along their path? Is three rounds of k-means enough? Was three centroids optimal? The remainder of this chapter details the implementation of the k-means algorithm and answers these questions.

You may have also wondered how we generated plots in the terminal. That would be too much fun for one chapter, so we leave that until Chapter 14 [313].

## 3.2 Centroid Initialization

To perform k-means clustering, we must first initialize k centroids—one for each of the k clusters we desire. Quick convergence of the k-means algorithm critically depends on the initial centroid positions. Selecting initial centroids that are close together causes the k-means algorithm to take longer to converge. We will review three initialization schemes: the Forgy, random partition and k-means++ methods.

### Forgy Method

Our example above used the .ml.forgy function to pick random coordinates from each dimension of the data set.

```
q).ml.forgy[3] X
5.5 5.2 6.2
2.8 3   3
5.7 1.3 1.4
0.3 1.6 1.3
```

Choosing an initial centroid from the provided data increases our chance that we've started the algorithm with centroids somewhere close to the optimal values and is known as the Forgy method after E. W. Forgy.[1]

**.ml.forgy**

---

[1] E. W. Forgy, "Cluster analysis of multivariate data: efficiency versus interpretability of classifications," *Biometrics*, Jan. 1965.

## 3.2. CENTROID INITIALIZATION

```
/ generate (k) centroids by randomly choosing (k) samples from matri(X)
forgy:{[k;X]neg[k]?/:X}          / Forgy method
```

The function accepts two parameters: the number of desired centroids k and the data X. The implementation uses the ? operator to randomly select k values from each feature of the X matrix. We supplied a negative left operand to the ? operator to prevent any single point from being chosen more than once. A positive argument to the ? operator randomly selects values *with* replacement while negative arguments randomly select values *without* replacement.

> **Centroid vs. Medoid**
>
> Note that the generated centroids are not points from the original data set. They are just a combination of their coordinates. In other words, the centroid could be (x1;y2;z3) not necessarily (x1;y1;z1). If we require the centroids to be elements from the original data set, we would need to use a different algorithm called k-medoids (discussed in Section 3.7 [62]).

### Random Partition

Instead of creating k random centroids, we can randomly assign each data point to one of k groups (or clusters) and then compute a centroid from each group. This is called random partition initialization. We can, for example, use the ? operator to generate a vector of random values from a universe of k integers.

```
q)count[X 0]?3
0 1 2 0 2 2 2 0 2 2 0 2 1 2 1 1 1 2 2 2 1 1 0 1 1 1 2 0 0 1 2 1 0 2 1 1 2..
```

Using the group operator, we can then generate the indices for k clusters,

```
q)value group count[X 0]?3
0 2 3 5 8 10 11 16 18 19 23 28 29 30 32 34 36 39 41 42 45 46 51 57 58 61 ..
1 4 6 12 13 20 21 24 26 35 38 47 48 50 53 54 55 56 60 67 74 77 80 81 83 8..
7 9 14 15 17 22 25 27 31 33 37 40 43 44 49 52 59 64 65 69 70 72 76 78 79 ..
```

which can be used to index back into the data to generate k clusters.

```
q)X@\:value group count[X 0]?3
5.1 4.7 4.6 4.6 4.4 4.8 5.7 5.7 4.6 5.1 5.2 4.7 4.8 5.2 5 4.9 5.1 4.5 4.4..
3.5 3.2 3.1 3.4 2.9 3.4 4.4 3.8 3.6 3.3 3.4 3.2 3.1 4.1 3.2 3.6 3.4 2.3 3..
```

```
1.4 1.3 1.5 1.4 1.4 1.6 1.5 1.7 1 1.7 1.4 1.6 1.6 1.5 1.2 1.4 1.5 1.3 1.3..
0.2 0.2 0.2 0.3 0.2 0.2 0.4 0.3 0.2 0.5 0.2 0.2 0.2 0.1 0.2 0.1 0.2 0.3 0..
```

And finally, we can generate the k centroids by aggregating each dimension of each cluster with the avg operator.

```
q)(avg'')X@\:value group count[X 0]?3
5.886275 5.766667 5.879167
3.05098  3.041176 3.08125
3.794118 3.6      3.8875
1.182353 1.133333 1.2875
```

The .ml.rpart random-partition function generalizes this approach by allowing us to specify any aggregating function—referred to here as the centroid function cf.

**.ml.rpart**

```
/ generate (k) centroids by applying (c)entroid (f)unction to (k) random
/ partitions of matri(X)
rpart:{[cf;k;X](cf'') X@\:value group count[X 0]?k} / random partition
```

This will come in handy when we discuss k-harmonic means in the section called "K-Harmonic Means" [63].

## 3.3 K-Means++ Initialization

Picking random points or assigning points to random clusters to define centroids runs the risk of unluckily starting in a bad state. Instead of resorting to luck to initialize our centroids, we can take a more proactive approach and pick initial centroids that minimize our chance of being unlucky. To differentiate between a good and bad cluster, we must first agree upon a metric that encapsulates cluster compactness.

### Cluster Quality

Cluster quality is typically defined by computing the sum of squared distances between each point in a cluster and its centroid. For a single cluster, this can be defined as $\sum_{i=1}^{n_j}\|x_i - \bar{x}\|^2$ where $n_j$ represents the number of elements in the $j^{th}$

## 3.3. K-MEANS++ INITIALIZATION

cluster. The .ml.sse sum-of-squared-error (SSE) function implements this statistic.

**.ml.sse**

```
/ given matri(X) compute the sum of squared errors (distortion)
sse:{[X]sum edist2[X] avg each X}
```

To evaluate the total errors across all clusters, sometimes referred to as "distortion", we merely sum the SSE across each cluster. This is also referred to as the sum of squares *within* (SSW) clusters to distinguish it from the sum of squares *between* (SSB) clusters. The .ml.ssw function accepts the complete data set and the cluster indices and returns the total distortion.

**.ml.ssw**

```
/ given matri(X) and cluster (I)ndices, compute within-cluster sse
ssw:{[X;I]sum (sse X@\:) peach I}
```

Beginning with randomly generated centroids, we can generate the cluster indices with .ml.cgroup and compute the SSW.

```
q).ml.ssw[X] .ml.cgroup[.ml.edist2;X] .ml.forgy[3] X
154.947
```

The function

The .ml.cgroup centroid-grouping function applies the supplied distance function over the second dimension of the centroid matrix C, determines the index of the minimum distance with the .ml.imin function and finally groups the results. It is actually possible for the algorithm to generate degenerate clusters which are empty. In this case, the number of clusters returned from the function will be fewer than the number of centroids supplied. The key of the grouped indices is removed because the assigned centroids are no longer relevant.

**.ml.cgroup**

```
/ using the (d)istance (f)unction, group matri(X) based on the closest
/ (C)entroid and return the cluster indices
cgroup:{[df;X;C]value group imin f2nd[df X] C}
```

Generating clusters and computing the SSW is conveniently combined into a single distortion function .ml.distortion.

**.ml.distortion**

```
/ using (d)istance (f)unction, matri(X) and (C)entroids, compute total
/ cluster distortion
distortion:{[X;C]ssw[X] cgroup[edist2;X] C}
```

We can see how the cluster quality continues to improve at each iteration of k-means.

```
q).ml.distortion[X] each .ml.kmeans[X] scan .ml.forgy[3] X
113.0468 90.97388 81.17606 79.54151 78.85144 78.85144
```

## Contrived Example

We now turn to an example—perhaps contrived—to demonstrate why letting fortune choose our initial centroids is such a bad idea. Take the rectangular shaped data set R displayed in Example 3.8 [54].

**Example 3.8** Contrived K-Means

```
q).ut.plt R:(0 1 5 9 10 0 1 5 9 10;0 0 0 0 0 1 1 1 1 1)
1.2|  "                              "
1   | "++         +         ++"
    |  "                              "
0.8|  "                              "
0.6|  "                              "
    |  "                              "
0.4|  "                              "
    |  "                              "
0.2|  "                              "
0   | "++         +         ++"
```

If we run k-means a few times and compute the total distortion exhibited over all clusters, we can see a very wide divergence based on the initial cluster choice.

```
q)f:.ml.distortion[R] .ml.kmeans[R] over .ml.forgy[2]::
q)f each 10#enlist R
31.5 31.5 164 166.5 31.5 166.5 31.5 31.5 166.5 31.5
```

## 3.3. K-MEANS++ INITIALIZATION

### Generalized K-Means++ Initialization

The popular way to minimize the chance of poor cluster initialization is to purposely pick centroids that are as far apart as possible. The k-means++ initialization algorithm achieves this by randomly picking the first centroid and then picking each subsequent centroid by randomly picking from the remaining points with a probability proportional to the square of their distance from the nearest already chosen centroid. This algorithm is encapsulated in the .ml.kpp generalized-initialization function.

**.ml.kpp**

```
/ k-means++ initialization algorithm
/ using (d)istance (f)unction and matri(X), append the next centroid to the
/ min centroid (d)istance and all (C)entroids
kpp:{[df;X;d;C]
 if[not count C;:(0w;X@\:1?count X 0)];    / first centroid
 if[count[X 0]=n:count C 0;:(d;C)];         / no more centroids
 d&:df[X] C[;n-1];                          / update distance vector
 C:C,'X@\: first iwrand[1] d;               / pick next centroid
 (d;C)}
```

The .ml.kpp generic k-means++ function accepts a distance function, the data X as well as the minimum distance between each data point and any centroid seen prior to the current iteration and the list of accumulated centroids.

It begins by detecting an empty list and then uniformly picks an initial centroid from the data—setting the *previous* distance to all centroids to infinity.

```
q).ml.kpp[.ml.edist2;R;();()]
0w
(,10;,0)
```

The function then proceeds to detect the condition where all points have been chosen as centroids. In this case, it returns the previously computed list of centroids. Distances from each data point to the most recently chosen centroid are then computed. The third line of the function stores the minimum of these distances and the values supplied from the previous iteration into d. The final line uses the .ml.iwrand weighted-random-value function to find the index of a random element using the distances as weights.

**.ml.iwrand**

```
/ return the index of n (w)eighted samples
iwrand:{[n;w]s binr n?last s:sums w}
```

To compute a weighted probability, the function begins by using the ? operator to uniformly generate values between zero and sum of all weights. It then uses the binr operator to find the index of each random value within the cumulative sums. We can see that calling the function with a weight of 0 never picks that index, while a weight of infinity always picks that index. Similarly, equal weights return indices in equal proportions.

```
q).ml.iwrand[10] 0 1f
1 1 1 1 1 1 1 1 1 1
q).ml.iwrand[10] 1 0w
1 1 1 1 1 1 1 1 1 1
q).ml.iwrand[10] 1 1f
0 1 1 1 1 0 0 1 0 0
```

## Iterating with Complex State

Returning to the .ml.kpp function, we notice that although the function accepts the distance vector and centroid list as two distinct arguments, it returns the new values as a pair. Because the function requires two data structures during each iteration, it is not possible to simply use the / or over adverbs. We can see how the . apply operator is required.

```
q).ml.kpp[.ml.edist2;R] . .ml.kpp[.ml.edist2;R;();()]
81 64 16 0 1 82 65 17 1 2f
(9 0;0 1)
```

The / and over adverbs allow us to iteratively call a function—using the output of the previous function call as the input for the next call. We now have a case where the state required for each iteration is not a simple table, matrix or list.

We could have implemented .ml.kpp to accept a single argument, which was the same (d;C) pair that is returned by the function, but that would then require extra code at the beginning of the function to *unpack* the pair of values into local variables. Instead, we implemented the function to take the distance vector and list of clusters as separate parameters. We therefore need some way of automatically splitting the (d;C) pair into distinct arguments.

## 3.3. K-MEANS++ INITIALIZATION

Similar to the example demonstrated above, we can use the . apply operator to transform the parameter list into a list of parameters.

```
q)2 (.ml.kpp[.ml.edist2;R] .)/ 2#()
100 81 25 1 0 101 82 26 2 1f
(10 0;0 0)
```

The same effect can be achieved with a slightly different syntax.

```
q)2 .[.ml.kpp[.ml.edist2;R]]/ 2#()
2 1 17 65 82 1 0 16 64 81f
(1 10;1 1)
```

The first requires a pair of widely spaced parentheses, and the second, a pair of widely spaced brackets. We can do better. First note that the / adverb can sometimes be used in-place of the . apply operator.

```
q)(*) . 1 2
2
q)(*/) 1 2
2
```

A double dose of the / adverb solves our problem—iterating a fixed number of times while automatically unpacking the distance vector and the list of clusters during each iteration.

```
q)2 .ml.kpp[.ml.edist2;R]// 2#()
1 0 16 64 81 2 1 17 65 82f
(1 10;0 0)
```

### K-Means++ Implementation

The .ml.kmeanspp k-means++ function is a specific parameterization of .ml.kpp that uses the Euclidean distance as its distance metric. We will see how .ml.kpp can be used with the Hamming distance metric in Section 5.5 [98].

#### .ml.kmeanspp

```
kmeanspp:kpp[edist2]              / k-means++ initialization
```

Using the k-means++ initialization algorithm on this hypothetical data set no longer results in centroids with large distortions.

```
q)f:.ml.distortion[R](.ml.kmeans[R]/)last .ml.kmeanspp[R]//[2;]::
q)f each 10 2#()
36.8 31.5 31.5 31.5 31.5 31.5 31.5 31.5 31.5 31.5
```

Applying the k-means algorithm to the Iris data produces the following centroids.

```
q)show C:.ml.kmeans[X] over last 3 .ml.kmeanspp[X]// 2#()
5.006 6.853846 5.883607
3.428 3.076923 2.740984
1.462 5.715385 4.388525
0.246 2.053846 1.434426
```

## 3.4 Lloyd's Algorithm

We now turn to Lloyd's algorithm, which is the basis for the k-means algorithm. Lloyd's algorithm involves iteratively performing an Assignment and Update step until centroids are formed that minimize the intra-cluster dispersion.

Assignment   Assign each data point to the *nearest* of the k centroids.

Update       Create k new centroids by *merging* the points of each group created in the Assignment step.

These two steps—assignment and update—are together known as Lloyd's algorithm after Stuart P. Lloyd and are implemented in .ml.lloyd.

**.ml.lloyd**

```
lloyd:{[df;cf;X;C]cf X@\: cgroup[df;X;C]}
```

Lloyd's algorithm requires us to provide a distance function, a centroid function, the data to be clustered and the initial centroids. Using the distance function, the algorithm first performs the update step by calling the .ml.cgroup centroid-grouping function to assign each data point to the nearest cluster.

Then, using the centroid function, the .ml.lloyd function computes and returns the new centroids.

The .ml.kmeans function is a specific parameterization of Lloyd's algorithm.

## 3.4. LLOYD'S ALGORITHM

### .ml.kmeans

```
kmeans:lloyd[edist2;avg'']      / k-means
```

Specifically, the k-means algorithm uses the Euclidean distance metric and averages the data points within each cluster to create new clusters. There are, however, other choices for these two parameters. The choice of distance metric affects the speed and stability of the algorithm as well as the shape of the clusters.

The k-means algorithm uses the Euclidean (or L2) distance. Similar to k-nearest neighbors, it is common to use the Euclidean distance squared for performance.

Using the .ml.cgroup function, the .ml.lloyd function groups the data based on each point's nearest centroid.

```
q).ml.cgroup[.ml.edist2;X] .ml.forgy[3] X
60 106 113
100 102 104 105 107 108 109 112 117 118 120 122 124 125 129 130 131 135 1..
0 1 2 3 4 5 6 7 8 9 10 11 12 13 14 15 16 17 18 19 20 21 22 23 24 25 26 27..
```

The algorithm then moves to the Update step and averages each of the elements within each grouping to compute the new centroids.

```
q)show C:(avg'') X@\:.ml.cgroup[.ml.edist2;X] .ml.forgy[3] X
5.006 6.301031 5
3.428 2.886598 2.4
1.462 4.958763 3.2
0.246 1.695876 1.033333
```

Using the mplt projection defined above, we can demonstrate how the algorithm clustered the data.

```
q)mplt .ml.cgroup[.ml.edist2;X] C
3| "                         "
 | "            + +++        "
 | "            +++++++     "
2| "            ++++++++"
 | "           ++++  +       "
 | "         @@+++   +       "
1| "         @@@@+           "
 | "    .                    "
 | "  ...                    "
0| " ....                    "
```

The key to rendering this plot is determining which samples belong to which clusters. This was achieved using the .ut.ugrp utility.

## 3.5 Ungrouping Clusters

The .ut.ugrp utility reverses the effect of the group operator. It accepts a dictionary and returns a vector where each value was obtained from the dictionary key that corresponded to the index stored in the dictionary value.

**.ut.ugrp**

```
/ given a dictionary mirroring the group operator return value, reconstruct
/ the original ungrouped list.  generate the dictionary key if none provided
ugrp:{
 if[not type x;x:til[count x]!x];
 x:@[sum[count each x]#k;value x;:;k:key x];
 x}
```

With a simple example, we can see how grouping and then ungrouping a list returns the initial list.

```
q).ut.ugrp group 4 4 1 1 2 3 3 5
4 4 1 1 2 3 3 5
```

The .ut.ugrp utility has also been overloaded to accept just the nested list of indices corresponding to the grouped values—the return value of the group operator without the key. This is useful because the .ml.cgroup function returns the cluster indices without the centroid-identifying key. We will see in Chapter 4 [67] how clusters can be defined without reference to corresponding centroids. Clusters are defined by their cohorts, not their centroid.

To ungroup a nested list of indices without the original labels, the first line of the .ut.ugrp utility assigns a unique integer value to each cluster. The position and cluster membership of each sample remains the same, but the labels change.

```
q).ut.ugrp value group 4 4 1 1 2 3 3 5
0 0 1 1 2 3 3 4
```

Using the .ut.ugrp utility on the return value of the .ml.cgroup function results in a vector of labels that can be associated with x and y coordinates for plotting.

```
q)(-2#X),enlist .ut.ugrp .ml.cgroup[.ml.edist2;X] C
1.4 1.4 1.3 1.5 1.4 1.7 1.4 1.5 1.4 1.5 1.5 1.6 1.4 1.1 1.2 1.5 1.3 1.4 1..
0.2 0.2 0.2 0.2 0.2 0.4 0.3 0.2 0.2 0.1 0.2 0.2 0.1 0.1 0.2 0.4 0.4 0.3 0..
0   0   0   0   0   0   0   0   0   0   0   0   0   0   0   0   0   0   0..
```

## 3.6. THE ELBOW METHOD

With the implementation of k-means under our belt, we now move to the critical question: how many clusters should we generate? What is the optimal value for k?

## 3.6 The Elbow Method

We know from the Iris species labels that there are, in fact, three species. But will the k-means algorithm actually partition the data into three clusters? What is, in fact, the optimal number of clusters? Using the .ml.distortion function, we can compute the total distortion across all clusters for each choice of k.

### Sum of Squared Errors Within

Example 3.9 [61] plots each of the distortion values. We can see the graph resembles a bent arm—where the optimal number of clusters k is found at the elbow.

**Example 3.9** Sum of Squared Errors Within

```
q)C:{[X;k].ml.kmeans[X] over last k .ml.kmeanspp[X]// 2#()}[X] each 1+til 10
q).ut.plt .ml.distortion[X] each C
800|  "                  "
   |  "+                 "
600|  "                  "
   |  "                  "
400|  "                  "
   |  "                  "
   |  "                  "
200|  "                  "
   |  "    +             "
 0 |  "       + + + + + + + +"
```

Total distortion continues to drop significantly through three clusters, and adding extra clusters only reduces the distortion by a small amount. This matches our knowledge that the data contained three species of Iris—but it needn't be so.

### Percentage of Total Variance

The sum of squares *within* statistic has an arbitrarily large range of values. This can cause details in the graph to be lost. An alternate approach is to plot the percentage of total variance explained by the sum of squares *between*.

If the sum of squares within details the sum of all distances squared from each point in a cluster to its centroid, the remaining error is computed by summing the distances from each centroid to the centroid of all points. This is called the sum of squares between. The two combined produce the total sum of squares, which can be computed by treating the data as a single cluster and computing the sum of squares within.

**.ml.ssb**

```
/ given matri(X) and cluster (I)ndices, compute between-cluster sse
ssb:{[X;I]count'[I] wsum edist2[(avg '')G] (avg raze::) each G:X@\:I}
```

Plotting the percentage of total variance as a function of k always gives a plot, seen in Example 3.10 [62], with a range of values from zero to one.

**Example 3.10** Percentage of Total Variance

```
q)I:.ml.cgroup[.ml.edist2;X] each C
q).ut.plt (.ml.ssb[X] each I)%.ml.sse X
1   | "        + + + + + + +"
0.8 | "   +                  "
    | "  +                   "
0.6 | "                      "
    | "                      "
0.4 | "                      "
    | "                      "
0.2 | "                      "
    | "                      "
0   | "+                     "
```

## 3.7 Partitional Clustering

We've written the k-means clustering algorithm as a specific parameterization of the more generic Lloyd's algorithm. This allows us to use alternate "assignment" and "update" functions to build new partitional clustering algorithms.

## K-Medians

If we use the Manhattan (L1) distance function .ml.mdist instead of the Euclidean (L2) distance function squared .ml.edist2 for the assignment function and compute the median of the points instead of taking the average when performing the update function, we can build the k-medians algorithm.

**.ml.kmedians**

```
kmedians:lloyd[mdist;med'']         / k-medians
```

Using the k-medians algorithm creates clusters that minimize the absolute distance from the points to their centroids while k-means minimizes the variance. In addition, the result of using k-medians produces centroids with coordinates obtained from the actual data.

```
q).ml.kmedians[X] over last 3 .ml.kmedianspp[X]// (0w;())
5   5.9 6.7
3.4 2.8 3
1.5 4.5 5.7
0.2 1.4 2.1
```

The previous example initialized the centroids using the .ml.kmedianspp k-medians++ projection. It uses the same .ml.kpp function, but computes distances using the Manhattan distance instead of the Euclidean distance squared.

**.ml.kmedianspp**

```
kmedianspp:kpp[mdist]               / k-medians++ initialization
```

## K-Harmonic Means

The k-harmonic means (KHM) algorithm attempts to reduce the dependence on the initial cluster choice by using the harmonic mean instead of the average or median during the update phase.

**.ml.hmean**

```
hmean:1f%avg 1f%                    / harmonic mean
```

Each iteration of the k-harmonic means algorithm is less sensitive to points with large distances. This also means the centroids move slower and the algorithm can, therefore, take many more iterations to converge. The k-harmonic means algorithm can be initialized using the random partition method instead of the Forgy method to allow the centroids to be chosen with the .ml.hmean aggregating function. After averaging the initial groups, this typically creates centrally located centroids.

```
q).ml.rpart[.ml.hmean;3] X
5.727008  5.710083  5.749889
3.013871  3.013791  2.955854
2.639311  2.658697  2.805569
0.5058747 0.4940317 0.4815996
```

## K-Medoids

The last algorithm in the partitional clustering family of algorithms that we will discuss is k-medoids. Instead of minimizing the squared distance like k-means, k-medoids minimizes the actual distance like k-medians. In addition, centroids (or medoids) of the k-medians algorithm are constrained to actual points within the data set. At the cost of a more complicated algorithm, k-medoids has the benefit of being less sensitive to outliers—regardless of the distance metric used.

The k-medoids algorithm is implemented using the .ml.pam partitioning-around-medoids (PAM) function.

**.ml.pam**

```
/ given a (d)istance (f)unction, return a new function that finds a medoid
/ during the "update" step of lloyd's algorithm
pam:{[df]lloyd[df;flip f2nd[medoid df]::]} / partitioning around medoids
```

The .ml.pam higher-order function does not implement the PAM algorithm directly. Taking advantage of q's functional nature it accepts a distance function and returns another function—a projection of .ml.lloyd with the update function customized to return a medoid instead of a centroid. Finding a medoid is more computationally intensive than finding a centroid. The process involves assuming each point is the medoid and computing the total distance between that point and each and every other point in the cluster. To identify the medoid, we simply return the point which minimized the intra-cluster distance.

**.ml.medoid**

```
/ using (d)istance (f)unction, find the medoid in matri(X)
medoid:{[df;X]X@\:imin f2nd[sum df[X]::] X}
```

## 3.7. PARTITIONAL CLUSTERING

Although the k-medoids algorithm does not specify the actual distance function to use, the most popular choices are the Manhattan distance and the Euclidean distance. Regardless of this choice, the effect of outliers is still limited.

To run k-medoids clustering we first generate a list of medoids—3 in this case. This is done by generating three random integers that we use for indexing into each dimension of the Iris data set. This ensures that each medoid is an actual point from the data set.

```
q)show M:X@\:-3?count X 0
6.2 6.7 5.9
2.8 3   3
4.8 5   4.2
1.8 1.7 1.5
```

We then use the .ml.pam function to generate a function projection of .ml.lloyd and iterate until convergence. We see that the medoids are quite close to the centroids determined by the previous algorithms. The k-medoids algorithm would only generate a significantly different solution if the data had large outliers.

```
q)cplt M:.ml.pam[.ml.edist][X] over M
3| "                      "
 | "            ....      "
 | "           .@.. ."
2| "           .......   "
 | "         .@...    "
 | "          ..... . "
1| "          ....     "
 | " .                 "
 | "...                "
0| ".@.                "
```

To confirm these medoids are in fact elements of the data set, we can find the exact indices.

```
q)flip[X] ? flip M
27 70 82
```

This chapter focused on the partitional clustering techniques k-means, k-medians, k-harmonic means and k-medoids. Each cluster was uniquely identified by a single centroid (or medoid), around which the other points were associated. We now turn to a hierarchical clustering technique that builds clusters by iteratively merging smaller clusters into ever larger clusters. Each cluster does, of course, have a centroid but it is not necessarily used in determining how the cluster is built.

# Chapter 4

# Hierarchical Agglomerative Clustering

> Every seeming equality conceals a hierarchy.
>
> — Mason Cooley

Hierarchical Cluster Analysis (HCA) builds a model by iteratively splitting (or combining) clusters of data points. Divisive clustering begins with a single cluster and then iteratively divides the clusters until all data points are in their own cluster. Agglomerative clustering starts with each data point in its own cluster and then iteratively merges two clusters until a single cluster containing all the data points remains. In both cases, we can then compare the total intra-cluster distance at each stage of the process and pick the number of clusters that provides the best trade-off between model complexity (increased number of clusters) and error (greater intra-cluster distance).

We will focus on hierarchical agglomerative clustering (HAC) and the ingenious Lance-Williams algorithm.

## 4.1 Hierarchical Agglomerative Clustering Example

Before delving into the implementation of the Lance-Williams algorithm, let's see how hierarchical agglomerative clustering is used. We begin by loading the funq.q [339] library and downloading the uef clustering benchmark data set from the University of Eastern Finland[1] with the uef.q [383] library.

```
q)\l funq.q
q)\l uef.q
[down]loading uef data sets
```

We then build a dissimilarity matrix D between every point in the data set. Choosing the "ward" linkage function, we generate the linkage statistics L with the .ml.link linking function. The linkage statistics can then be used with the .ml.clust clustering function to generate any number of clusters between 1 and the number of data points. In this example, we use a 32 dimensional data set that has 1,024 data points. We model the data using between 1 and 32 clusters.

```
q)X:uef.d32
q)D:sqrt .ml.pedist2[X;X]
q)L:.ml.link[`.ml.lw.ward] D
q)I:.ml.clust[L] ks:1+til 32
```

Using the .ut.ugrp utility, we can convert the cluster indices into cluster labels. This allows us to see how the clusters are distributed. Knowing apriori that there are 16 clusters, we generate a graph, seen in Example 4.1 [69], where each cluster is rendered with a different character.

To determine an optimal number of clusters, we can use the .ml.silhouette function to compute the silhouette metric for each data point, compute the average across each cluster and find the number of clusters that maximize this average silhouette.

Example 4.2 [69] shows that 16 clusters maximizes the average silhouette metric. We now expand upon each of these concepts.

---

[1] P. Fränti and S. Sieranoja "K-means properties on six clustering benchmark data sets", *Applied Intelligence*, 48 (12), 4743-4759, December 2018 doi: s10489-018-1238-7.

## 4.1. HIERARCHICAL AGGLOMERATIVE CLUSTERING EXAMPLE

**Example 4.1** Large HAC Clusters

```
q)plt:.ut.plot[39;20;.ut.c68;.ml.mode]
q)plt X[0 1],enlist y:.ut.ugrp I 15
220| "           111 1              ??? ?    "
200| "            11                ????####  "
   | "                               ? ####   "
180| "                                        "
   | "                                        "
160| "                                        "
   | "             .    ....                  "
140| "              .....        qqq          "
   | "                           qqqq         "
120| "xxx           ,                         "
   | "xxxx        ,,,,,,,              lll    "
100| " x           ,,,,,             l llll   "
   | "         0                       l      "
80 | " 00000                                  "
   | "  0000              ccccc/c//           "
60 | "              kJJJJ cc    /// /         "
   | "             88kkJJJ~$$$$               "
40 | "             8888~~~~~ $$$              "
   | "                 8                      "
20 | "                                        "
```

**Example 4.2** Silhouette I

```
q).ut.plt (avg raze .ml.silhouette[.ml.edist;X] ::) peach I
1  | "           +              "
0.8| "         ++ ++            "
   | "        ++   ++           "
0.6| "       ++    +++          "
   | "      +        +          "
0.4| "    +         ++          "
   | "   +          ++          "
0.2| " +                        "
   | "+                         "
0  | "+                         "
```

## 4.2 Cluster Benchmark Data Sets

This chapter uses the cluster benchmark data sets compiled by the University of Eastern Finland, which correspond to published papers about clustering algorithms. To use these data sets, we can load the uef.q [383] library, which downloads the s, a and dim data sets. The s data sets have 5,000 data points distributed over 15 clusters. Each set has a varying amount of cluster overlap. The a data sets have 150 data points per cluster, but vary the number of total clusters: 20, 35 and 50. The s and a data sets are limited to two dimensions while the dim data set defines clusters with 32, 64, 128 and 256 dimensions—each representing 16 clusters over 1,024 data points. These data sets can be used to benchmark performance characteristics of different clustering algorithms. The performance of the hierarchical agglomerative clustering algorithm is highly sensitive to the number of data points, and less sensitive to the number of dimensions. We will use the 32 dimension data set with 1,024 data points to keep the problem tractable.

## 4.3 Dissimilarity Matrix

Similar to the k-nearest neighbors algorithm, hierarchical agglomerative clustering begins by creating a matrix of distances. Instead of computing the distance between a training set and a test or validation set, the generated matrix contains the distances between each data point in the data set and every other data point in the set. This is often referred to as a dissimilarity matrix. Remember that there is no such thing as test, train and validation partitions in clustering analysis because, while it may be interesting to compare against the "ground truth" labels, the performance of clustering algorithms is judged by how tight each cluster is as well as how distant each cluster is from the nearest cluster. Observation labels are not considered.

The Lance-Williams algorithm is a popular implementation of hierarchical agglomerative clustering. Although it supports different inter-cluster distance metrics, it requires the dissimilarity matrix be generated using the Euclidean distance. For performance, we can use the .ml.pedist2 function and then take the square root.

```
q)show D:sqrt .ml.pedist2[X;X]
0        27.11088 12.04159 39.03844 34.56877 7.549834 5.477226 12.24745 5..
27.11088 0        26.30589 43.2088  38.62642 26.72078 26.40076 29.44486 2..
12.04159 26.30589 0        39.33192 34.87119 13.2665  10.81665 16.03122 1..
39.03844 43.2088  39.33192 0        52.41183 38.37968 38.0526  37.94733 3..
```

```
34.56877 38.62642 34.87119 52.41183 0        33.82307 34.21988 36.01389 3..
7.549834 26.72078 13.2665  38.37968 33.82307 0        7.549834 14.38749 7..
5.477226 26.40076 10.81665 38.0526  34.21988 7.549834 0        12.56981 5..
..
```

## 4.4 Lance-Williams Algorithm

The Lance-Williams algorithm starts with each point in its own cluster. It then scans the dissimilarity matrix and merges the two closest clusters. After throwing away the merged cluster, it updates the distances to the remaining clusters for the newly merged cluster. The beauty of the Lance-Williams algorithm is the simplicity in which it can recompute the new distances between clusters given the existing cluster distances.

### Linkage Statistics

The Lance-Williams algorithm can be written recursively, but q will only permit 2,000 layers of recursion. Unlike other functional programming languages, q does not implement tail recursion, which allows a recursive call to replace the existing function on the stack when it is the last call in the function. This means that each recursive call adds a new layer on the stack is therefore limited by q's maximum stack depth.

The alternative to recursion is iteration with an additional data-structure that maintains state. To prepare the state object, the .ml.link function generates the dissimilarity matrix D, a cluster-assignment vector a and a linkage-statistics matrix L. These are then passed to the .ml.lancewilliams function that implements the Lance-Williams algorithm.

**.ml.link**

```
/ given a (l)inkage (f)unction and (D)issimilarity matrix, run the
/ Lance-Williams linkage algorithm for hierarchical agglomerative clustering
/ and return the linkage stats: (from index j;to index i)
link:{[lf;D]
 D:@'[D;a:til count D;:;0n];    / define cluster assignments and ignore loops
 if[-11h=type lf;lf:get lf];    / dereference lf
 L:last .[lancewilliams[lf]] over (D;a;2#()); / obtain linkage stats
 L}
```

The closest point to any point is obviously the point itself. To prevent merging clusters with themselves, the `.ml.link` function begins by replacing the diagonal zero values with null values. This clever trick works because, unlike the & operator, which treats null values as the smallest possible value (even smaller than negative infinity), the `min` operator ignores null values.

```
q)-0w&0n
0n
q)min -0w 0n
-0w
```

The second line of the `.ml.link` function dereferences the linkage function. This is not normally necessary because q allows function names to be called as if they were the functions themselves.

```
q)`.ml.mode 1 2 2 3
2
```

But the `.ml.lancewilliams` function accepts the linkage function parameter `lf` as either a vector of floats or a function that generates a vector of floats. To allow the function to distinguish between these two cases, we dereference the `lf` parameter before passing it through.

The last two arguments required by the `.ml.lancewilliams` function are needed for bookkeeping and accumulating the function's results. The first is a vector of cluster assignments a. All data points initially belong to their own cluster, so th cluster assignments begin as a list of distinct integers. By the completion of the algorithm, however, the cluster assignments will all have the same value because all data points will belong to one large cluster. The last argument L contains two vectors for storing the linkage statistics generated by the algorithm. The linkage statistics are not used in the algorithm itself, but are returned so the caller can later partition the data into the desired number of clusters.

We are now ready to tackle the Lance-Williams algorithm proper.

## Lance-Williams Implementation

The first line of the `.ml.lancewilliams` function stores the number of data points in n. The second line scans each row of the dissimilarity matrix looking for closest distance d and stores the associated indices in di. Using these minimum distances, the third line finds the indices i and j indicating the two closest clusters. If this

## 4.5. LINKAGE FUNCTIONS

minimum distance is null, we have reached the end of the algorithm and can return early.

### .ml.lancewillams

```
/ implementation of Lance-Williams algorithm for performing hierarchical
/ agglomerative clustering. given (l)inkage (f)unction to determine distance
/ between new and remaining clusters, (D)issimilarity matrix, cluster
/ (a)ssignments and (L)inkage stats: (j;i). returns updated (D;a;L)
lancewilliams:{[lf;D;a;L]
  n:count D;
  d:D@'di:imin peach D;                 / find closest distances
  if[null d@:i:imin d;:(D;a;L)]; j:di i; / find closest clusters
  c:$[9h=type lf;lf;lf(freq a)@/:(i;j;til n)]; / determine coefficients
  nd:sum c*nd,(d;abs(-/)nd:D (i;j));    / calc new distances
  D[;i]:D[i]:nd;                        / update distances
  D[;j]:D[j]:n#0n;                      / erase j
  a[where j=a]:i;                       / all elements in cluster j are now in i
  L:L,'(j;i);                           / append linkage stats
  (D;a;L)}
```

Briefly skipping the next two lines, the final four lines amend the dissimilarity matrix with the new distances nd and erase the merged cluster j by filling the row and column of the dissimilarity matrix with null values. All cluster assignments for cluster j are then re-assigned to cluster i and the from-index j and the to-index i are appended to the linkage statistics L.

We now return to the two skipped lines: 4 and 5. The crux of the Lance-Williams algorithm is the calculation of inter-cluster distance. This is determined by the supplied linkage function.

## 4.5 Linkage Functions

Once we've settled on using the Euclidean distance, the distance between any two points is not up for discussion. The first round of the Lance-Williams algorithm will use these distances to merge the closest two points. Subsequent rounds, however, must deal with the possibility that clusters are composed of more than one point. There are many ways to define the distance between a point and a cluster or even a cluster and another cluster.

For example, imagine we have three clusters $C_i$, $C_j$ and $C_k$. After we combine $C_i$ and $C_j$, we will need to compute the distance between the new cluster $C_{ij}$ and $C_k$.

Is the distance between these clusters defined as the distance between the closest two points? Perhaps it is the distance between the furthest points. Or maybe it should be defined as the distance between the centers of the two clusters.

The Lance-Williams algorithm generalizes and simplifies this problem into a formula (Equation 4.1 [74]) that only depends on the *existing* distances between clusters: $d_{ij}$, $d_{ik}$ and $d_{jk}$ and coefficients $\alpha_i$, $\alpha_j$, $\beta$ and $\gamma$ that may depend on the number of elements in the cluster.

$$d_{(ij)k} = \alpha_i d_{ik} + \alpha_j d_{jk} + \beta d_{ij} + \gamma |d_{ik} - d_{jk}|$$

Equation 4.1: Lance-Williams Recursive Update

The distance between the new cluster $C_{ij}$ and the existing cluster $C_k$ is the weighted average of the distance between each cluster and the absolute difference between the distance of the original clusters $C_i$ and $C_j$ from the existing cluster $C_k$.

Herein lies the magic. Suppose we define the distance between the new cluster $C_{ij}$ and the existing cluster $C_k$ as the minimum distance from $C_k$ to the original clusters $C_i$ and $C_j$. Setting $\alpha_i = .5$, $\alpha_j = .5$, $\beta = 0$ and $\gamma = -.5$ achieves this goal. Merely changing $\gamma = .5$ changes the distance definition to use the maximum distance from $C_k$ to the original clusters. A summary of commonly used coefficients can be found in Table 4.1 [74].

Table 4.1: Lance-Williams Recursive Update Coefficients

| Method | $\alpha_i$ | $\alpha_j$ | $\beta$ | $\gamma$ |
|---|---|---|---|---|
| Single | .5 | .5 | 0 | -.5 |
| Complete | .5 | .5 | 0 | .5 |
| Average | $\frac{n_i}{n_i+n_j}$ | $\frac{n_j}{n_i+n_j}$ | 0 | 0 |
| Weighted | .5 | .5 | 0 | 0 |
| Centroid | $\frac{n_i}{n_i+n_j}$ | $\frac{n_j}{n_i+n_j}$ | $-\frac{n_i n_j}{(n_i+n_j)^2}$ | 0 |
| Median | .5 | .5 | -.25 | 0 |
| Ward | $\frac{n_i+n_k}{n_i+n_j+n_k}$ | $\frac{n_j+n_k}{n_i+n_j+n_k}$ | $-\frac{n_k}{n_i+n_j+n_k}$ | 0 |

Single linkage is the same as using the minimum distance while complete linkage is the same as using the maximum distance. Average linkage adds a small twist to

## 4.5. LINKAGE FUNCTIONS

the Lance-Williams algorithm because, in addition to using the distance between clusters, it also requires the number of points within each cluster. Average linkage uses the number of elements in the cluster to produce a weighted average distance. Centroid linkage uses the number of points within each cluster to define the distance between clusters as the distance from the center of each cluster.

Ward linkage is the most popular linkage function. It is named after Joe H. Ward, Jr. who proposed weights for the Lance-Williams algorithm that minimizes the intra-cluster variance.[2] At each stage, the "closest" point is the point that minimizes the increase in total cluster variance.

These linkage functions are defined in the .ml.lw namespace. Some are defined as float vectors and others as functions that accept the cluster counts $n_i$, $n_j$ and $n_k$.

**.ml.lw**

```
/ Lance-Williams algorithm linkage functions. can be either a vector of four
/ floats or a function that accepts the cluster counts of i, j and list of
/ all cluster counts
lw.single:.5 .5 0 -.5
lw.complete:.5 .5 0 .5
lw.average:{(x%sum x _:2),0 0f}
lw.weighted:.5 .5 0 0
lw.centroid:{(((x,neg prd[x]%s)%s:sum x _:2),0f}
lw.median:.5 .5 -.25 0
lw.ward:{(((k+/:x 0 1),(neg k:x 2;0f))%\:sum x}
```

These linkage coefficients and functions are used by the Lance-Williams algorithm to generate the post-merge cluster distances for the next iteration.

The fourth line of the .ml.lancewilliams function checks the type of the supplied linkage function lf. If it is a vector of coefficients, it is used as-is. Otherwise, it is treated as a function and called with the cluster counts generated by the .ml.freq function. These results are then used as the required vector of coefficients.

The fifth line implements the Lance-Williams Update Function and assigns the post-merge distances computed as a weighted sum of the coefficients and the pre-merge distances to the new distance variable nd.

---

[2] J. H. W. Jr, "Hierarchical Grouping to Optimize an Objective Function," *Journal of the American Statistical Association*, vol. 58, no. 301, pp. 236–244, Mar. 1963, doi:10.1080/01621459.1963.10500845.

## 4.6 Building Clusters

The linkage statistics L returned by the .ml.link function provides the step-by-step instructions to merge clusters—one at a time—until finally only one remains.

```
q)L
445 493 703 739 767 906 1017 946 992 43 246 295 382 633 891 973 311 377 4..
391 486 684 706 740 904 984  904 984 41 193 288 344 598 840 967 300 351 3..
```

Each pair of indices indicates which clusters are merged for that stage of the algorithm. In the above example, the 445th cluster (a single data point in this case) is merged with the 391st cluster (again a single data point) to form a new cluster (now with 2 data points). These two clusters were chosen because they were the closest clusters based on our choice of the linkage function lf.

By cutting this process short, we can generate any number of clusters—from one through the number of data points. The .ml.clust cluster-generation function has been overloaded to handle the generation of clusters represented by a single value of k as well as a list of cluster definitions represented by a vector of k values.

### Cluster Implementation

The clustering function .ml.clust starts by checking the type of the k argument. Since the function has been generalized to handle a list of k values, we must special case an atomic k. Uniformly handling both atomic and vector k values is achieved by recursively calling the function with the .z.s system variable and passing it an enlisted k. The result will be a single-element list containing the cluster definition for the atomic value k. To conform with the caller's expectations, we return a single cluster definition by choosing the first element of the list.

**.ml.clust**

```
/ use (L)inkage stats to create (k) clusters
clust:{[L;k]
 if[0h>type k;:first .z.s[L] k,()]; / special case atoms
 c:1 cut til 1+count L 0;           / initial clusters
 k@:i:idesc k;                      / sort k descending
 fl:(1-mk:last k)_ flip L;          / drop unwanted links
 fls:(0,-1_count[c]-k) cut fl;      / list of flipped link stats
 c:{[c;fl]{x[y 1],:x y 0;x[y 0]:();x}/[c;fl]}\[c;fls]; / link into k clusters
 c:c except\: enlist ();            / remove empty clusters
```

## 4.6. BUILDING CLUSTERS

```
  c:c iasc i;                    / reorder based on original k
  c}
```

The algorithm begins on the second line by generating a cluster for each data point. It then sorts the list of k values on the third line and in the process saves the sorting indices i so the clusters can be returned in the originally requested order.

The fourth line of .ml.clust drops linkage instructions that combine clusters beyond the minimum number of requested clusters and stores a flipped copy of these linkage instructions in fl. Along the way to generating a set of clusters to represent the minimum requested value of k, we also generate the set of clusters for all previous values. The fourth line of the function cuts the flipped linkage statistics into stages that represent each of the requested values for k so that we can store these intermediate cluster definitions.

With the setup complete, the work of iteratively combining clusters occurs on line six. There are two iterations on this line. The inner iteration merges the clusters and returns the final cluster definition for a given vector of linkage instructions. The outer iteration generates cluster definitions for each of the requested values of k.

Although, the cluster definitions are now complete, some cleanup work must be performed. Line seven removes empty clusters from each of the cluster definitions and line eight reorders the cluster definitions based on the supplied values of k.

### Cluster Example

We can see how supplying a single value for k generates a single cluster of indices.

```
q).ml.clust[L] 3
0 47 6 10 21 39 41 43 40 12 61 8 45 9 5 20 29 63 15 19 33 51 18 46 62 26 ..
64 85 115 65 111 68 98 109 100 112 94 116 73 93 84 88 95 118 99 69 113 81..
128 191 187 186 137 143 180 140 148 188 190 153 156 160 162 129 157 130 1..
```

Supplying multiple k values returns a cluster definitions for each value.

```
q).ml.clust[L] 1 2 3
,0 47 6 10 21 39 41 43 40 12 61 8 45 9 5 20 29 63 15 19 33 51 18 46 62 26..
(0 47 6 10 21 39 41 43 40 12 61 8 45 9 5 20 29 63 15 19 33 51 18 46 62 26..
(0 47 6 10 21 39 41 43 40 12 61 8 45 9 5 20 29 63 15 19 33 51 18 46 62 26..
```

While centroids have no inherent use in hierarchical agglomerative clustering, they can be generated by using the group indices to index back into the original data set and average each of the dimensions.

```
q)(avg'') X@\:.ml.clust[L] 3
79.26875 75.10938 119.0357
85.8375  137.9648 109.2589
127.2656 103.8906 107.4442
118.2687 152.4805 120.0759
106.9969 129.2734 167.6406
157.4187 106.9453 124.7121
176.2125 105.0977 138.9821
..
```

Alternatively, we can use the .ut.ugrp utility to "uncluster" the data into a single vector such that each observation can be mapped to a cluster identifier. These clusters can be seen in Example 4.3 [78].

**Example 4.3** Small HAS Clusters

```
q)plt:.ut.plot[19;10;.ut.c10;.ml.mode]
q)plt X[0 1],enlist .ut.ugrp .ml.clust[L] 3
250| "                                "
200| "       +++           @@@@       "
   | "                     @@@        "
150| "            ...                 "
   | " .    + ..      ++              "
100| ".. ++++             @@@"
   | "+++         @@@@   @            "
50 | "       @@.@@.@@@@               "
   | "          @@.....               "
0  | "                                "
```

## 4.7 The Silhouette Method

In Section 3.6 [61], we saw how the number of clusters k could be chosen by examining the total distortion for each choice of k and picking the maximum value of k which continued to give a considerable drop in total distortion. By graphing these values, it was possible to choose the point that was positioned at an imaginary

## 4.7. THE SILHOUETTE METHOD

elbow of the graph. The distance from every point to its centroid is central to partitional clustering. Centroids, however, have no role in hierarchical agglomerative clustering.

## Silhouette Implementation

The silhouette method is an alternate approach to evaluating cluster quality. Instead of measuring the total Euclidean distance squared from each point to the centroid, the silhouette method assigns a value between -1 and 1, which indicates how likely each point belongs to the assigned cluster rather than the next closest cluster. A silhouette metric of 1 indicates a perfect assignment of each data point to its cluster, while -1 indicates that assigning the point to the next-closest cluster would be better. By using distance metrics, instead of squared metrics, the silhouette method is less affected by outliers.

### .ml.silhouette

```
/ given (d)istance (f)unction, matri(X), and cluster (I)ndices, compute the
/ silhouette statistic. group I if not already grouped
silhouette:{[df;X;I]
 if[type I;s:.z.s[df;X]I:value group I;:raze[s] iasc raze I];
 if[1=n:count I;:count[I 0]#0f]; / special case a single cluster
 a:{[df;X](1f%-1+count X 0)*sum f2nd[df X] X}[df] peach G:X@\:/:I;
 b:{[df;G;i]min{f2nd[avg x[z]::]y}[df;G i]'[G _ i]}[df;G] peach til n;
 s:0f^(b-a)%a|b;              / 0 fill to handle single point clusters
 s}
```

The .ml.silhouette function accepts a distance function, a matrix of data X and a vector of cluster indices I. The first line of the function detects the case where the I cluster-index parameter is passed in as an ungrouped vector. In this case, the data is grouped, the function is called recursively, and the results are ungrouped back to the original order. If the I cluster-index parameter was already grouped, the results are returned grouped as well.

In cases where there is only a single cluster, the silhouette method is undefined. Since there is no "next closest" cluster, the second line returns 0.

The third line uses the cluster indices to cluster the data and compute the average distance a from every point to every other point within its *own* cluster. Note that the divisor of the average is N-1 instead of N because the point itself does not contribute to the summation. The fourth line is quite complex. Stated simply, it computes the average distance b from every point to all points in the *next closest* cluster. To achieve this, the average distance to all the clusters are computed and the minimum value is chosen. This is obviously an expensive computation.

Finally, the silhouette value s is computed by subtracting these two distances and dividing by the larger of the two. The silhouette metric is not defined for clusters with only one point because the division of N-1 results in a division by 0. The .ml.silhouette function handles these cases by filling the resulting null values with 0.

## Silhouette Example

We can now use the .ml.clust and .ml.silhouette functions to compute the silhouette metric for every observation. Although we will use the Euclidean distance to generate the silhouette values, it is also possible to use the Manhattan distance. Too few clusters tends to generate positive values closer to zero than one.

```
q).ml.silhouette[.ml.edist;X] .ml.clust[L] 3
0.229359 0.2281797 0.2296652 0.2278801 0.2287029 0.2287349 0.2290454 0.22..
0.2928064 0.3047495 0.3061881 0.2976858 0.3003607 0.308594 0.3116868 0.30..
0.09701692 0.1019648 0.1008343 0.1003151 0.09503871 0.09923577 0.1010464 ..
```

Too many clusters, on the other hand, can generate negative silhouette values indicating that some points are closer (on average) to points in nearby clusters than the cluster to which they currently belong.

```
q).ml.silhouette[.ml.edist;X] .ml.clust[L] 20
0.7195888 0.7269278 0.7248759 0.7535088 0.7568341 0.7594867 0.759572 0.76..
-0.2551708 -0.3067475 -0.2991338 -0.1645346 -0.4508158 -0.3636373 -0.3164..
0.8906743 0.9011288 0.8846408 0.9079411 0.9111029 0.9130201 0.9217505 0.9..
0.9590069 0.9598579 0.9553711 0.9570317 0.9598228 0.9599733 0.9593234 0.9..
0.7292028 0.7347848 0.7266056 0.7349496 0.7352072 0.7284465 0.7284017 0.7..
-0.3191184 -0.3112321 -0.2766274 -0.3458856 -0.2319964 -0.2240288 -0.3569..
0.9146191 0.9177481 0.9119146 0.9395019 0.9330372 0.9421496 0.940136 0.95..
..
```

An optimal number of clusters generates the highest possible average silhouette value.

```
q).ml.silhouette[.ml.edist;X] .ml.clust[L] 16
0.9561579 0.9566273 0.9570651 0.9582289 0.9581007 0.9580687 0.9581933 0.9..
0.8906743 0.9011288 0.8846408 0.9079411 0.9111029 0.9130201 0.9217505 0.9..
0.9590069 0.9598579 0.9553711 0.9570317 0.9598228 0.9599733 0.9593234 0.9..
```

## 4.7. THE SILHOUETTE METHOD

```
0.9547821 0.955049  0.9545952 0.9551677 0.9552043 0.9548584 0.9543827 0.9..
0.9146191 0.9177481 0.9119146 0.9395019 0.9330372 0.9421496 0.940136  0.9..
0.9639938 0.9675258 0.9667758 0.9653723 0.9595012 0.9652693 0.9633534 0.9..
0.9485899 0.9439072 0.9486784 0.9443508 0.9365609 0.9361671 0.9420633 0.9..
..
```

Example 4.4 [81] shows the average silhouette value for different values of k. This allows us to visually determine the optimal number.

**Example 4.4** Silhouette II

```
q)I:.ml.clust[L] 1+til 32
q).ut.plt (avg raze .ml.silhouette[.ml.edist;X] ::) peach I
1   | "          +             "
0.8| "        ++ ++            "
   | "        ++  ++           "
0.6| "       ++    +++         "
   | "     +         +         "
0.4| "    +          ++        "
   | "   +           ++"
0.2| " +                        "
   | "+                         "
0  | "+                         "
```

The k-means and hierarchical agglomerative clustering methods assume that a point belongs to a cluster with 100% certainty. During the assignment phase of k-means clustering, a point is assigned to the closest cluster, regardless its density. This method does not take into consideration the compactness or denseness of the points surrounding the centroid. Given a point equidistant between two centroids, it is more likely to be a member of a more disperse cluster than a dense cluster. The k-means algorithm does not take this probability into consideration. We now turn our attention to the expectation-maximization algorithm, which takes this into account by treating all values as observations from a probability distribution.

# Chapter 5

# Expectation-Maximization

> Probability is expectation founded upon partial knowledge. A perfect acquaintance with all the circumstances affecting the occurrence of an event would change expectation into certainty, and leave nether room nor demand for a theory of probabilities.
> — George Bool *An Investigation of the Laws of Thought*

The implementation of the k-means algorithm cycles through grouping data points into their nearest centroid and then recomputing the centroid's location by summarizing all the points within the cluster by a single point. This centroid assignment tends to form spherical clusters—regardless of the distribution of the actual data. At each stage of the algorithm, each point is assigned to a single cluster, regardless of the conviction. Instead of performing a hard-assignment like the k-means algorithm, the expectation-maximization algorithm performs a soft-assignment by assigning a probability that a given point belongs to *each* of the clusters. Using these probabilities, an estimate of the distribution's parameters is made and the cycle continues with an assignment of new probabilities for each point.

The k-means algorithm requires us to provide a distance and a centroid function. Similarly, the expectation-maximization algorithm requires us to provide a likelihood function and a maximum-likelihood-estimator function. The k-means algorithm is a special case of expectation-maximization where the likelihood function returns either a 0 or 1 depending on the data point's distance to the nearest centroid. The associated k-means maximum-likelihood-estimator function assumes independence between points and only computes a single parameter—the centroid.

Once we begin talking about probabilities, we are forced to specify the data's assumed distribution. The expectation-maximization algorithm then estimates the distribution parameters. If, for example, we assume the data points come from a Gaussian (normal) distribution, the expectation-maximization algorithm determines the mean (which corresponds to the centroid location of the k-means algorithm) and the deviation (which is not estimated at all in the k-means algorithm). The expectation-maximization algorithm can be used with any distribution as long as we can provide the likelihood function that returns the probability that a point belongs to a distribution and a maximum-likelihood-estimator function that returns the distribution parameters that best fit the data.

Before using the Gaussian distribution to demonstrate the soft-assignment version of k-means, let's review how the expectation-maximization algorithm can be used to estimate the parameters of a few other distributions.

## 5.1 Bernoulli Distribution

Our first example of the expectation-maximization algorithm will use multiple Bernoulli distributions to model biased coins. A Bernoulli distribution returns one of two values with a fixed probability. An unbiased coin flip can, therefore, be represented by draws from Bernoulli distribution with a probability of 50%.

```
q)\l funq.q
q).ml.rbern[10] .5
1001110001b
```

A biased coin flip will generate true values with a different probability.

```
q).ml.rbern[10] .2
0011000000b
```

The .ml.rbern random-Bernoulli-generator function generates n uniform variates with the .ml.runif function and returns true if the value is less than the provided probability p.

**.ml.rbern**

```
/ generate (n) Bernoulli distribution variates with (p)robability of success
rbern:{[n;p]p>runif n}
```

The `.ml.runif` random-uniform-generator function is a thin wrapper around the ? operator. Passing the value 1f as the right operand to the ? operator returns uniformly distributed values between zero and one.

**.ml.runif**

```
/ generate (n) uniform distribution variates
runif:{[n]n?1f}
```

Now suppose that I have 3 (potentially biased) coins in my pocket. I then randomly select one coin and record the results of flipping it 10 times. If I then repeat this process 20 times, would you be able to determine how biased each coin is, and which coin I selected for each flip?

If I told you which coin was used for each trial, you could estimate its bias by averaging the number of heads that appear each time. Alternatively, if I told you how biased each coin was, you could use a maximum-likelihood estimator to guess the most likely coin given the number of heads that appeared. But if I don't tell you either, the problem seems intractable.

## 5.2 Expectation-Maximization Algorithm

The expectation-maximization algorithm takes turns assuming it knows either the distribution parameters or the likelihood of each data point belonging to a distribution. Lucky for us, switching back and forth between these two routines converges on a single solution. With this added flexibility comes uncertainty. The converged solution will be locally optimal, but we have no guarantee that it is the globally optimal solution. Because of this, it is typical to run the algorithm a few times with different random initial conditions.

**.ml.em**

```
/ using (l)ikelihood (f)unction, (w)eighted (m)aximum likelihood estimator
/ (f)unction with prior probabilities (p)hi and distribution parameters
/ (THETA), optionally (f)it (p)hi and perform expectation maximization
em:{[fp;lf;wmf;X;phi;THETA]
 W:prb likelihood[0b;lf;X;phi;THETA];  / weights (responsibilities)
 if[fp;phi:avg each W];                / new phi estimates
 THETA:wmf[;X] peach W;                / new THETA estimates
 (phi;THETA)}
```

The expectation-maximization algorithm requires us to provide a likelihood function lf to determine the likelihood that a data point belongs to a distribution. Next, we need to provide a weighted-maximum-likelihood-estimator function wmf that estimates new distribution parameters given weights determined by the likelihood function lf. We must, of course, provide the training data X, the prior probability that each coin will be selected phi and a list of distribution parameters THETA—one for each coin. The result of the function will be a new estimate of phi and THETA that takes us one step closer to an optimal parameterization. We can then iterate over this function a fixed number of times, until an error estimate falls below a pre-specified threshold or until convergence. There is one extra parameter fp, which is used to enable or disable the fitting of phi. If we know the actual probability that each coin will be picked, we can make the expectation-maximization converge faster by setting fp to false and phi will always be the values we initially pass in.

## 5.3 Binomial Distribution

Let's play our game with three coins that show up heads 10%, 30% and 80% of the time.

```
q)show x:.ml.rbern[10] each 20?.1 .3 .8
0001011001b
1111100100b
1101111101b
0000000000b
0010110001b
1111101111b
0100001010b
..
```

To simplify things, we can summarize each trial by the number of times a head appears.

```
q)show x:sum each x
4 6 8 0 4 9 3 10 2 2 0 2 9 4 7 0 2 7 0 3i
```

This is, in fact, the binomial distribution which is implemented in .ml.rbinom.

**.ml.rbinom**

```
/ generate (n) binomial distribution (sum of Bernoulli) variates with (k)
/ trials and (p)robability
```

## 5.3. BINOMIAL DISTRIBUTION

```
rbinom:{[n;k;p](sum rbern[k]::) each n#p}
```

Using the .ml.rbinom function, we can generate 20 variates coming from 10 coin flips, where each of the coins has a 1% probability of coming out heads.

```
q).ml.rbinom[20;10] .1
0 0 0 1 2 1 3 1 0 2 1 1 1 1 1 0 2 1 0 0i
```

Or, alternatively, we can generate 20 variates coming from 10 coin flips where each of the coins has a different probability of coming out heads.

```
q).ml.rbinom[20;10] 20?.1 .3 .8
1 9 2 0 8 10 3 7 8 6 2 3 5 9 2 7 1 1 2 3i
```

We will use the binomial distribution, its likelihood function and its maximum-likelihood estimator to demonstrate the expectation-maximization algorithm.

## Parameter Initialization

To initialize the expectation-maximization algorithm, we need to estimate how often each coin appears in the data. Without prior knowledge, we can give each coin equal probability.

```
q)show phi:3#1%3
0.3333333 0.3333333 0.3333333
```

We must also estimate the bias on each of the coins. Again, without prior knowledge of the actual coin biases, we can pick three random numbers between 0 and 1. It is important that each of these values be different to prevent the algorithm from collapsing into two solutions (or even a single solution).

```
q)show THETA:3?1f
0.8999132 0.6989981 0.4640775
```

We can now set the likelihood function and weighted-maximum-likelihood-estimator function to their binomial variants.

```
q)lf:.ml.binl[10]
q)mf:.ml.wbinmle[10;0]
```

The first parameter n of each function specifies how many times we flipped the coin (10 in this case).

Given a probability p and k observed flips, the .ml.binl function returns the likelihood that the sample was from the provided distribution.

**.ml.binl**

```
/ binomial likelihood (without the binomial coefficient nCk)
binl:{[n;p;k](p xexp k)*(1f-p) xexp n-k}
```

The actual binomial likelihood function, shown in Equation 5.1 [88], includes the binomial coefficient $\binom{n}{k}$ which is the expensive combinatorial calculation $\frac{n!}{k!(n-k)!}$.

$$\mathcal{L}(p|n,k) = \binom{n}{k} p^k (1-p)^{n-k}$$

Equation 5.1: Binomial Likelihood

It turns out that for a fixed k, the parameters obtained by maximizing the likelihood with the binomial coefficient are equivalent to maximizing the likelihood without the coefficient. For computational efficiency, therefore, we drop the coefficient.

Given the observation weights w and number of observations x, the .ml.wbinmle weighted-binomial-maximum-likelihood-estimator function returns the best estimate of the distribution's probability parameter p. This would be the coin's probability of turning up heads.

**.ml.wbinmle**

```
/ weighted binomial mle with Dirichlet smoothing (a)
wbinmle:{[n;a;w;x]enlist w wavg a+x%n}
```

Notice that the returned value is enlisted to create a list of one value. Even though the binomial distribution has a single estimated parameter $\hat{p}$, other distributions have more than one estimated parameter. The Gaussian distribution's maximum likelihood estimator, for example, returns two parameters: $\hat{\mu}$ and $\hat{\sigma}$. To ensure our functions can be generalized to any likelihood function, the maximum likelihood estimators always return a list (even if it is a list of just one element), so the parameters can be passed to their corresponding likelihood function with the . operator.

The .ml.wbinmle function has a second parameter a (which we will set to 0 to disable) that allows us to add smoothing to prevent numerical instability when parameters come close to zero. Although we have implemented the weighted average

## 5.3. BINOMIAL DISTRIBUTION

across multiple observations, the binomial maximum-likelihood-estimator equation for a single observation is provided in Equation 5.2 [89].

$$\hat{p} = \frac{k}{n}$$

Equation 5.2: Binomial Maximum Likelihood Estimator

## Algorithm Iteration

Running the algorithm once takes us a step closer to optimal values of phi and THETA.

```
q).ml.em[1b;lf;mf;x] . (phi;flip enlist THETA)
0.1587248 0.1754012 0.665874
0.894992  0.6690673 0.22615
```

Running the algorithm 10 times takes us even closer.

```
q)10 .ml.em[1b;lf;mf;x]// (phi;flip enlist THETA)
0.1640413 0.2075941 0.6283647
0.8857198 0.6853291 0.1948473
```

And running until convergence gives us parameters of phi and THETA (prior probabilities and coin biases) that best fit the given data.

```
q)(.ml.em[1b;lf;mf;x]//) (phi;flip enlist THETA)
0.1267688 0.2379131 0.6353181
0.9044606 0.7152367 0.1970326
```

We can see these values are not very close to the actual prior probabilities (1/3) and biases (10%, 30% and 80%). We can get much closer to the actual values if we flipped the coin more times per trial or performed more trials. Let's perform 100,000 trials—saving each flip's bias into y so we can calculate our accuracy later.

```
q)x:.ml.rbinom[count y;10] .1 .3 .8 y:100000?3
q)show pT:(.ml.em[1b;lf;mf;x]//) (phi;flip enlist THETA)
0.3355016 0.3262065 0.3382919
0.7992075 0.3011412 0.1027082
```

## Algorithm Accuracy

We can see by visual inspection that the algorithm has done a pretty good job. These numbers, however, would be meaningless if we didn't already know the biases of each coin. To judge the algorithm we need to compute the accuracy by using the phi and THETA values to predict the biases of each coin.

The expectation-maximization algorithm uses the .ml.likelihood function to estimate the likelihood that each coin has each of the provided biases. We can use this function ourselves to classify each coin.

### .ml.likelihood

```
likelihood:{[l;lf;X;phi;THETA]
  p:(@[;X]lf .) peach THETA;    / compute [log] probability densities
  p:$[l;p+log phi;p*phi];       / apply prior probabilities
  p}
```

The .ml.likelihood function is capable of using the likelihood function of a distribution or the *log* likelihood function. Many likelihood functions (like the binomial likelihood function) are implemented with exponentiation and multiplication. When the order (and not the actual value) of the likelihood function matters most, it is common practice to use the *log* likelihood function instead of the likelihood function because the exponentiations are replaced with logarithms and multiplications are replaced with additions—making the calculation faster and often more numerically stable. The first parameter of the .ml.likelihood function l specifies if we are passing the likelihood or the log likelihood function. This is followed by the likelihood function itself lf and the data X. The final two parameters are the phi and THETA values.

After computing the likelihood of the data against each of the phi and THETA values, we can map which parameters correspond to which classification. This can be achieved by grouping the data and finding the label y which occurs most frequently within the group. We store the mapping from our classification to y in m.

```
q)p:.ml.imax .ml.likelihood[0b;lf;x] . pT
q)show m:.ml.mode each y group p
2| 0
1| 1
0| 2
```

To confirm the algorithm's effectiveness, we can now use this mapping to compare against which coin was used for each trial and compute the accuracy by taking the average.

## 5.3. BINOMIAL DISTRIBUTION

```
q)avg y=m p
0.83611
```

In practice, we would not know the true labels, but this comparison provides evidence that the algorithm is on the right track. The algorithm is typically used to derive hidden parameters. Had we already known which coin was used for each flip, we could have used a more precise supervised learning algorithm.

## Confusion Matrix

In addition to computing the accuracy, an intuitive way of understanding how a classification algorithm behaves is to create a confusion matrix as seen in Example 5.1 [91].

**Example 5.1** Binomial EM Confusion Matrix

```
q).ut.totals[`TOTAL] .ml.cm[y;m p]
y| 0     1     2     TOTAL
-| ----------------------
0| 24400 8781  9     33190
1| 4960  26789 1583  33332
2| 0     1056  32422 33478
 | 29360 36626 34014 100000
```

The .ml.cm confusion-matrix function accepts the true and predicted labels (y and p respectively) and returns a table with the count for each combination of y and p value. The table lists the unique true y labels as the primary key and the unique predicted labels p as column headers. Each row indicates how many times the label associated with the key was predicted as each of the labels. A perfect predictor would have values along the diagonal and nowhere else. The more off-diagonal elements there are, the worse the algorithm was at classifying the data. Commonly confused elements can be found with large off-diagonal values.

Remembering that the biases of our coins are 10%, 30% and 80%, it is not surprising to see that the first row shows that coins with biases of 10% were more often mistaken as 30% (8,781 times) than mistaken as 80% (9 times). It is also not surprising to see that the coin with the most accurate (maximum value along the diagonal) predictions is the coin with a bias of 80%. It is the furthest from the other two.

**.ml.cm**

```
/ given true labels y and predicted labels p, return a confusion matrix
cm:{[y;p]
 n:count u:asc distinct y,p;
 m:./[(n;n)#0;flip (u?p;u?y);1+];
 t:([]y:u)!flip (`$string u)!m;
 t}
```

The .ml.cm function begins by creating a sorted list u of all the unique y and p values. It then creates an n x n square zero matrix and iteratively increments the matrix values corresponding to the y and p pairs. The last line of the function casts the unique values to symbols and uses them as column names and primary-key values.

After building the confusion matrix with the .ml.cm function, we used the .ut.totals utility function to add a "TOTAL" column as well as a total row. Separating these two functions not only allows us to use them together but also allows us to use the .ut.totals function independently.

**.ut.totals**

```
/ append a total row and (c)olumn to (t)able
totals:{[c;t]
 t[key[t]0N]:sum value t;
 t:t,'flip (1#c)!enlist sum flip value t;
 t}
```

The first line of .ut.totals sums the columns and adds a new row that is keyed with a null value. All rows—including the newly added total row—are then summed and the resulting vector is transformed into a one-column table. To prevent potential collisions with existing columns, the name of the total column is provided as a parameter c to the function. This one-column table is then appended to the original table.

## 5.4 Multinomial Distribution

The expectation-maximization function .ml.em was designed to be used with any distribution. The only difference is the supplied likelihood function lf and weighted-maximum-likelihood-estimator function wmf. Our next example demonstrates a slightly more complicated distribution—the multinomial distribution.

## 5.4. MULTINOMIAL DISTRIBUTION

Now, instead of reaching into our pocket and pulling out a coin, we have three 6-sided (potentially biased) dice. Instead of recording a single value representing the total number of heads flipped in each trail, we will now record a vector indicating how many times each side of the dice was rolled. For example, if we reset the random number generator seed and rolled a fair dice 10 times, we could expect to see the following distribution of outcomes.

```
q)\S -314159
q).ml.rmultinom[1;10;6#1%6]
0 2 3 3 2 0
```

If we performed this exercise 5 times, we could expect to see the following outcomes.

```
q).ml.rmultinom[5;10;6#1%6]
1 2 2 3 2 0
0 1 3 3 0 3
3 2 1 0 1 3
2 1 4 1 2 0
3 3 0 1 1 2
```

The .ml.rmultinom random-multinomial-generator function resembles the .ml.rbinom random-binomial-generator function in that it computes a summation of boolean values. Instead of representing a single true or false value (a coin flip), however, each sample returns multiple boolean values to indicate the class of the sample. The function still chooses values from a uniform distribution, but instead of having a single cutoff to determine true or false, there are multiple cutoffs—corresponding to each of the classes.

**.ml.rmultinom**

/ generate (n) multinomial distribution variate-vectors with (k) trials and
/ (p)robability vector defined for each class
rmultinom:{[n;k;p](sum til[count p]=/:sums[p] binr runif::) each n#k}

To play a game similar to the coin flipping experiment, we would need to define the biases of each face of each of three dice, pick one of each dice randomly from our pocket and record the results of 10 rolls.

First we define the biases of each of the three coins.

```
q)show b:(6#1f%6;.5,5#.1;(2#.1),4#.2)
0.1666667 0.1666667 0.1666667 0.1666667 0.1666667 0.1666667
0.5       0.1       0.1       0.1       0.1       0.1
```

| 0.1 | 0.1 | 0.2 | 0.2 | 0.2 | 0.2 |

Next we run through 100,000 trials (again recording which coin was used in y).

```
q)show X:flip raze .ml.rmultinom[1;10] each b y:100000?3
3 0 1 0 4 1 2 4 1 2 3 2 6 1 1 1 1 5 5 1 6 0 6 5 1 0 1 5 2 0 5 3 1 2 2 2 5..
3 1 1 1 3 0 1 2 4 1 2 2 1 1 1 2 0 1 1 0 1 1 1 0 3 1 0 1 0 3 0 1 1 2 1 2..
1 3 3 2 0 0 1 2 1 0 0 1 0 2 0 3 0 1 2 3 0 1 0 0 1 3 2 0 2 4 2 2 5 1 0 1 1..
0 2 0 3 3 3 2 2 3 0 2 2 1 2 5 2 3 1 2 3 1 3 1 2 1 2 4 0 0 0 0 2 0 1 2 3 1..
1 2 1 1 2 2 2 1 2 1 3 3 0 2 1 1 0 2 0 2 0 5 1 1 4 2 1 4 2 2 0 1 0 3 3 0 1..
2 2 4 3 0 1 3 0 1 3 1 0 1 2 2 2 4 1 0 0 3 0 1 1 3 0 1 1 3 4 0 2 3 2 1 3 0..
```

We must remember that in order to take advantage of q's vectorization, the first dimension corresponds to the features (each of the six sides) and the second dimension corresponds to the trials. This choice is made clearer by viewing the data as a table.

```
q)flip `1`2`3`4`5`6!X
1 2 3 4 5 6
-----------
3 3 1 0 1 2
0 1 3 2 2 2
1 1 3 0 1 4
0 1 2 3 1 3
4 1 0 3 2 0
..
```

Moving on, we define the likelihood function lf and the weighted-maximum-likelihood-estimator function wmf and apply the expectation-maximization algorithm. Again, we are assuming 10 rolls of the dice. And this time, we are applying a small bit of smoothing for the second parameter of .ml.wmmmmle so infinities don't appear when it produces absolute certain results.

```
q)lf:.ml.mmml
q)mf:.ml.wmmmmle[10;1e-8]
```

A series of trials from different distributions is commonly called a mixture model. The multinomial mixture model likelihood is defined as a product of individual multinomial likelihoods whose formula is shown in Equation 5.3 [95], where the multinomial coefficient $\binom{n}{k_i}$ expands to $\binom{n}{k_1,k_2,...,k_i}$ and is computed as $\frac{n!}{k_1!k_2!\cdots k_i!}$.

The individual multinomial likelihoods are defined in .ml.multil, and here again, we drop the multinomial coefficient because the probabilities obtained with the maximum likelihood are not effected by its inclusion.

## 5.4. MULTINOMIAL DISTRIBUTION

$$\mathcal{L}(p_i|n, k_i) = \binom{n}{k_i} p_i^{k_i}$$

Equation 5.3: Multinomial Likelihood

**.ml.multil**

```
/ multinomial likelihood approximation (without the multinomial coefficient)
multil:{[p;k]p xexp k}
```

To create a multinomial-mixture-model-likelihood function, we merely compute the product of individual multinomial likelihoods. This is implemented in .ml.mmml.

**.ml.mmml**

```
/ multinomial mixture model likelihood
mmml:prd multil::
```

With the likelihood function complete, we now turn our attention to the maximum likelihood estimator. The .ml.wmmmmle function implements the weighted multinomial mixture model maximum likelihood estimator. It computes a weighted average over multiple observations and includes an extra term a for Dirichlet smoothing.

**.ml.wmmmmle**

```
/ weighted multinomial mixture model mle with Dirichlet smoothing (a)
wmmmmle:{[n;a;w;x]enlist w wavg/: a+x%n}
```

The corresponding multinomial mixture model maximum-likelihood estimator is defined in Equation 5.4 [95].

$$\hat{p}_i = \frac{x_i}{n}$$

Equation 5.4: Multinomial Mixture Model Maximum Likelihood Estimator

## Parameter Initialization

We again initialize phi assuming an equal probability of picking each of the dice. And to initialize the THETA, we randomly select three of the trials and use the .ml.prb function to convert the number of faces to a probability.

```
q)phi:3#1f%3
q)show THETA:flip .ml.prb 3?/:X
0         0.1818182  0.2727273  0.2727273  0.09090909 0.1818182
0.5833333 0.08333333 0.1666667  0          0          0.1666667
0.3333333 0.2222222  0          0.1111111  0.1111111  0.2222222
```

## Aggregation-based Transformations

To transform a list of values representing frequencies into probabilities, we can divide each value by the sum of all values.

```
q)prb:{x%sum x}
q)prb 1 1 2 2 4
0.1 0.1 0.2 0.2 0.4
```

This implementation can then be used with the each adverb to be applied across multiple lists.

```
q)prb each (1 1 2 2 4;2 2 3 3 6)
0.1   0.1   0.2    0.2    0.4
0.125 0.125 0.1875 0.1875 0.375
```

If we wish to apply the operator across the second dimension of a matrix, however, we need to be more creative because the naive application fails us. The .ml.prb function is implemented as a projection of the .ml.dax function to handle this case.

**.ml.prb**

```
/ convert densities into probabilities
prb:dax[%;sum]
```

It accepts a dyadic operator as its first argument and an aggregating function as its second argument. The last argument is obviously the data x.

**.ml.dax**

```
/ apply (d)yadic function to the result of (a)ggregating
/ vector/matrix/dictionary/table x
dax:{[d;a;x]daxf[d;a;x] x}
```

## 5.4. MULTINOMIAL DISTRIBUTION

The `.ml.dax` function is itself implemented in terms of the `.ml.daxf` higher-order function that partially evaluates its arguments and returns a new function.

**.ml.daxf**

```
/ return a function that applies (d)yadic function to the result of
/ (a)ggregating vector/matrix/dictionary/table x
daxf:{[d;a;x]$[0h>type first x; d[;a x]; d[;a x] peach]}
```

We will discuss the benefits of providing a function that returns another function when we introduce feature scaling in Section 9.10 [195]. For now, let's focus on the functionality, rather than the implementation, of `.ml.daxf` and therefore `.ml.dax`.

The `.ml.daxf` function behaves differently depending on the type of the first element of x. As previously mentioned in the section called "Find" [35], checking the type of the first element, instead of the type of x directly, allows a function to be used with simple vectors and dictionaries as well as matrices and tables. If the type of the first element is an atom, we intuitively apply the dyadic and aggregating functions as demonstrated in the example above. If, on the other hand, the first element is not an atom, the results of the aggregation are applied to *each* element of x. Applying the `.ml.prb` function to a matrix converts the values into probabilities normalized across each column.

```
q).ml.prb (1 1 2 2 4;2 2 3 3 6)
0.3333333 0.3333333 0.4 0.4 0.4
0.6666667 0.6666667 0.6 0.6 0.6
```

We will see the `.ml.dax` and `.ml.daxf` functions a few more times because transforming data based on an aggregation of the data itself appears often.

### Algorithm Iteration

Running the expectation-maximization algorithm until convergence discovers dice biases very similar to what we defined. We can even turn off fitting of `phi` to speed up convergence.

```
q)last pT:(.ml.em[0b;lf;mf;X]//) (phi;flip enlist THETA)
0.1003825 0.09959829 0.2013954 0.202444  0.1988795 0.1973005
0.5000714 0.1001468  0.09995779 0.1002758 0.09958262 0.09996568
0.1656837 0.167635   0.1642931 0.1639278 0.1690072 0.1694532
```

Again, we can compute accuracy by using `phi` and `THETA` to classify the trials.

```
q)p:.ml.imax .ml.likelihood[0b;lf;X] . pT
q)m:.ml.mode each y group p
q)avg y=m p
0.71182
```

Checking the diagonal of the confusion matrix in Example 5.2 [98], we see that the second die is the most accurately predicted.

**Example 5.2** Multinomial EM Confusion Matrix

```
q).ut.totals[`TOTAL] .ml.cm[y;m p]
y| 0     1     2     TOTAL
-| ----------------------
0| 20902 2343  9955  33200
1| 5337  27608 392   33337
2| 10389 402   22672 33463
 | 36628 30353 33019 100000
```

It is clearly easy to differentiate a die that produces a one 50% of the time and all other faces 10% each.

```
q)b 1
0.5 0.1 0.1 0.1 0.1 0.1
```

## 5.5 Bernoulli Mixture Models

We now move on to a more interesting application of the expectation-maximization algorithm. A popular data set for machine learning is the MNIST handwritten-digit database.[1] It contains 7,000 black and white images of the handwritten digits 0 through 9. 6,000 of the images are segregated for training and 1,000 for testing. Each image is a 28 x 28 square with a total of 784 bytes ranging from 0 to 255. Importing the mnist.q [381] library[2] loads six variables. mnist.X and mnist.Xt are the training and testing byte matrices, while mnist.Y and mnist.Yt are the classification matrices (numeric values 0 through 9). Finally, mnist.y and mnist.yt store

---

[1] Y. LeCun, C. Cortes, and C. Burges, "MNIST handwritten digit database." [Online]. Available: http://yann.lecun.com/exdb/mnist/. [Accessed: 22-Jan-2020].

[2] The utility used to load the MNIST data, .ut.mnist, leverages q's ability to reshape a vector for an arbitrary list of dimensions. This requires a minimum kdb+ version of 3.4 with a release date of 2016.04.10 or later.

## 5.5. BERNOULLI MIXTURE MODELS

the classification values in simple vectors that are sometimes more convenient to use.

```
q)\l mnist.q
[down]loading handwritten-digit data set
loading mnist training data
loading mnist testing data
```

After defining a custom plotting function to transform the image vectors into 28 x 28 pixel heat maps, Example 5.3 [99] demonstrates how we can render a few digits.

**Example 5.3** MNIST Digits
```
q)plt:value .ut.plot[28;14;.ut.c10;avg] .ut.hmap flip 28 cut
q)-1 (,'/) plt each mnist.X @\:/: 0 1;
```

```
            --: :+=-                    +%@%+
      ++x%%@@@@@x+x+=.           .+@@@%x@x-
       +%#@@@=:+#                .#@@%#@@-+@x
           =@#                  -x@#x:   .    @@+
         x@%#-                   +@%.         @@#
         :x@#=                  :@@-         -@%:
         -:@@@.                 :@#         :#%=.
        -+#@@@%x:               :@@-   .:=#@%=
       :=x@@@%x=.               -%@@@@@@#:-
     :%@@@##+-                      -===-
```

An interesting approach to analyzing this data is to convert each image to black and white and assume that each pixel comes from a Bernoulli distribution. In other words, each pixel has a different probability of being on or off. When the distributions of all pixels are analyzed together, patterns will emerge for each handwritten digit. This combination of Bernoulli observations is called a Bernoulli mixture model.

Before running the expectation-maximization algorithm against this data set we first copy the data to the global namespace, limit the number of samples to 10,000 and convert the images to black and white by setting all values greater than 128 to 1 and the rest to 0.

```
q)`X`y set' mnist`X`y;
```

```
q)X:10000#/:X;y:10000#y
q)X>:128
```

## Parameter Initialization

Due to the variety of hand writing behaviors, it is expected that limiting ourselves to exactly 10 clusters will perform worse than if we allow more. Taken to the extreme, allowing as many clusters as data points will obviously classify our training data set quite well but with added model complexity. We will use 20 clusters for this demonstration and initialize phi to assume equal probability.

```
q)phi:20#1f%20
```

Initializing theta is a bit more tricky. One option is to select 20 random images from the training data set. Alternatively, we could create 20 images with random pixel values. The first option initializes the clusters with logical values—permitting faster convergence but exposes us to numeric instability because the pixel values are concretely 0 or 1. The second option makes no assumptions about the cluster values and results in longer convergence times. A compromise picks initial clusters from the training set using the k-means++ initialization algorithm such that the images are as different as possible, and then averages these images with some random noise such that the values are not too close to 0 or 1.[3]

The first step is to use the k-means++ .ml.kpp function to pick 20 prototypes that are as different as possible.

```
q)\S -314159
q)THETA:flip last 20 .ml.kpp[.ml.hdist;X]// 2#()
```

Since the images are black and white (vectors of booleans), we used the Hamming-distance function .ml.hdist that counts the number bytes in two vectors that are not equal.

**.ml.hdist**

```
hdist:sum (<>)::           / Hamming distance
```

We then average this data with uniformly distributed random values between .15 and .85.

---

[3]A. Juan, J. García-Hernández, and E. Vidal, "EM Initialisation for Bernoulli Mixture Learning," in *Structural, Syntactic*, and Statistical Pattern Recognition, Berlin, Heidelberg, 2004, pp. 635–643, doi: 10.1007/978-3-540-27868-9_69.

## 5.5. BERNOULLI MIXTURE MODELS

```
q)THETA:.5*THETA+.15+count[X]?/:20#.7
```

Two of the resulting prototypes are demonstrated in Example 5.4 [101].

**Example 5.4** Prototypical Digits with Random Noise

```
q)-1 (,'/) plt each 2#THETA;
.:--   ...  -.-.-. =.::--:.- :. ...- -:.-:.-.--- -:-::-- :.
-.--...- ....-:.. ..-:..-:.:-.-... ::.--==@%=:..:-- ---
 - :. ::..=+x@x#%@x+.:::-..:..-. .:.-. :x..=:#=..----.-
:..--- :.+:---.-.%#.::- ::.---..:..-..-.- -x#+-:.:.-.
----.-...:.--.-..-%##-....:.---. .:--.--:- .+%#...:-..
.:-:. ...-....-.:x%xx.: --:.-. - ----:-xxx:::--%##.......
::--:..:-..:++xx=.-.-:.:.-..-..----:%+x++=x@@x+#% : -..:
 . :.---:=#+=---...-.-..--. .:. -@#- -.--=#%%+-. -- .--
-.-.-:+#x=.--:-:- -.-..-..----..-x%-...: :@@%#=.. -....:
.---=@+ ::---::-:--:--:.--..-- :. %#%++###=--:%#+ .- --
.- -.:+@##%+x%x@x%x@=+: .:-...: --- +::+:...:- :.:.--
---  --.-=:.....-:-- +:  -...:-.-..-..:   .- -:..:: - -
-.:. .---.:- -:----.-.-:---.-.---...-.:.:......-.. .:..
```

And finally, we can define the likelihood function lf and weighted-maximum-likelihood-estimator function mf with the Bernoulli mixture model variants. Noting that the Bernoulli distribution is just a binomial distribution with one dimension, we pass 1 in as the first parameter to both functions. And in order to preserve numerical stability, we pass 1e-8 as the smoothing parameter.

```
q)lf:.ml.bmml[1]
q)mf:.ml.wbmmmle[1;1e-8]
```

The Bernoulli mixture model likelihood function is defined in Equation 5.5 [101] as the product of individual Bernoulli likelihoods.

$$\mathcal{L}(p|x) = \prod_{i=1}^{n} p_i^{x_i}(1-p_i)^{1-x_i}$$

Equation 5.5: Bernoulli Mixture Model Likelihood

We obtain a deeper understanding of the Binomial-mixture-model-likelihood function .ml.bmml by implementing it as the product of individual Binomial likelihoods.

**.ml.bmml**

```
/ binomial mixture model likelihood
bmml:prd binl::
```

The weighted Binomial mixture model maximum-likelihood-estimator function is defined in .ml.wbmmmle and can also be used for a Bernoulli mixture model by fixing n as 1.

**.ml.wbmmmle**

```
/ weighted binomial mixture model mle with Dirichlet smoothing (a)
wbmmmle:{[n;a;w;x]enlist w wavg/: a+x%n}
```

We can see in Equation 5.6 [102] how the binomial mixture model maximum-likelihood estimator is again just the sample proportion of success.

$$\hat{p}_i = \frac{x_i}{n}$$

Equation 5.6: Binomial Mixture Model Maximum Likelihood Estimator

## Algorithm Iteration

Running the expectation-maximization algorithm 10 times clusters the images. Although we are not performing classification, it is still instructive to see if the clusters match our recognition of the handwritten digits.

```
q)pT:10 .ml.em[1b;lf;mf;X]// (phi;flip enlist THETA)
q)p:.ml.imax .ml.likelihood[0b;lf;X] . pT
q)m:.ml.mode each y group p
q)avg y=m p
0.7018
```

Example 5.5 [103] demonstrates how the random noise around the edges of the prototypes has disappeared, but yet the digits themselves remain slightly blurry—resulting from the variation in how people draw digits.

## Confusion Matrix

The diagonal of the confusion matrix in Example 5.6 [104] demonstrates that the digit 1 is least often confused, while the digit 5 is very hard to identify and is often

## 5.6. GAUSSIAN MIXTURE MODEL

**Example 5.5** Prototypical Digits

```
q)-1 (,'/) plt each  first each 2#last pT;
```

```
        .:=+xx#x+=-.                        .-::::-.
       -:+x#####%#+:.                  .-=x%%%%##x=-
      .-::::::+xx=-                  .=#%@@%#xxx#%#=.
      .-=++x###+:.                  -+%@%#+=----:x%%x-
      -=x####%#x=.                  -+%@%+:-.    .=#%#=.
      ......-=#%x:.                 .x@@#=.       .-=#%#+-
      ....     .=#%x-               :%@%+-.....-:+#@%x:.
     .-=++=:-.--=#@@x:.             -%@%x+++x#%@@%x:.
     .:x%@@@@@@%x:.                 :x#%%%%#x+:.
        .::==:-.                       .---..
```

clustered with the digits 3 and 8. Understandably, the digits 7 and 4 are often added to clusters dominated by the digit 9. We can improve this by using more clusters and/or by iterating over the expectation-maximization algorithm more times.

## 5.6 Gaussian Mixture Model

For the final example, let's use the expectation-maximization algorithm to cluster the Iris data set. Performing expectation-maximization using a Gaussian distribution is very similar to the k-means algorithm. Instead of summarizing each cluster by a single point and classifying data points based on the closest cluster, the Gaussian distribution describes the cluster with a location and a variance. Each point, therefore, has a probability of being in each cluster. In addition, the Gaussian mixture model incorporates the covariance between features as well.

We begin by loading the Iris data set and creating a reference to the data in the global namespace.

```
q)\l iris.q
[down]loading iris data set
q)`X`y set' iris`X`y;
```

**Example 5.6** Bernoulli Mixture Model EM Confusion Matrix

```
q).ut.totals[`TOTAL] .ml.cm[y;m p]
y| 0    1    2   3    4    5    6    7   8   9   TOTAL
-| ----------------------------------------------------
0| 880  0    2   42   0    11   57   0   9   0   1001
1| 0    1021 6   10   1    65   6    0   6   12  1127
2| 7    16   796 31   4    7    95   0   30  5   991
3| 4    26   23  851  10   17   8    4   73  16  1032
4| 0    4    6   1    650  65   38   2   0   214 980
5| 21   4    1   284  29   321  28   1   163 11  863
6| 10   4    1   6    0    7    982  0   3   1   1014
7| 2    35   7   1    163  42   3    552 8   257 1070
8| 9    31   7   152  14   43   33   1   653 1   944
9| 2    6    3   17   546  55   9    19  9   312 978
 | 935  1147 852 1395 1417 633  1259 579 954 829 10000
```

## Parameter Initialization

With the knowledge that there are three different species in the data, we equal-weight phi.

```
q)phi:3#1f%3
```

Until now, we have been using distributions characterized by a single parameter. The multivariate Gaussian distribution has two parameters: mu (the central location vector) and SIGMA (the variance-covariance matrix). To initialize these parameters, we pick three random points from the data set for mu and the sample covariance of the data for each of the three SIGMA parameters.

```
q)\S -314159
q)mu:X@\:/:-3?count y
q)SIGMA:3#enlist X cov\:/: X
```

We can now declare the likelihood function lf and the weighted-maximum-likelihood-estimator function mf with the multivariate Gaussian distribution variants.

```
q)lf:.ml.gaussmvl
q)mf:.ml.wgaussmvmle
```

## 5.6. GAUSSIAN MIXTURE MODEL

The Gaussian multivariate likelihood equation is listed in Equation 5.7 [105] where $d$ is the dimension of the multivariate problem. This can be interpreted as the size of the $x$ vector or the dimension of the $d \times d$ variance-covariance matrix $\Sigma$.

$$\mathcal{L}(x|\mu, \Sigma) = \frac{1}{\sqrt{(2\pi)^d |\Sigma|}} e^{-\frac{1}{2}(x-\mu)^T \Sigma^{-1}(x-\mu)}$$

Equation 5.7: Multivariate Gaussian Likelihood

This is implemented in the .ml.gaussmvl Gaussian-multivariate-likelihood function that accepts vector values for mu and a variance-covariance matrix SIGMA.

**.ml.gaussmvl**

```
/ Gaussian multivariate
gaussmvl:{[mu;SIGMA;X]
 if[type SIGMA;SIGMA:diag count[X]#SIGMA];
 p:exp -.5*sum X*mm[minv SIGMA;X-:mu];
 p%:sqrt mdet[SIGMA]*twopi xexp count X;
 p}
```

In addition to the .ml.minv matrix-inversion function which we will describe in Section 9.5 [187], the .ml.gaussmvl function requires the calculation of a matrix determinant. The .ml.mdet function recursively calls itself until a 2 x 2 matrix is found and the determinant can be calculated.

**.ml.mdet**

```
mdet:{[X]                    / determinant
 if[2>n:count X;:X];
 if[2=n;:(X[0;0]*X[1;1])-X[0;1]*X[1;0]];
 d:dot[X 0;(n#1 -1)*(.z.s (X _ 0)_\:) each til n];
 d}
```

The .ml.wgaussmvmle function implements a weighted version of the Gaussian multivariate maximum-likelihood-estimator equation detailed in Equation 5.8 [106].

**.ml.wgaussmvmle**

```
/ weighted Gaussian multivariate mle
wgaussmvmle:{[w;X](mu;w wavg X (*\:/:)' X:flip X-mu:w wavg/: X)}
```

$$\hat{\mu} = \frac{1}{n}\sum_{i=1}^{n} x_i$$

$$\hat{\Sigma} = \frac{1}{n}\sum_{i=1}^{n} (x_i - \hat{\mu})(x_i - \hat{\mu})^T$$

Equation 5.8: Multivariate Gaussian Maximum Likelihood Estimator

## Algorithm Iteration

With such a small data set, we can iterate the expectation-maximization algorithm until convergence,

```
q)pT:(.ml.em[lb;lf;mf;X]//) (phi;flip (mu;SIGMA))
```

and calculate the accuracy by computing the predicted cluster assignments p and cluster mappings m.

```
q)p:.ml.imax .ml.likelihood[0b;.ml.gaussmvl;X] . pT
q)m:.ml.mode each y group p
q)avg y=m p
0.8866667
```

## Confusion Matrix

Viewing the confusion matrix in Example 5.7 [106] makes it evident that the algorithm accurately identifies Iris setosa, but often confuses Iris virginica with Iris versicolor.

**Example 5.7** Gaussian Mixture Model EM Confusion Matrix

```
q).ut.totals[`TOTAL] .ml.cm[y;m p]
x               | Iris-setosa Iris-versicolor Iris-virginica TOTAL
----------------| -----------------------------------------------
Iris-setosa     | 50          0               0              50
Iris-versicolor | 0           49              1              50
Iris-virginica  | 0           16              34             50
                | 50          65              35             150
```

The k-means, hierarchical agglomerative clustering and expectation-maximization algorithms are known as unsupervised learning algorithms because they don't require classification labels during the training process. The algorithms depended only on distance and distribution parameters of the data. We actually have the labels for the MNIST and Iris data set, and used them to see if the clusters happened to match the labels. Wouldn't it have been better if we used these labels while building our model?

The next chapter builds upon the likelihood and weighted-maximum-likelihood-estimator functions that we introduced in this chapter, combines them with each observation's label, and builds a much more efficient, and hopefully accurate, model.

# Chapter 6

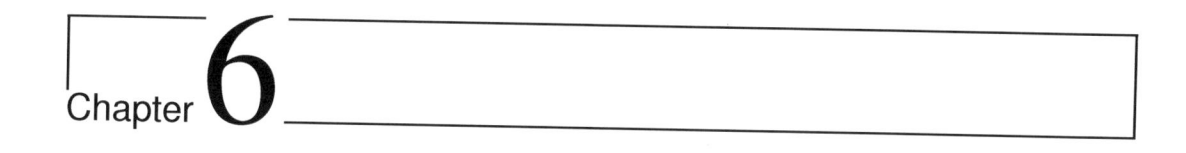

# Naive Bayes

> Naiveté is the most important attribute of genius.
>
> — Johann Wolfgang von Goethe

On first pass, being naive has a negative connotation. One might understandably be insulted by being labeled naive. But as Goethe indicates, taking a simple and open-minded view of a problem can result in creative insights. The naive Bayes algorithm is an example where taking a simplistic view of a problem can yield powerful results.

The "naive" in naive Bayes is not a reflection of the algorithm's weakness. In fact, the algorithm is very powerful and can be used efficiently on large amounts of data. Similar to the expectation-maximization algorithm, the naive Bayes algorithm uses the weighted-maximum-likelihood-estimator function to determine the model parameters for a given distribution. Similarly, it also uses the likelihood (or log likelihood) function to classify new data with the generated model. The main difference between the two algorithms is that the naive Bayes algorithm uses the fact that we know the class of each observation when building the model. This allows the algorithm to perform a single pass across the training data set—it does not need to iterate like the k-means and expectation-maximization algorithms.

More importantly, the algorithm assumes conditional independence between the different training features. In other words, conditional on being a member of a specific class, it is assumed there is no relationship between the values of any the training features. It is therefore possible to multiply the likelihood probabilities of each of the observed data points by the probability of being a member of the class itself to perform the final classification. This assumed conditional independence is where the "naive" in naive Bayes comes from. Even if all the features are not perfectly independent, the naive Bayes algorithm can still be used—with much success.

## 6.1 Fit Naive Bayes

The naive Bayes fitting function requires four parameters. The first parameter wmf is the weighted-maximum-likelihood-estimator function for the data's assumed distribution. This is followed by the weight vector w—one weight for each training data observation or the null :: if each data point should get the same weight. The final two parameters, y and X, are the observation classes and training data set respectively.

**.ml.fnb**

```
/ fit parameters given (w)eighted (m)aximization (f)unction returns a
/ dictionary with prior and conditional likelihoods
fnb:{[wmf;w;y;X]
 if[(::)~w;w:count[y]#1f];      / handle unassigned weight
 pT:(odds g; (wmf . (w;X@\:) @\:) peach g:group y);
 pT}
```

Given the ground we've already covered, it really is that simple. The first line handles the case where all weights should be equal. This is followed by the algorithm itself. The second and final line of the function groups the data by the class values y and computes the phi and THETA variables we introduced in Chapter 5 [83]. These correspond to the prior probability of observing each class and the associated model parameters for each feature.

A new function, .ml.odds, is used to compute the prior probabilities. It accepts a dictionary generated by the group operator and returns the odds of each value occurring within the data set.

**.ml.odds**

```
/ given (g)rouped dictionary, compute the odds
odds:{[g]prb count each g}
```

A quick example demonstrates how the .ml.odds function can be used.

```
q).ml.odds group 1 1 2 2 3 3 4 4 4 4
1| 0.2
2| 0.2
3| 0.2
4| 0.4
```

As with many statistical functions, a weighted variant also exists. Instead of counting the number elements corresponding to each unique value, the .ml.wodds weighted-odds function sums the weights of the elements corresponding to each unique value.

**.ml.wodds**

```
/ given (w)eight vector and (g)rouped dictionary, compute the weighted odds
wodds:{[w;g]prb sum each w g}
```

Giving observations different weights will be useful in Chapter 7 [131] for redistributing each observation's importance in the presence of null values. Section 8.5 [173] will also depend heavily on assigning custom weights to each observation in order to dynamically improve a model by explicitly increasing the weight on observations that were previously incorrectly classified. By providing a weight vector to .ml.wodds we can obtain the weighted odds of observing each value.

```
q).ml.wodds[10#til 5] group 1 1 2 2 3 3 4 4 4 4
1| 0.05
2| 0.25
3| 0.2
4| 0.5
```

## 6.2 Gaussian Naive Bayes

Returning to our faithful Iris data set, we can build a classification model assuming that, like most things in nature, the features of the Iris flower follow a Gaussian (normal) distribution.

```
q)\l funq.q
q)\l iris.q
[down]loading iris data set
q)`X`y set' iris`X`y
q)pT:.ml.fnb[.ml.wgaussmle/:;:::;y;X]
```

```
q)pT 0
Iris-setosa    | 0.3333333
Iris-versicolor| 0.3333333
Iris-virginica | 0.3333333
q)pT 1
Iris-setosa    | 5.006 0.121764 3.428 0.140816 1.462 0.029556 0.246 0.010884
Iris-versicolor| 5.936 0.261104 2.77  0.0965   4.26  0.2164   1.326 0.038324
Iris-virginica | 6.588 0.396256 2.974 0.101924 5.552 0.298496 2.026 0.073924
```

The prior probabilities are identical because the training data set has an equal number of observations (50) for each species. The Gaussian distribution parameters (mu and SIGMA) for each feature are returned for each class. Note that in contrast to the expectation-maximization algorithm, the phi and THETA values are dictionaries instead of vectors and matrices. The difference here is that each value is no longer anonymous, but assigned to a class.

With these parameters, we can use the .ml.pnb predict-naive-Bayes function to classify our training data set and measure the algorithm's accuracy.

```
q)avg y=p:.ml.pnb[0b;.ml.gaussl;pT] X
0.96
```

## Predict Naive Bayes

The .ml.pnb function accepts a boolean l specifying if the supplied likelihood function computes the *log* likelihood instead of the likelihood. Prior probabilities phi and distribution parameters THETA are supplied as a single parameter pT, and X is the data to be classified.

### .ml.pnb

```
/ using a [log](l)ikelihood (f)unction and prior probabilities (p)hi and
/ distribution parameters (T)HETA, perform naive Bayes classification
pnb:{[l;lf;pT;X]
  d:{(x . z) y}[lf]'[X] peach pT[1]; / compute probability densities
  c:imax $[l;log[pT 0]+sum flip d;pT[0]*prd flip d];
  c}
```

The first line of the .ml.pnb uses the THETA values in pT along with the data in X to compute the probability densities that each observation belongs to the given probability distribution. Note that these values are not actual probabilities because they do not sum to one. They are, however, comparable across distributions and can be used for ranking. The second line classifies the observations by finding the class with the maximum total probability density. The total probability density is computed by summing the log likelihoods for the conditionally independent observations and the class probabilities phi if l is true, or multiplying them together if the value is false.

Even with perfect knowledge of each observation's class, using the naive Bayes algorithm with a Gaussian distribution still can't get 100% accuracy. Plotting the petal length and width in Example 6.1 [113], we can see that the mistakes (rendered with the "@" character) occurred at the boundary between two classes.

**Example 6.1** Naive Bayes Mistakes

```
q).ut.plt X[2 3], enlist 1 0N y=p
3| "                            "
 | "                  ....      "
 | "                  .... .    "
2| "              @......       "
 | "            .@@@ .          "
 | "              ..... .       "
1| "          ....              "
 | " .                          "
 | "...                         "
0| "...                         "
```

## 6.3 Multinomial Naive Bayes

Identifying email or SMS messages as spam is an important example of how the naive Bayes algorithm can be used with a multinomial distribution. As introduced in Section 5.4 [92], a multinomial distribution represents the result of n independent trials when there are a fixed set of k possible values. This time, instead of rolling a six-sided dice, our k possible values will be a collection of words—scoured from an SMS training data set. The n independent trials will be the actual number of words in the SMS messages.

To begin, we download the SMS Spam Collection[1] from UCI's machine-learning

---

[1] T. A. Almeida, J. M. Gómez, and A. Yamakami, "Contributions to the Study of SMS Spam Filtering: New Collection and Results," in *Proceedings of the 2011 ACM Symposium on Document Engineering*, Mountain View, 2011, pp. 259–262.

data archive with the smsspam.q [382] library. The imported data set is a table with two columns: the class (spam or not) and the actual SMS text. Note that SMS messages that are not "spam" are humorously classified as "ham". We drop the first 18 messages in the following demonstration to provide good examples of the text cleaning pipeline.

```
q)\l smsspam.q
[down]loading sms spam data set
q)18_smsspam.t
class text                                                              ..
-----------------------------------------------------------------------..
ham   "Fine if that\302\222s the way u feel. That\302\222s the way its go..
spam  "England v Macedonia - dont miss the goals/team news. Txt ur nation..
ham   "Is that seriously how you spell his name?"                        ..
ham   "I\342\200\230m going to try for 2 months ha ha only joking"       ..
ham   "So \303\274 pay first lar... Then when is da stock comin..."      ..
..
```

Any text-based analysis requires pre-processing of the data. In short, we must focus our attention on text with information content and throw away the rest. In addition, some words may be spelled differently, but represent the same piece of information. Let's address these two issues in-turn.

## ASCII text

In order to display characters outside the basic ASCII character set, text documents often represent special characters (such as letters with accents, fancy quotation marks and currency symbols) in UTF-8 or Unicode encoding. These characters are represented by more than a single byte. Q can read these bytes, but displays them by their octal value. The .ut.ua Unicode-to-ASCII dictionary maps common Unicode characters to their ASCII equivalent. We only show the first few lines below because the list is long. The complete list is located in the ut.q [339] library.

**.ut.ua**

```
/ map (u)nicode characters to their (a)scii equivalents
ua:(!/) 2 1 0#""
ua["\342\200\223"]:"--"                 / endash
ua["\342\200\224"]:"---"                / emdash
ua["\342\200[\231\230]"]:"'"            / single quotes
ua["\342\200[\234\235]"]:"\""           / double quotes
```

## 6.3. MULTINOMIAL NAIVE BAYES

HTML entities for the "<", ">" and "&" characters are also scattered throughout the SMS messages. The `.ut.ha` HTML-to-ASCII dictionary maps a few of the common HTML entities to their ASCII equivalent.

**.ut.ha**

```
/ map (h)tml entities to their (a)scii equivalents
ha:(!/) 2 1 0#""
ha["&lt;"]:"<"                              / <
ha["&gt;"]:">"                              / >
ha["&amp;"]:"&"                             / &
ha["&apos;"]:"'"                            / '
ha["&quot;"]:"\""                           / "
ha[" "]:" "                            /
ha:1_ha
```

Given these two maps, we can now use the `.ut.sr` search-and-replace utility to transform the SMS messages into pure ASCII characters.

```
q)18_t:update .ut.sr[.ut.ua,.ut.ha] peach text from smsspam.t
class text                                                              ..
------------------------------------------------------------------------..
ham   "Fine if that's the way u feel. That's the way its gota b"        ..
spam  "England v Macedonia - dont miss the goals/team news. Txt ur nation..
ham   "Is that seriously how you spell his name?"                       ..
ham   "I'm going to try for 2 months ha ha only joking"                 ..
ham   "So u pay first lar... Then when is da stock comin..."            ..
..
```

The `.ut.sr` search-and-replace utility accepts a character-mapping dictionary and a string as parameters. It iteratively uses the `ssr` string search-and-replace operator to apply each transformation.

**.ut.sr**

```
/ search (s)tring for all instances of key[d] and replace with value[d]
sr:{[d;s] ssr/[s;key d;value d]}
```

The resulting text is a bit cleaner, but we still need to remove punctuation marks and numeric values, so we can focus on individual words. The `.ut.pw` punctuation-to-whitespace dictionary maps punctuation and numeric values to appropriate whitespace alternatives: some get converted to a single space, while others are removed altogether.

**.ut.pw**

```
/ map (p)unctuation characters to their (w)hitespace replacements
pw:(!/) 2 1 0#""
pw["[][\n\\/()<>@#$%^&*=_+.,;:!?-]"]:" " / replace with whitespace
pw["['\"0-9]"]:""                         / delete
pw:1_pw
```

By reusing the .ut.sr search-and-replace utility, we can remove all punctuation and numeric values—leaving us with pure text.

```
q)18_t:update .ut.sr[.ut.pw] peach text from t
class text                                                              ..
------------------------------------------------------------------------..
ham   "Fine if thats the way u feel  Thats the way its gota b"          ..
spam  "England v Macedonia   dont miss the goals team news  Txt ur nation..
ham   "Is that seriously how you spell his name "                       ..
ham   "Im going to try for  months ha ha only joking"                   ..
ham   "So u pay first lar   Then when is da stock comin   "             ..
..
```

## Stop Words

Our analysis moves from character- to word-based filtering. Not all words convey meaning and including meaningless words will weaken our model. A lot of research has gone into generating lists of words that should be removed from vocabularies. These words are referred to as *stop words*. The stopwords.q [382] library sources a few such lists that we can choose from.

```
q)\l stopwords.q
q)stopwords.xpo6
""
,"a"
"about"
"above"
"across"
"after"
"afterwards"
..
```

The next step is to tokenize the words by splitting on spaces and then remove all stop words. We also convert all characters to lowercase with the lower operator to ensure our analysis is case-insensitive.

## 6.3. MULTINOMIAL NAIVE BAYES 117

```
q)18_t:update (except[;stopwords.xpo6] " " vs) peach lower text from t
class text                                                              ..
-----------------------------------------------------------------------..
ham   ("fine";"thats";"way";,"u";"feel";"thats";"way";"gota";,"b")      ..
spam  ("england";,"v";"macedonia";"dont";"miss";"goals";"team";"news";"tx..
ham   ("seriously";"spell")                                             ..
ham   ("im";"going";"try";"months";"ha";"ha";"joking")                  ..
ham   (,"u";"pay";"lar";"da";"stock";"comin")                           ..
..
```

We can see how words like "the", "is" and "you" have been removed from the SMS text.

### Lemmatization

The last step in the data preparation phase is to combine similar words with variations in spelling. One approach is to map words to their underlying meaning. The words "better", "best" and "well" can all be mapped to "good". This process is called lemmatization. The simplest approach to lemmatize a document is to use a word dictionary to map each word to its root. More advanced approaches use information in the sentence structure to determine the word's part of speech—and therefore make better mappings.

### Porter Stemmer

Another approach converts "seriously" into "serious" and "months" to "month" so that our model has a more compact vocabulary on which to learn. Algorithms that strip word suffixes to generate word roots are called "stemmers". The Porter stemmer was developed in 1980.[2] The Porter2 stemmer (also known as the English stemmer) stems words more accurately, but is also many times slower. We will use the Porter stemmer implemented in the porter.q [376] library for our analysis.

```
q)18_t:update (.porter.stem') peach text from t
class text                                                              ..
-----------------------------------------------------------------------..
ham   ("fine";"that";"wai";,"u";"feel";"that";"wai";"gota";,"b")        ..
```

---
[2] M. F. Porter, "An algorithm for suffix stripping," *Program: electronic library and information systems*, vol. 40, no. 3, pp. 211–218, Jul. 2006, doi 10.1108/00330330610681286.

```
spam    ("england";,"v";"macedonia";"dont";"miss";"goal";"team";"new";"txt"..
ham     ("serious";"spell")                                                 ..
ham     ("im";"go";"try";"month";"ha";"ha";"joke")                          ..
ham     (,"u";"pai";"lar";"da";"stock";"comin")                             ..
..
```

Notice how the word "seriously" was converted to "serious" and the word "going" was replaced with "go". These replacements were intuitive. Notice, too, how "way" was converted to "wai" and the spelling of "pay" was changed to "pai". Neither has lost its meaning, but we need to recognize new spellings for common words.

We now have 5574 SMS messages cleaned, lowered, tokenized and stemmed—ready for analysis. We will save 25% of the data for testing our model. The remaining 75% will be used for training. To ensure we have a representative frequency of spam vs. ham messages, we will also use the `class` column to perform stratified sampling.

```
q)d:.ut.part[`train`test!3 1;t.class] t
```

The next step in our processing pipeline is to define the vocabulary of our model. This step extracts the training corpus and classes into c and y respectively.

```
q)c:d . `train`text
q)y:d . `train`class
```

We can now build the vocabulary vector v by combining all the stemmed terms in all the training SMS messages. The resulting list is sorted for clarity, but this is not necessary.

```
q)v:asc distinct raze c
q)v
"aa"
"aah"
"aaniy"
"aaooooright"
"aathi"
"ab"
"abbei"
..
```

## Term Document Matrix

We are now ready to generate a term document matrix. The .ml.tdm function generates a matrix listing the number of times each word in our vocabulary appears in each document of our corpus. Analyzing text with a term document matrix makes a serious assumption about the data—the actual order of appearance in the document does not matter. This is also referred to as a Bag of Words model because it's as if we dumped all the words of the document into a bag and only the word frequencies matter.

**.ml.tdm**

```
/ term document matrix built from (c)orpus and (v)ocabulary
tdm:{[c;v](-1_@[(1+count v)#0;;+;1]::) each v?c}
```

The term document matrix has exactly the same form as our multinomial dice example. We can, therefore, use the weighted multinomial maximum-likelihood estimator to generate our naive Bayes model.

```
q)X:flip .ml.tdm[c;v]
q)pT:.ml.fnb[.ml.wmultimle[1];::;y;X]
```

The naive Bayes algorithm found 14% of the training data set was spam and assigned a weight to each term relative to its strength in determining if a message was spam or ham.

```
q)pT 0
ham | 0.8660287
spam| 0.1339713
q)pT 1
ham | 6.239276e-05 9.358914e-05 6.239276e-05 6.239276e-05 0.0002183747 6...
spam| 7.392622e-05 7.392622e-05 7.392622e-05 7.392622e-05 7.392622e-05 7...
```

Notice that if we sum each of the classes, the weights add to 1.

```
q)sum each pT 1
ham | 1
spam| 1
```

## Algorithm Accuracy

It's time to put our model to the test. How well will it classify the messages we partitioned for validation? After extracting the corpus and classes from the test data, we use the `.ml.pnb` function to classify our naive Bayes model (storing the predicted values in `p` for later analysis).

```
q)ct:d . `test`text
q)yt:d . `test`class
q)Xt:flip .ml.tdm[ct] v
q)avg yt=p:.ml.pnb[0b;.ml.multil;pT] Xt
0.982066
```

Not bad. I bet you are wondering what words helped the model classify the messages so well. Is there a single word that every spam message had? Here is a list of the words that most identified spam.

```
q)select[>spam] from ([]word:v)!flip last pT
word  | ham          spam
------| -----------------------
"free"| 0.00146623   0.0135285
"txt" | 0.0003119638 0.01094108
,"u"  | 0.02904383   0.009832187
"ur"  | 0.005802527  0.008649368
,"p"  | 0.0002807674 0.008575442
..
```

It makes sense that an SMS offering something for "free" would be classified as spam. What about the character "u" (obviously a shorthand for "you")? Even though it is one of the highest weighted spam words, it's weight for ham is even higher. It is, in fact, the highest ranked ham word.

```
q)select[>ham] from ([]word:v)!flip last pT
word  | ham         spam
------| -----------------------
,"u"  | 0.02904383  0.009832187
"im"  | 0.01135548  0.0008131884
"come"| 0.007299953 0.0003696311
"ok"  | 0.007143971 0.0002957049
"just"| 0.006956793 0.004139868
..
```

It makes more sense to sort by the relative weight of spam vs. ham.

```
q)select[>spam%ham] from ([]word:v)!flip last pT
word   | ham          spam
-------| -----------------------
"claim"| 3.119638e-05 0.006209803
```

## 6.4. BINARY CLASSIFICATION

```
"prize"| 3.119638e-05 0.005248762
"tone" | 3.119638e-05 0.005100909
"nokia"| 3.119638e-05 0.004657352
"uk"   | 3.119638e-05 0.0045095
..
```

Notice how each of the top five spam words have the same ham weight. This occurs because the words didn't appear in any of the ham messages. These words received the same weight because we "smoothed" the model by calling .ml.wmultimle with a smoothing parameter of 1—claiming that all the words appeared in each message one more time than they actually did.

## 6.4 Binary Classification

Was our model actually that good? Simply declaring all messages as ham would have achieved an accuracy of 86%. On the surface looks great, but in reality we didn't filter any spam. Accuracy is a quick estimate of a model's performance, but when a classification problem is limited to two values, there are actually many ways we can measure the quality of a model. Binary classification can result in one of four outcomes:

| | |
|---|---|
| **True Positive** | Correctly identifying a positive value |
| **True Negative** | Correctly identifying a negative value |
| **False Positive** | Incorrectly identifying a positive value |
| **False Negative** | Incorrectly identifying a negative value |

These four values represent the four quadrants of the binary classification confusion matrix pictured in Example 6.2 [121].

**Example 6.2** Binary Classification Confusion Matrix

```
q).ml.cm . `spam=(yt;p)
y| 0    1
-| --------
0| 1193 14
1| 11   176
```

These same statistics can be calculated with the .ml.tptnfpfn function.

### .ml.tptnfpfn

```
/ given actual values (y) and (p)redicted values, compute (tp;tn;fp;fn)
tptnfpfn:{[y;p]tp,(("i"$count y)-tp+sum f),f:(sum p;sum y)-/:tp:sum p&y}
```

The function expects boolean values, so we must convert "ham" and "spam" to 0b and 1b before calling the function.

```
q)show tptnfpfn:.ml.tptnfpfn . `spam=(yt;p)
176 1193 14 11i
```

## Accuracy

Accuracy is only concerned with the True Positive and True Negative values as a percentage of the total predictions. This is equivalent to computing avg yt=p as we've done previously.

### .ml.accuracy

```
accuracy:{[tp;tn;fp;fn](tp+tn)%tp+tn+fp+fn}
```

Checking the statistics, we see that even though 162 spam messages were correctly flagged, 14 ham messages were incorrectly flagged as spam. If we turned on the spam filter, those 14 messages would have been isolated, and perhaps never read—regardless of the importance of their contents. Alternatively, we can focus on the 12 spam messages that were incorrectly labeled as ham—and were therefore not filtered. When building a spam filtering algorithm (just like diagnosing cancer), there is a tradeoff between being too aggressive with positive predictions and not being aggressive enough. In a perfect world, our algorithm would be 100% accurate, and we wouldn't have to worry about false positives and false negatives. Lacking perfection, however, we need statistics that evaluate the performance of an algorithm based on how often we generate false positives and false negatives. There are two statistics that incorporate this information: precision and recall.

## Precision

Precision is defined as the percentage of positive predictions that were—in fact—positive. Precision is computed by dividing the number of true positives by the total number of *predicted* positives (true positives plus false positives).

### .ml.precision

## 6.4. BINARY CLASSIFICATION

```
precision:{[tp;tn;fp;fn]tp%tp+fp}
```

## Recall

Recall is defined as the percentage of all positive values that were—in fact—predicted as positive. It is computed by dividing the number of true positives by the total number of *actual* positives (true positives plus false negatives). Recall is often referred to by other names as well: sensitivity, hit rate and true positive ratio (TPR).

**.ml.recall**

```
recall:sensitivity:hitrate:tpr:{[tp;tn;fp;fn]tp%tp+fn}  / true positive rate
```

We can now see how these values compare.

```
q).ml.precision . tptnfpfn
0.9263158
q).ml.recall . tptnfpfn
0.9411765
```

## F1 Statistic

When judging the quality of a model, how do you choose how much weight should be given to precision and how much to recall? A common approach is to use the F1 statistic, which takes the harmonic mean of the two.

**.ml.f1**

```
/ f measure: given (b)eta and tp,tn,fp,fn compute the harmonic mean of
/ precision and recall
f:{[b;tp;tn;fp;fn]
 f:1+b2:b*b;
 f*:r:recall[tp;tn;fp;fn];
 f*:p:precision[tp;tn;fp;fn];
 f%:r+p*b2;
 f}
f1:f[1]

q).ml.f1 . tptnfpfn
0.933687
```

## Matthews Correlation Coefficient

Another robust binary classification performance measure is the Matthews correlation coefficient (MCC).

```
/ Matthews correlation coefficient
/ correlation coefficient between the observed and predicted
/ -1 0 1 (none right, same as random prediction, all right)
mcc:{[tp;tn;fp;fn]((tp*tn)-fp*fn)%prd sqrt(tp;tp;tn;tn)+(fp;fn;fp;fn)}
```

The MCC is defined as the correlation between the observed and predicted values. Unlike other statistics, which vary between 0 and 1, the Matthews correlation coefficient varies between -1 and 1. It does a good job handling data sets like the SMS spam collection where the size of one population is much smaller than the other. In effect, it punishes algorithms for random guessing by returning a value close to 0.

If, for example, our algorithm returned ham for all predictions, the MCC would be undefined,

```
q).ml.mcc . .ml.tptnfpfn . `ham=(yt;count[yt]#`ham)
0n
```

even though the accuracy and F1 statistics look good.

```
q).ml.accuracy . .ml.tptnfpfn . `ham=(yt;count[yt]#`ham)
0.8658537
q).ml.f1 . .ml.tptnfpfn . `ham=(yt;count[yt]#`ham)
0.9281046
```

Taking a step back from such an extreme, if one value was predicted as spam, the MCC correctly highlights that our model is not much better than flipping a coin.

```
q).ml.mcc . .ml.tptnfpfn . `ham=(yt;`spam,1_count[yt]#`ham)
-0.01054609
```

The MCC indicates that our SMS spam naive Bayes classifier is indeed doing a good job—and not as naive as the name implies.

```
q).ml.mcc . tptnfpfn
0.9233577
```

## 6.5 Text Classification

Instead of looking at a large corpus of small documents (SMS messages), we can also look at a small corpus of large documents. Single words lose their primary importance, and the distribution of words becomes relevant. The Bag of Words model (where each document was summarized by a vector of word frequencies) emphasized words with high frequencies. We tried to improve the model by removing common meaningless (stop) words. As our documents get longer, we run the risk of common *meaningful* words diluting our analysis.

### Term Frequencies—Inversion Documents Frequency

To address this issue, the field of Natural Language Processing (NLP) has developed a few methods of scaling word frequencies to highlight infrequent words that provide out-sized insight. They are all variants of a ratio called TF-IDF, which stands for Term Frequency—Inverse Document Frequency. The basic idea is that even though a term may appear many times in a document, its importance decreases as its occurrence across other documents in the corpus increases. In other words, we divide the term frequency by the document frequency.

"Frequency" can be interpreted in many ways and the TF-IDF statistic, therefore, has many variants. We implement `tfidf` as a function which accepts two frequency functions: the term-frequency function `tff` and the inverse-document-frequency function `idff`.

**.ml.tfidf**
```
tfidf:{[tff;idff;x]tff[x]*\:idff x}
```

In its most basic from, the term frequency is simply the count of each word within each document and the document frequency is the percentage of documents that contain the term.

### Jane Austen Example

To see how this would be used in practice, we define our corpus as Jane Austen's 6 novels, which are readily available from Project Gutenberg[3] (a site which contains the full text of many out-of-copyright books). Our task will be to classify an

---
[3]"Project Gutenberg," Project Gutenberg. http://www.gutenberg.org/ (accessed Apr. 12, 2020).

unseen chapter from the book it was extracted from. We start by loading her size novels: Emma (emma.q [379]), Pride and Prejudice (pandp.q [381]), Sense and Sensibility (sands.q [382]), Mansfield Park (mansfield.q [380]), Northanger Abbey (northanger.q [381]) and Persuasion (persuasion.q [382]). Each chapter is stored as a vector of terms. These will be stored in the "text" column of a table with the "class" column holding a symbol identifying the book: EM, PP, SS, MP, NA and PE.

```
q)\l funq.q
q)\l emma.q
q)\l pandp.q
q)\l sands.q
q)\l mansfield.q
q)\l northanger.q
q)\l persuasion.q
q)t:flip `text`class!(emma.s;`EM)          / emma
q)t,:flip `text`class!(pandp.s;`PP)        / pride and prejudice
q)t,:flip `text`class!(sands.s;`SS)        / sense and sensibility
q)t,:flip `text`class!(mansfield.s;`MP)    / mansfield park
q)t,:flip `text`class!(northanger.s;`NA)   / northanger abbey
q)t,:flip `text`class!(persuasion.s;`PE)   / persuasion
```

The text of each book has already been stripped of Unicode characters. We are left with the task of removing punctuation and stop words, converting the text to lowercase and stemming the words.

```
q)t:update .ut.sr[.ut.pw] peach text from t
q)t:update (except[;stopwords.xpo6] " " vs ) peach lower text from t
q)t:update (.porter.stem') peach text from t
```

To test our algorithm, we partition the chapters into a training set and a testing set in a three to one ratio. Once again, we use stratified sampling.

```
q)d:.ut.part[`train`test!3 1;t.class] t
q)c:d . `train`text
q)y:d . `train`class
```

The training corpus c now contains a matrix of terms,

```
q)c
("mr";"elton";"left";"himself";"longer";"emma";"power";"superintend";"hap..
("charl";"mari";"remain";"lyme";"longer";"mr";"mr";"musgrov";"go";"ann";"..
("discuss";"mr";"collinss";"offer";"nearli";"end";"elizabeth";"suffer";"u..
("second";"week";"young";"ladi";"set";"gracechurch";"street";"town";"hert..
```

## 6.5. TEXT CLASSIFICATION

```
("quarter";"hour";"minut";"pass";"awai";"fanni";"think";"edmund";"miss";"..
("week";"return";"soon";"gone";"second";"began";"regiment";"stai";"meryto..
("morn";"fair";"catherin";"expect";"attack";"assembl";"parti";"mr";"allen..
..
```

and the training labels y now contain a vector of classes.

```
q)y
`EM`PE`PP`PP`MP`PP`NA`MP`PP`EM`NA`EM`EM`PE`SS`PP`PE`PP`NA`NA`MP`MP`SS`MP`..
```

If you've read Pride and Prejudice, like my wife has, you know that Mr. Collins proposes to Elizabeth Bennet. Without reading the book five times, as my wife has, we can assume the chapter came from Pride and Prejudice merely by seeing the terms "mr", "collinss", "elizabeth" and "offer". It is possible, however, that Jane Austen included Mr. Collins in more than one book. In this case, it would not be obvious from which of her books the chapter came. That is unless, like my wife, you've read every other book by Jane Austen. Without relying on my wife, we can apply the naive Bayes algorithm to this text to help clarify the situation.

Once again, we create a vocabulary v and build a term document matrix tdm.

```
q)v:asc distinct raze c
q)show tdm:.ml.tdm[c] v
0 0 1 0 0 0 0 0 0 0 0 0 0 0 0 0 0 0 0 0 0 1 0 0 0 0 0 0 0 0 0 0 0..
0 0 0 0 0 0 0 0 0 0 2 0 0 0 0 0 0 0 0 0 0 0 0 0 0 0 0 0 0 0 0 0 0..
0 1 0 0 0 0 0 0 0 0 1 0 0 0 0 0 1 0 0 0 0 3 0 0 0 0 0 0 0 0 0 0 0..
0 0 0 0 0 0 0 0 0 0 0 0 0 0 0 0 0 0 0 0 0 0 0 0 0 0 0 0 0 0 1 0 0..
0 0 0 0 0 0 0 0 0 0 1 0 0 0 0 0 0 0 0 0 2 0 0 0 0 0 0 0 1 0 0 0 0..
0 0 0 0 0 0 0 0 0 0 1 0 0 0 0 0 0 0 0 0 0 1 0 0 0 0 0 1 0 0 0 0 0..
0 0 0 0 0 0 0 0 0 1 3 0 0 0 0 0 0 1 0 0 0 0 0 0 0 0 0 0 0 0 0 0 0..
..
```

Instead of fitting the naive Bayes model on these raw frequencies, we can first apply the TF-IDF adjustment.

```
q)show "i"$X:0f^.ml.tfidf[.ml.lntf;.ml.idf] tdm
0 0 2 0 0 0 0 0 0 0 0 0 0 0 0 0 0 0 0 0 1 0 0 0 0 0 0 0 0 0 0 0 0..
0 0 0 0 0 0 0 0 0 0 1 0 0 2 0 0 0 0 0 0 0 0 0 0 0 0 0 0 0 0 0 0 0..
0 0 0 0 0 0 0 0 0 0 1 0 0 0 0 0 0 0 0 0 1 0 1 0 0 0 0 0 0 0 0 0 0..
0 0 2 0 0 0 0 0 0 0 0 0 0 0 0 0 0 0 0 0 1 1 0 0 0 0 1 0 0 0 0 0 0..
0 0 3 0 0 0 0 0 0 0 0 0 0 0 0 0 0 0 0 0 1 0 0 0 0 0 0 2 0 0 0 0 0..
0 0 2 0 0 0 0 0 0 0 0 0 0 0 0 0 0 0 0 3 2 0 0 1 0 0 0 0 0 0 0 0 0..
0 0 0 0 0 0 0 0 0 0 0 0 0 0 0 0 0 0 0 0 0 1 0 0 0 0 0 0 0 2 0 0 0..
..
```

## Log Normalized Term Frequency

In this case, we adjusted the term frequencies with the log-normalized-term-frequency function .ml.lntf, which adds one to the frequency and then takes the log. Adding one to the frequency ensures that terms with zero frequency continue to be zero after the log transform (instead of negative infinity).

**.ml.lntf**

```
lntf:log 1f+                        / log normalized term frequency
```

## Inverse Document Frequency Smooth

The inverse document frequency is similarly computed by taking the natural logarithm of one plus the ratio of total documents to the number of documents with each term.

**.ml.idfs**

```
idfs:{log 1f+count[x]%sum 0<x}    / inverse document frequency smooth
```

We can once again use the multinomial maximum-likelihood estimator to fit the naive Bayes model.

```
q)pT:.ml.fnb[wmf:.ml.wmultimle[1];w:(::);y;flip X]
```

Without knowing anything about the terms in the documents, we already have a bias as to the which book any further chapters come from. Since Pride and Prejudice leads the books in the number of chapters with 61, it is not surprising that it has the highest prior probabilities.

```
q)pT 0
EM| 0.205
PP| 0.225
SS| 0.185
MP| 0.18
NA| 0.115
PE| 0.09
```

## 6.5. TEXT CLASSIFICATION

## Algorithm Accuracy

Sorting the terms by probability of being from the book Pride and Prejudice clarifies our question about the importance of Mr. Collins.

```
q).ut.rnd[1e-4]`PP xdesc ([]v)!flip pT 1
v          | EM     PP     SS MP     NA PE
-----------| -------------------------------
"elizabeth"| 0.0001 0.0041 0  0.0001 0  0.0011
"darci"    | 0      0.004  0  0      0  0
"bennet"   | 0      0.0037 0  0      0  0
"binglei"  | 0      0.0035 0  0      0  0
"wickham"  | 0      0.0029 0  0      0  0
"collin"   | 0      0.0028 0  0      0  0
"lydia"    | 0      0.0027 0  0      0  0
"jane"     | 0.0016 0.0025 0  0      0  0
"longbourn"| 0      0.0021 0  0      0  0
"lizzi"    | 0      0.0021 0  0      0  0
..
```

> **Rounding Values**
>
> The .ut.rnd function accepts a rounding factor as its first parameter and the values to round as the second. The function can be applied to all numeric data types and is useful at the final stage of analysis for generating visually appealing results.
>
> **.ut.rnd**
>
> ```
> / round y to nearest x
> rnd:{x*"j"$y%x}
> ```

It seems that not only does Mr. Collins play a pivotal role in the book, but a certain Bingley and Darcy do as well.

With our model in place, we can extract the test data and evaluate the model. This time, however, instead of using the multinomial likelihood function, we change to use the .ml.multill multinomial *log*-likelihood function—and therefore pass 1b as the first argument.

**.ml.multill**

```
/ multinomial log likelihood
multill:{[p;k]k*log p}
```

It turns out that as the size of the problems grows, the multinomial likelihood function can generate probabilities with values of 0 due to exponent underflow. Multiplying these values with the other probabilities forces all total probability to be zero as well. Log likelihoods, on the other hand, do not face this problem because the results are added together, making the calculations more tractable.

```
q)ct:d . `test`text
q)yt:d . `test`class
q)Xt:0f^.ml.tfidf[.ml.lntf;.ml.idf] .ml.tdm[ct] v
q)avg yt=p:.ml.pnb[lb;.ml.multiLL;pT] flip Xt
1f
```

It seems that the model performed extremely well. Either that, or the problem we designed was a bit too easy.

Natural Language Processing is a deep field with many innovations and dedicated libraries. While q cannot compare with other languages in its ability to manipulate text (most specifically due to its lack of an advanced regular expression engine), once a problem has been converted to term document model, q's strength (and flexibility) in manipulating vectors make it a powerful environment to analyze large documents.

Transforming complicated relationships into matrices is a common technique used to allow existing algorithms to be applied to new problem. We now transition to a technique which uses a series of logical questions to partition data into a predictive tree. The next chapter discusses the intuitive decision tree algorithm.

# Chapter 7

# Decision Trees

> Decision trees are like grapevines: They are productive only if they are vigorously pruned.
>
> — R. Brealey and S. Myers *Principles of Corporate Finance (1981)*

Decision trees are a popular and relatively old machine-learning algorithm. Easily represented as a chart of distinct choices, their predictions can be explained by a few intuitive yes-no or multiple choice questions. While enhancements and adjustments have been made over the years, their fundamental premise has remained constant. Using one feature at a time, a decision tree algorithm partitions the data into two or more buckets that can then be sub-divided again using another feature. The goal of each division is to make each sub-division more uniform than the parent.

The classic childhood game "Guess Who?", originally manufactured by Milton Bradley in 1979, pits two players against each other trying to determine which of the 24 diverse faces has been chosen by their opponent. Among the different physical traits, the faces vary in, hair length, hair color and eye color. Opponents take turns asking yes-no questions attempting to narrow the universe of possible faces as fast as possible. A typical question would be "Is your face bald", or "Does your face wear glasses". The game was designed such that approximately 5 faces will have an attribute and 19 will not. This means that if you are lucky, you will be able to narrow down the possibilities to 5 faces after your first question. If you are unlucky, however, you will be left with 19 faces. A bad question would be "Is your face Sam?". In this case, you either win, or are stuck with 23 faces still at large. An optimal question would therefore throw away 12 faces (and therein lies the creativity in the game).

The challenges encountered in playing the game "Guess Who?" are exactly the same as those in building a decision tree. Which feature should I ask a question about first? What question should I ask? Fundamentally, we are trying to divide the populations into equal size buckets. If we are limited to yes-no questions like the game, we hope to split the population in half. Some decision tree implementations, however, allow us to ask questions such as "What color is your hair". In this case, we can narrow the population down even more.

## 7.1 Impurity Functions

How do we quantify "evenness of split"? There are a few choices for this measure but in practice they are very similar—they obtain a maximum value when there are equal numbers of each category and obtain a minimum value when all the values are the same category.

### Mean Squared Errors

When the values we are trying split are numeric, the most common choice is mean squared errors (MSE).

This was used in the "Automatic Interaction Detection" (AID) algorithm in 1963.

**.ml.mse**

```
mse:{enorm2[x-avg x]%count x}        / mean squared error
```

We can see how its value achieves a minimum when all values are the same and how it increases the more diverse the values become.

```
q).ml.mse 1 1 1 1 1
0f
q).ml.mse 1 1 1 1 2
0.1388889
q).ml.mse 1 1 1 2 2
0.2222222
q).ml.mse 1 1 1 2 2 2
0.25
```

## 7.1. IMPURITY FUNCTIONS

We can graphically demonstrate how the values change as the relative frequencies of two values vary. Starting with all zeros, and finishing with all ones, we have continuously varied the distribution.

```
q)show x:(0N?where@) each flip (reverse x;x:til 11)
0 0 0 0 0 0 0 0 0
0 0 0 0 0 1 0 0 0
0 0 0 0 1 0 0 0 1 0
1 0 0 0 0 1 0 0 0 1
1 1 0 0 1 0 0 1 0 0
0 1 0 0 1 1 0 1 1 0
1 1 1 0 1 0 1 0 1 0
1 1 1 1 0 0 1 0 1 1
1 0 1 1 1 1 0 1 1 1
1 1 1 1 0 1 1 1 1 1
1 1 1 1 1 1 1 1 1 1
```

Example 7.1 [133] provides us with an intuition into how the MSE statistic varies with changes in the distribution.

**Example 7.1** Mean Squared Errors
```
q).ut.plt .ml.mse each x
0.3|   "                           "
   |   "           + + +           "
   |   "        +         +        "
0.2|   "                           "
   |   "     +                +    "
   |   "                           "
0.1|   " +                    +  "
   |   "                           "
   |   "                           "
0  |   "+                       +"
```

Decision trees that are applied to numeric (also known as continuous) values are called regression trees. We will return to this concept later in the chapter.

The remaining splitting functions apply to categorical values and are used for classification instead of regression.

## Misclassification

Misclassification is the most intuitive splitting function because it returns the percentage of observations which are misclassified. Binary classification problems only generate values between 0 and .5 because the correct class is determined by the majority. The "Theta Automatic Interaction Detection" (THAID) algorithm published in 1973[1] uses this impurity function when building trees.

**.ml.misc**

```
misc:{1f-avg x=mode x}                    / misclassification
```

We can see how the misclassification function .ml.misc behaves in the presence of different distributions of a binary values.

```
oq).ml.misc 000000b
0f
q).ml.misc 000001b
0.1666667
q).ml.misc 000011b
0.3333333
q).ml.misc 000111b
0.5
```

The misclassification statistic, demonstrated in Example 7.2 [135], *linearly* increases (and then decreases) with changes in relative frequency. This is an undesired property that is corrected in the next two impurity functions.

## Entropy

The entropy statistic has its roots in information theory and tells us how spread out (or mixed up) the values in a population. Where the misc statistic linearly approaches a maximum when the values are equally distributed, the entropy statistic rises quickly and plateaus near the maximum value. The first use of entropy as the impurity function for a decision tree was in Ross Quinlan's Iterative Dichotomizer 3 (ID3).[2]

**.ml.entropy**

---

[1] J. N. Morgan and R. C. Messenger, *THAID: A Sequential Search Program for the Analysis of Nominal Scale Dependent Variables*. Ann Arbor: Institute for Social Research, University of Michigan, 1973.

[2] J. R. Quinlan, "Induction of decision trees," *Mach Learn*, vol. 1, no. 1, pp. 81–106, Mar. 1986, doi: 10.1007/BF00116251.

## 7.1. IMPURITY FUNCTIONS

**Example 7.2** Misclassification

```
q).ut.plt .ml.misc each x
0.6| "                          "
   | "                          "
   | "         +                "
   | "                          "
0.4| "                          "
   | "      +   +               "
   | "    +       +             "
   | "                          "
0.2| "  +             +         "
   | "                          "
   | " +                 +      "
0  | "+                     +   "
```

```
entropy:{neg sum x*log x:odds group x}    / entropy
```

```
q).ml.entropy `a`a`a`a`a`a
-0f
q).ml.entropy `a`a`a`a`a`b
0.4505612
q).ml.entropy `a`a`a`a`b`b
0.6365142
q).ml.entropy `a`a`a`b`b`b
0.6931472
```

Example 7.3 [136] illustrates that the behavior of the entropy statistic closely resembles that of the MSE statistic.

## Gini Impurity

The last impurity function is the Gini impurity statistic. While it does not have an information-theoretic backing like the entropy statistic, the Gini impurity is often used because it behaves similar to the entropy statistic, but is more efficient to compute.

### .ml.gini

```
gini:{1f-enorm2 odds group x}             / Gini
```

**Example 7.3** Entropy

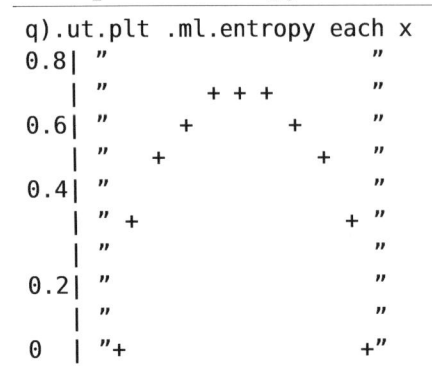

```
q).ut.plt .ml.entropy each x
0.8| "                        "
  | "         + + +           "
0.6| "      +       +         "
  | "    +           +        "
0.4| "                        "
  | "  +               +      "
  | "                         "
0.2| "                        "
  | "                         "
 0 | "+                     +"
```

Instead of using logarithms, the Gini impurity merely squares the probabilities (similar to how the MSE statistic squares the difference from the mean). The Gini impurity algorithm is used in modern Classification And Regression Trees (CART), which combine (as the name implies) both classification and regression trees.

As we can see in Example 7.4 [136], the behavior across the spectrum of value distributions mirrors both the MSE and entropy statistic. The maximum value reached in each statistic is different, but as long as we are consistent in our use of a single statistic, it is only the relative values that matter.

**Example 7.4** Gini

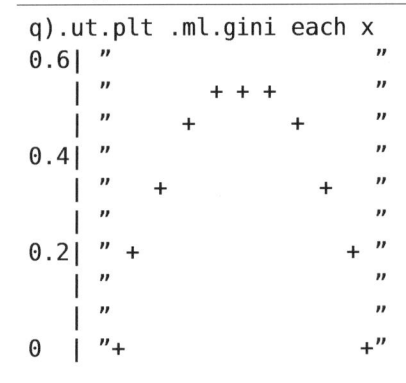

```
q).ut.plt .ml.gini each x
0.6| "                        "
  | "         + + +           "
  | "      +       +          "
0.4| "                        "
  | "    +           +        "
  | "                         "
0.2| "  +               +     "
  | "                         "
  | "                         "
 0 | "+                    +"
```

## 7.2 Iterative Dichotomizer 3

Let's drill down and focus on the implementation of an intuitive and simple decision tree implementation: the Iterative Dichotomizer 3 by Ross Quinlan. The "weather" data set is a canonical ID3 data set used for demonstrating decision tree analysis and can be loaded with the weather.q [383] library. It has four features: outlook, temperature, humidity and wind.

```
q)\l weather.q
q)weather.t
Play Outlook  Temperature Humidity Wind
-----------------------------------------
No   Sunny    Hot         High     Weak
No   Sunny    Hot         High     Strong
Yes  Overcast Hot         High     Weak
Yes  Rain     Mild        High     Weak
Yes  Rain     Cool        Normal   Weak
No   Rain     Cool        Normal   Strong
Yes  Overcast Cool        Normal   Strong
No   Sunny    Mild        High     Weak
Yes  Sunny    Cool        Normal   Weak
Yes  Rain     Mild        Normal   Weak
Yes  Sunny    Mild        Normal   Strong
Yes  Overcast Mild        High     Strong
Yes  Overcast Hot         Normal   Weak
No   Rain     Mild        High     Strong
```

Using these four features, we are supposed to predict whether an individual will play tennis, soccer, football or other outdoor sport.

The ID3 algorithm was an early entrant into the decision tree family. It differentiates itself by:

- using the entropy impurity function

- treating all features as categorical variables

- permitting multi-valued (not just binary) splits

- treating missing (or null) values as distinct values

- growing trees to full depth

Based on a parameterized decision-tree function .ml.dt (which we will discuss next), the id3 function is defined as follows.

**.ml.id3**

```
id3:dt[ig;ig;wentropy]          / iterative dichotomizer 3
```

Accepting these parameters as given for now, we can transform the weather data set into a decision tree.

```
q)show tr:.ml.id3[();::] weather.t
`Outlook
::
`Sunny`Overcast`Rain!((`Humidity;::;`High`Normal!((0.07142857 0.07142857 0...
```

## 7.3 Visualizing Decision Trees

Q does not have a native tree structure, so we are forced to build one ourselves. Through experience, and necessity, I have used a three element list at each level of the tree. The first element is the feature to split on, the second element is the function used to split and the third element is either a dictionary representing the sub-tree or a pair of elements representing the classification (or regression) data and their respective weights. This is not an intuitive structure to manipulate so it is important to have utilities to graphically render it.

### ASCII Trees

One way is by displaying each node as a line of text, with each sub-branch indented to reflect its depth within the tree.

```
q)-1 .ml.ptree[0] tr;
Yes (n = 14, err = 35.7%)
|   Outlook :: Overcast: Yes (n = 4, err = 0%)
|   Outlook :: Rain: Yes (n = 5, err = 40%)
|   |   Wind :: Strong: No (n = 2, err = 0%)
|   |   Wind :: Weak: Yes (n = 3, err = 0%)
|   Outlook :: Sunny: No (n = 5, err = 40%)
|   |   Humidity :: High: No (n = 3, err = 0%)
|   |   Humidity :: Normal: Yes (n = 2, err = 0%)
```

## 7.3. VISUALIZING DECISION TREES

The `.ml.ptree` print-tree function accepts the level of indentation as its first argument and the tree (or sub-tree) as its second argument.

**.ml.ptree**

```
/ print (tr)ee with i(n)dent
ptree:{[n;tr]
 if[not n;:(pleaf . first xs),last xs:.z.s[n+1;tr]];
 if[2=count tr;:(tr;"")];
 s:1#"\n";
 s,:raze[(n)#enlist "| "],raze string[tr 0 1],\:" ";
 s:s,/:string k:asc key tr 2;
 c:.z.s[n+1] each tr[2]k;         / child
 x:first each c;
 s:s,'": ",/:(pleaf .) each x;
 s:raze s,'last each c;
 x:(,'/) x;
 (x;s)}
```

The function recursively calls itself—each time incrementing the level of indentation—until a leaf is reached. Leaves are then displayed with the `.ml.pleaf` print-leaf function, which takes the weights and node values as parameters and either prints the classification error for categorical values or the sum of squared errors (SSE) for ordered values.

**.ml.pleaf**

```
/ print leaf: prediction followed by classification error% or regression sse
pleaf:{[w;x]
 v:waom[w;x];                    / value
 e:$[isord x;string sum e*e:v-x;string[.1*"i"$1e3*1f-avg x = v],"%"];
 s:string[v], " (n = ", string[count x],", err = ",e, ")";
 s}
```

## Graphviz

ASCII trees are a compact format to view decision trees, but graphs are more popular. This, however, requires the use of a separate program called Graphviz.[3] Using the `.ml.pgraph` print-graph function, we can generate a graphical decision tree.

---

[3] "Graphviz - Graph Visualization Software." [Online]. Available: https://www.graphviz.org/. [Accessed: 12-Mar-2020].

```
q)-1 .ml.pgraph tr;
digraph Tree {
graph[dpi=300]
node [shape = box]
0 [label = "Yes (n = 14, err = 35.7%)\nOutlook :: "]
00 [label = "No (n = 5, err = 40%)\nHumidity :: "]
0 -> 00 [label = "Sunny"]
000 [label = "No (n = 3, err = 0%)"]
00 -> 000 [label = "High"]
001 [label = "Yes (n = 2, err = 0%)"]
00 -> 001 [label = "Normal"]
01 [label = "Yes (n = 4, err = 0%)"]
0 -> 01 [label = "Overcast"]
02 [label = "Yes (n = 5, err = 40%)\nWind :: "]
0 -> 02 [label = "Rain"]
020 [label = "Yes (n = 3, err = 0%)"]
02 -> 020 [label = "Weak"]
021 [label = "No (n = 2, err = 0%)"]
02 -> 021 [label = "Strong"]
}
```

The .ml.pgraph print-graph function generates the Graphviz pre-amble and post-amble,

### .ml.pgraph

```
/ print graph text for use with the 'dot' Graphviz command, graph-easy or
/ http://webgraphviz.com
pgraph:{[tr]
 s:enlist "digraph Tree {";
 s,:enlist "node [shape = box]";
 s,:last pnode["";"0";`;tr];
 s,:1#"}";
 s}
```

while the real work is done in the .ml.pnode print-node function. It generates the text for the current node and calls itself recursively to append the text for all sub-nodes. Once again, text for the classification and regression errors are generated by the .ml.pleaf function.

### .ml.pnode

*/ given (p)arent id, (n)ode id, label and (tr)ee print Graphviz node*

## 7.4. DECISION TREE CLASSIFICATION 141

```
pnode:{[p;n;l;tr]
  s:n," [label = \"";                                            / label
  st:$[b:2=count tr;();tr 2];                                    / sub tree
  cn:n,/:"0"^(neg max count each cn)$ cn:string til count st;    / child node ids
  c:$[b;enlist (tr;st);.z.s[n]'[cn;key st;value st]];            / children
  s,:pleaf . x:(,'/) first each c;                               / error stats
  if[not b;s,:"\\n",raze string[2#tr],\: " "];                   / node title
  s:enlist s,"\"]";
  if[count p;s,:enlist p," -> ",n," [label = \"",string[l],"\"]"]; / edge
  s,:raze last each c;
  (x;s)}
```

Without going through the effort of installing Graphviz, it is also possible to render your graphs using the web-based WebGraphviz.[4] Running Graphviz on the above output of .ml.pgraph generates Figure 7.1 [141].

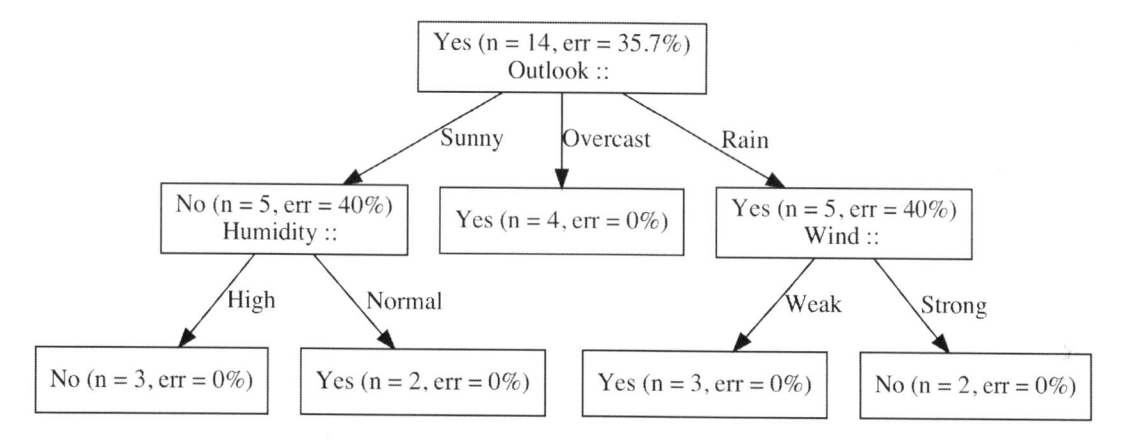

Figure 7.1: Weather Decision Tree

## 7.4 Decision Tree Classification

Based on the first line of the displayed tree, we can see that lacking any other information, we should predict that *yes*, they will play (but expect to have an approximate 36% error). Knowing the Outlook improves our ability to respond. If the

---
[4]"Webgraphviz." [Online]. Available: http://www.webgraphviz.com/. [Accessed: 12-Mar-2020].

Weather is Overcast, for example, they will play tennis regardless of the wind conditions or humidity level. We have no test data set, but can apply the tree to the original weather data with the .ml.pdt predict-decision-tree function to obtain the predicted classifications.

**.ml.pdt**

```
/ use decision (tr)ee to make predictions for (d)ictionary
pdt:{[tr;d]
 if[98h=type d;:.z.s[tr] peach d]; / iterate on a table
 p:waom . pdtr[tr;d];
 p}
```

The first line of .ml.pdt checks to see if the passed-in dictionary is, in fact, a table. In this case, the function calls itself recursively for each row—passed as a dictionary—of the table. The second line delegates the processing of the tree to the recursive function .ml.pdtr.

**.ml.pdtr**

```
/ use decision (tr)ee to recursively find leaf/leaves for (d)ictionary
pdtr:{[tr;d]
 if[2=count tr;:tr];                  / (w;a)
 if[not null k:d tr 0;if[(a:tr[1][k]) in key tr[2];:.z.s[tr[2] a;d]]];
 v:(,'/) tr[2] .z.s\: d;   / dig deeper for null values
 v}
```

It recurses through the tree until it finds a leaf that is identified by a two-element list. The first element is a list of observation weights and the second element is a list of the associated observation values. If a leaf has not been found, a decision must be made. To decide which branch of the tree to descend, the .ml.pdtr function uses the rule at the current node to test a single dictionary value. If the value is null, all branches at this node of the tree are pursued and the resulting weights and values are combined. Once the tree has been fully applied and a final set of weights and values are obtained, they are passed back to .ml.pdt for processing.

```
q).ml.pdtr[tr] first weather.t
0.07142857 0.07142857 0.07142857
No         No         No
```

The .ml.pdt function uses the values returned by .ml.pdtr and either computes a weighted average or, as in this case, a weighted mode. The decision to use an average or mode is based on the type of the data. A weighted mode is calculated in this example because "Yes" and "No" are categorical values. The distinction between regression trees and classification trees comes down to this final step, which is encapsulated in the .ml.waom function. As discussed in Section 2.10 [32], .ml.waom calculates the weighted average or mode of the provided data.

Applying the decision tree to the original table returns a classification for each record.

```
q).ml.pdt[tr] weather.t
`No`No`Yes`Yes`Yes`No`Yes`No`Yes`Yes`Yes`Yes`Yes`No
```

We can see how our tree perfectly fits (or perhaps overfits) the data.

```
q)avg weather.t.Play=.ml.pdt[tr] weather.t
1f
```

## 7.5 Building the Decision Tree

We return now to the implementation and parameterization of the core decision-tree function .ml.dt. The responsibility of a decision tree algorithm is to determine the order in which we split features and how many splits we should make. There are many ways of picking the best feature to split and many ways of limiting the bushiness of the tree. To accommodate all of these options, the .ml.dt decision-tree function has many parameters: five required parameters as well as a dictionary of optional parameters.

**.ml.dt**

```
/ given a vector of (w)eights (or ::) and a (t)able of features where the
/ first column is the target attribute, create a decision tree using the
/ (c)ategorical (g)ain (f)unction and (o)rdered (g)ain (f)unction. the
/ (i)m(p)urity (f)unction determines which statistic to minimize. a dict of
/ (opt)ions specify the (max) (d)epth, (min)imum # of (s)amples required to
/ (s)plit, (min)imum # of (s)amples at each (l)eaf, (min)imum (g)ain and the
/ (max)imum (f)eature (f)unction used to sub sample features for random
/ forests.  defaults are: opt:`maxd`minss`minsl`ming`maxff!(0N;2;1;0;::)
dt:{[cgf;ogf;ipf;opt;w;t]
  if[(::)~w;w:n#1f%n:count t];      / compute default weight vector
  if[1=count d:flip t;:(w;first d)]; / no features to test
  opt:(`maxd`minss`minsl`ming`maxff!(0N;2;1;0;::)),opt; / default options
  if[0=opt`maxd;:(w;first d)];      / check if we've reached max depth
```

```
if[identical a:first d;:(w;a)];  / check if all values are equal
if[opt[`minss]>count a;:(w;a)];  / check if insufficient samples
d:((neg floor opt[`maxff] count d)?key d)#d:1 _d;    / sub-select features
d:{.[x isord z;y] z}[(cgf;ogf);(ipf;w;a)] peach d;   / compute gains
d:(where (any opt[`minsl]>count each last::) each d) _ d; / filter on minsl
if[0=count d;:(w;a)];            / check if all leaves have < minsl samples
if[opt[`ming]>=first b:d bf:imax d[;0];:(w;a)]; / check gain of best feature
c:count k:key g:last b;          / grab subtrees, feature names and count
/ distribute nulls down each branch with reduced weight
if[c>ni:null[k]?1b;w:@[w;n:g nk:k ni;%;c-1];g:(nk _g),\:n];
if[(::)~b 1;t:(1#bf)_t];         / don't reuse exhausted features
b[2]:.z.s[cgf;ogf;ipf;@[opt;`maxd;-;1]]'[w g;t g]; / split sub-trees
bf,1_b}
```

## Decision Tree Parameters

The first two parameters of the .ml.dt function are functions used to compute the information gain (or impurity reduction) of every possible split for categorical and ordered data (cgf and ogf respectively). The idea is to find the split that results in a more ordered sub-tree. We will delve into the differences between the possible gain functions in Section 7.6 [147]. The third parameter, ipf, is the impurity function (covered in Section 7.1 [132]) we wish to use.

A dictionary, opt, which allows us to control how deep (and bushy) the tree becomes is supplied as the second parameter. Default values for the dictionary are chosen such that the options are disabled if not supplied. To control the tree depth, for example, we can specify the maxd option. A maxd value of 0 results in a *tree* with all the values at the root node. In other words, there are no splits at all. The value of maxd is decremented by one at each sub-tree until it becomes 0 and the tree stops growing. To disable the parameter, the default value of maxd is set to 0N. No matter how many times we subtract 1 from 0N, it will never become zero.

The minss option prevents the algorithm from splitting unless the node has at least a minimum number of samples. It is not possible to spit on a single sample, so the default value is 2. If there are fewer than minss samples, no splitting is performed. The minsl option, which defaults to 1, is applied after the sub-tree is split and confirms that each leaf has at least minsl samples. Limiting the split behavior based on the number of samples in each leaf, therefore, requires more computations than limiting based on the number of samples in a node.

## 7.5. BUILDING THE DECISION TREE 145

Overfitting can also be prevented by using the `ming` option, which allows us to specify a minimum gain that is required to accept a split. The units of `ming` may be an actual minimum gain or a minimum gain ratio depending on the functions specified by `cgf` and `ogf`, which we will review in Section 7.6 [147].

By using the `maxff` option, we may also specify how many features we should sub-select when finding the best split. For a basic decision tree, this should be *all* the features, and the default value achieves this by having the value `::` . We will see how other values can be beneficial in Section 8.4 [169].

The last two parameters are a weight vector and a table with the training data. If all weights are equal, we can pass the null value `::` and the algorithm will equal-weight each of the observations for us. Being able to supply a weight for each observation is important when samples have missing (or null) values. It is also useful when we want to over/under-weight observations to build trees that fit specific observations better. This will be covered in Section 8.5 [173].

Note that the function expects the first column of the table to be the target feature—either categorical for a decision tree or ordered for a regression tree.

## Decision Tree Implementation

The decision tree algorithm `.ml.dt` begins by converting the weight parameter to a uniform weight vector if it was passed-in as the null value `::`. It then checks for conditions that will cause the tree to stop growing. This can occur if there are no more features to search, the maximum depth has been reached, all remaining values are equal, or there are not enough samples. To detect equality among all values, `.ml.dt` uses the `.ml.identical` function, which only returns true if all values in the supplied list are exactly equal.

### .ml.identical

```
/ returns true if all values are exactly equal
identical:{min first[x]~':x}
```

The function then shuffles the features. This prevents the algorithm from always picking the same feature when two or more have the same gain. This means that building a decision tree on the same data multiple times can result in different trees. We shall also see in Section 8.4 [169] how this line is used to sub-select the features to add a bit more randomness into the tree generation process.

The algorithm then computes the gain on each feature—switching between the categorical gain function or the ordered gain function as the case may be. It then discards all sub-trees that have less than the minimum number of leaves required and exits early if there are no more features left.

The feature that provides the maximum gain is chosen and the function exits early if this gain is insufficient. The next line proceeds to prepare a few variables for building the sub-tree.

To support null values, the algorithm redistributes sample weights down all remaining branches—reduced in proportion to the number of branches. This is in-effect saying that since our training data had unknown values, we will defer to each of the other features with equal weight.

Finally, before splitting the sub-trees, the algorithm removes the feature just used for splitting if new branches were created for each distinct feature value. This is typically all categorical features except for the case when the split was created with the .ml.sig set-information-gain function. These, and all ordered features, are left in the training data so that they may be used to split again—if required by the data.

Returning to the weather example, you can imagine that we would need to split an ordered temperature feature more than once. The first split is required to separate the hot days vs. everything else. The second split is needed to separate the cold days as well. Since each categorical temperature value is assigned its own branch, the whole feature can be removed.

The algorithm returns a triplet: the feature, the split function and either a sub-tree or a pair of weight and sample vectors indicating a leaf has been created.

We can now revisit the ID3 parameterization and see that it uses the .ml.ig function for both categorical and ordered data, and uses a weighted variant of .ml.entropy for the impurity function. Although we reviewed the unweighted versions of each impurity function, .ml.dt requires weighted variants in order to correctly handle null values.

### .ml.wodds

```
wodds:{[w;g]prb sum each w g}
```

### .ml.wmode

```
wmode:imax wfreq::            / weighted mode
```

### .ml.wmse

```
wmse:{[w;x]enorm2[x-w wavg x]%count x} / weighted mean squared error
```

### .ml.wmisc

```
wmisc:{[w;x]1f-avg x=wmode[w;x]}    / weighted misclassification
```

### .ml.wentropy

```
wentropy:{[w;x]neg sum x*log x:wodds[w] group x} / weighted entropy
```

### .ml.wgini

```
wgini:{[w;x]1f-enorm2 wodds[w] group x} / weighted Gini
```

## 7.6 Gain Functions

We've covered different impurity functions used to measure how homogeneous each leaf is and also stepped through the tree-building algorithm .ml.dt. It's time to discuss how to measure the improvement gained by splitting on a feature. How do we know that splitting the weather data on Outlook was better than splitting on Humidity? Just as there are multiple choices for impurity functions, there are multiple choices for gain functions. At their core, however, they are all variants on a single concept: given a feature, find a way to split its values that maximizes the homogeneity of each branch. The performance of the split is judged by comparing the value obtained by using the impurity function (such as .ml.wentropy) on the current node to the weighted average of the values obtained by applying the same impurity function on each of the branches. Using the ID3 algorithm's nomenclature, this would be called the "information gain".

### Information Gain

#### .ml.ig

```
/ use (i)m(p)urity (f)unction to compute the (w)eighted information gain of
/ x after splitting on y
ig:{[ipf;w;x;y]                      / information gain
 g:ipf[w] x;
 g-:sum wodds[w;gy]*(not null key gy)*w[gy] ipf' x gy:group y;
 (g;::;gy)}
```

Assuming all the weights in the weight vector w are equal, we can compute the information gain by splitting the x values by the values in y. In this example, we split the Play vector by the values in Outlook.

```
q).ml.ig[.ml.wentropy;14#1;weather.t.Play;weather.t.Outlook]
0.1710339
::
`Sunny`Overcast`Rain!(0 1 7 8 10;2 6 11 12;3 4 5 9 13)
```

The function returns a three element list: the gain, the operator used to perform the splitting (which is merely a null value for this function, but will take on different values for other gain implementations) and a dictionary of the split tree mapping the split values to the indices in the original data set.

Splitting on Humidity confirms that Outlook is indeed a better choice for splitting the tree.

```
q).ml.ig[.ml.wentropy;14#1;weather.t.Play;weather.t.Humidity]
0.1052443
::
`High`Normal!(0 1 2 3 7 11 13;4 5 6 8 9 10 12)
```

## Set Information Gain

Based on the ID3 specification, the .ml.ig information-gain function creates a branch for each unique value in the y vector. The AID algorithm took a more complicated approach by searching through all combinations of the feature's categorical values. The .ml.sig set-information-gain function implements a set variant of the .ml.ig function.

### .ml.sig

```
/ use (i)m(p)urity (f)unction to pick the maximum (w)eighted information
/ gain of x after splitting across all sets of distinct y
sig:{[ipf;w;x;y]                / set information gain
  c:raze cmb[;u] peach 1+til 1|count[u:distinct y] div 2;  / combinations of y
  g:(ig[ipf;w;x] y in) peach c;                            / all gains
  g@:i:imax g[;0];                                         / highest gain
  g[1]:in[;c i];                  / replace split func
  g}
```

## 7.6. GAIN FUNCTIONS

It begins by using the .ml.cmb combination function to generate a unique list of all the combinations that the supplied feature can represent.

**.ml.cmb**

```
/ combinations of length x (or all lengths if null x) from count (or list) y
cmb:{
  if[not 0>type y;:y .z.s[x] count y];    / list y
  if[null x;:raze .z.s[;y] each 1+til y]; / null x = all lengths
  c:flip enlist flip enlist til y-:x-:1;
  c:raze c {(x+z){raze x,''y}'x#\:y}[1+til y]/til x;
  c}
```

The .ml.cmb function returns all the combinations of length x from the data y. For example, the unique combinations of Outlook pairs can be generated.

```
q).ml.cmb[2] distinct weather.t.Outlook
Overcast Sunny
Rain     Sunny
Rain     Overcast
```

If a null value is passed to the .ml.cmb function, it returns all the combinations of all sample counts.

```
q).ml.cmb[0N] distinct weather.t.Outlook
,`Sunny
,`Overcast
,`Rain
`Overcast`Sunny
`Rain`Sunny
`Rain`Overcast
`Rain`Overcast`Sunny
```

The .ml.sig function finds the set that maximizes the information gain.

```
q).ml.sig[.ml.wentropy;14#1;weather.t.Play;weather.t.Outlook]
0.1566514
in[;,`Overcast]
01b!(0 1 3 4 5 7 8 9 10 13;2 6 11 12)
```

## Gain Ratio

We can see that the gain obtained by splitting the tree into values that equal "Overcast" vs. values that are not equal to "Overcast" is less than the gain obtained by creating a tree with three branches: "Sunny", "Overcast" and "Rain". The information gain can by very high when the feature has many distinct values. With a different value for each element of the training data, it is possible to classify the data perfectly and maximize the information gain. This runs a serious risk of overfitting the training data. To punish features with many distinct features, Quinlan proposed to maximize the "gain ratio" instead of just the "information gain".

**.ml.gr**

```
/ use (i)m(p)urity (f)unction to compute the (w)eighted gain ratio of x
/ after splitting on y
gr:{[ipf;w;x;y]                 / gain ratio
  g:ig[ipf;w;x;y];              / first compute information gain
  g:@[g;0;%[;ipf[w;y]]];        / then divide by splitinfo
  g}
```

The gain ratio is computed by dividing the information gain by the impurity of the feature. Quinlan refers to this impurity as the *split info* (or the information embedded in the splitting criteria). The gain ratio is punished most by a feature with many unique values. We can see how this decreases the gain obtained by splitting across distinct values in the section called "Information Gain" [147].

```
q).ml.gr[.ml.wentropy;14#1;weather.t.Play;weather.t.Outlook]
0.1564276
::
`Sunny`Overcast`Rain!(0 1 7 8 10;2 6 11 12;3 4 5 9 13)
```

## Ordered Information Gain

The gain functions we've analyzed thus far have been designed for categorical features. Though they will return results for ordered data, their usefulness is limited. If, for example, our data set had Temperatures with varying degrees listed in Fahrenheit (or Centigrade), would we want to create a tree with as many branches as distinct temperatures? You may argue that using gain ratio instead of information gain should address this situation. The problem, however, is not that there are multiple values, the issue is that the order of the values has meaning. It may be meaningful that we don't play Tennis any time the temperature is above 90 degrees Fahrenheit. Similarly, the data may show that we don't play when the temperature is below 50 degrees Fahrenheit because it is too cold. Limiting the tree to just these splits would perform better at classifying unseen data than a tree with a branch at

## 7.6. GAIN FUNCTIONS

each different temperature. The way we accomplish this is by discretizing ordered data.

The goal is to find a value that maximizes the information gain when it is used to split the data into two groups: above and below. This is performed by first sorting the data and then computing the gain achieved by splitting on each change in the feature's value. The optimal split value is then chosen midway between the value that maximizes the information gain and the one prior.

**.ml.oig**

```
/ use (i)m(p)urity (f)unction to pick the maximum (w)eighted information
/ gain of x after splitting across all values of y
oig:{[ipf;w;x;y]                          / ordered information gain
 g:(ig[ipf;w;x] y >) peach u:asc distinct y; / all gains
 g@:i:imax g[;0];                         / highest gain (not gain ratio)
 g[1]:>[;avg u i+0 1];                    / replace split func
 g}
```

To see this in action, let's return to the Iris data set whose features are all ordered.

```
q)\l iris.q
[down]loading iris data set
q).ml.oig[.ml.wentropy;150#1;iris.t.species;iris.t.slength]
0.3862443
>[;5.55]
01b!(0 1 2 3 4 5 6 7 8 9 10 11 12 13 16 17 19 20 21 22 23 24 25 26 27 28 ..
```

We can see that—ignoring all other features—splitting the data by a sepal length of 5.55 maximizes the information gain for this feature. Using the .ml.ct classification-tree function, which resembles the SciKit Learn CART (Classification And Regression Tree) algorithm,[5] we can build a full tree for the Iris data.

**.ml.ct**

```
ct:dt[oig;oig;wgini]           / classification tree
```

Notice that the .ml.ct function uses .ml.wgini instead of .ml.wentropy. This is in-line with the CART algorithm, which presumably uses Gini impurity instead of entropy for efficiency. Another important difference with the CART algorithm is that it does not support categorical features. We drop support for categorical

---

[5] "Decision Trees - scikit-learn documentation." [Online]. Available: https://scikit-learn.org/stable/-modules/tree.html. [Accessed: 12-Mar-2020].

data in .ml.ct as well by supplying .ml.oig ordered-information-gain function for the cgf categorical-gain function argument. Note that there is, therefore, no bias to using features with a high number of distinct values. Using the .ml.ct classification-tree function, we can train a tree on the Iris data.

```
q)-1 .ml.ptree[0] tr:.ml.ct[();::] iris.t;
Iris-setosa (n = 150, err = 66.7%)
|  pwidth >[;0.8] 0: Iris-setosa (n = 50, err = 0%)
|  pwidth >[;0.8] 1: Iris-versicolor (n = 100, err = 50%)
|  |  pwidth >[;1.75] 0: Iris-versicolor (n = 54, err = 9.3%)
|  |  |  plength >[;4.95] 0: Iris-versicolor (n = 48, err = 2.1%)
|  |  |  |  pwidth >[;1.65] 0: Iris-versicolor (n = 47, err = 0%)
|  |  |  |  pwidth >[;1.65] 1: Iris-virginica (n = 1, err = 0%)
|  |  |  plength >[;4.95] 1: Iris-virginica (n = 6, err = 33.3%)
|  |  |  |  pwidth >[;1.55] 0: Iris-virginica (n = 3, err = 0%)
|  |  |  |  pwidth >[;1.55] 1: Iris-versicolor (n = 3, err = 33.3%)
|  |  |  |  |  plength >[;5.45] 0: Iris-versicolor (n = 2, err = 0%)
|  |  |  |  |  plength >[;5.45] 1: Iris-virginica (n = 1, err = 0%)
|  |  pwidth >[;1.75] 1: Iris-virginica (n = 46, err = 2.2%)
|  |  |  plength >[;4.85] 0: Iris-virginica (n = 3, err = 33.3%)
|  |  |  |  swidth >[;3.1] 0: Iris-virginica (n = 2, err = 0%)
|  |  |  |  swidth >[;3.1] 1: Iris-versicolor (n = 1, err = 0%)
|  |  |  plength >[;4.85] 1: Iris-virginica (n = 43, err = 0%)
```

## 7.7 Cost Complexity Pruning

Classification trees keep splitting until all the values are classified correctly. This tends to lead to very deep trees that overfit the training data, and therefore have high variance and predict poorly. To compensate for this tendency, we could pre-prune the tree by using the opt parameter to specify a maximum depth, minimum number of leaves at each node, and so on. A more robust method, however, is to post-prune. A method called Cost Complexity Pruning was first described by Breiman.[6] We grow the tree to its fullest depth and then begin cutting off nodes one by one—measuring the additive error for each snip. By combining this with a cost for each node in the tree, we can find an optimal tree size. The optimal tree size will obviously depend on how much cost we place on each extra node. The cost complexity measure is often represented as Equation 7.1 [153].

---

[6]L. Breiman, J. Friedman, C. J. Stone, and R. A. Olshen, *Classification and Regression Trees*: Taylor & Francis, 1984.

## 7.7. COST COMPLEXITY PRUNING

$$R_\alpha(T) = R(T) + \alpha|T|$$

where $R(T)$ = the error (or risk) of tree $T$
$\alpha$ = the complexity parameter and
$|T|$ = the number of leaves in tree $T$

Equation 7.1: Decision Tree Cost Complexity

When the complexity parameter is set to 0, the optimal tree is obviously the full tree $T$. And when the complexity parameter is infinite, the optimal tree is a tree with no nodes and whose prediction will always be the mode of the training data. How do we, then, pick the optimal $\alpha$? Let us first implement the decision-tree-cost-complexity function .ml.dtcc.

## Leaves

We begin by creating the function .ml.leaves, which returns each of the leaves of the provided tree.

### .ml.leaves

```
/ return the leaves of (tr)ee
leaves:{[tr]$[2=count tr;enlist tr;raze .z.s each last tr]}
```

Each leaf is a pair of vectors—a weight vector and a classification (or regression) vector. The .ml.leaves function returns a list of these vectors. Counting the results tells you how many leaves are in the tree.

```
q)count .ml.leaves tr
9
```

## Risk

We now progress to a function that computes error (or risk) of a tree. The .ml.dtriskn function returns the error and number of leaves for a given impurity function and tree.

### .ml.dtriskn

```
/ using (e)rror (f)unction, return the decision (tr)ee's risk R(T) and
/ number of terminal nodes |T|
dtriskn:{[ef;tr](sum'[l[;0]]wsum ef ./: l;count l:leaves tr)}
```

Even though it is better to use an impurity function like Gini impurity .ml.gini when building the classification tree (because it tends to create pure nodes), it is better to use misclassification .ml.misc for pruning because it is a more accurate calculation of the error. Applying the function to our tree, we should not be surprised that it has no misclassification error and 9 leaves.

```
q).ml.dtriskn[.ml.wmisc] tr
0f
9
```

With these building blocks, we can compute the cost complexity of a decision tree given an impurity function and cost parameter $T$.

### .ml.dtcc

```
/ using (e)rror (f)unction and regularization coefficient a, compute cost
/ complexity for (tr)ee
dtcc:{[ef;a;tr](1f;a)wsum dtriskn[ef;tr]}
```

But this is not our goal. The possible values for $\alpha$ are endless. How should we pick the best one? Breiman et al. also provide an algorithm that iteratively generates a minimum $\alpha$ for each tree size—beginning with the full tree and ending at the tree with no nodes.

## Subtrees

The first step in this algorithm is to define a function that returns all the sub-trees which share the same root as $T$.

### .ml.subtrees

```
/ given a decision (tr)ee, return all the subtrees sharing the same root
subtrees:{[tr]
 if[2=count tr;:enlist tr];
 str:tr 2; / subtree
 if[all l:2=count each str;:enlist (,'/) str]; / prune
 strs:(@[str;;:;].) each raze flip each flip (i;.z.s each str i:where not l);
 trs:@[tr;2;:;] each strs;
```

## 7.7. COST COMPLEXITY PRUNING

```
  trs,:enlist (,'/) leaves tr;  / collapse this node too
  trs}
```

The .ml.subtrees function calls itself recursively until it reaches a node that only has leaves and then prunes itself. All possible combinations of this pruning strategy are performed and the list of sub-trees is returned. It should not be surprising that there are eight sub-trees in our example.

```
q)count .ml.subtrees tr
8
```

We can see the tree with almost all the nodes collapsed.

```
q)-1 .ml.ptree[0] .ml.subtrees[tr] 6;
Iris-setosa (n = 150, err = 66.7%)
|  pwidth >[;0.8] 0: Iris-setosa (n = 50, err = 0%)
|  pwidth >[;0.8] 1: Iris-versicolor (n = 100, err = 50%)
```

## Minimum Alpha

The .ml.dtmina decision-tree-minimize-alpha function computes the error of the tree, and all its sub-trees, to find the one tree that minimizes the marginal increase in error per node pruned.

### .ml.dtmina

```
/ given an (i)m(p)urity function and the pair of values (a;tr), return the
/ minimum (a)lpha and its associated sub(tr)ee.
dtmina:{[ipf;atr]
 if[2=count tr:last atr;:atr];
 en:dtriskn[ipf;tr];
 ens:dtriskn[ipf] peach trs:subtrees tr;
 a:neg (%) . en - flip ens;
 atr:(a;trs)@\:i imin a i:idesc ens[;1]; / sort descending # nodes
 atr}
```

Calling it once returns a value for $\alpha$ and the associated tree. Calling it iteratively gives us a list of all the $\alpha$ values we can choose from.

```
q)atr:flip .ml.dtmina[.ml.wmisc] scan (0f;tr)
q)flip atr
0f              (`pwidth;>[;0.8];`s#01b!((0.006666667 0.006666667 0.006666667..
```

```
0.003333333   (`pwidth;>[;0.8];`s#01b!((0.006666667 0.006666667 0.006666667..
0.006666667   (`pwidth;>[;0.8];`s#01b!((0.006666667 0.006666667 0.006666667..
0.006666667   (`pwidth;>[;0.8];`s#01b!((0.006666667 0.006666667 0.006666667..
0.01333333    (`pwidth;>[;0.8];`s#01b!((0.006666667 0.006666667 0.006666667..
0.2933333     (`pwidth;>[;0.8];`s#01b!((0.006666667 0.006666667 0.006666667..
0.3333333     (0.006666667 0.006666667 0.006666667 0.006666667 0.006666667 ..
```

This indicates that an $\alpha$ between 0 and 0.003 results in an optimal tree with all its leaves intact while an $\alpha$ starting at 0.333 results in a fully pruned tree. How then, do we pick the right tree? Which tree would optimize the tradeoff between overfitting and underfitting the data. Using cross validation, we can use all the training data to train a few different trees and determine which $\alpha$ provides the best tradeoff between accuracy and parsimony.

## 7.8 K-Fold Cross Validation

To perform k-fold cross validation we partition our data set into k folds and then take turns fitting the model on k-1 partitions and validating the fitted model against the remaining partition. If we create 10 partitions, we fit and validate ten times. How, then, can we find the optimal value for k? Much thought and research has gone into suggesting the optimal number of partitions. If we use a low value for k, the trees we generate will have a much smaller training data set—resulting in trees that are very biased. On the other hand, if we have a very high value for k, the bias decreases because the k-th fold training set looks very similar to the full training set and the resulting trees will have low bias but much higher variance. Experience has shown that k values of 5 or 10 give a good bias-variance tradeoff. At the extreme, using a value of k that equals the number of training data points is called leave-one-out cross validation. Depending on the algorithm, this can be very computationally expensive, but produces good models. With our small Iris data set we can compare the models generated when using k=10.

The k-fold cross-validation algorithm begins by partitioning the training data into k-folds. We will use the .ut.part utility to randomly allocate the training data into k partitions.

```
q)ts:.ut.part[(k:10)#1;0N?]iris.t
```

The goal for cross validation is to use the original training data set to pick the decision tree that corresponds to the $\alpha$ which optimizes the tradeoff between prediction

## 7.8. K-FOLD CROSS VALIDATION

error and tree complexity. To do this, we iterate across each fold and fit a decision tree with all the training data except that fold. We then build a series of pruned trees that correspond to each $\alpha$. Finally, we use each of the sub-trees to predict the target value for the left-out fold. Using these predictions we can calculate the error for each $\alpha$ and finally pick the one with the smallest error. Let's walk through these steps before wrapping it up into a single function.

Excluding the first fold, we build the full decision tree.

```
q)b:sqrt (1_a,0w)*a:atr 0
q)t:raze ts _ 0
q)show tr:.ml.ct[()`;::] t
`pwidth
>[;0.8]
0 1b!((0.007407407 0.007407407 0.007407407 0.007407407 0.007407407 0.00740..
```

We then iteratively prune the tree for each increasing value for $\alpha$. The first tree remains the unpruned tree while the last tree has been fully pruned and contains all the training data in a single node.

```
q)show strs:tr .ml.dtmincc[.ml.wmisc]\ b
(`pwidth;>[;0.8];0 1b!((0.007407407 0.007407407 0.007407407 0.007407407 0...
(`pwidth;>[;0.8];0 1b!((0.007407407 0.007407407 0.007407407 0.007407407 0...
(`pwidth;>[;0.8];0 1b!((0.007407407 0.007407407 0.007407407 0.007407407 0...
(`pwidth;>[;0.8];0 1b!((0.007407407 0.007407407 0.007407407 0.007407407 0...
(`pwidth;>[;0.8];0 1b!((0.007407407 0.007407407 0.007407407 0.007407407 0...
(`pwidth;>[;0.8];0 1b!((0.007407407 0.007407407 0.007407407 0.007407407 0...
(0.007407407 0.007407407 0.007407407 0.007407407 0.007407407 0.007407407 ..
```

## Minimum Cost Complexity

These trees were generated with the .ml.dtmincc decision-tree-min-cost-complexity function that accepts an error function, a decision tree and an $\alpha$. It returns the sub-tree that minimizes the cost complexity for the given parameters.

**.ml.dtmincc**

```
/ given an (e)rror function, a cost parameter (a)lpha and decision (tr)ee,
/ return the subtree that minimizes the cost complexity
dtmincc:{[ef;tr;a]
  if[2=count tr;:tr];
  strs:subtrees tr;
```

```
    strs@:iasc (count leaves::) each strs; / prefer smaller trees
    str:strs imin dtcc[ef;a] each strs;
    str}
```

Using each of these sub-trees, we can now classify the left-out fold and compute an error for each tree.

```
q)avg ts[0;`species]=flip .ml.pdt[;ts 0] peach strs
1 1 1 1 1 0.4666667 0.1333333
```

In this example, we could prune a few leaves and still obtain perfect classification accuracy. With k-fold cross validation, we repeat this step k times and average the results across folds.

## Decision Tree Cross Validation

The .ml.dtxv function encapsulates this procedure by building a projection of the .ml.xv function specifically for decision trees.

### .ml.dtxv

```
/ k-fold cross validate (i)th table in (t)able(s) using (d)ecision (t)ree
/ (f)unction, (a)lphas and misclassification (e)rror (f)unction
dtxv:{[dtf;ef;a;ts]xv[dtmincc[ef]\[;a]dtf::;pdt\:/:;ts]}
```

Running k-fold cross validation across all folds we can get an accuracy rate for each choice of $\alpha$.

```
q)p:.ml.dtxv[.ml.ct[();::];.ml.wmisc;b;ts] peach til k
q)avg avg each ts[;`species]=p
0.96 0.9466667 0.92 0.8533333 0.76 0.44 0.2133333
```

This indicates that the full tree is over biased and that we can achieve greater accuracy on unseen data if we prune a few leaves. We can now pick the tree built using all the training data that corresponds to the optimal $\alpha$.

```
q)atr[1] .ml.imax avg avg each ts[;`species]=p
`plength
>[;2.45]
`s#01b!((0.006666667 0.006666667 0.006666667 0.006666667 0.006666667 0.00..
```

In this small example, pruning didn't accomplish much. The optimal tree is close to the full tree. Classification trees don't typically get very large because the target class can only take a concrete set of values. Regression trees, on the other hand, can grow until all errors are zero. In the worst case, this can cause the tree to have as many leaves as data points. Let's take a look at regression trees and how to prune them.

## 7.9 Regression Trees

It is easy to understand a decision tree when the trained (and predicted) values are categorical. Will we play or not? What is the species of this iris? The decision tree algorithm .ml.dt is easily extended to training (and predicting) ordered data as well. Instead of using impurity functions that are specific to categorical values such as .ml.entropy and .ml.gini, we can use .ml.mse, which operates on numeric values. The difference between the two types of impurity functions is that categorical impurity functions only care about equality of values, while ordered impurity functions take the distance between values into account—the closer the better. The .ml.rt regression-tree function is identical to the .ml.ct classification-tree function except that it uses .ml.mse as its impurity function.

**.ml.rt**

```
rt:dt[oig;oig;wmse]              / regression tree
```

To demonstrate how a regression tree works, it is important to find a data set where the target feature is ordered and not categorical. The UCI machine-learning data archive has a "Wine Quality" data set that provides objective features such as pH and a single subjective feature: quality.[7]

We begin by downloading the data with the winequality.q [383] library and examining a few summary statistics of the red-wine data.

```
q)\l winequality.q
[down]loading wine-quality data set
q)(min;avg;max;sdev)@\:/:flip winequality.red.t
quality        | 3e     5.636023    8e      0.8075694
fixedacidity   | 4.6e   8.319636    15.9e   1.741096
```

---

[7] P. Cortez, A. Cerdeira, F. Almeida, T. Matos, and J. Reis, "Modeling wine preferences by data mining from physicochemical properties," *Decision Support Systems*, vol. 47, pp. 547–553, 2009, doi: 10.1016/-j.dss.2009.05.016.

```
volatileacidity    | 0.12e     0.5278205  1.58e      0.1790597
citricacid         | 0e        0.2709757  1e         0.1948011
residualsugar      | 0.9e      2.538806   15.5e      1.409928
chlorides          | 0.012e    0.08746663 0.611e     0.0470653
freesulfurdioxide  | 1e        15.87492   72e        10.46016
totalsulfurdioxide | 6e        46.46779   289e       32.89532
density            | 0.99007e  0.996747   1.00369e   0.001887335
pH                 | 2.74e     3.311108   4.01e      0.1543865
sulphates          | 0.33e     0.6581495  2e         0.169507
alcohol            | 8.4e      10.42299   14.9e      1.065668
```

The subjective *quality* feature takes values within the range of 3 and 8 with average value of 5.6 and standard deviation of .8. Summarizing a few features by quality we can observe a few relationships.

```
q)s:(avg'') `quality xgroup `quality xasc winequality.red.t
q)`volatileacidity`citricacid`chlorides`sulphates`alcohol #/:s
quality| volatileacidity citricacid chlorides  sulphates alcohol
-------| -----------------------------------------------------------
3      | 0.8845          0.171      0.1225     0.57      9.955
4      | 0.6939622       0.174151   0.09067922 0.5964151 10.26509
5      | 0.5770414       0.2436856  0.09273578 0.6209692 9.899703
6      | 0.4974844       0.2738246  0.08495613 0.6753293 10.62951
7      | 0.4039197       0.3751759  0.07658796 0.7412562 11.46592
8      | 0.4233333       0.3911111  0.06844444 0.7677778 12.09444
```

There is a positive relationship between quality and citric acid, sulphates, and (not surprisingly) alcohol. There is also a negative relationship between quality and volatile acidity and chlorides values.

Let's see what a single node regression tree would look like.

```
q)-1 .ml.ptree[0] .ml.rt[(1#`maxd)!1#1;::] winequality.red.t;
5.636023 (n = 1599, err = 1042.165)
|   alcohol >[;10.525] 0: 5.366226 (n = 983, err = 424.1587)
|   alcohol >[;10.525] 1: 6.066558 (n = 616, err = 432.2711)
```

Instead of displaying percent accuracy for each leaf, a regression tree displays the sum of squared errors. With one split, we can see the sum of squared errors drops from 1042 to 856. Allowing the tree to continuously split creates more than 400 leaves!

```
q)count .ml.leaves .ml.rt[();::] winequality.red.t
418
```

## 7.9. REGRESSION TREES

We have the tools, now, to prune back this regression tree. Let's first start by splitting our data into a training and testing partitions.

```
q)d:.ut.part[`train`test!3 1;0N?] winequality.red.t
```

We then define our decision tree function as .ml.rt and error function as .ml.wmse because we are growing and pruning a regression tree. The fully grown tree on the training partition has fewer leaves than before because there are fewer data points in total. It still grows, however, until all misclassification error is zero.

```
q)dtf:.ml.rt[();::]
q)ef:.ml.wmse
q)tr:dtf d`train
q)count .ml.leaves tr
324
```

We now prune one node at a time, generating the characteristic tree for each alpha.

```
q)atr:flip .ml.dtmina[ef] scan (0f;tr)
q)flip atr
0f           (`alcohol;>[;10.525];10b!((`volatileacidity;>[;0.905];10b!((..
0.0003475118 (`alcohol;>[;10.525];10b!((`volatileacidity;>[;0.905];10b!((..
0.0003648874 (`alcohol;>[;10.525];10b!((`volatileacidity;>[;0.905];10b!((..
0.0003706793 (`alcohol;>[;10.525];10b!((`volatileacidity;>[;0.905];10b!((..
0.0003706793 (`alcohol;>[;10.525];10b!((`volatileacidity;>[;0.905];10b!((..
0.0003738748 (`alcohol;>[;10.525];10b!((`volatileacidity;>[;0.905];10b!((..
0.0003753128 (`alcohol;>[;10.525];10b!((`volatileacidity;>[;0.905];10b!((..
..
```

Taking the geometric mean of each alpha gives us a list of betas to use with k-fold cross validation.

```
q)b:sqrt (1_a,0w)*a:atr 0
```

We then partition the training data into k folds and validate.

```
q)ts:.ut.part[(k:10)#1;0N?]d`train
q)p:.ml.dtxv[dtf;ef;b;ts] peach til k
q)e:avg each e*e:ts[;`quality]-p
```

The best tree has a minimum average error across all folds, and drastically drops the number of leaves.

```
q)count .ml.leaves btr:atr[1] .ml.imin avg e
12
```

### Root Mean Squared Error

Regression models are typically quantified by taking the square root of the average squared prediction errors—or the root mean squared error RMSE. The .ml.rms root-means-square function implements this.

**.ml.rms**

```
rms:{sqrt avg x*x}              / root mean square error
```

We can now use this tree on the test data to make predictions and quantify the quality of the model.

```
q).ml.rms d.test.quality - .ml.pdt[btr] d`test
0.6916861
```

Our average prediction error is close to .5 of a quality point. We now return to the weather data set and describe a transformation that allows us to use a classification tree algorithm with categorical data.

## 7.10 One Hot

The .ml.ct classification-tree function follows the CART implementation and does not support categorical features. How, then, can we generate a classification tree on the weather data? At first glance it would seem that this is a deficiency in the algorithm. Are we limited to ordered features? Not if we can convert categorical features into numbers. But how? If we merely map each categorical value into a numeric value (something akin to enumeration), the relative ordering of, and the distance between, the values would take on a meaning which we do not intend. Our transformation process must, therefore, ensure each distinct value of each categorical feature creates a branch that is mutually exclusive to all other values.

We do this by adding one new column for each distinct value. This new column will be limited to 2 values: one (or true) when the column matches the categorical value and zero (or false) everywhere else. This is called one-hot encoding--sometimes referred to as one-of-k encoding. The .ut.onehot one-hot function implements this algorithm.

**.ut.onehot**

## 7.10. ONE HOT

163

```
/ one-hot encode vector, (symbol columns of) table or (non-key symbol
/ columns of) keyed table x.
onehot:{
 if[98h>t:type x;:u!x=/:u:distinct x];        / vector
 if[99h=t;:key[x]!.z.s value x];              / keyed table
 D:.z.s each x c:where 11h=type each flip x;  / list of dictionaries
 D:string[c] {(`$(x,"_"),/:string key y)!value y}' D; / rename uniquely
 x:c _ x,' flip raze D;                       / append to table
 x}
```

Using the function on a vector of values generates a dictionary that we can flip to see a table where each row corresponds to the initial vector.

```
q)flip .ut.onehot weather.t.Outlook
Sunny Overcast Rain
-------------------
1    0        0
1    0        0
0    1        0
0    0        1
0    0        1
..
```

This is such a common operation that the function has been overloaded to perform one-hot encoding on every column of a table that has type *symbol*. It is possible, though not in this case, that the different columns with type *symbol* have the same values. To prevent these non-unique values from overwriting each other, the .ut.onehot function prepends the original column name to the resulting one-hot columns.

```
q).ut.onehot weather.t
Play_No Play_Yes Outlook_Sunny Outlook_Overcast Outlook_Rain Temperature_..
---------------------------------------------------------------------------..
1       0        1             0                0            1           ..
1       0        1             0                0            1           ..
0       1        0             1                0            1           ..
0       1        0             0                1            0           ..
0       1        0             0                1            0           ..
..
```

But this has gone a bit too far. We need the Play column to remain unencoded. The .ut.onehot function supports this by excluding any keyed columns from being encoded.

```
q)0!.ut.onehot 1!weather.t
Play Outlook_Sunny Outlook_Overcast Outlook_Rain Temperature_Hot Temperat..
-----------------------------------------------------------------------------
No   1             0                0            1                0        ..
No   1             0                0            1                0        ..
Yes  0             1                0            1                0        ..
Yes  0             0                1            0                1        ..
Yes  0             0                1            0                0        ..
..
```

We can now use the .ml.ct function to generate a classification tree.

```
q)-1 .ml.ptree[0] .ml.ct[();::] 0!.ut.onehot 1!weather.t;
Yes (n = 14, err = 35.7%)
| Outlook_Overcast >[;0.5] 0: No (n = 10, err = 50%)
| | Humidity_Normal >[;0.5] 0: No (n = 5, err = 20%)
| | | Outlook_Rain >[;0.5] 0: No (n = 3, err = 0%)
| | | Outlook_Rain >[;0.5] 1: No (n = 2, err = 50%)
| | | | Wind_Weak >[;0.5] 0: No (n = 1, err = 0%)
| | | | Wind_Weak >[;0.5] 1: Yes (n = 1, err = 0%)
| | Humidity_Normal >[;0.5] 1: Yes (n = 5, err = 20%)
| | | Wind_Strong >[;0.5] 0: Yes (n = 3, err = 0%)
| | | Wind_Strong >[;0.5] 1: No (n = 2, err = 50%)
| | | | Outlook_Sunny >[;0.5] 0: No (n = 1, err = 0%)
| | | | Outlook_Sunny >[;0.5] 1: Yes (n = 1, err = 0%)
| Outlook_Overcast >[;0.5] 1: Yes (n = 4, err = 0%)
```

Instead of creating a node with multiple branches, our tree will successively create binary splits on each value of each feature. And although the algorithm doesn't explicitly exclude these pseudo-features from being used more than once, the fact that they only take on two values ensures it never happens in practice. Once split, there are no other values to split upon.

Decision trees are popular because each decision is easy to interpret. Our decision tree algorithm has many parameters and options to control the complexity of the tree. Decision trees are so flexible, they can fit our training sets perfectly. We've spent a lot of time and effort trying to introduce parameters and generate algorithms that prevent decision trees from over fitting their data. We've discussed methods of pre- and post- pruning to optimize the balance between bias and variance. Instead of making the decision tree algorithm more complex, however, we can address this tradeoff by building multiple trees. The next chapter shows how multiple trees can be more powerful than a single tree.

# Chapter 8

# Decision Tree Ensembles

> Two heads are better than one, not because either is infallible, but because they are unlikely to go wrong in the same direction.
>
> — C.S. Lewis

Ensemble learning is a machine-learning technique that combines multiple underlying algorithms to create a new model that has better predictive power than each underlying model by itself. An ensemble does not necessarily have to be the same underlying machine-learning algorithm. But when they are all decision trees, the result is called a decision tree ensemble. There are two approaches to combining decision trees: in parallel (Bagging) and sequentially (Boosting).

## 8.1  Ensemble Example

Our first example loads the Wisconsin Diagnosis Breast Cancer data set, partitions the data, uses bootstrap aggregation to build a model and evaluates its accuracy on the test data set.

```
q)\l funq.q
q)\l wdbc.q
[down]loading wisconsin diagnostic breast cancer data set
q)count each d:.ut.part[`train`test!3 1;0N?] wdbc.t
train| 426
```

```
test | 143
q)k:30
q)m:.ml.bag[k;.ml.ct[();::]] d.train
q)avg d.test.diagnosis = .ml.pbag[k;m] d.test
0.965035
```

By changing one option on the classification tree, we can use a random forest to model the data.

```
q)m:.ml.bag[k;.ml.ct[(1#`maxff)!1#sqrt;::]] d.train
q)avg d.test.diagnosis = .ml.pbag[k;m] d.test
0.979021
```

Our third example transforms the target diagnosis features benign "B" and malignant "M" to -1 and 1, re-partitions the data, declares a decision "stump" projection, builds an adaptive boosting model and finally evaluates the accuracy on test data.

```
q)t:update -1 1 "M"=diagnosis from wdbc.t
q)count each d:.ut.part[`train`test!3 1;0N?] t
train| 426
test | 143
q)stump:.ml.ct[(1#`maxd)!1#1]
q)m:.ml.fab[k;stump;.ml.pdt] d.train
q)avg d.test.diagnosis = .ml.pab[k;.ml.pdt;m] d.test
0.965035
```

The first two examples, bootstrap aggregation and random forest generate multiple full-sized decision trees and allow each tree to vote on the predicted value. The last ensemble example sequentially builds and then averages multiple decision stumps—each one specifically grown to correct errors from the earlier stumps. We introduced the Wisconsin Diagnosis Breast Cancer data set because discrete adaptive boosting requires a binary classification problem. Let's review this data set.

## 8.2 Wisconsin Diagnosis Breast Cancer Data Set

Detecting cancer is not only a noble goal, but also a good binary classification problem. We will load the Wisconsin Diagnosis Breast Cancer data set[1] from the

---

[1] W.N. Street, W.H. Wolberg and O.L. Mangasarian. Nuclear feature extraction for breast tumor diagnosis. *IS&T/SPIE 1993 International Symposium on Electronic Imaging: Science and Technology*, volume 1905, pages 861-870, San Jose, CA, 1993.

University of California at Irvine's server with the wdbc.q [383] library.

The breast cancer data set was generated by measuring 10 features on digitized images of cell nuclei. From each of these 10 features, three values were recorded: the mean, standard error and worst measurement.

```
q)flip 10 cut 1_cols wdbc.t
radius_mean              radius_se              radius_worst
texture_mean             texture_se             texture_worst
perimeter_mean           perimeter_se           perimeter_worst
area_mean                area_se                area_worst
smoothness_mean          smoothness_se          smoothness_worst
compactness_mean         compactness_se         compactness_worst
concavity_mean           concavity_se           concavity_worst
concave_points_mean      concave_points_se      concave_points_worst
symmetry_mean            symmetry_se            symmetry_worst
fractal_dimension_mean   fractal_dimension_se   fractal_dimension_worst
```

In addition to providing these 30 objective values, the data set indicates whether the tumor was malignant or benign.

```
q)wdbc.t`diagnosis
"MMMMMMMMMMMMMMMMMMMMBBBMMMMMMMMMMMMMMMMBMMMMMMMMBMBBBBBMMBMMBBBBMBMMBBBBMB..
```

Starting with bootstrap aggregation, let's see how these algorithms can be applied to this data set to predict the existence of a malignant tumor.

## 8.3 Bootstrap Aggregation

The first approach to creating a decision tree ensemble is to train multiple independent trees on randomly (with replacement) sampled subsets of the training data. Due to its dependence on re-sampled subsets of the data, this technique is known as bootstrap aggregation (or bagging). The .ml.bag algorithm is a simple layer on top of our decision tree code.

**.ml.bag**

```
/ generate (n) decision trees by applying (f) to a resampled (with
/ replacement) (t)able
bag:{[n;f;t](f ?[;t]::) peach n#count t}  / (b)ootstrap (ag)gregating
```

It starts by generating a vector with n copies of the count of t. This vector is then used with the ? operator to generate copies of t that have the same number of rows, but whose data have been randomly sampled (with replacement). These re-sampled copies of t are then passed to f, which generates a decision tree for each copy. The combination of re-sampling and application of f is applied in parallel with the peach adverb.

Bootstrap aggregation benefits from using multiple, fully grown, trees. This allows each tree to specialize but the final average (or mode) reduces the resulting variance. The more trees we add, the higher our accuracy.[2] We first build models from 1 through 50 trees.

```
q)k:50
q)m:.ml.bag[k;.ml.ct[();::]] d.train
```

## Predicting Bootstrap Aggregation

We can then plot the prediction accuracy as a function of the number of trees by using the .ml.pbag predict-boosted-aggregating function, which is written to handle multiple values for k.

### .ml.pbag

```
/ given an atom or list (k), and bootstrap aggregating (m)odel, make
/ prediction on (d)ictionary
pbag:{[k;m;d]
 if[count[m]<max k;'`length];
 if[98h=type d;:.z.s[k;m] peach d]; / iterate on a table
 p:k {aom x#y}\: pdt[;d] peach m;
 p}
```

The function begins by ensuring the requested number of trees k is less than or equal to the number of trees in the aggregation. It then detects that a table has been supplied instead of a dictionary and the function recurses over each record of the table. Predictions for each decision tree in m are then made by applying the .ml.pdt function. The last step computes the average (or mode) for every value of k.

Example 8.1 [169] shows how the accuracy quickly increases as we add more trees to the ensemble, and then levels off.

---

[2] P. Probst and A.-L. Boulesteix, "To tune or not to tune the number of trees in random forest?," arXiv:1705.05654 [cs, stat], May 2017.

## 8.4. RANDOM FOREST 169

**Example 8.1** Bootstrap Aggregation Accuracy

```
q).ut.plt avg d.test.diagnosis = .ml.pbag[1+til k;m] d.test
0.98|  "           +++        "
     |  "       +  ++++ +++++"
0.96|  "  ++++++++       +   "
     |  "    + +  +              "
0.94|  " +                       "
     |  " +                      "
     |  "+                       "
0.92|  "++                       "
     |  "                        "
0.9 |  "+                        "
```

Our goal, therefore, should be to generate as many trees as computationally feasible.

## 8.4 Random Forest

We can extend the process of making independent trees by not only randomly selecting samples from the data set, but also randomly selecting a subset of the features. To add diversity to our trees, we don't always want the strongest feature to used first. An ensemble works best when consistent variations in the data are closely fit by their own model. We have two choices: filter the features before building a complete tree or filter the features at each node of the tree generation process. Most decision tree implementations follow Leo Breiman's proposal[3] to filter at each node. The difference between these two choices is subtle. If feature A is superior to feature B, the tree will always be split on feature A first. To allow feature B to be split before feature A, we need to temporarily hide feature A, and then allow it to reappear later in the tree-building algorithm. This happens when we randomly filter the features at each node, but does not happen when we filter the features before generating the tree.

We now arrive at the purpose for the `maxff` option to the `.ml.dt` decision-tree function. The `maxff` option is used in combination with the `?` operator to randomly sub-sample the features before computing the information gain associated with

---
[3]L. Breiman, "Random Forests," *Machine Learning*, vol. 45, no. 1, pp. 5–32, Oct. 2001, doi: 10.1023/-A:1010933404324.

each feature. If the null value :: is supplied, the full feature count is supplied as the left operand of the ? operator and a random shuffle of all features will be used. Other functions can be supplied to achieve different behaviors.

Although the actually number of features used for each split is a tunable parameter, a few reasonable defaults have been suggested. Leo Breiman originally recommended using $\lfloor log_2(M+1) \rfloor$ features, where M is the number of available features, for random forest classification problems. He also identified that classification and regression problems should be treated differently. Breiman's *randomForest* R package defaults classification trees to use $\lfloor \sqrt{M} \rfloor$ features at each split while regression trees use $\lfloor M/3 \rfloor$ features as a default.[4]

With 50 trees, we use the .ml.rt regression-tree projection, the .ml.bag bootstrap-aggregation function and one third of the available features to fit the red-wine-quality data.

```
q)\l winequality.q
q)count each d:.ut.part[`train`test!3 1;0N?] winequality.red.t
train| 1199
test | 400
q)m:.ml.bag[k;.ml.rt[(1#`maxff)!1#%[;3];::]] d.train
```

Example 8.2 [170] shows how adding more trees achieves ever-increasing accuracy on the training data.

**Example 8.2** Random Forest Regression Training Error
```
q).ut.plt .ml.rms d.train.quality - .ml.pbag[1+til k;m] d.train
0.6| "                        "
   |  "                       "
0.5| "+                       "
   |  "                       "
0.4| "                        "
   |  "+                      "
   |  "+                      "
0.3| "  +                     "
   |  "    ++++               "
0.2| "        ++++++++++++++" 
```

We can also see in Example 8.3 [171] how the test data improves as well—but not as much.

---

[4]Fortran original by L. Breiman and A. Cutler and R port by A. Liaw and M. Wiener, *randomForest: Breiman and Cutler's Random Forests for Classification and Regression*. 2018.

## 8.4. RANDOM FOREST

**Example 8.3** Random Forest Regression Test Error

```
q).ut.plt .ml.rms d.test.quality - .ml.pbag[1+til k;m] d.test
0.9| "+                "
   | "                 "
0.8| "                 "
   | "                 "
0.7| "+                "
   | "++               "
   | " +++             "
0.6| "    +++++++++++++"
   | "                 "
0.5| "                 "
```

With 50 trees, we use the .ml.ct classification-tree projection, the .ml.bag bootstrap-aggregation function and the square root of the available features to build a random forest classification model of the iris data set.

```
q)\l iris.q
[down]loading iris data set
q)count each d:.ut.part[`train`test!3 1;0N?] iris.t
train| 112
test | 38
q)m:.ml.bag[k;.ml.ct[(1#`maxff)!1#sqrt;::]] d.train
```

Once again, Example 8.4 [171] shows the training accuracy continuously approaches 100%.

**Example 8.4** Random Forest Classification Training Error

```
q).ut.plt avg d.train.species = .ml.pbag[1+til k;m] d.train
1.01| "                 "
    | "                 "
1   | " ++++++++++++++++"
    | "                 "
0.99| "++               "
    | "                 "
    | "+                "
0.98| "                 "
    | "                 "
0.97| "+                "
```

And Example 8.5 [172] illustrates how the testing accuracy levels off at a lower value.

**Example 8.5** Random Forest Classification Test Error
```
q).ut.plt avg d.test.species = .ml.pbag[1+til k;m] d.test
0.96| "                           "
0.94| " +                         "
    | "                           "
0.92| "+++++++++++++++++++++++++++"
    | "                           "
    | "                           "
0.9 | "                           "
0.88| "                           "
    | "                           "
0.86| "+                          "
```

Permitting the user to supply the maximum feature function `maxff` allows the user to supply any custom function. Other approaches include using the base-2 logarithm,

```
q)m:.ml.bag[k;.ml.ct[(1#`maxff)!1#xlog[2];::]] d.train
q)avg d.test.species = .ml.pbag[k;m] d.test
0.9210526
```

as well as a fixed fraction of features,

```
q)m:.ml.bag[k;.ml.ct[(1#`maxff)!1#*[.5];::]] d.train
q)avg d.test.species = .ml.pbag[k;m] d.test
0.9210526
```

or even a fixed number of features.

```
q)m:.ml.bag[k;.ml.ct[(1#`maxff)!1#&[3];::]] d.train
q)avg d.test.species = .ml.pbag[k;m] d.test
0.9210526
```

Note how we never implemented a function specifically for random forests. A random forest is just bootstrap aggregation with randomized feature sub-sampling.

## 8.5 Adaptive Boosting

Instead of generating many trees in parallel like bootstrap aggregation or random forest, adaptive boosting (AdaBoost) generates classifiers sequentially. The idea is to build the first classifier on data with all data points having equal weight. We then build the next classifier using weights specifically adjusted to underweight the samples we previously classified correctly, and overweight the samples we classified incorrectly. In this manner, we can progressively keep adding new classifiers to our ensemble that correct the points we were previously unable to classify correctly. In addition to modifying the sample weights when building each subsequent classifier, we also keep track of a specific multiplier that will be used when combining the results of each classifier to make a composite prediction. As we will see, this multiplier is intuitively related to the total prediction error of the classifier: the lower the error, the higher the multiplier.

The adaptive boosting algorithm does not specifically require the use of a decision tree. It merely needs a classifier that has an accuracy better than a random guess. For binary classification it must have an accuracy greater than 50%. Adaptive boosting combines multiple "weak learners" into an ensemble, which is itself a "strong learner". Adaptive boosting is not limited to binary classification, but the binary classification implementation is quite intuitive and elegant.

**.ml.adaboost**

```
/ given (t)rain (f)unction, discrete (c)lassifier (f)unction, initial
/ (w)eights, and (t)able with -1 1 discrete target class values in first
/ column, return ((m)odel;(a)lpha;new (w)eights)
adaboost:{[tf;cf;w;t]
  if[(::)~w;w:n#1f%n:count t];    / initialize weights
  m:tf[w] t;                       / train model
  p:cf[m] t;                       / make predictions
  e:sum w*not p=y:first flip t;    / compute weighted error
  a:.5*log (c:1f-e)%e;             / compute alpha (minimize exponential loss)
  / w*:exp neg a*y*p;                 / increase/decrease weights
  / w%:sum w;                        / normalize weights
  w%:2f*?[y=p;c;e];                / increase/decrease and normalize weights
  (m;a;w)}
```

The .ml.adaboost discrete-adaptive-boosting function accepts four arguments. The first two arguments are the training and classification functions: tf and cf respectively. Unlike other machine-learning algorithms, the .ml.adaboost function requires a classification function so it can detect which samples were incorrectly classified. The next argument to the function is a vector of weights w—one for each sample. A table of samples t, whose first column indicates the discrete class -1 or 1, is supplied as the last argument.

The algorithm starts by handling the case of a null weight vector. Similar to the decision tree algorithm, a null weight vector is replaced by an equal-weight vector matching the length of the table t. The function then builds a model m using the training function tf, which is expected to accept two parameters, a weight vector and the table of samples—exactly the last two parameters of the .ml.dt function. This model is then used with the classification function cf to make predictions on the samples just used when we built the model.

The .ml.adaboost function then compares the predicted classes (-1 or 1) to the actual classes in the first column of the table and computes a total error e—accounting for the different weights of each sample. By scaling the correct term c by the error term e, a new alpha is computed which is used as the multiplier for this tree in the ensemble. Computing the sample weights for building the next tree requires some explanation.

## 8.6 Discrete Adaboost

After completing our ensemble of "weak classifiers" that independently vote on the correct class (either -1 or 1), we have a "strong classifier" represented as Equation 8.1 [174].

$$H(x) = \sum_{t=1}^{T} a_k h_t(x)$$

where $h_t(x) \in \{+1, -1\}$ and

$T =$ the number of weak learners

Equation 8.1: AdaBoost Strong Classifier

To find the optimal values for $a_t$, the AdaBoost algorithm minimizes the exponential loss function (Equation 8.2 [175]), which accumulates small values when the sign of the predicted value $H(x_i)$ matches the sign of actual value $y_i$.

Minimizing this error function and solving for $a_t$ results in the following formula.

$$a_{t+1} = \frac{1}{2} \log \frac{1 - e_t}{e_t}$$

## 8.6. DISCRETE ADABOOST

$$\mathcal{L}(H) = \sum_{i=1}^{n} \exp\left(-y_i H(x_i)\right)$$

where $y_i \in \{+1, -1\}$

Equation 8.2: Exponential Loss

The last step of the AdaBoost algorithm is to increase the weight for the incorrectly classified samples and decrease the weight for the correctly classified samples so that the next iteration can improve the ensemble by building a "weak classifier" specifically for the samples we missed. The next two lines, which are commented out, first increase (decrease) the sample weights if the predicted value p and the true value y have the same (opposite) sign,

$$w_{t+1}(i) = w_t(i) e^{-ah(x_i)p}$$

and then normalize the weights such that they sum to 1.

These two lines are commented out because although the implementation is intuitive, there is a more efficient implementation that does not require the expensive exp operator, uses values we've already computed and updates the weights while at the same time ensuring they continue to sum to 1. The function ends by returning the decision tree model m, the computed alpha a (used for weighting this addition to the ensemble) and finally the new weight vector w, which will be used to build the next classifier.

To use the data set with the AdaBoost algorithm, we must first transform the diagnosis values from characters to the numeric values -1 and 1. By comparing the values to the letter "M" and indexing into a two-element list, we define 1 as malignant and -1 as benign. We will also limit our feature set to just the mean values of the 10 independent features plus the target diagnosis feature.

```
q)show t:update -1 1 "M"=diagnosis from wdbc.t
diagnosis radius_mean texture_mean perimeter_mean area_mean smoothness_me..
-----------------------------------------------------------------------------
1         17.99       10.38        122.8          1001      0.1184         ..
1         20.57       17.77        132.9          1326      0.08474        ..
1         19.69       21.25        130            1203      0.1096         ..
1         11.42       20.38        77.58          386.1     0.1425         ..
1         20.29       14.34        135.1          1297      0.1003         ..
..
```

We can then split the data into training and testing partitions.

```
q)count each d:.ut.part[`train`test!3 1;0N?] t
train| 426
test | 143
```

The next step is to define a "weak classifier". Decision stumps, which are decision trees with one branch, are commonly used with AdaBoost because they are interpretable and meet the requirement that the classifier have greater than 50% accuracy. We can generate a decision stump by specifying that the tree has a maximum depth of 1.

```
q)stump:.ml.ct[(1#`maxd)!1#1]
```

In this example, the decision stump splits on the "area_worst" feature. If the largest area in the sample is less than or equal to 880.75, the stump classifies the sample as benign with a 91.8% accuracy. If, on the other hand, the largest area in the sample is greater than 880.75, the stump classifies the sample as malignant with a 95.2% accuracy. We can see that large tumors are likely to be malignant.

```
q)-1 .ml.ptree[0] stump[::] d.train;
-1 (n = 426, err = 38%)
|   area_worst >[;880.75] 0: -1 (n = 280, err = 8.2%)
|   area_worst >[;880.75] 1: 1 (n = 146, err = 4.8%)
```

## Fitting Adaptive Boosting

AdaBoost will increase the weight on the samples we got wrong so the next use of the decision stump will improve our model. Running multiple rounds of AdaBoost is made easier by the .ml.fab fit-adaptive-boosting function.

**.ml.fab**

```
/ given an atom or list (k), (t)rain (f)unction, discrete (c)lassifier
/ (f)unction, and (t)able perform max(k) iterations of adaboost
fab:{[k;tf;cf;t] 1_max[k] (adaboost[tf;cf;;t] last::)\ (::)}
```

There are a few items to note. Firstly, even though the .ml.adaboost function returns three elements (the model, alpha and weight vector), we are only iterating over the weight vector. In order to use .ml.adaboost with the scan operator \, we had to create a composition so that only the last element of the previous iteration

## 8.6. DISCRETE ADABOOST

was used. We also had to start iterating with equal weights across all samples. We did this by starting the iteration with the generic null ::. Finally, we throw away the first element of the returned list because it is our starting null weight vector and not a member of our ensemble.

If we run the model 2 times, we can see that using the worst concave points feature will improve the classification of our mistakes.

```
q).ml.fab[2;stump;.ml.pdt] d.train
(`area_worst;>[;880.75];10b!((0.002347418 0.002347418 0.002347418 0.00234..
(`concave_points_worst;>[;0.1223];01b!((0.001262626 0.001262626 0.0012626..
```

Using .ml.fab to iterate many times allows our ensemble to fit the training data with increasing accuracy. We can run 50 rounds of AdaBoost and store the model in m.

```
q)m:.ml.fab[k;stump;.ml.pdt] d.train
```

### Predicting Adaptive Boosting

The result of .ml.fab is a list of sequential decision stumps, alpha values and weights. We can then compute a weighted average of all the decision trees, or just a subset of them. The .ml.pab predict-adaptive-boosting function accepts a single (or list of) k value(s) and returns predictions for each value of k.

**.ml.pab**

```
/ given an atom or list (k), discrete (c)lassifier function, adaboost
/ (m)odel, make prediction on (d)ictionary
pab:{[k;cf;m;d]
 if[count[m]<mx:max k;'`length];
 if[98h=type d;:..z.s[k;cf;m] peach d]; / iterate on a table
 p:m[;1] * cf[;d] peach m[;0];
 p:signum $[0h>type k;sum k#p;sums[mx#p] k-1];
 p}
```

The function starts by comparing the maximum value of k to the number of decision trees in m. If the value is too large, the function throws a "length" exception. It then detects that the supplied dictionary is actually a table and then recursively calls itself for each record. The next line applies the classification function cf over each decision tree (stored in m[;0]) and then multiplies the results by the alpha values (stored in m[;1]).

Finally, the last line of the `.ml.pab` function handles the differences between a single k value and a list of k values. If k is an atom, we simply need to add each of the first k elements of m. If on the other hand k is a list, the code accumulates a running sum from the first decision tree through the maximum requested value of k. Finally, the function uses the `signum` operator to convert the weighted sums into the values -1 and 1.

After we use the `.ml.pab` function to compute predictions on the training data, we can plot the relationship between accuracy and increasing number of decision stumps in the ensemble. Example 8.6 [178] demonstrates this relationship.

**Example 8.6** AdaBoost Training Accuracy
```
q)P:.ml.pab[1+til k;.ml.pdt;m] d.train
q).ut.plt avg d.train.diagnosis = P
1.02| "                              "
1    | "          +++++++++++"
     | "      +++++           "
0.98| "   +++                 "
     | " +++                  "
0.96| "++                     "
     | "                      "
0.94| "                      "
     | "                      "
0.92| "+                     "
```

Applying the same model against the test data set, seen in Example 8.7 [179], shows that the additional benefit of each extra element of our ensemble trails off.

As with any parameter tuning, the number elements in our ensemble should be determined with cross validation.

## 8.7 AdaBoost Cross Validation

We first split our training data set into 10 folds.
```
q)n:10
q)ts:.ut.part[n#1;0N?] t
```

The next step is to define our fitting function `ff` and our prediction function `pf`.

## 8.7. ADABOOST CROSS VALIDATION 179

**Example 8.7** AdaBoost Test Accuracy

```
q)Pt:.ml.pab[1+til k;.ml.pdt;m] d.test
q).ut.plt avg d.test.diagnosis = Pt
0.98|  "       +++   ++++++   +"
0.96|  "           +++   ++++++"
    |  " +++++ ++++       +  "
0.94|  "  +                  "
    |  "+  +                 "
    |  "                     "
0.92|  " ++                  "
0.9 |  "                     "
    |  "                     "
0.88|  "+                    "
```

```
q)ff:.ml.fab[;stump;.ml.pdt]
q)pf:.ml.pab[;.ml.pdt]
```

After defining our ensemble lengths in ks, we can perform cross validation and compute predicted values P for each one.

```
q)ks:1+til 20
q)P:.ml.xv[ff ks;pf ks;ts] peach til n
```

Now we can compare the predicted values with the actual test diagnosis and compute accuracy statistics. Picking the k value with maximum accuracy gives us our optimal ensemble size.

```
q)k:0N!ks .ml.imax avg avg each e:ts[;`diagnosis] = P
16
```

Finally, we can confirm the accuracy of using this optimal k value on the test partition.

```
q)avg d.test.diagnosis = pf[k;;d.test] ff[k] d.train
0.972028
```

Decision trees are very flexible and create intuitive models of our data. These models can be described by a series of "if" statements and graphically visualized. Given enough nodes, a decision tree can model any relationship. Adding ensembles reduces the variance caused by this flexibility but introduces more complexity. When there is a linear relationship in the data, we may be better served with other modeling tools such as linear regression. To this we now turn.

# Chapter 9

# Linear Regression

> When you're fundraising, it's AI, when you're hiring, it's ML, when you're implementing, it's linear regression, when you're debugging, it's printf().
>
> — Baron Schwartz *Vivid Cortex*

If we define machine learning as a statistical technique that allows a computing device to "learn" relationships within data without explicitly being taught, linear regression can be considered the oldest machine-learning algorithm. Although it pre-dates the first use of the term "machine learning" by Arthur Samuel in 1959,[1] linear regression has been the workhorse of the scientific community since the 1800s.

We are, perhaps, most familiar with a version of linear regression known as least squares regression that finds the slope (and potentially intercept) of a line drawn through a plot of a two-dimensional data set. As we will see, linear regression can, in fact, be used on multi-dimensional data sets. Least squares regression, also referred to as ordinary least squares (OLS) is named after the choice of error that it attempts to minimize—the sum of squared errors. We could, however, have chosen to minimize the sum of absolute errors or even the maximum error. The choice of minimizing the sum of squared errors results in an elegant closed-form solution. This does not mean, however, it is the best, or only, algorithm that can be used for modeling, and therefore predicting, data.

---

[1] A. L. Samuel, "Some Studies in Machine Learning Using the Game of Checkers," *IBM Journal of Research and Development*, vol. 3, no. 3, pp. 210–229, Jul. 1959, doi: 10.1147/rd.33.0210.

We will start this chapter by reviewing q's built-in matrix operators, deriving our own implementation of least squares regression, re-implementing least squares regression with gradient descent, and then introducing regularization to make our solutions more resistant to overfitting.

## 9.1 Matrices

Although q represents atoms by negative types

```
q)type each (0b;0x00;0h;0i;0j;0e;0f)
-1 -4 -5 -6 -7 -8 -9h
```

and vectors by positive types,

```
q)type each (01b;0x0001;0 1h;0 1i;0 1j;0 1e;0 1f)
1 4 5 6 7 8 9h
```

matrices do not have a specific type. A matrix, which is entered as a list of float vectors, has the same type as a mixed list: 0h.

```
q)type (1 1f;1 1f)
0h
```

Because q lacks a distinct matrix type, matrix operations must ensure each vector within the matrix is of type 9h and equal length. The following .ml.ismatrix function mirrors this check by first confirming the supplied argument is a mixed list. It then ensures all elements within the list are themselves float vectors. And finally, the function confirms all vectors are the same length.

**.ml.ismatrix**

```
/ returns true if x is a matrix as defined by q
ismatrix:{
 if[type x;:0b];
 if[not all 9h=type each x;:0b];
 b:identical count each x;
 b}
```

## 9.2 Matrix Operators

The q matrix operators `mmu` (matrix multiplication), `lsq` (least squares) and `inv` (matrix inversion) are—in fact—overloaded versions of primitive k operators.

```
q)inv
!:
q)lsq
!
q)mmu
$
```

There is nothing unique about these operators and their behavior merely depends on the fact that their arguments are matrices. The `!:` k operator is also the underlying implementation of the key q operator. The `!` operator is commonly used to create a dictionary by binding the key and value vectors and the `$` operator is typically used to cast values between types. If we use these matrix operators with parameters that are not matrices, the results will reflect the fact that the underlying k operator is overloaded.

For example, if we were to attempt to take the inverse of a dictionary, we would merely obtain the key,

```
q)inv `a`b`c!1 2 3
`a`b`c
```

because it has the same underlying k operator.

```
q)key
!:
```

These operators will only behave as matrix operators if their operands are matrices.

```
q)(1 2 3f;1 2 3f) mmu (1 2f;1 2f;1 2f)
6 12
6 12
```

As a special case, q treats simple float vectors of length N as 1 x N or N x 1 matrices as the case may be. For example, we can matrix multiply a matrix with a simple vector,

```
q)enlist[1 2 3f] mmu 1 2 3f
,14f
```

or even two simple vectors to compute a dot product. We can even use the underlying $ operator for clarity instead of mmu.

```
q)1 2 3f $ 1 2 3f
14f
```

## 9.3 Least Squares Regression

Returning to least squares regression, we can now call lsq with two matrices to find the slope of a line that passes through the origin that minimizes sum of squared errors.

```
q)enlist[1 2 3f] lsq enlist 2 3 4f
0.6896552
```

To fit the y intercept as well, we must add a degree of freedom by prepending a vector of ones to the right operand.

```
q)enlist[1 2 3f] lsq (1 1 1f;2 3 4f)
-1 1
```

In this case, the y intercept is -1 and the slope is 1.

## 9.4 Multi-Dimensional Least Squares

To demonstrate multi-dimensional least squares regression, let's use the wine-quality data set again.

```
q)\l winequality.q
[down]loading wine-quality data set
```

We can obtain a rough intuition into the linear relationship between the subjective quality feature and the objective features by computing the correlation between each of them. Based on our analysis of the data set with decision trees, it should be no surprise that quality and alcohol have the highest correlation.

## 9.4. MULTI-DIMENSIONAL LEAST SQUARES

```
q)t:winequality.red.t
q)t.quality cor/: 1_flip t
fixedacidity       | 0.1240516
volatileacidity    | -0.3905578
citricacid         | 0.2263725
residualsugar      | 0.01373164
chlorides          | -0.1289066
freesulfurdioxide  | -0.05065606
totalsulfurdioxide | -0.1851003
density            | -0.174919
pH                 | -0.05773139
sulphates          | 0.2513971
alcohol            | 0.4761663
```

Using least squares regression, we can find how wine quality is linearly related to alcohol.

```
q)enlist[t.quality] lsq enlist t.alcohol
0.5388704
```

In other words, the red-wine quality is equal to the alcohol content multiplied by .539.

$$\text{quality} = .539 \times \text{alcohol}$$

To fit the y intercept as well, we can use the `.ml.prepend` function to prepend a vector of ones.

```
q)enlist[t.quality] lsq .ml.prepend[1f] enlist t.alcohol
1.874975 0.3608418
```

The `.ml.prepend` function prepends a matrix with a row of repeated values. Its counterpart, the `.ml.append` function, likewise appends a row of repeated values to the supplied matrix.

### .ml.prepend

```
prepend:pend[1]              / prepend 1 row of repeated x to matri(X)
```

### .ml.append

```
append:pend[-1]              / append  1 row of repeated x to matri(X)
```

Both functions are implemented in terms of the generic .ml.pend function that can prepend or append multiple rows of repeated values to a matrix. If the supplied parameter n is positive, n rows are prepended to the matrix. If n is negative, the rows are appended to the matrix.

**.ml.pend**

```
pend:{[n;x;X]$[n>0;,[;X];X,](abs n;count X 0)#x}
```

The results of this regression indicate that the relationship between red-wine quality and alcohol content can be described by the following formula.

$$\text{quality} = 1.87 + .36 \times \text{alcohol}$$

We can now move beyond this single variable regression and use all the provided features.

```
q)flip winequality.red.Y lsq .ml.prepend[1f] winequality.red.X
21.96521
0.02499055
-1.08359
-0.1825639
0.01633127
-1.874225
0.004361333
-0.00326458
-17.88116
-0.4136531
0.9163344
0.2761977
```

Splitting the data between training and testing partitions allows us to estimate the quality of a linear regression model on the red-wine-quality data set.

```
q)d:.ut.part[`train`test!3 1;0N?] winequality.red.t
q)`Y`X set' 0 1 cut value flip d.train;
q)THETA:Y lsq .ml.prepend[1f] X
```

The .ml.plin function encapsulates the process of prepending an X matrix with a vector of ones and then multiplying by the THETA coefficients.

**.ml.plin**

```
/ linearly predict Y values by prepending matri(X) with a vector of 1s and
/ multiplying the result to (THETA) coefficients
plin:{[X;THETA]mm[THETA] prepend[1f] X}
```

We can now apply the fitted THETA coefficients to the test wine-quality data set and measure the accuracy of the prediction by again computing the root mean squared error with the .ml.rms function.

```
q)`Yt`Xt set' 0 1 cut value flip d.test;
q).ml.rms first Yt-p:.ml.plin[Xt] THETA
0.7059337
```

## 9.5 Custom Matrix Operators

The ml.q [345] library does not use the native q matrix operators directly. Instead, it calls variants declared within the .ml namespace. This is done for three reasons. The first is to enable parallel execution of standard matrix multiplication. Q's native matrix multiplication operator mmu serially computes the results of matrix multiplication over each row. The rows are independent, however, and it is possible to achieve large performance gains by using the peach operator across all the rows. Though this is overkill for small matrices, the performance gain is substantial for larger matrices.

**.ml.mm**

```
mm:{$[;y] peach x}            / X * Y
```

The second reason the ml.q [345] library uses its own matrix operators is to reduce the number of matrix transpositions.

> **Matrix Multiplication Optimizations**
>
> Other languages, such as Matlab, recognize an attempt to multiply a matrix and the transpose of another matrix: X * Y'. Instead of performing the wasteful transpose, the language merely iterates over the columns (rows) of the matrix instead of the rows (columns). Q strictly parses from right to left and therefore cannot perform this optimization.

This is very important for large matrices because the time taken to allocate and copy memory for the new matrix is considerable. Avoiding a flip of the matrix also reduces the memory footprint of the algorithm, which can mean the difference between successfully computing the solution and crashing with a wsfull error.

The .ml.mmt function is similar to the .ml.mm function but is implemented such that the algorithm understands that the right operand should be transposed before the matrix multiplication—even though no transpose is actually performed.

**.ml.mmt**

```
mmt:{(y$) peach x}                    / X * Y'
```

Similarly, we have implemented the .ml.mtm function, which understands that the left operand should be transposed before performing the multiplication.

**.ml.mtm**

```
mtm:{f2nd[$[;y];x]}                   / X' * Y
```

This function is in-turn implemented in terms of the .ml.f2nd function, which applies the supplied function in parallel over each element of the second dimension of the supplied matrix.

Matrix inverse .ml.minv and matrix least squares .ml.mlsq are also defined within the .ml namespace, and default to the native q operators. This is done so that they, in addition to the previously defined matrix operators, can be externally redefined with faster implementations. Enabling function redefinition is the third reason the ml.q [345] library uses its own matrix operators.

One example of such an implementation is the Q Math Library (QML).[2] In addition to providing access to statistics and optimization functions, QML includes linear algebra primitives, which can be used instead of ml.q's default implementation. Loading qmlmm.q redefines the .ml.mm, .ml.mmt, .ml.mtm, .ml.minv, .ml.mlsq, .ml.dot, .ml.mdet and .ml.mchol functions. The QML library in-turn transforms the kdb+ data into a format appropriate for calling Basic Linear Algebra Subprograms (BLAS) functions. When QML is installed, the user has a choice of using a pre-compiled BLAS library or downloading and compiling a new installation. BLAS libraries are optimized for the hardware on which they run. In addition to AMD and Intel BLAS libraries, which take advantage of CPU-based SIMD vectorized instructions, there are even libraries such as NVBLAS that execute the instructions on GPUs. Compiled properly, BLAS operators can also execute routines in parallel across multiple cores.

Simple vectors can be passed directly to the BLAS routines. Matrices, however, need to be massaged before they can be passed as arguments to the BLAS routines. Unlike q, which stores matrices as a list of lists, BLAS expects the matrix to be

---

[2] A. Zholos, "Q Math Library." [Online]. Available: http://althenia.net/qml. [Accessed: 20-Dec-2019].

unwound into a single vector. Although there is overhead involved in reshaping the memory, it is typically small compared to the complexity of the math operation. In Big O notation, unwrapping the matrix into a single vector of contiguous memory is $O(n^2)$ while matrix multiplication, for example, is $O(n^3)$ for a naive implementation. Offloading linear algebra routines to a BLAS library is not new. Both commercial applications such as Mathematica and Matlab, as well as open source applications such as R, GNU Octave and Numpy, offload their linear algebra computations to a BLAS library.

## 9.6 Normal Equations

We finally return to our own implementation of least squares regression. The most intuitive linear least squares algorithm involves inverting a matrix containing the normal equations. Given the equation

$$X\theta = Y$$

a solution for $\theta$ can be obtained by first multiplying both sides by $X^T$.

$$X^T X \theta = X^T Y$$

We can then obtain an equation for $\theta$ by multiplying both sides by the inverse of $X^T X$ (the normal matrix),

$$(X^T X)^{-1} X^T X \theta = (X^T X)^{-1} X^T Y$$

and noting that the equation simplifies to Equation 9.1 [189] because $X^{-1} X = I$.

$$\theta = (X^T X)^{-1} X^T Y$$

Equation 9.1: Normal Equations

This is implemented in the .ml.normeq normal-equations function and involves three matrix multiplications and a matrix inversion.

**.ml.normeq**

```
/ given target matrix Y and data matri(X), return the THETA matrix resulting
/ from minimizing sum of squared residuals
normeq:{[Y;X]mm[mmt[Y;X]] minv mmt[X;X]} / normal equations ols
```

We can see that the function produces the same results as the native lsq operator.

```
q)(lsq;.ml.normeq) .\: (winequality.red.Y;.ml.prepend[1f] winequality.red.X)
21.96521 0.02499055 -1.08359 -0.1825639 0.01633127 -1.874225 0.004361333 ..
21.96521 0.02499055 -1.08359 -0.1825639 0.01633127 -1.874225 0.004361333 ..
```

To be precise, our implementation of least squares regression is not exactly the same as q's implementation. While we are using the inv operator, which is implemented in terms of the LU decomposition, the lsq operator uses the Cholesky decomposition internally to improve numerical stability.

Least squares regression based on the normal equations works well for small to medium-sized data sets that fit into memory and data sets that have more observations than features. As the data set grows in size, however, the complexity of the computation grows polynomially. The whole matrix may not even fit into memory. It is not feasible to solve the normal equations in these cases. In addition, there are cases where it is not possible to obtain a solution because there are more features than observations. To obtain solutions in both of these cases, we can drop the requirement of obtaining a unique solution that fits all the data. Instead, we can randomly pick an initial set of parameters, and then iteratively adjust them in a direction that reduces the overall regression error. This process is called gradient descent. We will see how this technique also allows us to customize our definition of *error* to influence the selection of parameters.

## 9.7 Gradient Descent

Gradient descent is an algorithm by which we minimize a function by successively adjusting parameters in the direction of the steepest descent. In mathematics, the gradient is a multi-dimensional vector that points in the direction of the steepest *ascent*. To use gradient descent, we compute (either numerically or analytically) the negative of the gradient and adjust the parameters accordingly. A simple example would be to find the x coordinate corresponding to the minimum value of the sin function. Example 9.1 [191] uses the .ut.nseq utility to plot values between $-\pi$ and $\pi$.

**.ut.nseq**

```
/ generate a sequence of (n) steps between (b)egin and (e)nd
nseq:{[n;b;e]b+til[1+n]*(e-b)%n}
```

## 9.7. GRADIENT DESCENT

**Example 9.1** Sine

```
q).ut.plt sin .ut.nseq[21] . -1 1*.ml.pi
1    | "           ++++     "
     | "         +    +     "
0.5  | "        +      +    "
     | "                +"
0    | "       +        +"
     | "+            +       "
     | "+                    "
-0.5 | "  +        +.        "
     | "    +    +           "
-1   | "      ++++           "
```

The .ut.nseq function accepts a number of steps n as its first parameter and the beginning and ending values as the second and third parameters respectively. The function returns n+1 values demarcating the n steps.

We can, for example, use the .ut.nseq utility to create 10 steps between -20 and 20.

```
q).ut.nseq[10;-20;20]
-20 -16 -12 -8 -4 0 4 8 12 16 20f
```

The value of $\pi$ is precomputed and stored in the variable .ml.pi.

**.ml.pi**

```
pi:acos -1f
```

Knowing that the sin function has a period (or wave length) of $2\pi$, we would expect the minimum value to be at $-\pi/2$.

```
q)-.5 * .ml.pi
-1.570796
```

To confirm this, we can use the .ml.gd function, which implements a numeric gradient descent. It accepts a learning rate alpha a, gradient function gf and initial coefficients THETA.

**.ml.gd**

```
/ (a)lpha: learning rate, gf: gradient function
gd:{[a;gf;THETA] THETA-a*gf THETA} / gradient descent
```

Each call of the function takes a step in the opposite direction of the gradient. Starting at zero, we would expect each step to slowly fall down the sin function's slope and settle in the well centered at -1.57. Knowing that the slope of the sin function is, in fact, the cos function, we can call .ml.gd a few times to see the progression.

```
q)5 .ml.gd[.5f;cos]\ 0f
0 -0.5 -0.9387913 -1.234173 -1.399324 -1.484641
```

Running until convergence we can obtain the exact location.

```
q).ml.gd[.5f;cos] over 0f
-1.570796
```

The .ml.gd function is overly simplistic. It requires us to pick a learning rate alpha that is not so small that convergence is extremely slow, nor too big that we overshoot the minimum and begin bouncing back and forth (and hopefully converging) on either side of the minimum. As the next example shows, bouncing on either side of the minimum can still result in convergence, but at a very slow pace.

```
q).ut.rnd[.01] 10 .ml.gd[2f;cos]\ 0f
0 -2 -1.17 -1.95 -1.21 -1.92 -1.24 -1.89 -1.26 -1.87 -1.28
```

## 9.8 Linear Regression Cost

To use gradient descent for linear regression, we need to find parameters THETA that minimize the mean squared errors. To use the .ml.gd function, we must provide a function that returns the gradient of the loss function (mean squared errors). We first define the cost function (Equation 9.2 [192]).

$$J(\theta) = \frac{1}{2m} \sum_{i=1}^{m} \left( h_\theta(x^{(i)}) - y^{(i)} \right)^2 + \frac{\lambda_1}{m} \sum_{j=1}^{n} |\theta_j| + \frac{\lambda_2}{2m} \sum_{j=1}^{n} \theta_j^2$$

where: $h_\theta(x^{(i)}) = \theta^{(i)} x^{(i)}$ (the predicted value of item $i$)

$m$ = number of samples

$n$ = number of features

Equation 9.2: Regularized Linear Regression Cost

## 9.8. LINEAR REGRESSION COST

Note that this equation demonstrates a regularized cost function that includes two extra terms at the end used to penalize large coefficients. We will discuss regularization later in this chapter in Section 9.14 [208]. The equation also references a general prediction function $h_\theta$ that has a simple definition for linear regression. This function will become more complicated in the next three chapters when we encounter logistic regression, neural networks and recommender systems. It is convenient to refer to $h_\theta$ for consistency—understanding that the definition will change for each type of model.

The linear regression cost equation is implemented in the .ml.lincost function. The choice of regularization is passed in as the first argument. If no regularization is needed, we can pass in an empty list. It is worth noting, even before we define regularization, that the implementation deviates from the equation by setting the first THETA value of each dimension to 0. This excludes the bias term coefficient from the regularization penalty. The implementation follows the standard convention to not penalize a mere translation of the data.

**.ml.lincost**

```
/ linear regression cost
lincost:{[rf;Y;X;THETA]
  J:(.5%m:count X 0)*revo[sum] E*E:plin[X;THETA]-Y;      / cost
  if[count rf,:();THETA[;0]:0f; J+:sum rf[;m][;0][;THETA]]; / regularization
  J}
```

After the regularization function rf parameter, .ml.lincost accepts the Y, X and THETA matrices. The first line calculates the prediction error E and then uses the .ml.revo function to sum the squared errors across all observations. We will review the implementation of .ml.revo in the section called "Summing Over Tensors" [209] when we discuss regularization.

There are two scaling adjustments that need to be addressed. The first is the seemingly superfluous division by 2 (multiplication by .5). Defining the cost with this extra factor is a linear adjustment and does not change the location of the minimum value. It helps when computing the gradient because an extra factor of 2 is obtained when taking the partial derivative of a squared value. These two values cancel each other and result in a simpler gradient function.

The second scaling adjustment is the division by the number of observations. This renders the computation a mean (not a sum) of squared errors, and allows the optimal learning rate alpha to be independent of the number observations.

## 9.9 Linear Regression Gradient

To perform gradient descent, we need a function (Equation 9.3 [194]) that computes the gradient of this cost function with respect to THETA.

$$G(\theta_j) = \frac{\partial J(\theta)}{\partial \theta_j} = \frac{1}{m}\left(h_\theta(x^{(i)}) - y^{(i)}\right)x_j^{(i)} + \frac{\lambda_1}{m}\text{sign}(\theta_j) + \frac{\lambda_2}{m}\theta_j$$

where: $h_\theta(x^{(i)}) = \theta^{(i)} x^{(i)}$ (the predicted value of item $i$)

$m$ = number of samples

$n$ = number of features

Equation 9.3: Regularized Linear Regression Gradient

This is implemented in the .ml.lingrad linear-regression-gradient function, which accepts the same four parameters as the .ml.lincost linear-regression cost function. Following our choice to exclude the bias term from the regularization cost, we must also amend the bias term's gradient. Given that we set the value of the bias regularization term to a constant value of 0, the slope must also be 0.

**.ml.lingrad**

```
/ linear regression gradient
lingrad:{[rf;Y;X;THETA]
  G:(1f%m:count X 0)*mmt[0f^mm[THETA;X]-Y] X:prepend[1f] X; / gradient
  if[count rf,:();THETA[;0]:0f; G+:sum rf[;m][;1][;THETA]]; / regularization
  G}
```

Combining the .ml.gd gradient-descent function and the .ml.lingrad function, we can fit coefficients to the wine-quality data—initializing the default THETA values to 0f.

```
q)THETA:(1;1+count X)#0f
q).ut.rnd[.01] 100 .ml.gd[.0001;.ml.lingrad[();Y;X]]/ THETA
0.01 0.11 0.01 0 0.03 0 0.06 0.02 0.01 0.04 0.01 0.14
```

Using the .ml.lincost function, we can compare the mean square errors with that of the optimal coefficients.

Running 100 rounds of gradient descent results in a total cost of 1.531005,

```
q).ml.lincost[();Y;X] 100 .ml.gd[.0001;.ml.lingrad[();Y;X]]/ THETA
1.531005
```

## 9.10. FEATURE SCALING

while the optimal coefficients have a cost of 0.1957852.

```
q).ml.lincost[();Y;X] .ml.normeq[Y;.ml.prepend[1f] X]
0.1957852
```

## 9.10 Feature Scaling

How fast does the algorithm converge? How many iterations would it take for us to obtain the optimal coefficients? If we store the intermediate THETA values, we can plot the total cost in Example 9.2 [195] to see how it converges.

**Example 9.2** Linear Regression Cost Convergence
```
q)THETAS:100 .ml.gd[.0001;.ml.lingrad[();Y;X]]\ THETA
q).ut.plt .ml.lincost[();Y;X] each THETAS
20|  "                           "
  | "+                           "
15|  "                           "
  |  "                           "
10|  "                           "
  | "+                           "
  | "+                           "
 5 | "++++                       "
  |  "     +++++++++++++         "
 0 |  "                   +++++  "
```

We'd like to increase the learning rate, but if our steps are too large, the coefficients start jumping past the minimum with ever-increasing values.

```
q)raze (first'') 6 .ml.gd[.001;.ml.lingrad[();Y;X]]\ THETA
0 0.005627189 -0.003337306 0.02625007 -0.04756687 0.1545253 -0.3809038
```

What makes matters worse is that the variability of each feature can be quite different.

```
q)dev each flip winequality.red.t
quality        | 0.8073169
fixedacidity   | 1.740552
volatileacidity| 0.1790037
citricacid     | 0.1947402
```

```
residualsugar      | 1.409487
chlorides          | 0.04705058
freesulfurdioxide  | 10.45689
totalsulfurdioxide | 32.88504
density            | 0.001886744
pH                 | 0.1543382
sulphates          | 0.169454
alcohol            | 1.065334
```

This means that if we pick a small learning `alpha` to cater to features with small variance, it will take extremely long to fit high variance features. There are two approaches to solving this. The first is to scale the data so the features lie in similar ranges. And the second is to use an algorithm that dynamically adjusts the learning rate. Let's review these two techniques in-turn.

## Min-Max Normalization

The first feature-scaling algorithm is called min-max normalization. It scales each of the values such that the minimum value maps to 0 while the maximum value maps to 1.

**.ml.minmax**

```
minmax:fxx minmaxf:{daxf[%;{max[x]-min x};x] daxf[-;min;x]::}
```

The .ml.minmax composition is implemented in terms of the higher-order function .ml.minmaxf (which is itself implemented in terms of the .ml.daxf higher-order function introduced in the section called "Aggregation-based Transformations" [96]). In this case, .ml.minmaxf applies the min and max operators to the data passed as the x argument and returns a function that can be used to scale the data. By applying .ml.minmaxf to each feature of X we generate a list of min-max functions mmf that can be reused.

```
q)show mmf:.ml.minmaxf each X
%[;11f]-[;4.6]
%[;1.21]-[;0.12]
%[;1f]-[;0f]
%[;14.5]-[;0.9]
%[;0.598]-[;0.012]
%[;71f]-[;1f]
%[;283f]-[;6f]
```

## 9.10. FEATURE SCALING

```
%[;0.01362]-[;0.99007]
%[;1.27]-[;2.74]
%[;1.63]-[;0.37]
%[;5.6]-[;8.4]
```

Not only can we use the functions stored in mmf to scale the training data X so that all values fall within the range [0, 1],

```
q)(min;max)@/:\: mmf @' X
0 0 0 0 0 0 0 0 0 0
1 1 1 1 1 1 1 1 1 1
```

but we can also use the same functions to scale test data features Xt as well. For consistency, it is important to make the same transformations on the training and testing data sets. But as we see, the scaled features of the testing data set do not strictly fall within the range [0, 1].

```
q).ut.rnd[.01] (min;max)@/:\: mmf @' Xt
-0.03 0    0    0    0.04 0.03 0    0    0.12 0.04 0
1.03  1.38 0.76 0.99 0.68 0.94 0.53 1.04 0.91 0.97 1.16
```

If we have no need to reuse the mmf min-max function list, we can apply the results of .ml.minmaxf directly to the data.

```
q)(min;max)@/:\: .ml.minmaxf'[X]@'X
0 0 0 0 0 0 0 0 0 0
1 1 1 1 1 1 1 1 1 1
```

But that syntax is too onerous. It can be simplified by using the .ml.minmax composition, which combines the .ml.fxx function with the .ml.minmaxf function.

```
q)(min;max)@/:\: .ml.minmax each X
0 0 0 0 0 0 0 0 0 0
1 1 1 1 1 1 1 1 1 1
```

The .ml.fxx function simply applies a function f to its argument x and applies the results to x again.

**.ml.fxx**

```
/ apply the result of f[x] to x
fxx:{[f;x]f[x] x}
```

## Z-Score Normalization

A second—and more popular—method for scaling features is to center the values around 0 and change the standard deviation to be 1. This is also referred to as z-score normalization or z-scoring.

**.ml.zscore**

```
/ feature normalization (centered/unit variance)
zscore:fxx zscoref:{daxf[%;nsdev;x] demeanf[x]::}
```

The .ml.zscore composition is also implemented in terms of a function-generating function: .ml.zscoref. Once again, this allows us to use the same scaling functions on both the training and testing data.

```
q)show zsf:.ml.zscoref each X
%[;1.760852]-[;8.288324]
%[;0.1741116]-[;0.5252877]
%[;0.1970534]-[;0.2695079]
%[;1.34447]-[;2.515888]
%[;0.04671413]-[;0.08690492]
%[;10.18203]-[;15.80692]
%[;33.01345]-[;46.49124]
%[;0.001900936]-[;0.9967343]
%[;0.1548955]-[;3.313987]
%[;0.1697552]-[;0.6588741]
%[;1.04835]-[;10.4149]
```

The similarities with the .ml.minmaxf function are striking. Both translate and then scale the features, but do so with different values.

Z-scoring the training data results in values with an average of 0 and standard deviation of 1.

```
q).ut.rnd[.01] (avg;sdev)@/:\: X:zsf @' X
0 0 0 0 0 0 0 0 0 0 0
1 1 1 1 1 1 1 1 1 1 1
```

The distribution of the testing data is not exactly the same, but it does come close.

```
q).ut.rnd[.01] (avg;sdev)@/:\: Xt:zsf @' Xt
0.07 0.06 0.03 0.07 0.05 0.03 0    0.03 -0.07 -0.02 0.03
0.95 1.11 0.95 1.18 1.03 1.11 0.99 0.97 0.99  1     1.07
```

## 9.11. FMINCG

After using the `.ml.demeanf` higher-order function to generate functions that center the data around 0, the `.ml.zscoref` higher-order function uses `.ml.daxf` to generate functions that normalize the standard deviation of the data to 1. The `.ml.demeanf` higher-order function is itself implemented in terms of `.ml.daxf` as well.

**.ml.demean**

```
/ centered
demean:fxx demeanf:daxf[-;navg]
```

Scaling each of the features to have a similar standard deviation allows us to quickly run gradient descent and achieve convergence.

```
q).ut.rnd[.01] .ml.gd[.5;.ml.lingrad[();Y;X]] over THETA
5.63 0.08 -0.2 -0.06 0.05 -0.09 0.07 -0.12 -0.05 -0.04 0.16 0.28
```

We can now use the scaled testing data along with the fitted parameters THETA to evaluate the goodness of fit.

```
q).ml.lincost[();Yt;Xt] .ml.gd[.5;.ml.lingrad[();Y;X]] over THETA
0.2491712
```

If you read carefully, you may have noticed that `.ml.demeanf` and `.ml.zscoref` used custom versions of the `avg` and `sdev` operators: `.ml.navg` and `.ml.nsdev`. Like the `.ml.nwavg` null-aware-weighted-average function introduced in the section called "Weighted Mode" [33], these are null-aware variants of the average and standard deviation functions. Performing linear regression on data with null values produces null THETA coefficients. Our data, therefore, must be null-free. Once again, permit me to delay discussing the implementations of these null-aware functions until Section 12.4 [271], when we face data sets that are interesting specifically because they are dominated by null values.

## 9.11 FMINCG

The other way to improve the efficiency of finding parameters that minimize a function is to use an algorithm that detects how steep the gradient is and dynamically adjusts the learning rate for each feature. Q does not have a native minimization function. The QML library provides functions for unconstrained minimization

.qml.min and constrained minimization .qml.conmin, which call algorithms implemented in Fortran. These functions are more convenient to use than the gradient-descent function .ml.gd because they only require the caller to supply the cost (and not the gradient) function. The algorithm computes the gradient numerically by evaluating the cost function multiple times. This is, of course, less efficient. Convergence can be hastened by also passing the gradient function.

Hope is not lost if you do not have access to the QML library. The fmincg.q [372] library implements a function minimization routine that is written in q. Originally written for Matlab/Octave by Carl Edward Rasmussen in 1999, the algorithm closely resembles the native Matlab/Octave unconstrained minimization function fminunc. The .fmincg.fmincg function, however, uses far less memory and can efficiently deal with large data sets.

Porting the fmincg.q [372] library was not straight forward. Q limits the number of local variables as well as the number of bytes within a branch statement (if, do, while, and the conditional operator $[.;.;.]). To get around these limitations, the single fmincg function needed to be broken up into smaller (hopefully logical) pieces. This required passing many variables around. Making the problem worse, q also limits the number of function arguments to 8. To get around this limitation, fmincg was modified to store each variable in a dictionary. This dictionary could then be passed as a single argument.[3]

Another problem encountered when porting the fmincg library was the lack of a break operator in q. This wasn't a show stopper, however. The solution was to create a variable called BREAK and loop until its value became false.

Finally, to mirror the original implementation, .fmincg.fmincg prints the iteration number and the cost of each iteration. By printing a carriage return "\r" instead of a newline "\n", each iteration is printed over the previous without proceeding to the next line. This has the effect of allowing the caller to watch iterations fly by as the total cost decreases. After the last iteration is complete, or an error is encountered, a newline "\n" is printed so any subsequent logging does not overwrite the cost of the last iteration.

To use .fmincg.fmincg we need to supply a function that returns two values: the predicted value (cost in our case) given the supplied parameters and each of their gradients. The .ml.lincostgrad function returns both the linear regression mean

---

[3] Prior to kdb+ 3.6, each function could only have 23 local variables and branches could only be 255 bytes long. As of kdb+ 3.6, these restrictions have been relaxed a bit. The maximum number of local variables has now been increased to 110 while the number of bytes allowed within a branch statement has been increased to 65025.

# 9.12. STOPPING CONDITIONS

squared error and the gradient of each parameter. The function minimization routine `.fmincg.fmincg` assumes the parameter vector is a simple vector. It is up to us to reshape the vector into a matrix to compute the cost and gradient.

**.ml.lincostgrad**

```
/ linear cost & gradient
lincostgrad:{[rf;Y;X;theta]
 THETA:(count Y;0N)#theta; X:prepend[1f] X;         / unroll theta
 J:(.5%m:count X 0)*revo[sum] E*E:0f^mm[THETA;X]-Y; / cost
 G:(1f%m)*mmt[E] X;                                 / gradient
 if[count rf,:();THETA[;0]:0f;JG:rf[;m][;;THETA];J+:sum JG@'0;G+:sum JG@'1];
 (J;raze G)}
```

Using `.fmincg.fmincg` we can come enticingly close to the optimal values with merely 1,000 iterations.

```
q).ut.rnd[.01] .fmincg.fmincg[1000;.ml.lincostgrad[();Y;X];THETA 0]
Iteration 1000 | cost: 0.1957852
5.63 0.08 -0.2 -0.06 0.05 -0.09 0.07 -0.12 -0.05 -0.04 0.16 0.28
0.75 0.57 0.3 0.22 0.2 0.2 0.2 0.2 0.2 0.2 0.2 0.2 0.2 0.2 0.2 0.2 0...
1000f
```

The `.fmincg.fmincg` function returns a vector with three elements. The first element is the final parameter vector. A vector of each iteration's total cost is returned as the second element. The final element is the number of iterations that were attempted before returning.

## 9.12 Stopping Conditions

Our data set is relatively small, and we obtained convergence quickly. For bigger problems, however, we may not want to wait for complete and total convergence. Instead of guessing how many iterations we need, we can use the `.ml.iter` function to compute the cost during each iteration and stop after the reduction is less than a specified tolerance.

**.ml.iter**

```
/ keep calling (m)inimization (f)unction on (THETA) and logging status to
/ (h)andle until the % decrease in the (c)ost (f)unction is less than
/ (p). return (cost vector;THETA)
iter:{[h;p;cf;mf;THETA](continue[h;p]last::)acccost[cf;mf]//(::;cf)@\:THETA}
```

The .ml.iter function iteratively calls the minimization function over the THETA values. To find the stopping point, the function delegates the minimization call to the .ml.acccost accumulate-cost function, which appends the cost of each iteration to the variable c.

**.ml.acccost**

```
/ accumulate cost by calling (c)ost (f)unction on the result of applying
/ (m)inimization (f)unction to THETA.   return (THETA;new cost vector)
acccost:{[cf;mf;THETA;c] (THETA;c,cf THETA:mf THETA)}
```

To demonstrate how these functions are implemented, we declare a minimization function mf and cost function cf, which are projections of the .ml.gd and .ml.lincost functions respectively.

```
q)mf:.ml.gd[.5;.ml.lingrad[();Y;X]]
q)cf:.ml.lincost[();Y;X]
```

Note that the .ml.acccost function only returns the cost after applying the function. We must therefore initialize the cost vector ourselves by applying the cost function and the identity function :: to THETA before starting the iterations.

```
q)(::;cf)@\:THETA
,0 0 0 0 0 0 0 0 0 0 0f
16.14554
```

The progressively decreasing cost can be seen by calling the .ml.acccost function a fixed number of times.

```
q)5 .ml.acccost[cf;mf]// (::;cf)@\:THETA
,5.45134 0.0614432 -0.1773707 0.01925037 0.05120929 -0.09118131 0.0404165..
16.14554 4.165692 1.19054 0.4463399 0.2597086 0.2126549
```

Returning the vector of cost values is convenient, but also required if we need to stop once the percent reduction in cost drops below a specified threshold. The .ml.iter function uses the .ml.continue continuation predicate to determine if the iteration should continue.

**.ml.continue**

```
/ print # of iterations, current (c)ost and % decrease to (h)andle, return a
/ continuation boolean: % decrease > float (p) or iterations < integer (p)
continue:{[h;p;c]
 pct:$[2>n:count c;0w;1f-(%/)c n-1 2];
```

## 9.12. STOPPING CONDITIONS

```
  b:$[-8h<type p;p>n;p<pct];
  s:" | " sv ("iter: ";"cost: ";"pct: ") ,' string (n;last c;pct);
  if[not null h; h s,"\n\r" b];
  b}
```

The function begins by calculating the percent change in cost. If there are less than two elements in the vector, the percent change is assumed to be infinite. The second line checks if iteration should continue. If the percent parameter is an integer type, we treat it as an exact number of iterations. If, however, the parameter is a floating-point value, we use it confirm we are reducing the cost. The third line generates an informative string to scroll with the number of iterations, the current cost and the percentage decrease over the last iteration. Finally, the last line of the function checks the provided handle and logs the message if the handle is not null.

We can now use the .ml.iter function to perform gradient descent until the percent reduction in cost is less than .001.

```
q).ut.rnd[.01] .ml.iter[1;.001;cf;mf] THETA
iter: 11 | cost: 0.1960607 | pct: 0.0007148247
,5.62 0.07 -0.19 -0.02 0.05 -0.1 0.06 -0.12 -0.07 -0.03 0.16 0.26
16.15 4.17 1.19 0.45 0.26 0.21 0.2 0.2 0.2 0.2 0.2
```

We see that it took 11 iterations, obtained a final cost of 0.196 and stopped when the percent reduction in cost was 0.0007. Although we may recognize the return values from the .ml.iter function as the final THETA coefficients and the vector of costs computed along the way, the first parameter passed to the function is new. Instead of hard-coding all logging to be printed to STDOUT (by using the integer 1), the .ml.iter allows us to change the logging behavior by passing different values for the file descriptor. We can, for example, turn off logging by passing a null value.

```
q).ut.rnd[.01] .ml.iter[0N;.001;cf;mf] THETA
,5.62 0.07 -0.19 -0.02 0.05 -0.1 0.06 -0.12 -0.07 -0.03 0.16 0.26
16.15 4.17 1.19 0.45 0.26 0.21 0.2 0.2 0.2 0.2 0.2
```

By passing a negative file handle, we can cause each status update to be printed on a new line.

```
q).ut.rnd[.01] .ml.iter[-1;.001;cf;mf] THETA
iter: 1 | cost: 16.14554 | pct: 0w
iter: 2 | cost: 4.165692 | pct: 0.7419911
iter: 3 | cost: 1.19054  | pct: 0.7142036
iter: 4 | cost: 0.4463399 | pct: 0.6250946
```

```
iter: 5  | cost: 0.2597086 | pct: 0.4181372
iter: 6  | cost: 0.2126549 | pct: 0.1811788
iter: 7  | cost: 0.2006262 | pct: 0.05656469
iter: 8  | cost: 0.1974387 | pct: 0.0158875
iter: 9  | cost: 0.1965177 | pct: 0.004664666
iter: 10 | cost: 0.1962009 | pct: 0.001611998
iter: 11 | cost: 0.1960607 | pct: 0.0007148247

,5.62  0.07 -0.19 -0.02 0.05 -0.1 0.06 -0.12 -0.07 -0.03 0.16 0.26
16.15  4.17 1.19 0.45 0.26 0.21 0.2 0.2 0.2 0.2 0.2
```

Returning the vector of costs along with the final THETA values is a useful byproduct of the routine. To mirror q's ability to run for a fixed number of iterations and also return the cost vector, the .ml.iter function allows the iteration tolerance to be specified as an integer.

```
q).ut.rnd[.01] .ml.iter[-1;5;cf;mf] THETA
iter: 1 | cost: 16.14554  | pct: 0w
iter: 2 | cost: 4.165692  | pct: 0.7419911
iter: 3 | cost: 1.19054   | pct: 0.7142036
iter: 4 | cost: 0.4463399 | pct: 0.6250946
iter: 5 | cost: 0.2597086 | pct: 0.4181372

,5.28  0.05 -0.17 0.03 0.05 -0.09 0.03 -0.1 -0.08 -0.01 0.15 0.25
16.15  4.17 1.19 0.45 0.26
```

## 9.13 Stochastic Gradient Descent

Our data set is small and the matrix multiplications are fast. What happens as the size our data set increases? Do we experience a slow down proportional to the growth of the data set? Actually, no. The cost grows super-linearly with the number of samples. Matrix multiplications have a complexity somewhere between $O(n^2)$ and $O(n^3)$—depending on the implementation. Without an alternative, performing gradient descent on very large data sets becomes unwieldy.

Let's take a step back and reconsider if really need to use all the samples on every iteration? Is gradient descent so sensitive to each data point that dropping a few items meaningfully changes the gradient? It would seem that even if we dropped a few—if not many—samples, the gradient may not be perfect, but it would still point us in the correct general direction. This is, in fact, a common trick to solving problems with very large data sets—especially ones where the full data set cannot simultaneously fit in memory.

The alternative to running gradient descent on the full data set is to run gradient descent on a subset of the samples and then repeat the process multiple times across other subsets of the data. Each iteration of gradient descent may not take us on a straight path to the optimal solution, but it will arrive at the approximate solution much faster.

Like a drunkard walking home, stochastic gradient descent may take a few detours along the way, but will eventually arrive at the destination. This process of running multiple iterations of gradient descent on a random selection of samples is called stochastic gradient descent. It is not a new machine-learning algorithm, per se, but a way to use existing algorithms more efficiently. In fact, the addition of a little randomness gives the gradient descent algorithm the opportunity to jump out of local minima and increase the odds of finding a global minimum.

With the addition of a utility function, we can leverage the algorithms we've already built. The stochastic gradient descent algorithm is not specific to linear regression. It can be used anywhere we perform gradient descent.

**.ml.sgd**

```
/ optimize (THETA) by using gradient descent with learning rate (a) and
/ (g)radient (f)unction over (n) subsamples of (X) and (Y) generated with
/ (s)ampling (f)unction: til = no shuffle, 0N? = shuffle, {x?x} = bootstrap
sgd:{[a;gf;sf;n;Y;X;THETA]           / stochastic gradient descent
  I:(n;0N)#sf count X 0;
  THETA:THETA (gd[a] . (gf .;::)@'{(x[;;z];y)}[(Y;X)]::)/ I;
  THETA}
```

Similar to the .ml.gd function, the .ml.sgd stochastic-gradient-descent function also requires a learning rate alpha a, the gradient function gf and the THETA matrix. The .ml.sgd function, however, also requires the full X and Y matrices in order to generate subsets of them. To customize the sampling, we also need to pass two more parameters: the number of samples (or mini-batches) and the sampling function.

Instead of reshaping the X and Y matrices directly, which would allocate a large amount memory simultaneously, the first line of the .ml.sgd function only generates the indices for each mini-batch. To do this, it first passes the number of samples to the sampling function sf, which is expected to return a list of indices in the desired order. We will soon review a few different examples of sampling functions. The first line then finishes by reshaping the list of indices into n mini-batches with the # reshape operator.

The second line of the .ml.sgd function iterates over each of the mini-batch indices—passing the mini-batch to the gradient function, which is in-turn passed along with the THETA values to the minimization function. After each mini-batch is processed, the final THETA values are returned.

We can begin our example by resetting the THETA matrix and redefining the gradient function gf without projecting the X and Y parameters. They will be applied within the .ml.sgd function for each mini-batch.

```
q)THETA:(1;1+count X)#0f
q)gf:.ml.lingrad[()]
```

The stochastic gradient descent algorithm obtains its name from the fact that each iteration of gradient descent is provided a random mini-batch. When it comes to picking a method of randomizing the data, we have a few choices. One option is to first permute the data and then run gradient descent over each mini-batch. In this case, any subsequent rounds—often referred to as epochs—of stochastic gradient descent would not further randomize the data.

We first define the shuffled row indices i and then permute the X and Y variables by using i to re-indexing them.

```
q)i:0N?count X 0
q)X:X[;i];Y:Y[;i]
```

Then we can run two epochs of gradient descent without further randomizing the mini-batches by passing the til operator as the sampling function. When called within .ml.sgd, it merely returns the original indices. In this example, we run with 10 mini-batches.

```
q)2 .ml.sgd[.01;gf;til;10;Y;X]/ THETA
1.025068 0.01509093 -0.05252054 0.0267542 0.004910349 -0.01996575 -0.0019..
```

Instead of pre-shuffling the data before running multiple epochs, we can shuffle the data within each epoch. To accomplish this, we pass 0N? as the sampling function.

```
q)2 .ml.sgd[.01;gf;0N?;10;Y;X]/ THETA
1.025031 0.01478395 -0.05229643 0.02528082 0.004811812 -0.01991488 -0.002..
```

Passing a null integer as the number of random elements causes the ? operator to return a full permutation.

## 9.13. STOCHASTIC GRADIENT DESCENT

```
q)0N?5
1 2 0 3 4
```

Instead of permuting the data, another choice is to randomly select elements from the data but this time allowing replacement. Similar to the method introduced in Section 8.3 [167], this is referred to as bootstrapping.

```
q)2 .ml.sgd[.01;gf;{x?x};10;Y;X]/ THETA
1.02474 0.03795894 -0.0176098 0.01712377 -0.00133503 -0.01025919 -0.00680..
```

By passing {x?x} as the sampling function, we can generate a list of indices equal in length to the original data, while allowing the samples to be uniformly selected from the complete data set.

```
q){x?x}5
4 2 3 4 1
```

Finally, by declaring a cost function cf and a projection of the .ml.sgd function as the minimization function, we can use the .ml.iter iteration utility to keep running stochastic gradient descent until the reduction in cost is less than or equal to our threshold. In this case, we set the parameter p to 0 to iterate until the cost either remains the same or increases—which can happen.

```
q)cf:.ml.lincost[();Y;X]
q)mf:.ml.sgd[.01;gf;{x?x};10;Y;X]
q).ut.rnd[.01] .ml.iter[1;0f;cf;mf] THETA
iter: 58 | cost: 0.1961678 | pct: -3.661286e-05
,5.61 0.08 -0.19 -0.02 0.06 -0.1 0.06 -0.12 -0.07 -0.04 0.16 0.26
16.15 13.27 10.92 8.95 7.34 6.02 4.97 4.11 3.4 2.82 2.33 1.95 1.63 1.37 1..
```

The size of the mini-batch controls the behavior of stochastic gradient descent. At one extreme, a single mini-batch encompasses all samples within a data set. In this case, stochastic gradient descent collapses into gradient descent. At the other extreme, each mini-batch has a single sample. Each new observation slowly imparts a nudge towards the optimal THETA coefficients. We can use this configuration when we require the model to learn over time. If the observations are taken from a static system, the THETA coefficients would converge to their optimal values. If the system is dynamic, however, the THETA coefficients would change as our samples reflect different realities. This is referred to as online gradient descent.

```
q)cf .ml.sgd[.01;gf;til;count X 0;Y;X] THETA
0.2017697
```

## 9.14 Regularization

Including the intercept (also referred to as the bias term), we are fitting 12 coefficients to the wine-quality data. The more features we include in our regression, the more likely we are to overfit the training data and produce a model with high variance. Small fluctuations in the training data may have an over-sized effect on the parameters, resulting in poor estimates on the test data. To reduce the variance and therefore increase the bias—but hopefully not as much as the variance is reduced—we can add a regularization term to the cost function. This regularization term adds an extra cost related to values of the coefficients. The higher the coefficients, the higher the cost. The more regularization we use, the more likely the minimum cost solution will have small coefficients. This all sounds like a good idea, but it leaves us with two questions. How does the cost relate to the coefficients? How much regularization should we use? We first discuss two different regularization techniques: L1 and L2 regularization.

A naive approach to incorporating the fitted coefficients into the cost function would be to add each of their values. This does not work because negative coefficients would actually decrease the cost. We must therefore pick a way to transform the coefficients to positive values.

### L1 Regularization

An obvious solution would be to take the absolute value of each coefficient. This is called L1 regularization because of its relation to the L1 norm (where norm is often used to refer to a function that assigns a strictly positive value to the length of a vector). We used the L1 norm already in the section called "Manhattan Distance" [21].

L1 regularization is implemented in the .ml.l1 function.

**.ml.l1**

```
/ given l1 regularization (l)ambda and size of dimension (m), return two
/ function compositions that compute the cost and gradient
l1:{[l;m]((l%m)*revo[sum] abs::;(l%m)*signum::)}
```

It accepts the regularization parameter l and number of observations m, which correspond to the $\lambda_1$ and $m$ coefficients in Equation 9.2 [192] and Equation 9.3 [194]. The function returns a two-element list: function compositions that calculate the L1 regularization cost and gradient. Given a set of regression parameters

## 9.14. REGULARIZATION

THETA, the first composition takes the absolute value of each element, sums them and scales the result by l and m. The second function returns the similarly scaled gradient—the sign of the THETA coefficients.

L1 regularization has the desirable quality that it tends to force coefficients to 0 if they are weaker than the coefficients of other features. This helps create a parsimonious model. In other words, using L1 regularization also performs feature selection. Given a data set with many features, it may be difficult to determine which ones are the most descriptive. Using L1 regularization quickly drives the weak features to zero, thus allowing us to perform regression *and* feature selection at the same time.

One prickly point about L1 regularization is that the gradient does not strictly exist when the coefficient is zero. Any value between 1 and -1 can be used for the gradient, but we will use the value of zero because it elegantly allows us to use the `signum` operator. Restated, all positive values have slope of 1, all negative values have a slope of -1 and the value 0 has a slope of 0.

Introducing L1 regularization by passing a projection of the .ml.l1 function begins to knock out the weakest coefficients.

```
q)rf:.ml.l1[100]
q).ut.rnd[.01] 1#.fmincg.fmincg[1000;.ml.lincostgrad[rf;Y;X];THETA 0]
Iteration 1000 | cost: 0.254067
5.65 0 -0.15 0 0 -0.01 0 -0.01 0 0 0.07 0.24
```

Note that the total cost has increased, but the hope is that the error on the test data set has decreased.

Performing linear regression with L1 regularization is also known as LASSO (least absolute shrinkage and selection operator).

### Summing Over Tensors

The THETA coefficients for linear regression are two-dimensional tensors, i.e., matrices. The implementation of .ml.l1 could have been precise and summed over the second dimension of THETA and then summed the resulting vector. But as we will see in Chapter 11 [237] and Chapter 12 [261], we also need to regularize a two-dimensional tensor (a list of THETA matrices). To ensure .ml.l1 can be generically used for any dimension of THETA, we have implemented the unoriginally-named .ml.revo function, which implements the functionality of the over operator in reverse.

**.ml.revo**

```
/ reverse of over (start deep and end shallow)
revo:{[f;x]$[type x;f x;type first x;f f peach x;f .z.s[f] peach x]}
```

Instead of starting from the outer-most layer of the tensor and iteratively applying the supplied function until convergence, `.ml.revo` recursively drills into the data structure x and applies the supplied function f at the inner-most layer first, and then again over each outer layer of the x parameter.

Using the take # operator, we can build a tensor of any dimension.

```
q)0N!2 2 3#til 12
((0 1 2;3 4 5);(6 7 8;9 10 11))
0 1 2  3 4 5
6 7 8  9 10 11
```

We can actually use the over operator to compute the sum of all elements of this matrix.

```
q)sum over 2 2 3#til 12
66
```

But this has two drawbacks. The first is that summing across matrices is less efficient than recursively summing vectors. The second—and more important—drawback is that the vector of THETA matrices in neural networks are not of equal dimensions. It would not be possible to sum across each THETA matrix.

```
q)sum over ((2 2#til 4);2 3#til 6)
'length
  [0]  sum over (2 2#til 4),2 3#til 6
                ^
```

It is possible, however, to first sum each row of each THETA matrix, then sum the resulting vectors and finally sum the single vector.

```
q).ml.revo[sum] ((2 2#til 4);2 3#til 6)
21
```

## L2 Regularization

Another approach to transforming the regression coefficients into positive values is to square them. This is referred to as L2 regularization due to its use of the

## 9.14. REGULARIZATION

L2 norm that was introduced in the section called "Euclidean Distance" [22]. Unlike L1 regularization, which creates a sparse solution, L2 regularization smooths the coefficient weights across each of the features. This ensures a stable (but not sparse) solution. A benefit of L2 regularization is that unlike L1 regularization, the optimal coefficients vary smoothly with small changes in the training data.

L2 regularization is implemented in the .ml.l2 function.

**.ml.l2**

```
/ given l2 regularization (l)ambda and size of dimension (m), return two
/ function compositions that compute the cost and gradient
l2:{[l;m]((.5*l%m)*revo[sum] {x*x}::;(l%m)*)}
```

The function has the same interface as .ml.l1. It accepts the regularization parameter l and number of observations m, which correspond to the $\lambda_2$ and $m$ coefficients in Equation 9.2 [192] and Equation 9.3 [194]. The function also returns a two-element list: function compositions that calculate the L2 regularization cost and gradient. Given a set of regression parameters THETA, the first composition squares each coefficient, sums them and scales the values by l and m—this time multiplying by .5 so the gradient doesn't need to multiply by 2. The second function returns the similarly scaled gradient—the THETA coefficients themselves.

We can see how using L2 regularization generally dampens all the coefficients.

```
q)rf:.ml.l2[100]
q).ut.rnd[.01] 1#.fmincg.fmincg[1000;.ml.lincostgrad[rf;Y;X];THETA 0]
Iteration 1000 | cost: 0.2028672
5.63 0.07 -0.18 -0.02 0.05 -0.09 0.05 -0.11 -0.06 -0.03 0.15 0.25
```

Performing linear regression with L2 regularization is also known as ridge regression, which has a closed-form solution seen in Equation 9.4 [211].

$$\theta = (X^T X + \lambda I)^{-1} X^T Y$$

Equation 9.4: Ridge Regression

Notice how the equation reduces to the Normal Equations formula derived in Equation 9.1 [189] when $\lambda = 0$. This can be seen in the .ml.ridge ridge-regression function as well.

**.ml.ridge**

```
/ given (l2) regularization parameter, target matrix Y and data matri(X),
/ return the THETA matrix resulting from performing ridge regression
ridge:{[l2;Y;X]mm[mmt[Y;X]] minv mmt[X;X]+diag count[X]#l2}
```

Passing the same value for the l2 regularization parameter results in the same theta coefficients.

```
q).ut.rnd[.01] .ml.ridge[0f,count[X]#100f;Y;.ml.prepend[1f]X]
5.63 0.07 -0.18 -0.02 0.05 -0.09 0.05 -0.11 -0.06 -0.03 0.15 0.25
```

Like .ml.normeq and unlike the .ml.lincost and .ml.lincostgrad functions, the .ml.ridge function does not prepend a vector of ones to explicitly fit the intercept. This is left to the caller of the function. If we choose not to fit an intercept, a single atomic value of lambda can be supplied and .ml.ridge will expand it to the correct dimension. If, on the other hand, we desire to fit an intercept, we must pass a vector of lambdas that conform to the size of our X matrix and ensure the first lambda is set to zero.

## L1 + L2 Regularization

When the number of features is less than the number of data points, L1 regularization will pick at most as many features as there are data points. In addition, among highly correlated features, L1 regularization typically picks just one of them. Introducing the ability to perform both L1 and L2 regularization simultaneously removes these limitations and expands the solution space from which we can search for optimal coefficients. Using a combination of both forms of regularization also stabilizes the regularization path, which may be jumpy if we only used L1 regularization.

Performing linear regression with both L1 and L2 regularization is also known as elastic net regression.

Passing a list of regularization functions allows us to benefit from a combination of both. The .ml.enet elastic-net function accepts an alpha parameter that reflects the strength of regularization and a lambda ratio parameter that specifies how the alpha should be distributed between the l1 and l2 regularization parameters.

### .ml.enet

```
/ given (a)lpha and (l)ambda (r)atio elastic net parameters, convert them
/ into l1 and l2 units and return a pair of l1 and l2 projections
enet:{[a;lr](l1 a*lr;l2 a*1f-lr)}
```

## 9.15 Optimal Regularization

The function returns projections of `.ml.l1` and `.ml.l2`, which can then be passed as the first parameter to `.ml.lincostgrad`.

```
q)rf:.ml.enet[100;.5]
q).ut.rnd[.01] 1#.fmincg.fmincg[1000;.ml.lincostgrad[rf;Y;X];THETA 0]
Iteration   465 | cost: 0.2088352
5.63 0.02 -0.17 0 0 -0.04 0 -0.04 0 0 0.1 0.26
```

## 9.15 Optimal Regularization

We now return to the second question: how much regularization do we need? It is possible that each of the features in our data set are important and no regularization is needed at all. Or alternatively, we have so many features that we've seriously overfit the data and regularization will considerably improve test data set prediction. To find the best regularization parameter, we can run through a few different values and see where the test error stops decreasing. We'll first define a utility projection that performs a round of gradient descent and returns the test error associated with the fitted coefficients. The projection accepts the first two parameters of `.fmincg.fmincg`, which are the maximum number of iterations and cost-gradient function.

```
q)f:.ml.lincost[();Yt;Xt]1#.fmincg.fmincg[;;THETA 0]::
```

We first test a sequence of L2 regularization values. The `.ut.sseq` function makes generating these sequences more intuitive than using the `til` operator directly.

**.ut.sseq**

```
/ generate a sequence of (s)-sized steps between (b)egin and (e)nd
sseq:{[s;b;e]b+s*til 1+floor 1e-14+(e-b)%s}
```

Using the `.ut.sseq` function, we can generate a sequence of L2 coefficients from 0 to 500 with step size 50.

```
q)show l2:.ut.sseq[50;0;500]
0 50 100 150 200 250 300 350 400 450 500
```

Notice how the training error continues to rise as we increase the regularization.

```
q)e:(f[1000] .ml.lincostgrad[;Y;X] .ml.l2@) each l2
Iteration  1000 | cost: 0.1957852
```

```
Iteration 1000 | cost: 0.1994975
Iteration 949  | cost: 0.2028672
Iteration 453  | cost: 0.205964
Iteration 169  | cost: 0.2088352
Iteration 638  | cost: 0.2115144
Iteration 107  | cost: 0.2140272
Iteration 636  | cost: 0.2163937
Iteration 120  | cost: 0.2186299
Iteration 490  | cost: 0.2207489
Iteration 146  | cost: 0.2227618
```

We hope, however, that the test error begins to fall as we limit the overfitting.

**Example 9.3** Optimal Linear Regression Regularization

```
q).ut.plt e
0.249| "+                    "
     | "                     "
     | "                     "
0.248| "                     "
     | "  +              +"
     | "                     "
0.247| "             +  "
     | "    +       +   "
     | "      +  +      "
0.246| "       + +      "
```

We can see in Example 9.3 [214] that an L2 regularization parameter around 200 will give us the best tradeoff between bias and variance.

```
q).ml.imin l2!e
200
```

Alternatively, we can find the optimal parameters for elastic net regression by finding the optimal combination of L1 and L2 coefficients. We begin by using the `cross` operator to create a grid of alpha and lambda ratio values and storing them in the variable `alr`.

```
q)show alr:.ut.sseq[50f;0f;500f] cross .ut.sseq[.1;0f;1f]
0 0
0 0.1
0 0.2
0 0.3
```

## 9.15. OPTIMAL REGULARIZATION

```
0 0.4
0 0.5
0 0.6
..
```

Using the utility function f from above, we can compute the error each parameter pair produces when used to predict values on the test data set. Note that this can take a while to run and is a perfect candidate to use peach to perform the search across multiple cores.

```
q)alr .ml.imin e:(f[1000] .ml.lincostgrad[;Y;X] .ml.enet .) peach alr
50 0.7
```

As we've seen, ordinary least squares regression based on the normal equations can be performed using q's native lsq operator or our own .ml.normeq. For a more nuanced approach to regression, we must turn to gradient descent, which allows us to introduce regularization (both L1 and L2). These concepts take center stage in the next three chapter when we introduce logistic regression, neural networks and matrix factorization. Unlike the normal equations for least squares regression, there is no closed-form solution for logistic regression, neural networks or matrix factorization. Gradient descent becomes our workhorse and regularization becomes vital because a deep neural network can have so many coefficients that overfitting becomes the rule and not the exception.

# Chapter 10

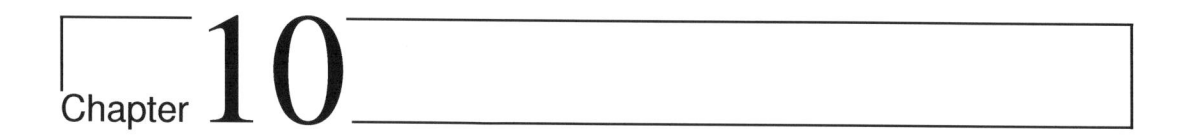

# Logistic Regression

> Logistic regression is based on this principle: it expresses the multiple linear regression equation in logarithmic terms (called the *logit*) and thus overcomes the problem of violating the assumption of linearity.
> — Andy Field *Discovering Statistics Using IBM SPSS Statistics*

Instead of modeling and predicting a continuous ordered value like wine quality, logistic regression is useful for predicting probabilities. Where linear regression predicts values along the full range of negative infinity to positive infinity, logistic regression predicts values between 0 and 1. If we round these probabilities to either 0 or 1, we can also use logistic regression to classify binary values. Let's start by using the Wisconsin Diagnosis Breast Cancer data set to see how logistic regression can be used to create a predictor of malignant vs. benign tumors.

## 10.1 Logistic Regression Example

We start by loading the Wisconsin Diagnosis Breast Cancer data set with the wdbc.q [383] library, converting the diagnosis feature into a boolean variable, selecting the first 11 features (10 independent features plus the target diagnosis feature) and splitting the data into training and test partitions.

```
q)\l funq.q
q)\l wdbc.q
```

[down]loading wisconsin diagnostic breast cancer data set
```
q)t:11#/:update "M"=diagnosis from wdbc.t
q)d:.ut.part[`train`test!3 1;0N?] "f"$t
```

We then assign the train and test partitions to global variables matching our X, Y, y and Xt, Y, yt naming conventions.

```
q)y:first get first `Y`X set' 0 1 cut value flip d`train
q)yt:first get first `Yt`Xt set' 0 1 cut value flip d`test
```

Z-scoring the data speeds convergence.

```
q)zsf:.ml.zscoref each X
q)X:zsf @' X
q)Xt:zsf @' Xt
```

Now we can initialize our THETA weight matrix, perform unregularized logistic regression to train the weights and compute the accuracy against the test data set.

```
q)THETA:enlist theta:(1+count X)#0f
q)THETA:1#.fmincg.fmincg[5;.ml.logcostgrad[();Y;X];THETA 0]
q)avg yt=first "i"$.ml.plog[Xt] THETA
0.9440559
```

Let's slow down and dissect these steps on at a time.

## 10.2 Wisconsin Diagnosis Breast Cancer Data Set

The Wisconsin Diagnosis Breast Cancer data set provides a diagnosis with the two characters "M" and "B" representing malignant and benign tumors respectively. To perform logistic regression, we must transform the diagnosis values from these characters to the numeric values 1 and 0. By comparing the values to the letter "M", we define 1 as malignant and 0 as benign.

```
q)show t:update "M"=diagnosis from wdbc.t
diagnosis radius_mean texture_mean perimeter_mean area_mean smoothness_me..
-----------------------------------------------------------------------------..
1         17.99       10.38        122.8          1001      0.1184        ..
1         20.57       17.77        132.9          1326      0.08474       ..
1         19.69       21.25        130            1203      0.1096        ..
1         11.42       20.38        77.58          386.1     0.1425        ..
```

## 10.2. WISCONSIN DIAGNOSIS BREAST CANCER DATA SET 219

```
1        20.29      14.34      135.1      1297       0.1003     ..
..
```

The data set provides the mean, standard error and worst value for 10 different measurements. For simplicity, we'll limit our analysis to just the *mean* values of each measurement.

```
q)4 cut cols t:11#/:t
`diagnosis`radius_mean`texture_mean`perimeter_mean
`area_mean`smoothness_mean`compactness_mean`concavity_mean
`concave_points_mean`symmetry_mean`fractal_dimension_mean
```

We can now set the random number generator seed to ensure our results are reproducible, split the data into train and test partitions and extract the X, Y, Xt and Yt matrices as well as y and yt diagnosis vectors. To comply with q matrix operator requirements, we also cast all the values to floating-point numbers.

```
q)\S -314159
q)d:.ut.part[`train`test!3 1;0N?] "f"$t
q)y:first get first `Y`X set' 0 1 cut value flip d`train
q)yt:first get first `Yt`Xt set' 0 1 cut value flip d`test
```

Logistic regression is similar to linear regression in that it determines coefficients for each feature (including a bias term) that are then used to scale each observation before being aggregated.

We start by initialize all our THETA coefficients to zero. By convention, the lowercase theta is a simple vector while the upper case THETA is a 1 x N matrix—each representation has its use.

```
q)show THETA:enlist theta:(1+count X)#0f
0 0 0 0 0 0 0 0 0 0
```

To make predictions, logistic regression begins like linear regression. We add a row of ones to the X matrix for the bias term and matrix multiply the result with THETA.

```
q).ml.plin[X] THETA
0 0 0 0 0 0 0 0 0 0 0 0 0 0 0 0 0 0 0 0 0 0 0 0 0 0 0 0 0 0 0 0 0 0 0 0 0 0..
```

## 10.3 Sigmoid

Logistic regression, however, adds one extra step. It passes these values through a specifically designed function that compresses them such that they lie between 0 and 1. This function, officially named the logistic function, is commonly referred to as the sigmoid function (Equation 10.1 [220]) because it is the archetype of many S-shaped functions.

$$S(x) = \frac{1}{1 + e^{-x}}$$

Equation 10.1: Sigmoid

**.ml.sigmoid**

```
sigmoid:1f%1f+exp neg::                              / sigmoid
```

We can see in Example 10.1 [220] how the values ranging between -5 and 5 are transformed into an S shape with values approaching 0 and 1.

**Example 10.1** Sigmoid
```
q).ut.plt .ml.sigmoid .ut.nseq[10;-5;5]
1   | "              + ++"
0.8|  "           +     "
   |  "         +       "
0.6|  "                 "
   |  "       +         "
0.4|  "                 "
   |  "                 "
0.2|  "     +           "
   |  "   +             "
0   | "++ +             "
```

Applying this function to the results of our analysis produces values that we can interpret as a probability of being malignant. With no information, we have guessed with 50% probability that each observation is malignant.

```
q).ml.sigmoid .ml.plin[X] THETA
0.5 0.5 0.5 0.5 0.5 0.5 0.5 0.5 0.5 0.5 0.5 0.5 0.5 0.5 0.5 0.5 0.5 0..
```

## 10.4. LOG-LOSS COST

These two operations are combined in the .ml.plog predict-logistic-regression function.

**.ml.plog**

```
/ logistic regression predict
plog:sigmoid plin::
```

## 10.4 Log-Loss Cost

Unlike linear regression, which used the sum of squared errors to measure prediction performance for continuous numbers that can take any value, logistic regression uses the log-loss statistic (Equation 10.2 [221]) to rate the quality of fit for binary values that can be either 0 or 1.

$$\text{LogLoss}(y, p) = -(y \log(p) + (1 - y) \log(1 - p))$$

Equation 10.2: Log-Loss

The log-loss function encodes an `if` statement with multiplication and addition. The true value y can only take on values 0 and 1. If the true value is 1, only the first half of the function will evaluate to a non-zero value. If, on the other hand, the true value is 0, the second half will return a non-zero value. The log of values between 0 and 1 are negative, so the final step in computing the log-loss function is to negate the computation.

To prevent the function from taking the log of 0, which would result in the value negative infinity and cause numeric instability, .ml.logloss floors the predicted value p and 1-p at 1e-15. This also ensures that when the true and predicted values are exactly equal, the log-loss is 0.

**.ml.logloss**

```
/ given true (y) and (p)redicted values return the log loss
logloss:{[y;p]neg (y*log 1e-15|p)+(1f-y)*log 1e-15|1f-p}
```

Minimizing the log-loss is similar to maximizing the accuracy of a model except that the log-loss takes into account the uncertainty of the prediction. As can be seen in Example 10.2 [222], the loss slowly increases for predictions close to the true value, but then grows exponentially as more conviction is placed on a wrong prediction.

### Example 10.2 Log-Loss

```
q).ut.plt .ml.logloss[1f] -1_.ut.nseq[100;1f;0f]
5|  "                   +"
4|  "                    "
 |  "                   +"
3|  "                   +"
 |  "                  ++"
2|  "                  ++ "
 |  "                 +++ "
1|  "                 +++  "
 |  "            ++++++    "
0|  "++++++++              "
```

## 10.5 Logistic Regression Cost

Matching linear regression, we've also implemented the logistic-regression cost function (Equation 10.3 [222]) with the option of supplying regularization functions to activate L1 and L2 regularization.

$$J(\theta) = \frac{1}{m}\left[\sum_{i=1}^{m} \text{LogLoss}(y^{(i)}, h_\theta(x^{(i)}))\right] + \frac{\lambda_1}{m}\sum_{j=1}^{n}|\theta_j| + \frac{\lambda_2}{2m}\sum_{j=1}^{n}\theta_j^2$$

where: $h_\theta(x^{(i)}) = S(\theta^{(i)} x^{(i)})$ (the predicted value of item $i$)

$m$ = number of samples

$n$ = number of features

Equation 10.3: Regularized Logistic Regression Cost

The function accepts four parameters: the regularization function rf (or a list of regularization functions), and the Y, X and THETA matrices. The regularized logistic-regressions cost function is implemented in .ml.logcost.

**.ml.logcost**

```
/ logistic regression cost
logcost:{[rf;Y;X;THETA]
  J:(1f%m:count X 0)*revo[sum] logloss[Y] plog[X;THETA];    / cost
  if[count rf,:();THETA[;0]:0f; J+:sum rf[;m][;0][;THETA]]; / regularization
  J}
```

After computing the predicted values with the provided Y and THETA matrices, the logistic-regression cost function `.ml.logcost` applies the `.ml.logloss` log-loss cost function to compute the error of each observation. The function then averages each of the errors before proceeding to apply regularization on the second line.

```
q).ml.logcost[();Y;X] THETA
0.6931472
```

To ensure the cost of all features are comparable and our fit is not dominated by a single feature, we normalize the training and testing data.

```
q)zsf:.ml.zscoref each X
q)X:zsf @' X
q)Xt:zsf @' Xt
```

## 10.6 Logistic Regression Gradient

We then define a regularized gradient function (Equation 10.4 [223]) to use with gradient descent to improve our THETA coefficients.

$$G(\theta_j) = \frac{\partial J(\theta)}{\partial \theta_j} = \frac{1}{m}\left(h_\theta(x^{(i)}) - y^{(i)}\right)x_j^{(i)} + \frac{\lambda_1}{m}\text{sign}(\theta_j) + \frac{\lambda_2}{m}\theta_j$$

where: $h_\theta(x^{(i)}) = S(\theta^{(i)} x^{(i)})$ (the predicted value of item $i$)

$m$ = number of samples

$n$ = number of features

Equation 10.4: Regularized Logistic Regression Gradient

Notice how similar the gradient for logistic regression is to linear regression's gradient—the fitted error multiplied by the observed data. This "coincidence" is a result of the specific pairing of the sigmoid function, which has an exponent, and the log-loss cost function, which has a logarithm. They cancel each other out and therefore simplify the gradient.

The syntax should start to be familiar. The first line of the `.ml.loggrad` logistic-gradient function implements the unregularized gradient, while the last line adds the regularization.

**.ml.loggrad**

```
/ logistic regression gradient
loggrad:{[rf;Y;X;THETA]
  G:(1f%m:count X 0)*mmt[sigmoid[mm[THETA;X]]-Y] X:prepend[1f] X; / gradient
  if[count rf,:();THETA[;0]:0f; G+:sum rf[;m][;1][;THETA]]; / regularization
  G}
```

After 10,000 iterations, the cost has come down considerably.

```
q).ml.logcost[();Y;X] 10000 .ml.gd[.1f;.ml.loggrad[();Y;X]]/ THETA
0.1397237
```

We can even use .fmincg.fmincg for a dynamic learning rate if we first define a function .ml.logcostgrad that returns both the regularized cost and gradient.

### .ml.logcostgrad

```
logcostgrad:{[rf;Y;X;theta]
  THETA:(count Y;0N)#theta; X:prepend[1f] X; / unroll theta
  J:(1f%m:count X 0)*revo[sum] logloss[Y] P:sigmoid mm[THETA] X; / cost
  G:(1f%m)*mmt[P-Y] X;                                          / gradient
  if[count rf,:();THETA[;0]:0f;JG:rf[;m][;;THETA];J+:sum JG@'0;G+:sum JG@'1];
  (J;raze G)}
```

Although the .ml.logcostgrad function is very similar to the linear-regression-cost-and-gradient function .ml.lincostgrad, there are two key differences. The first is the inclusion of the .ml.sigmoid function to compress the predicted values into the range [0,1]. The second difference is the use of the .ml.logloss function instead of the sum of squared errors. Handling of regularization is identical in both functions.

## 10.7 Optimal Regularization

Defining a utility function to test different regularization parameters against the test data allows us to pick the best value.

```
q)f:.ml.logcost[();Yt;Xt]1#.fmincg.fmincg[;;THETA 0]::
```

We now generate a sequence of L2 coefficients between 0 and .05.

```
q)show l2:.ut.sseq[.005;0;.05]
0 0.005 0.01 0.015 0.02 0.025 0.03 0.035 0.04 0.045 0.05
```

## 10.7. OPTIMAL REGULARIZATION

As expected, the training error rises. We hope, however, to find a set of parameters that cause the test error to fall.

```
q)e:(f[1000] .ml.logcostgrad[;Y;X] .ml.l2@) each l2
Iteration 1000 | cost: 0.135389
Iteration 1000 | cost: 0.1370365
Iteration 1000 | cost: 0.1377742
Iteration 1000 | cost: 0.138272
Iteration 1000 | cost: 0.1386478
Iteration 1000 | cost: 0.1389498
Iteration 1000 | cost: 0.1392032
Iteration 1000 | cost: 0.1394226
Iteration 1000 | cost: 0.1396173
Iteration 1000 | cost: 0.1397933
Iteration 1000 | cost: 0.1399549
```

A visual inspection in Example 10.3 [225] shows that we found the correct range of L2 regularization parameters.

**Example 10.3** Optimal Logistic Regression Regularization

```
q).ut.plt e
0.118|  "                              "
0.117|  "+                             "
     |  "                              "
0.116|  "                              "
0.115|  "                              "
     |  "                              "
0.114|  "                              "
     |  "                              "
0.113|  " +           + + + ++"
0.112|  "    + + + +              "
```

The best L2 regularization parameter for this normalized data set is 0.015.

```
q).ml.imin l2!e
0.015
```

Using this value for our regression produces our optimal THETA coefficients.

```
q)THETA:1#.fmincg.fmincg[1000;.ml.logcostgrad[.ml.l2[.015];Y;X];THETA 0]
Iteration 1000 | cost: 0.138272
```

The predicted values from logistic regression are probabilities that vary between zero and one.

```
q).ut.rnd[.01] p:first .ml.plog[Xt] THETA
1 0.02 0 0 0.96 0.07 0.01 0 1 0.79 0 0.06 0.69 0.02 0.72 0 0 0.65 1 1 0 0..
```

## 10.8 Receiver Operating Characteristic

Although the logistic regression model returned probabilities between 0 and 1, the actual class labels only indicate a binary choice without uncertainty: benign or malignant. If we are forced to choose a value, our best option would be to round the predicted values to the nearest integer.

```
q)"i"$p
1 0 0 0 1 0 0 0 1 1 0 0 1 0 1 0 0 1 1 1 0 0 1 0 0 0 0 1 0 1 0 1 1 0 1 1 1..
```

Comparing these values with the true diagnosis reveals a close match.

```
q)yt
1 0 0 0 1 0 0 0 1 1 0 0 0 0 0 0 0 1 1 1 0 0 1 0 0 0 0 1 0 1 0 1 1 0 1 1 1..
```

How good is it? Computing the accuracy gives us the impression that we've done quite well.

```
q)avg yt="i"$p
0.951049
```

A glance at the confusion matrix in Example 10.4 [226] gives us a more granular picture.

**Example 10.4** Logistic Regression Binary Classification Confusion Matrix

```
q).ut.totals[`TOTAL] .ml.cm . "i"$(yt;p)
y| 0  1  TOTAL
-| -----------
0| 89 5  94
1| 2  47 49
 | 91 52 143
```

Out of 94 benign tumors, we incorrectly labeled 5 of them as malignant. That is embarrassing, but not likely to cause us to lose our job. On the other hand, there

## 10.8. RECEIVER OPERATING CHARACTERISTIC

were 2 out of 49 malignant tumors that we incorrectly identified as benign. Those patients will surely be back to question our methods of using machine learning to diagnose cancer.

If instead of rounding the probabilities to 0 and 1, we compare them with the actual rates of malignancy, we should hope for a high degree of correlation. In other words, we might accept being wrong when the model predicts a value close to .5, but we expect to be correct when the model indicates either a very low or high probability. It would be extra embarrassing if we told the client that we were 99% confident that the tumor was benign, when it turns out to be malignant. That same conversation would have been remembered differently if we indicated that we were only 51% confident that the tumor was benign, but that there was still a 49% chance that it could be malignant. If calculating the accuracy of our predictor gave us a black and white picture, and the confusion matrix gave us a few shades of gray, then the receiver operating characteristic (ROC) curve gives us a color picture.

The ROC curve is a visual representation of how capable a model is in distinguishing the negatives from the positives, the 0s from the 1s and the benign from the malignant. Instead of picking a single threshold (.5) to divide the outcomes, the ROC curve picks multiple thresholds and computes the true positive rate (TPR) and false positive rate (FPR) at each threshold. The TPR statistic, which was introduced in the section called "Recall" [123], is also knows as the recall, while the FPR statistic is referred to as the fallout.

**.ml.fallout**

```
fallout:fpr:{[tp;tn;fp;fn]fp%fp+tn}                    / false positive rate
```

It is defined as the percentage of all negative values that were—in fact—predicted as positive. Fallout is computed by dividing the number of false positives by the total number of *actual* negatives (false positives plus true negatives).

Assume, for example, that we use a threshold of .1 instead of .5 when deciding if a tumor was benign or malignant. Example 10.5 [228] shows that the false positives are higher, but the false negatives are lower.

And yet, the TPR is quite high and the FPR is low.

```
q)`.ml.tpr`.ml.fpr  .\: .ml.tptnfpfn . "i"$(yt;.1<p)
0.9795918 0.1276596
```

At the opposite extreme, we can use a threshold of .9 and see in Example 10.6 [228] that the false positives have dropped to zero, but the false negatives are higher.

Even though the TPR dropped a bit, it is still close to 1 and the FPR dropped to 0.

**Example 10.5** Low Threshold Binary Classification Confusion Matrix

```
q).ut.totals[`TOTAL] .ml.cm . "i"$(yt;.1<p)
y| 0  1  TOTAL
-| -----------
0| 82 12 94
1| 1  48 49
 | 83 60 143
```

**Example 10.6** High Threshold Binary Classification Confusion Matrix

```
q).ut.totals[`TOTAL] .ml.cm . "i"$(yt;.9<p)
y| 0   1  TOTAL
-| ------------
0| 94  0  94
1| 6   43 49
 | 100 43 143
```

```
q)`.ml.tpr`.ml.fpr .\: .ml.tptnfpfn . "i"$(yt;.9<p)
0.877551 0
```

The .ml.roc receiver-operating-characteristic function accepts the actual y labels and the predicted p values and returns three vectors: the false positive rate, the true positive rate, and the sorted p values, which correspond to the thresholds used to compute the false and true positive rates.

**.ml.roc**

```
/ receiver operating characteristic
roc:{[y;p]
  r:(til[count s]-s;s:0f,sums y i:idesc p);  / (fp;tp)
  r:(r%last each r),enlist 0w,p i;           / (fpr;tpr;threshold)
  r:r@\:where reverse differ reverse r 2;    / filter duplicate thresholds
  r}
```

Instead of using the .ml.tptnfpfn function for each and every threshold p, the .ml.roc uses vector operators to efficiently compute the false and true positive ratios directly. The function starts by computing the running sum of the false and true positive counts. The second line of the function converts these to ratios by dividing by the total number of false and true positives and appends the sorted

## 10.8. RECEIVER OPERATING CHARACTERISTIC

threshold list. An additional element is added to the front of each vector corresponding to a threshold of 0w and false and true positive rates of 0. The final line of the function removes duplicate thresholds. By plotting the false positive rates against the true positive rates, we can obtain an intuition about how well the model can separate the classes.

**Example 10.7** Discriminating Receiver Operating Characteristic
```
q).ut.plt 2# .ml.roc . (yt;p)
1.2| "                               "
1   | "   +++++++++++++++++"
    | "+++                          "
0.8| "+                             "
0.6| "+                             "
    | "+                            "
0.4| "+                             "
    | "+                            "
0.2| "+                             "
0   | "+                            "
```

Example 10.7 [229] starts at the origin and rises quickly before leveling off. This is great result. By using the ? operator to randomize the predicted values p, Example 10.8 [229] shows how a model with no predictive power generates a diagonal line starting from the origin.

**Example 10.8** Non-discriminating Receiver Operating Characteristic
```
q).ut.plt 2# .ml.roc . (yt;0N?p)
1.2| "                               "
1   | "                     ++"
    | "                  +++  "
0.8| "                 +++    "
0.6| "               +        "
    | "            +++        "
0.4| "       +++++++          "
    | "    ++                 "
0.2| " +++                    "
0   | "+++                    "
```

Though this rarely happens in practice, Example 10.9 [230] shows a model that consistently predicts the wrong value and therefore has an ROC curve below the diagonal.

**Example 10.9** Negative Discriminating Receiver Operating Characteristic

```
q).ut.plt 2# .ml.roc . (yt;1f-p)
1.2| "                      "
1  | "                     +"
   | "                     +"
0.8| "                     +"
0.6| "                     +"
   | "                     +"
0.4| "                     +"
   | "                     +"
0.2| "                     +"
0  | "+++++++++++++++++++++"
```

## 10.9 Area Under the Curve

Although the ROC curve satisfies our need for a visual representation of the model, the curve itself is often summarized by a single value—the area under the curve (AUC). To compute the area under the curve, we sum the area between (and below) each pair of data points. We don't know the exact shape of the curve between the points, but by assuming that points are connected with a straight line, the area between (and below) them can be represented by a trapezoid. The AUC can then be computed by summing the area of each trapezoid.

**.ml.auc**

```
auc:{[x;y] .5*sum (x-prev x)*y+prev y} / area under the curve
```

As the number of points on the chart increases, the quality of the calculation improves and our linear approximation of the curve becomes more precise.

```
q).ml.auc . 2# .ml.roc . (yt;p)
0.9906644
```

The AUC for our tumor model is very close to 1—the maximum possible value. Although the lowest AUC we expect to see in the wild is approximately .5, it is possible to engineer values close to 0 in the lab.

```
q).ml.auc . 2# .ml.roc . (yt;1f-p)
0.009335649
```

## 10.10 Multi-Class Classification

Classifying a tumor as either benign or malignant is called binary classification. There are only two categories. Logistic regression will always return a value between 0 and 1—so it doesn't seem obvious how we can use it to classify a data set into one of more than two categories. We will see in the next chapter how neural networks are built from the ground up to accomplish multi-class (or even multi-label) classification. But hope is not lost with logistic regression.

The MNIST handwritten-digit data set is a great example of multi-class classification. Given an image, we need to classify it as one of 10 numeric digits. This can be broken down into 10 different binary classification problems—one for each digit. We will use the MNIST training data to train 10 different models. Each model will be specialized to answer a different question: Does the image represent a 0, 1, 2, ...? Once training is complete, we will have 10 sets of THETA coefficients, which can then be used to provide a probability that each image is—in fact—a specific digit. We will then classify the image as being the digit assigned the highest probability of being a match for the image. Building multiple binary classification models and then classifying new observations with the class associated with the highest probability is called a one-vs.-all (or one-vs.-rest) classifier.

## 10.11 One-vs.-All Classifier

We begin by loading the MNIST handwritten-digit data set.

```
q)\l mnist.q
[down]loading handwritten-digit data set
```

The full data set has 60,000 observations. The next three lines copy the data from the `mnist` namespace into the global namespace, limit the training set to only 1,000 observations and normalize the X and Xt values to be between 0 and 1.

```
q)`X`Xt`Y`y`yt set' mnist`X`Xt`Y`y`yt;
q)X:1000#'X;Y:1000#'Y;y:1000#y;
q)X%:255f;Xt%:255f
```

Mirroring Section 5.5 [98], we plot a few samples in Example 10.10 [232].

### Example 10.10 MNIST Digits

```
q)plt:value .ut.plot[28;14;.ut.c10;avg] .ut.hmap flip 28 cut
q)-1 (,'/) plt each X @\:/: 2 3;
```

```
                    .=                          -=+.
      :=           +#.                         =@@@-
     %x           =@+                          .+@@x
    =@+           -%@.                         -%@%:
    x@-     ---=+x#@@-                         .x@%=
-#%###%xx=:-.    -@@                           :@@@:
                 x@:                           +@@%:
                 x@-                           :@@@-
                 x@=                           -@@@-
                 +@x                           .%@%
```

## 10.12 Fitting One vs. All

The one-vs.-all model fitting algorithm has been implemented in .ml.fova.

**.ml.fova**

```
/ given binary classification fitting (f)unction, fit a one-vs.-all model
/ against Y for each unique (lbls)
fova:{[f;Y;lbls] (f "f"$Y=) peach lbls}
```

It accepts a binary classification fitting function, a matrix of the multi-class Y labels that correspond to the X matrix and a unique list of Y labels we want models generated for. The function iterates across each of the labels and fits a new binary classification model to a matrix whose values are 0 in all places except where the labels match.

The Y matrix has integer values ranging from 0 through 9—corresponding to each of the handwritten digits.

```
q)distinct Y 0
5 0 4 1 9 2 3 6 7 8i
```

We therefore define our unique list of labels accordingly.

## 10.12. FITTING ONE VS. ALL 233

```
q)lbls:"i"$til 10
```

If our data set had contained the 26 letters of the alphabet, we would have to map each the letters to a numeric equivalent. You might consider this mapping obvious, but would the letters map to values starting from 0 through 25 or would we map them to the values 1 through 26? Things get less obvious when dealing with images that have no inherent ordering such as Chinese and Japanese characters (unless we limit ourselves to the characters for the numeric digits 0 through 9). We don't have this debate with the MNIST data set because the labels provided in the Y matrix are the exact values we need.

We now turn our attention to generating the binary classification fitting function. Following the approach we took for simple logistic regression, we will use the `.fmincg.fmincg` minimization routine with the `.ml.logcostgrad` logistic-regression-cost-gradient function. We will initialize the theta vector to be all zeros and can introduce L2 regularization.

```
q)rf:.ml.l2[1]
q)theta:(1+count X)#0f
q)f:first .fmincg.fmincg[5;;theta] .ml.logcostgrad[rf;;X]@
```

> **:: vs. @**
>
> This is one case where we need to use @ instead of :: to create our projection. `.ml.logcostgrad` takes a total of four arguments. Our projection has specified rf and X, the `.ml.fova` function will specify Y and `.fmincg.fmincg` will specify theta. Using @ for our projection causes `.ml.logcostgrad` to be passed along to `.fmincg.fmincg` as we desire. Had we used :: instead, our projection would not be evaluated until *both* the remaining arguments of `.ml.logcostgrad` had been supplied.

Returning to our one-vs.-all analysis, we now generate 10 different theta vectors—each one specialized at identifying a single handwritten digit.

```
q)THETA:.ml.fova[f;Y;lbls]
Iteration  5 | cost: 0.06259449
Iteration  5 | cost: 0.102219
Iteration  5 | cost: 0.05938054
Iteration  5 | cost: 0.1364373
Iteration  5 | cost: 0.0846071
Iteration  5 | cost: 0.07186039
```

```
Iteration 5 | cost: 0.1658782
Iteration 5 | cost: 0.06187736
Iteration 5 | cost: 0.1736208
Iteration 5 | cost: 0.1659348
```

## 10.13 Predicting One vs. All

Now that we've built our model, we can use the THETA matrix to classify the test data set Xt and compare the results with the test labels yt.

```
q).ut.rnd[.1] .ml.plog[Xt;THETA]
0 0   0   1 0   0 0   0   0   0   1   0 0   1 0 0   0   0   0   0   0 0..
0 0   1   0 0   1 0   0   0   0   0   0 0   0 1 0   0   0   0   0   0 0..
0 0.5 0.1 0 0.2 0 0   0   0.3 0   0.1 0 0   0 0 0   0   0   0   0   0 0..
0 0   0   0 0   0 0   0   0   0   0.1 0 0   0 0 0.2 0   0.1 0   0   0 0..
0 0   0   0 1   0 0.8 0   0   0   0   0 0.4 0 0 0   0.2 0   0.9 0   0 0..
0 0.4 0   0 0   0 0   0   0   0   0.1 0 0   0 0 0.4 0   0   0.1 0   0 0..
0 0.4 0   0 0   0 0   0   0   0   0   0 0   0 0 0   0   0   0   0   0 0..
1 0   0   0 0   0 0   0   0   0.6 0   0 0   0 0 0   0.1 1   0   0   0.4 0..
0 0   0   0 0   0 0   0   0   0   0   0 0   0 0 0   0   0   0   0   0 0..
0 0   0   0 0   0 0.1 0.2 0   0.1 0   0 0.6 0 0 0   0.1 0   0   0.4 0.2 0..
```

Each column of the above matrix corresponds to the probabilities that the observed digit is represented by each of the fitted labels. We can see that the first column has all small numbers except for the row representing 7. Moving to the right, we can assume the next few numbers are 2, 1, 0, 4 and 1. This can be performed programatically as well.

```
q)lbls .ml.imax .ml.plog[Xt;THETA]
7 2 1 0 4 1 4 9 2 7 0 2 9 0 1 5 4 7 5 4 7 6 4 5 4 0 7 4 0 1 3 1 3 4 7 2 7..
```

It may seem superfluous to index back into lbls because the values will be identical, but it would be required if we had modeled anything other than the first 10 digits. Let's see how well we did.

```
q)yt
7 2 1 0 4 1 4 9 5 9 0 6 9 0 1 5 9 7 3 4 9 6 6 5 4 0 7 4 0 1 3 1 3 4 7 2 7..
```

Pretty good—if I do say so myself! We can now compute the accuracy of our model,

## 10.13. PREDICTING ONE VS. ALL

```
q)avg yt=p:lbls .ml.imax .ml.plog[Xt] THETA
0.8107
```

and generate the confusion matrix as seen in Example 10.11 [235].

**Example 10.11** Logistic Regression One-vs.-All Confusion Matrix

```
q).ut.totals[`TOTAL] .ml.cm[yt;p]
y| 0    1    2    3   4   5   6   7    8   9   TOTAL
-| ---------------------------------------------------
0| 913  0    35   0   0   7   9   5    9   2   980
1| 0    1064 39   2   0   6   3   1    20  0   1135
2| 8    22   890  9   10  3   21  26   39  4   1032
3| 7    1    54   719 1   169 1   24   24  10  1010
4| 0    5    14   3   805 3   24  3    8   117 982
5| 14   9    21   48  35  609 9   30   79  38  892
6| 11   4    99   1   20  33  780 0    10  0   958
7| 2    17   36   3   13  5   1   927  2   22  1028
8| 4    13   35   22  11  73  9   33   690 84  974
9| 3    8    29   23  99  15  1   115  6   710 1009
 | 962  1143 1252 830 994 923 858 1164 887 987 10000
```

Understandably, it seems that 4 and 9 are the most often misclassified digits. Example 10.12 [236] shows two cases where we incorrectly classified an image as a 4.

Using multiple logistic binary classification models assumes each of our classes can be linearly separated. As we will see in Chapter 11 [237], we can improve our model by allowing for non-linear relationships between features. Additionally, each model of the one-vs.-all algorithm suffers from unequal distributions between positive and negative observations. Although we may have had an equal number of observations for each digit, each model sees 90% of the observations as 0s while only 10% are 1s. The problem worsens as the number of distinct classes increases. As we will see, using a neural network can simultaneously classify each of the observations. Logistic regression used many techniques such as regularization, the sigmoid function and one-vs.-all classification that we will use again with neural networks. The difference, however, will be the possibility of higher accuracy by allowing more flexibility in the relationship between features.

**Example 10.12** Incorrectly Classified MNIST Digits

```
q)-1 (,'/) plt each Xt@\:/:2#where not[yt=p]&p=4;


                                                 -+.
                                                 @#.
                  :x#%@%#.                       x@-
                :@@=.     =:.x+                  :@#              ...-.
                +@x         .@@+                 x@:           x@#==%x
                @@.          .@@#                x@:         %%.      x@:
                =@#:--:=#@@@.                    %@-    x@:         .%x
                 .=xx+=:-@@=                    .#@%x@@-..:x@+
                       =@@                        -+@@@#x:
                       .@@+                        -#@x+.
                       +@%
                       ::.
```

# Chapter 11

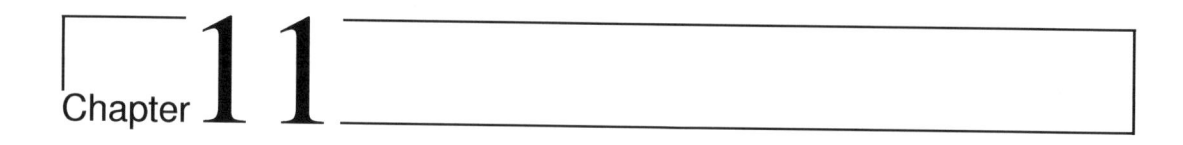

# Neural Networks

> A single neuron in the brain is an incredibly complex machine that even today we don't understand. A single "neuron" in a neural network is an incredibly simple mathematical function that captures a minuscule fraction of the complexity of a biological neuron.
>
> — Andrew Ng *Wired*

Artificial neural networks are modeled after their biological counterparts. Where biological neurons accept multiple signals on their dendrites, process the message in their nucleus and pass a single signal along their axons, an artificial neural networks accepts multiple values on each perceptron, combines each signal with pre-specified weights and then *squashes* (or activates) the resulting signal to behave like an on/off switch. As Andrew Ng points out, the biological neuron is a far more complex structure than the artificial neuron. By creating complex networks of artificial neurons, however, we can still achieve amazing computational feats.

## 11.1 Perceptron

Neural networks began as an attempt at reproducing the inner workings of the brain—an interconnected mesh of neurons. To create this mesh, scientists assumed a linear relationship between features that would generate a series of on/off values reflecting the activation of neurons. Passing these on/off values through another mesh would in-turn generate another series of on/off values. Passing the initial signal through enough layers could, in principle, replicate the anatomical process of a brain.

Frank Rosenblatt made the first attempt at creating a model of an anatomical neuron. His "perceptron" was a physical machine that combined photocell observations with learned weights. Modern perceptrons are computer programs that produce a linear combination of feature values and a bias term that are then passed through an activation function to produce a binary value. This is referred to as a binary linear classifier because it can only classify features that lie strictly on either side of a line (in two dimensions) or a hyperplane (in multiple dimensions). Figure 11.1 [238] demonstrates a perceptron with multiple inputs and the Heaviside activation function.

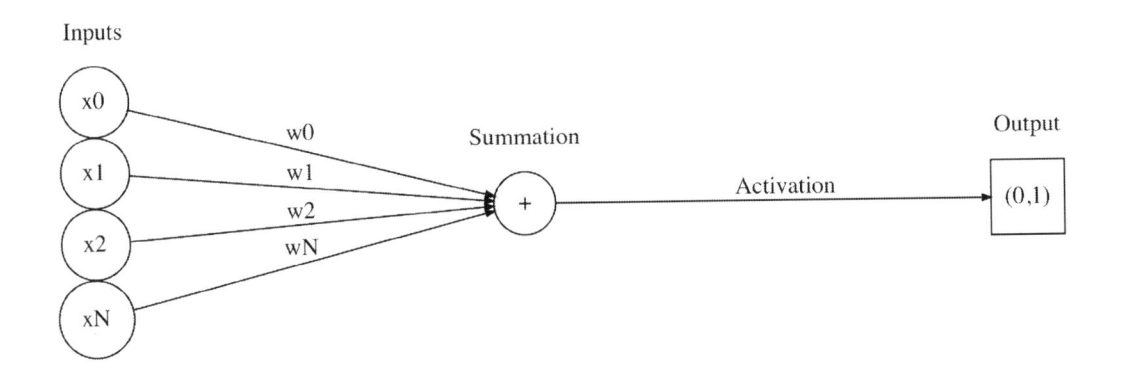

Figure 11.1: Perceptron with Heaviside Activation

The original perceptron implementation used the Heaviside step function (Equation 11.1 [238]), which returns 0 for all values less than 0, and 1 for all values greater or equal to 0.

$$\mathcal{H}(x) = \begin{cases} 0 & \text{if } x < 0 \\ 1 & \text{if } x \geq 0 \end{cases}$$

Equation 11.1: Heaviside Step

## 11.2 Neural Network

Though an important first step, which led to many improvements, the basic perceptron has many deficiencies that have been improved upon in modern neural networks. Even if you combine multiple perceptrons model multiple dimensions, it is not possible to model any arbitrary function. The most commonly cited example is a single-layer perceptron's inability to model the exclusive-OR (XOR) function. Adding multiple layers solves this but training the weights for a multi-layer perceptron with a Heaviside step function is difficult due to the discontinuous jump from 0 to 1.

Using a continuous activation function like the `.ml.sigmoid` function allows us to train multi-layer networks by a process called backpropagation. This involves the use of the chain-rule to allocate the final error back through the network allowing each perceptron's coefficient to be adjusted based on its gradient. Similar to the Heaviside step function, the sigmoid function produces values that lie between 0 and 1. When used as the activation function for a neural network, however, the sigmoid function is preferable for two reasons. The first is the obvious fact that the function is differentiable. The second, and less obvious, reason is that the gradient is not constant. This enables it to model non-linear functions. According to the universal approximation theorem, any continuous function can be approximated for inputs within a specified range by a neural network with a single hidden layer. This was initially proven with the use of the sigmoid function, and it is here we begin.

A neural network with a single hidden layer is built with three layers of perceptrons. The first layer accepts the observed feature X values, and the final layer generates the classification Y values. Because the middle layer is never directly observed, it is often referred to as hidden. The field of Deep Learning is focused on the generation of neural networks with many hidden layers. The neural networks we will create have every perceptron in each layer connecting to each and every perceptron of the adjacent layers. This is not a requirement, but layers that have every perceptron connected are intuitively called "fully connected". It is easy to imagine each layer of a Deep Neural Network encoding specific abstractions that are re-combined to build higher-order concepts. This is a convenient intuitive model, but adds level of consciousness that does not exist.

There are three basic architectures of neural networks: feed-forward neural networks FFNNs, recurrent neural networks RNNs and convolutional neural networks CNNs. Deep Neural Networks DNNs are typically FFNNs with many layers. We will focus on FFNNs, which are so-named because activations flow through the network without backtracking—or revisiting—any nodes.

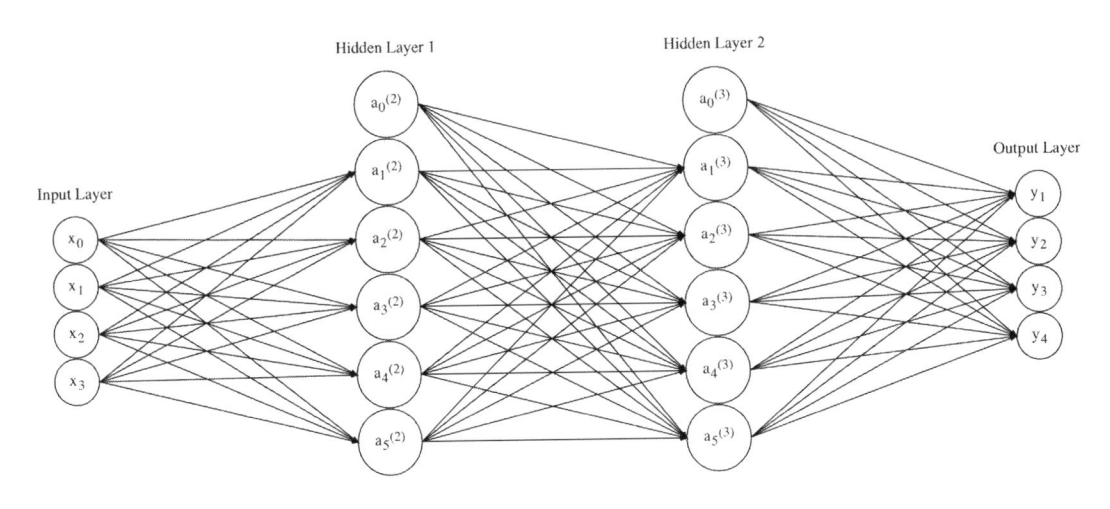

Figure 11.2: Neural Network with Two Hidden Layers

Figure 11.2 [240] is an example of a feed-forward neural network with two hidden layers. Data enters the front of the network, is transformed by the weights of each perceptron and exits the network as a final prediction. To train the model, the errors are backpropagated from the output layer back to the input layer. We will delve into the math behind this algorithm as well as demonstrate the different regularization and activation options that exist. But first, let's see a neural network in action.

## 11.3 Neural Network Example

This example loads the MNIST handwritten-digit data set first introduced in Section 5.5 [98]. We begin by loading the training and test data and limiting the training set to 1,000 (from the existing 60,000) training images to make our example run faster. We then normalize the values to be between 0 and 1 and generate the target Y matrix.

```
q)\l funq.q
q)\l mnist.q
[down]loading handwritten-digit data set
```

## 11.4. NEURAL NETWORK MATRICES INITIALIZATION

```
q)`X`Xt`y`yt set' mnist`X`Xt`y`yt;
q)X:1000#'X;y:1000#y;
q)X%:255f;Xt%:255f
q)Y:.ml.diag[(1+max y)#1f]@\:y
```

Next, we specify the neural network topology in the n variable, randomly initialize the perceptron weights in the theta variable and declare the rf regularization function to use L2 regularization.

```
q)n:"j"$.ut.nseq[2;count X;count Y];
q)theta:2 raze/ THETA:.ml.heu'[1+-1_n;1_n];
q)rf:.ml.l2[1];
```

To run the neural network we must specify the desired hidden layer's activation function (and its gradient) and the output layer's activation function along with the loss function.

```
q)show hgolf:`h`g`o`l!`.ml.sigmoid`.ml.dsigmoid`.ml.sigmoid`.ml.logloss
h| .ml.sigmoid
g| .ml.dsigmoid
o| .ml.sigmoid
l| .ml.logloss
```

Finally, we run 100 iterations of gradient descent and confirm that we've modeled the handwritten digits by checking the accuracy on the training data.

```
q)theta:first .fmincg.fmincg[100;.ml.nncostgrad[rf;n;hgolf;Y;X];theta]
Iteration 100 | cost: 0.4502275
q)avg y=p:.ml.imax .ml.pnn[hgolf;X] .ml.nncut[n] theta
0.999
```

Before explaining each of these pieces in detail, let's see how our model performs on the test data,

```
q)avg yt=p:.ml.imax .ml.pnn[hgolf;Xt] .ml.nncut[n] theta
0.8701
```

and view the confusion matrix in Example 11.1 [242].

## 11.4 Neural Network Matrices Initialization

Our example began by storing a 1,000-image subset of the 60,000 training images into the variable X. Each row of the X matrix contains 784 points corresponding to

> **Example 11.1** Neural Network Multinomial Classification Confusion Matrix

```
q).ut.totals[`TOTAL] .ml.cm[yt;"i"$p]
y| 0    1    2    3   4   5   6   7    8   9    TOTAL
-| ----------------------------------------------------
0| 947  0    6    1   0   3   13  4    3   3    980
1| 0    1096 4    1   0   2   3   1    27  1    1135
2| 9    11   901  14  12  1   22  19   33  10   1032
3| 8    2    43   787 3   93  5   16   38  15   1010
4| 2    2    8    4   847 0   17  3    12  87   982
5| 16   6    8    35  23  706 19  20   41  18   892
6| 12   5    22   0   11  26  875 1    5   1    958
7| 3    16   27   14  8   6   0   918  0   36   1028
8| 19   17   10   15  16  34  22  20   792 29   974
9| 10   5    5    27  45  10  1   66   8   832  1009
 | 1026 1160 1034 898 965 881 977 1068 959 1032 10000
```

each of the 28 x 28 image pixels. We then normalized the training and test data sets to have values between 0 and 1 by dividing the "pixel" values by 255.

```
q)\l funq.q
q)\l mnist.q
[down]loading handwritten-digit data set
q)`X`Xt`y`yt set' mnist`X`Xt`y`yt;
q)X:1000#'X;y:1000#y;
q)X%:255f;Xt%:255f
```

The y vector contains the values corresponding to the digit represented by the image.

```
q)y
5 0 4 1 9 2 1 3 1 4 3 5 3 6 1 7 2 8 6 9 4 0 9 1 1 2 4 3 2 7 3 8 6 9 0 5 6..
```

Our goal is to classify each image to the digit it represents. This is, therefore, a multi-class classification problem—not a regression problem. The results of our neural network cannot be a single number representing the numeric value of the image. The image 4 is not conceptually somewhere between the image 3 and 5. We need to model the problem such that the network produces 10 different values for each image. Each value represents the probability that the image represents each digit 0 through 9. To model this result, we generate a 10-row Y matrix such that each column only contains a single non-zero element indicating the digit rep-

## 11.5. NEURAL NETWORK TOPOLOGY 243

resented by the image. We can see that the first column has a 1 in the 6th row indicating the image represents a 5.

```
q)show Y:.ml.diag[(1+max y)#1f]@\:y
0 1 0 0 0 0 0 0 0 0 0 0 0 0 0 0 0 0 0 0 1 0 0 0 0 0 0 0 0 0 0 0 0 1 0 0..
0 0 0 1 0 0 1 0 1 0 0 0 0 0 1 0 0 0 0 0 0 0 0 1 1 0 0 0 0 0 0 0 0 0 0 0..
0 0 0 0 0 1 0 0 0 0 0 0 0 0 0 1 0 0 0 0 0 0 0 0 1 0 0 1 0 0 0 0 0 0 0 0..
0 0 0 0 0 0 1 0 0 1 0 1 0 0 0 0 0 0 0 0 0 0 0 0 0 1 0 0 1 0 0 0 0 0 0 0..
0 0 1 0 0 0 0 0 1 0 0 0 0 0 0 0 0 0 1 0 0 0 0 0 1 0 0 0 0 0 0 0 0 0 0 0..
1 0 0 0 0 0 0 0 0 0 0 1 0 0 0 0 0 0 0 0 0 0 0 0 0 0 0 0 0 0 0 0 0 0 1 0..
0 0 0 0 0 0 0 0 0 0 0 0 1 0 0 0 0 1 0 0 0 0 0 0 0 0 0 0 0 0 0 1 0 0 0 1..
0 0 0 0 0 0 0 0 0 0 0 0 0 0 0 1 0 0 0 0 0 0 0 0 0 0 0 0 0 1 0 0 0 0 0 0..
0 0 0 0 0 0 0 0 0 0 0 0 0 0 0 0 0 1 0 0 0 0 0 0 0 0 0 0 0 0 0 1 0 0 0 0..
0 0 0 0 1 0 0 0 0 0 0 0 0 0 0 0 0 0 0 0 1 0 0 1 0 0 0 0 0 0 0 0 1 0 0 0..
```

When we use the neural network to predict what digit the image represents, we will have values ranging from 0 through 1 in all the rows. Interpreting these values as probabilities, it will then be up to us to choose the digit that has the highest chances of being correct. Reviewing Example 11.1 [242], we can see that the images for the digit 3, which are distributed across the row associated with 3, are most often misinterpreted as 2, 5 and 8. We can also see that the images for the digit 4 are confused with the digit 9. Similarly, the images for the digit 7 are frequently confused with the digits 2 and 9. Even though we are asked to pick a single digit for each image, it is useful to see the distribution of probabilities so that we can also indicate the confidence of our prediction.

## 11.5 Neural Network Topology

With the data preparation complete, we turn our attention to the design of the topology of the neural network. The implementation of the .ml.nncostgrad neural-network-cost-gradient function permits us to pass a vector of dimensions as the second parameter. The first layer of this network must obviously have 784 nodes—one corresponding to each pixel of the image. Likewise, the number of nodes in the final layer are also fixed at 10—one for each distinct digit being trained.

Our example will demonstrate a neural network with a single hidden layer. Is there an optimal number of nodes that we should include in this layer? Making the hidden layer with only a few nodes throws away too much information too fast—high bias. Using too many nodes results in overfitting the training data—high variance. In reality, there is no rule specifying the optimal number of nodes per layer (or even the number of layers). This is something that must be determined by model validation. A good first attempt is to use the average number of nodes between the first and last layer.

```
q)0N!n:"j"$.ut.nseq[2;count X;count Y]
784 397 10
```

Supplying the network topology as a vector allows us to modify the number of hidden layers by adding more elements between the first and last layer. The implementation of .ml.nncostgrad is generic enough to handle any number of layers with any number of nodes per layer.

## 11.6  Neural Network Weight Initialization

We next initialize our THETA weight matrix—an art unto itself. If we initialized our THETA matrix with all values set to 0, each node of each layer, including the final layer, would become the same value—0. The learning adjustments for each node would also be the same. This same problem would occur had we used the value 1 for all weights. In fact the problem is endemic for all fully-connected networks. We must use randomly selected initial values to ensure we "break the symmetry".

The story does not end there, however. If the THETA values are too small or too large we end up with activation values that are very close to the tails of the activation function where the gradient asymptotically approaches 0. Because of these very small gradients, the learning rate in these regions becomes very slow. This is called the "vanishing-gradient problem" and is compounded for neural networks with many layers because the gradients are cumulatively multiplied. It is thus important to use values that are not too large in absolute value, and take into account the number of nodes at each layer.

To address these issues Xavier Glorot and Yoshua Bengio designed an algorithm[1] to initialize the THETA parameters in neural networks based on the average number of input and output nodes at each layer. The funq project provides one function .ml.glorotu for the uniformly distributed variate version,

### .ml.glorotu

---

[1] X. Glorot and Y. Bengio, "Understanding the difficulty of training deep feedforward neural networks," in *In Proceedings of the Thirteenth International Conference on Artificial Intelligence and Statistics*, 2010, pp. 249–256.

```
/ Xavier Glorot and Yoshua Bengio (2010) initialization
/ given the number of (i)nput and (o)utput nodes, initialize THETA matrix
glorotu:{[i;o]sqrt[6f%i+o]*-1f+i?/:o#2f}   / uniform
```

and another function .ml.glorotn for the normally distributed variate version.

**.ml.glorotn**

```
glorotn:{[i;o]rnorm'[o#i;0f;sqrt 2f%i+o]}   / normal
```

More recently, Kaiming He, Xiangyu Zhang, Shaoqing Ren and Jian Sun modified this algorithm[2] to only use the number of input nodes to scale the initial variates. Again, the funq project provides a function .ml.heu for the uniformly distributed variate version,

**.ml.heu**

```
/ Kaiming He, Xiangyu Zhang, Shaoqing Ren, Jian Sun (2015) initialization
/ given the number of (i)nput and (o)utput nodes, initialize THETA matrix
heu:{[i;o]sqrt[6f%i]*-1f+i?/:o#2f}    / uniform
```

and another function .ml.hen for the normally distributed variate version.

**.ml.hen**

```
hen:{[i;o]rnorm'[o#i;0f;sqrt 2f%i]}   / normal
```

Using the algorithm proposed by He et al., we initialize a list of THETA matrices and raze them into a simple vector that can be passed to .fmincg.fmincg. Note that we add one to the input layer because a bias term will be prepended at each layer of the network.

```
theta:2 raze/ THETA:.ml.heu'[1+-1_n;1_n];
```

## 11.7 Neural Network Cost

Let's recap the progress so far. We've loaded and normalized the data, built a target Y matrix, decided on the number of nodes in our neural network with a single

---

[2]K. He, X. Zhang, S. Ren, and J. Sun, "Delving Deep into Rectifiers: Surpassing Human-Level Performance on ImageNet Classification," in *2015 IEEE International Conference on Computer Vision (ICCV)*, 2015, pp. 1026–1034, doi 10.1109/ICCV.2015.123.

hidden layer and initialized the THETA matrix. Data preparation is now complete, and we can now implement a feed-forward network. We first introduce the neural-network cost function (Equation 11.2 [246]).

$$J(\Theta) = \frac{1}{m}\left[\sum_{i=1}^{m}\sum_{k=1}^{K}\text{Loss}(y_k^{(i)}, h_\Theta(x^{(i)})_k)\right] + \frac{\lambda_1}{m}\sum_{l=1}^{L-1}\sum_{i=1}^{s_l}\sum_{j=1}^{s_{l+1}}\left|\Theta_{ji}^{(l)}\right| + \frac{\lambda_2}{2m}\sum_{l=1}^{L-1}\sum_{i=1}^{s_l}\sum_{j=1}^{s_{l+1}}\left(\Theta_{ji}^{(l)}\right)^2$$

where $h_\Theta(x^{(i)})$ = the predicted value of item $i$
$m$ = number of samples
$K$ = the number nodes in the output layer
$L$ = the number of layers and
$s_l$ = the number of nodes in layer $l$

Equation 11.2: Neural Network Cost

This should be somewhat familiar. The algorithm is similar to the logistic regression algorithm, except that there are now multiple layers (which incurs an extra summation), the activation function is no longer required to be the sigmoid function and the loss function is not necessarily the logistic loss function. The .ml.nncost neural-network cost function implements this algorithm and introduces an extra parameter to allow these three choices to be specified.

**.ml.nncost**

```
/ (r)egularization (f)unction, holf: (h)idden (o)utput (l)oss functions
nncost:{[rf;holf;Y;X;THETA]
  J:(1f%m:count X 0)*revo[sum] holf[`l][Y] pnn[holf;X] THETA;  / cost
  if[count rf,:();THETA[;;0]:0f;J+:sum rf[;m][;0][;THETA]];   / regularization
  J}
```

In addition to the rf regularization function, Y, X and THETA matrices, the function also accepts a variable holf, which controls the activation of the hidden and output layers as well as the final loss function. The .ml.nncost function begins by using the .ml.pnn predict-neural-network function, which implements the feed-forward algorithm in order to compute the predicted values.

**.ml.pnn**

```
/ use (h)idden and (o)utput layer functions to predict neural network Y
pnn:{[hof;X;THETA]
  X:X (hof[`h] plin::)/ -1_THETA;
```

## 11.8. NEURAL NETWORK GRADIENT

```
  Y:hof[`o] plin[X] last THETA;
  Y}
```

The .ml.pnn function requires us to supply two functions—the hidden layer activation function hof[`h] and the output layer activation function hof[`o].

All hidden layers are activated with the supplied hidden layer activation function hgolf[`h]. The output layer is then activated with a potentially different activation function hgolf[`o] to compute the predicted values. The ability to use different activation functions on the hidden layers and the output layer is important. There are multiple activation functions we can use for the hidden layers, and they each have different benefits and drawbacks. Some vary between -1 and 1 (.ml.tanh), others vary between 0 and 1 (.ml.sigmoid) and yet others have no lower bound (.ml.lrelu). If we are attempting to classify an observation, however, we need to ensure the output layer produces a probability strictly between 0 and 1 such that we can pass the values to the log loss function to compute the error.

Using the .ml.sigmoid function in both cases resembles our logistic regression configuration.

```
q).ml.pnn[`h`o!`.ml.sigmoid`.ml.sigmoid;X;THETA]
0.8746094 0.8753624 0.8592557 0.8700098 0.9114427 0.9073142 0.8973078 0.8..
0.1290119 0.1369241 0.137734  0.1219405 0.1403382 0.1453568 0.1406521 0.1..
0.5751501 0.58141   0.5948391 0.6174419 0.5755223 0.5828165 0.6067813 0.5..
0.331568  0.3641328 0.3789833 0.416887  0.3788562 0.4204723 0.3952084 0.3..
0.6953199 0.7228154 0.6668734 0.6902265 0.7161018 0.706802  0.6719096 0.6..
0.6605288 0.6337911 0.6099245 0.5910219 0.6151377 0.6087636 0.667378  0.6..
0.3065307 0.2672851 0.2875652 0.3023932 0.3299548 0.2634653 0.3116421 0.2..
..
```

These predicted values are then passed to the specified loss function holf[`l] to compute the total cost J. The last line of .ml.nncost applies any regularization we require.

```
q).ml.nncost[();`h`o`l!`.ml.sigmoid`.ml.sigmoid`.ml.logloss;Y;X] THETA
8.472685
```

## 11.8 Neural Network Gradient

In order to perform gradient descent we also need a function that computes the gradient at each layer of the network. To do this, we need to remember the activation values at each layer as we performed the feed-forward loss computation. This considerably increases the complexity of the calculation—but given that we've kept the implementation down to a few lines, I hope you can follow along.

**.ml.nngrad**

```
/ (r)egularization (f)unction, hgof: (h)idden (g)radient (o)utput functions
nngrad:{[rf;hgof;Y;X;THETA]
 ZA:enlist[(X;X)],(X;X) {(z;x z:plin[y 1;z])}[hgof`h]\ -1_THETA;
 P:hgof[`o] plin[last[ZA]1;last THETA];     / prediction
 G:hgof[`g]@'`z`a!/:1_ZA;                    / activation gradient
 D:reverse{[D;THETA;G]G*1_mtm[THETA;D]}\[E:P-Y;reverse 1_THETA;reverse G];
 G:(1%m:count X 0)*(D,enlist E) mmt' prepend[1f] each ZA[;1];  / full grad
 if[count rf,:();THETA[;;0]:0f; G+:sum rf[;m][;1][;THETA]];   / regularization
 G}
```

The only difference between the interface of .ml.nncost and .ml.nngrad is the list of functions required no longer includes the loss function, but now requires a hidden layer gradient function.

```
q).ml.nngrad[();`h`g`o!`.ml.sigmoid`.ml.dsigmoid`.ml.sigmoid;Y;X] THETA
(0.02429655 0 0 0 0 0 0 0 0 0 0 0 0 0 0 0 0 0 0 0 0 0 0 0 0 0 0 0 0..
(0.7883735 0.4610106 0.3465189 0.4427025 0.4353606 0.3947486 0.4211609 0...
```

This time, instead of calling the .ml.pnn function, which uses the / over adverb, we must implement the iteration ourselves with the \ scan adverb. By accumulating the intermediate results, we will be able to adjust the THETA values for each layer in the network based on the final prediction error. In fact, we are required to save two matrices at each stage of the feed-forward process: the pre and post activated matrices—Z and A respectively. The variable ZA contains a list of these matrix pairs.

By using the gradient function supplied as hgof[`g], the third line of .ml.nngrad computes the gradient at each layer by supplying it with a dictionary of pre-activation and post-activation values. Line four reverses the layers and implements the chain rule by computing a cumulative product of each layer's gradient—dropping the bias term at each layer. The fifth line finishes the gradient computation by appending the output layer's gradient (the error itself) to the gradients of the hidden layers and multiplying each layer by its activation values. The function concludes by potentially adjusting the gradient G for regularization.

## 11.9 Neural Network Activation Functions

In principle, there is no need to keep the post activated values. The gradient at each layer is purely a function of the pre-activated values. The post activated values are cached and passed back to the activation functions because the derivative of some activation functions are, in fact, a function of the activated values. Recall the definition of the sigmoid function (Equation 11.3 [249]).

$$S(x) = \frac{1}{1 + e^{-x}}$$

Equation 11.3: Sigmoid

The gradient of the sigmoid function (Equation 11.4 [249]) looks a bit complex but simplifies to a function of the sigmoid function itself.

$$\frac{\partial S(x)}{\partial x} = \frac{e^{-x}}{(1 + e^{-x})^2} = S(x)(1 - S(x))$$

Equation 11.4: Sigmoid Gradient

By caching the activated values during the feed-forward process, we can skip the computationally expensive step of computing $e^{-x}$. By overloading the .ml.dsigmoid sigmoid-gradient function on type, we can handle the simple case where x is either a simple atom or vector,

```
q).ml.dsigmoid -0W -1 0 1 0W
0 0.1966119 0.25 0.1966119 0
```

but also the case where x is a dictionary of Z and A values.

```
q).ml.dsigmoid `z`a!(::;.ml.sigmoid)@\:-0W -1 0 1 0W
0 0.1966119 0.25 0.1966119 0
```

The funq project has provided implementations of the sigmoid, tanh, relu and leaky relu activation functions along with their gradient functions that have special handling for being passed the dictionary of pre- and post-activated values. We've seen the .ml.sigmoid function already, but here it is again alongside its gradient.

**.ml.sigmoid**
```
sigmoid:1f%1f+exp neg::                              / sigmoid
```

### .ml.dsigmoid

```
dsigmoid:{x*1f-x:$[99h=type x;x`a;sigmoid x]}    / sigmoid gradient
```

While the sigmoid function ranges from 0 to 1, a very similar .ml.tanh hyperbolic-tangent function (Equation 11.5 [250]) ranges from -1 to 1. It has the convenient property of being centered around 0 and is mathematically just a scaled and translated version of the .ml.sigmoid function.

$$\tanh(x) = \frac{e^x - e^{-x}}{e^x + e^{-x}} = \frac{e^{2x} - 1}{e^{2x} + 1} = 1 - \frac{2}{1 + e^{2x}}$$

Equation 11.5: Hyperbolic Tangent

For this reason, its gradient (Equation 11.6 [250]) is also a function of itself and can take advantage of the pre-calculated activation values.

$$\frac{\partial \tanh(x)}{\partial x} = 1 - \tanh(x)^2$$

Equation 11.6: Hyperbolic Tangent Gradient

### .ml.tanh

```
tanh:1f-2f%1f+exp 2f*                            / hyperbolic tangent
```

### .ml.dtanh

```
dtanh:{1f-x*x:$[99h=type x;x`a;tanh x]}          / hyperbolic tangent gradient
```

The sigmoid and hyperbolic tangent activation functions both suffer from the vanishing-gradient problem mentioned in Section 11.6 [244] when used with deep neural networks. An alternative that works surprisingly well is the .ml.relu Rectified Linear Unit or ReLU for short (Equation 11.7 [251]). The activation function returns the value itself for values greater than zero and returns zero for values less than zero. A purely linear activation function is incapable of modeling complex relationships, so although the ReLU activation function is linear when values are greater than zero, it is purposefully "rectified" for values below zero to add non-linearity to the model.

### .ml.relu

## 11.9. NEURAL NETWORK ACTIVATION FUNCTIONS

$$R(x) = \begin{cases} 0 & \text{if } x < 0 \\ x & \text{if } x \geq 0 \end{cases}$$

Equation 11.7: ReLU

$$\frac{\partial R(x)}{\partial x} = \begin{cases} 0 & \text{if } x < 0 \\ 1 & \text{if } x > 0 \end{cases}$$

Equation 11.8: ReLU Gradient

```
relu:0f|                              / rectified linear unit
```

### .ml.drelu

```
drelu:{"f"$0f<=$[99h=type x;x`z;x]}   / rectified linear unit gradient
```

Given that the .ml.relu activation function's gradient (Equation 11.8 [251]) is exactly zero for all values less than zero, you may wonder why we would use an activation function that suffers from the vanishing-gradient problem. Your question is valid, and data scientists[3] have created the "Leaky" Rectified Linear Unit or LReLU (Equation 11.9 [251]) to solve this problem. It allows for a non-zero, but still small, gradient (Equation 11.10 [252]) for values less than 0. The downside is that it introduces yet another parameter that needs tuning. The funq project hard-codes the leaky coefficient to .01.

$$R(x) = \begin{cases} .01x & \text{if } x < 0 \\ x & \text{if } x \geq 0 \end{cases}$$

Equation 11.9: LReLU

### .ml.lrelu

```
lrelu:{x*1 .01@0f>x}                  / leaky rectified linear unit
```

### .ml.dlrelu

---

[3] V. Nair and G. E. Hinton, "Rectified Linear Units Improve Restricted Boltzmann Machines," in *Proceedings of the 27th International Conference on International Conference on Machine Learning*, USA, 2010, pp. 807–814, Accessed: Dec. 21, 2019. [Online]. Available: http://dl.acm.org/citation.cfm?id=3104322.3104425.

$$\frac{\partial R(x)}{\partial x} = \begin{cases} .01 & \text{if } x < 0 \\ 1 & \text{if } x > 0 \end{cases}$$

Equation 11.10: LReLU Gradient

```
dlrelu:{1 .01@0f>$[99h=type x;x`z;x]}   / leaky rectified linear unit gradient
```

Neither .ml.drelu nor .ml.dlrelu take advantage of the pre-calculated activated values. In order to implement the same interface as .ml.dsigmoid and .ml.dtanh, however, they check their argument and extract the Z values from the dictionary if needed.

## 11.10 Neural Network Cost and Gradient

Following the model of .ml.lincostgrad and .ml.logcostgrad, we have also combined the .ml.nncost and .ml.nngrad functions in the .ml.nncostgrad function. In addition to the parameters required by the individual cost and gradient functions, .ml.nncostgrad requires the neural network topology vector n, which indicates the size of each layer of the network.

**.ml.nncostgrad**

```
/ (r)egularization (f)unction, (n)etwork topology dimensions, hgolf:
/ (h)idden (g)radient (o)utput (l)oss functions
nncostgrad:{[rf;n;hgolf;Y;X;theta]
 THETA:nncut[n] theta;                  / unroll theta
 ZA:enlist[(X;X)],(X;X) {(z;x z:plin[y 1;z])}[hgolf`h]\ -1_THETA;
 P:hgolf[`o] plin[last[ZA]1;last THETA];     / prediction
 J:(1f%m:count X 0)*revo[sum] hgolf[`l][Y;P]; / cost
 G:hgolf[`g]@'`z`a!/:1_ZA;                    / activation gradient
 D:reverse{[D;THETA;G]G*1_mtm[THETA;D]}\[E:P-Y;reverse 1_THETA;reverse G];
 G:(1f%m)*(D,enlist E) mmt' prepend[1f] each ZA[;1]; / full gradient
 if[count rf,:();THETA[;;0]:0f;JG:rf[;m][;;THETA];J+:sum JG@'0;G+:sum JG@'1];
 (J;2 raze/ G)}
```

The function begins by using the .ml.nncut neural-network-cut function to cut the unrolled theta vector passed by .fmincg.fmincg into a list of THETA matrices

## 11.10. NEURAL NETWORK COST AND GRADIENT

with dimensions matching those provided by the n vector. These are required to compute the cost and gradient.

### .ml.nncut

```
/ neural network cut
nncut:{[n;x]n cut' sums[prev[n+:1]*n:-1_n] cut x}

q).ml.nncut[n] theta
(-0.01875247 0.002988418 0.002794075 -0.01631996 -0.05628771 -0.03466053 ..
(-0.01265339 0.0201045 -0.0832128 -0.06208242 0.1183621 -0.0002805759 0.0..
```

By passing all the parameters required for the loss and gradient calculation, we can use gradient descent to find optimal parameters for our model.

```
q)rf:.ml.l2[1];
q)hgolf:`h`g`o`l!`.ml.sigmoid`.ml.dsigmoid`.ml.sigmoid`.ml.logloss
q)first .fmincg.fmincg[100;.ml.nncostgrad[rf;n;hgolf;Y;X];theta]
Iteration 100 | cost: 0.5097735
-0.03429903 0.00133391 0.001247163 -0.007284576 -0.02512458 -0.01547107 0..
```

We can now try different regularization, topology, activation and loss configurations. These parameters can have a significant impact on the predictive power of our model. Using a lightweight activation function can also help speed up the training process. For example, we can change the hidden layer's activation and corresponding gradient functions to use .ml.relu and .ml.drelu respectively.

```
q)hgolf:`h`g`o`l!`.ml.relu`.ml.drelu`.ml.sigmoid`.ml.logloss
q)first .fmincg.fmincg[100;.ml.nncostgrad[rf;n;hgolf;Y;X];theta]
Iteration 100 | cost: 0.1797125
-0.002017351 0.0009200652 0.0008602316 -0.005024541 -0.01732969 -0.010671..
```

Note that we are required to pass a hidden layer gradient function that corresponds to the activation function. It would make no sense to supply .ml.relu as the hidden layer activation function with the .ml.dsigmoid gradient function. Similarly, but perhaps not as obvious, the output layer activation function is inextricably tied to the loss function.

You may have noticed that we did not specify the gradient for the output layer activation function. You may also have wondered why the output layer's gradient is assumed to be the observation error E. These two facts are not coincidental. They are, in fact, by design. When the .ml.sigmoid activation function is combined with the .ml.logloss cost function, the combined gradient turns out to be $h_\Theta(x) - Y$, which is the error of our prediction P-Y. This *convenient* outcome is a result of using an exponent in our output activation layer and a natural logarithm in our loss function.

By assuming the gradient of the combined output layer and loss function is equal to the prediction error, we reduced the computational overhead of calculating the gradient of each individually. This obviously limits our choice of loss functions.

Machine-learning problems can be split into two types: classification and regression. We've seen how the .ml.logloss cost function can be used for binomial classification. There are, in fact two other cost functions that—when combined with the right output activation layer—can solve for multinomial classification and regression as well.

## 11.11 Neural Network Multinomial Classification

The .ml.logloss log-loss cost function is used when we have a single binary variable—as we did when we fit multiple logistic regression models on the MNIST data. Now that we have a neural network, however, our problem changes from binomial (with two classes) to multinomial (with more than two classes). The neural network fits all the possible digits simultaneously.

There are two types of multinomial classification: multi-label and multi-class. A multi-label classification problem exists when each observation can exist simultaneously in different classes. If our data was, for example, an image of a chest x-ray, it could potentially reflect pneumonia, emphysema, cardiomegaly or any of a number of pathologies.[4] Using an output layer with a sigmoid activation allows multiple classes to obtain a high output signal.

A multi-class classification problem, like classifying handwritten digits, only assigns each observation to a single class. For these problems, we need to use the softmax activation function (Equation 11.11 [254]) instead.

$$\sigma(x)_i = \frac{e^{x_i}}{\sum_{j=1}^{K} e^{x_j}}$$

Equation 11.11: Softmax

---

[4] I. M. Baltruschat, H. Nickisch, M. Grass, T. Knopp, and A. Saalbach, "Comparison of Deep Learning Approaches for Multi-Label Chest X-Ray Classification," *Sci Rep*, vol. 9, no. 1, pp. 1–10, Apr. 2019, doi: 10.1038/s41598-019-42294-8.

## 11.11. NEURAL NETWORK MULTINOMIAL CLASSIFICATION 255

The softmax activation function is a generalization of the sigmoid activation function to more than two dimensions. It ensures the probabilities across all classes sum to 1. As the network learns each image and increases the probability for a specific class, the probabilities associated with each of the other classes, by definition, must be lowered. We began our neural network classification demonstration by using the sigmoid activation function because it is easier to understand. Switching to the softmax activation function should improve our model by applying the extra constraint that each image can only represent a single digit. Our implementation of the .ml.softmax activation function is very short because it uses the .ml.prb function to convert each of the raw values into probabilities.

**.ml.softmax**

```
softmax:prb exp::           / softmax
```

One problem with the softmax function is its failure in the presence of large values.

```
q).ml.softmax 1 1000
0 0n
```

A common solution for this is to translate all values down by the largest value in the data—thus ensuring all values are less than or equal to 0. This has no effect on the resulting probabilities, other than ensuring numeric stability.

**.ml.ssoftmax**

```
ssoftmax:softmax dax[-;max]::   / stable softmax
```

The .ml.ssoftmax stable-softmax function uses the .ml.dax function to first subtract the maximum value from each element before calling the .ml.softmax function.

```
q).ml.ssoftmax 1 1000
0 1f
```

Once we choose to use .ml.softmax for output layers activation function, we need to use a different cost function to ensure the output layer's gradient remains equal to the prediction error. Just as the .ml.softmax activation function generalized the .ml.sigmoid activation function for more than 2 classes, the .ml.celoss loss function generalizes the .ml.logloss loss function for more than 2 classes as well.

The cross entropy loss function (Equation 11.12 [256]) iterates across all M classes and multiplies the boolean indicator y with the log of the predicted probabilities

$$H(y,p) = -\sum_{c=1}^{M} y_c \log(p_c)$$

Equation 11.12: Cross Entropy

p. Just as the log-loss function encodes an `if` statement by multiplying one half of the function by y and the other half by 1-y, the cross entropy loss function extends the `if` statement into a `switch` statement by multiplying the `log` of each of the predicted probabilities p by a vector of indicators y—where only one of the values can be 1. The result of the calculation will be the negative log of the probability associated with the correctly predicted class.

Again, to prevent the function from taking the log of 0, the .ml.celoss loss function floors the predicted values p at 1e-15.

**.ml.celoss**

```
/ given true (y) and (p)redicted values return the cross entropy loss
celoss:{[y;p]neg sum y*log 1e-15|p}
```

We can now combine the .ml.softmax activation function with the .ml.celoss loss function to classify the MNIST handwritten digits.

```
q)hgolf:`h`g`o`l!`.ml.sigmoid`.ml.dsigmoid`.ml.softmax`.ml.celoss
q)first .fmincg.fmincg[100;.ml.nncostgrad[rf;n;hgolf;Y;X];theta]
Iteration   100 | cost: 0.2276808
-0.01823797 0.0006513031 0.0006089476 -0.003556812 -0.01226748 -0.0075540..
```

Switching over to use the .ml.relu hidden layer activation function, we can achieve a much lower total cost.

```
q)hgolf:`h`g`o`l!`.ml.lrelu`.ml.dlrelu`.ml.softmax`.ml.celoss
q)theta:first .fmincg.fmincg[100;.ml.nncostgrad[rf;n;hgolf;Y;X];theta]
Iteration   100 | cost: 0.09748532
```

We can check how accurate this model is against the test data.

```
q)avg yt=p:.ml.imax .ml.pnn[hgolf;Xt] .ml.nncut[n] theta
0.8901
```

By using the .ml.prb probability function, we can review a row-normalized confusion matrix in Example 11.2 [257], where each row (representing the true class) sums to 1.

**Example 11.2** Row-Normalized Confusion Matrix
```
q).ut.rnd[.1] .ut.totals[`TOTAL] .ml.prb each .ml.cm[yt;"i"$p]
y| 0 1 2  3   4   5   6   7   8   9  TOTAL
-| ----------------------------------------
0| 1 0 0  0   0   0   0   0   0   0   1
1| 0 1 0  0   0   0   0   0   0   0   1
2| 0 0 0.9 0  0   0   0   0   0   0   1
3| 0 0 0  0.8 0   0.1 0   0   0   0   1
4| 0 0 0  0   0.9 0   0   0   0   0.1 1
5| 0 0 0  0   0   0.8 0   0   0   0   1
6| 0 0 0  0   0   0   0.9 0   0   0   1
7| 0 0 0  0   0   0   0   0.9 0   0   1
8| 0 0 0  0   0   0   0   0   0.8 0   1
9| 0 0 0  0   0   0   0   0.1 0   0.9 1
 | 1 1 1  0.9 1   1   1   1.1 0.9 1   10
```

Example 11.3 [258] shows a column-normalized confusion matrix, where each column (representing the predicted class) sums to 1.

## 11.12 Neural Network Regression

Although neural networks are often used for classification, they can also be used for non-linear regression. Given our flexible implementation of .ml.nncostgrad, all we need is a combination of output layer activation and regression cost functions that produce a gradient equal to the prediction error. Lucky for us, this is quite straight forward.

Regression predictions are not limited to probabilities between 0 and 1. They can take the full range of negative and positive values. Common regression cost functions include the L1 absolute distance and L2 squared distance, which we discussed in Section 3.7 [62]. The L2 squared distance is also referred to as the Mean Squared Error or MSE, and when combined with a linear activation function produces a gradient equal to the prediction error.

The linear activation function is very simple: it returns the supplied values without any transformation. The :: identity operator does exactly this.

**.ml.linear**
```
linear:(::)                                          / linear
```

**Example 11.3** Column-Normalized Confusion Matrix

```
q).ut.rnd[.1] .ut.totals[`TOTAL] .ml.prb .ml.cm[yt;"i"$p]
y| 0   1 2  3   4   5   6   7   8   9   TOTAL
-| ----------------------------------------------
0| 0.9 0 0  0   0   0   0   0   0   0   1
1| 0   1 0  0   0   0   0   0   0   0   1
2| 0   0 0.9 0  0   0   0   0   0   0   1
3| 0   0 0  0.9 0   0.1 0   0   0   0   1.1
4| 0   0 0  0   0.9 0   0   0   0   0.1 1
5| 0   0 0  0   0   0.8 0   0   0   0   1
6| 0   0 0  0   0   0   0.9 0   0   0   1
7| 0   0 0  0   0   0   0   0.9 0   0   1
8| 0   0 0  0   0   0   0   0   0.9 0   1
9| 0   0 0  0   0   0   0.1 0   0.8 1
 | 1   1 1  1   1   1   1   1   1   1   10
```

Though the name Mean Squared Error implies that the function averages the errors, the .ml.nncost and .ml.nncostgrad functions already sum the resulting cost calculations and divide by the number of elements—thus computing an average. The .ml.mseloss function, therefore, merely squares the error. The function also multiplies by an extra factor of .5 in order to offset the factor of 2 that arrives from taking the derivative of $x^2$.

**.ml.mseloss**

```
mseloss:{[y;p].5*y*y-:p}
```

For a concrete use case of neural network regression, we return to the wine-quality data.

```
q)\l winequality.q
[down]loading wine-quality data set
q)d:.ut.part[`train`test!3 1;0N?] winequality.red.t
q)`Y`X set' 0 1 cut value flip d.train;
q)`Yt`Xt set' 0 1 cut value flip d.test;
q)zsf:.ml.zscoref each X
q)X:zsf @' X
q)Xt:zsf @' Xt
```

Recall that ridge regression is linear regression with an L2 regularization penalty. Using this linear model, we are able to make predictions on the training data with a total cost of .25.

## 11.12. NEURAL NETWORK REGRESSION

```
q)l2:10f
q)THETA:.ml.ridge[0f,count[X]#l2;Y;.ml.prepend[1f]X]
q).ml.lincost[();Yt;Xt] THETA
0.2488384
```

A non-linear model, such as a neural network, should be able to do better.

```
q)n:"j"$.ut.nseq[2;count X;count Y]
q)rf:.ml.l2[l2]
q)theta:2 raze/ THETA:.ml.heu'[1+-1_n;1_n]
q)hgolf:`h`g`o`l!`.ml.relu`.ml.drelu`.ml.linear`.ml.mseloss
q)theta:first r:.fmincg.fmincg[1000;.ml.nncostgrad[rf;n;hgolf;Y;X]] theta
Iteration 1000 | cost: 0.1892778
q).ml.nncost[();hgolf;Yt;Xt] .ml.nncut[n] theta
0.2387781
```

Using gradient descent with regularization has proven to be a powerful technique to find model parameter weights. Over the past three chapters we used it for linear regression, logistic regression, neural network classification and neural network regression. We will use the technique one more time in the next chapter to find latent (or hidden) features to build a recommender system.

# Chapter 12

# Recommender Systems

> Recommendations and personalization live in the sea of data we all create as we move through the world, including what we find, what we discover, and what we love.
>
> — Brent Smith and Greg Linden *Two Decades of Recommender Systems at Amazon.com (2017)*

> We are leaving the age of information and entering the age of recommendation.
>
> — Chris Anderson *The Long Tail: Whey the Future of Business is Selling Less of More (2006)*

Our electronic interactions leave a trail of personal data. Between cookies in our browser, items we've purchased, songs we've listened to, or movies we've watched, we've unintentionally left footprints of what we like, and by extension, what we do not like. And although we may claim we want privacy, we actually benefit from, and enjoy the results of, recommendations made based on this data. When our data is combined with that of the millions (if not billions) of other digital profiles, patterns emerge that permit custom (and precise) recommendations for other items to purchase, songs to listen to and movies to watch.

We will cover four recommendation algorithms that fit into two groups. The first group is called *content-based filtering* and makes recommendations based on our own preferences combined with item-specific attributes. It does not, however, use other people's preferences. It makes recommendations based on similarities between item attributes for which we've indicated a preference. The second group is called *collaborative filtering* and makes recommendations based on our own and other people's preferences. It does not require any knowledge of item-specific attributes. Our first example of collaborative filtering will use a recommendation technique called user-user collaborative filtering.

We will begin by demonstrating two memory-based algorithms that require all the training data to be available at the time of recommendation. This memory-based approach was referred to as lazy learning in Chapter 2 [11]. We will then switch to a model-based, or eager learning, approach and describe three different ways to mathematically factor the rating matrix into a user specific matrix and an item specific matrix. By factoring the rating matrix, we will be able to find latent—or hidden—features that both describe the items (purchases, songs or movies) and specify our preferences for those features. By recombining the two latent-factor matrices, we can then recommend items, songs, or movies that we have not purchased, listened to or seen.

## 12.1 MovieLens Data Set

Recommender systems spiked in popularity when Netflix awarded US$1,000,000 to a team of data scientists that improved Netflix's movie recommendations by more than 10%. The competition started in 2006 and an annual price of US$50,000 was offered to the team that reduced the RMSE (root mean squared error) over the previous year's progress prize winner. The progress prize winner in 2009 was also the grand prize winner and the competition ended. One of the conditions of the prize was that the methodology used must be publicly shared. This created a surge in recommendation algorithms as well as research. Netflix no longer supplies the data set used for the competition and canceled a subsequent competition due to privacy concerns. Copies of the original Netflix Prize data set are still available, but we will use a more up-to-date data set.

GroupLens is a research lab that generates recommendations for a variety of products. It's MovieLens site allows users to create accounts and store their movie preferences. In addition to providing movie recommendations the site provides the raw rating data for download. Fixed-size data sets suitable for research are also available and vary in size from a small data set of 100K ratings up to a large data set consisting of 25M ratings.[1] The full "latest" data set is also available, but

---

[1] F. M. Harper and J. A. Konstan, "The MovieLens Datasets: History and Context," *ACM Trans. In-*

## 12.1. MOVIELENS DATA SET

is constantly changing. The mlens.q [380] library downloads a smaller version of the "latest" data set. Note that the data set may change by the time you run this code. The results may change, but will hopefully be more relevant to you.

The MovieLens data set consists of four files: movie.csv, ratings.csv, links.csv and tags.csv. To keep our model simple, we will only use movie.csv and ratings.csv. The mlens.q [380] library preprocesses the data to make it easier and more efficient to use. We first load the funq.q [339] and mlens.q [380] libraries and then create references to the movie and rating tables in the global namespace.

```
q)\l funq.q
q)\l mlens.q
[down]loading latest grouplens movie lens data set
"unzip -n ml-latest-small.zip"
loading movie definitions: integer movieIds and enumerated genres
removing movies without genres
converting unicode in titles to ascii
extracting the movie's year from the title
adding `u on movieId and enumerating genres
adding the decade as a genre
loading movie ratings
adding `p on userId and linking movieId to movie table
q)`rating`movie set' mlens`rating`movie;
```

The movie.csv file includes a unique identifier for each movie, its title and a list of genres. The mlens.q [380] library extracts the year from the title into a new column and adds the decade as a new genre.

```
q)5_movie
movieId| title           genres                                   year
-------| ---------------------------------------------------------------
6      | "Heat"          `genre$`Action`Crime`Thriller`1990       1995
7      | "Sabrina"       `genre$`Comedy`Romance`1990              1995
8      | "Tom and Huck"  `genre$`Adventure`Children`1990          1995
9      | "Sudden Death"  `genre$`Action`1990                      1995
10     | "GoldenEye"     `genre$`Action`Adventure`Thriller`1990   1995
..
```

Notice how the genres have been enumerated against the "genre" domain instead of the "sym" domain. This creates a new global variable genre. This is an important vector because we will need it later to map matrix indices back into genre names.

The index of the genre in the genre enumeration will match the index in the matrix. The actual index value does not matter, just the fact that we can map the genre symbols into indices starting from 0—and then map them back to symbols once our computations are complete.

```
q)8 cut genre
`Adventure`Animation`Children`Comedy`Fantasy`1990`Romance`Drama
`Action`Crime`Thriller`Horror`Mystery`Sci-Fi`War`Musical
`Documentary`1970`IMAX`1960`Western`Film-Noir`1980`1930
`1940`1950`1920`2000`1910`1900`2010
```

Each row of the rating.csv file includes an identifier for the user making the rating, the movie identifier, the rating, which ranges from .5 to 5 in increments of .5 and the timestamp at which the rating was recorded.

```
q)rating
userId movieId rating timestamp
-----------------------------------------------
1      1       4      2000.07.30D18:45:03.000000000
1      3       4      2000.07.30D18:20:47.000000000
1      6       4      2000.07.30D18:37:04.000000000
1      47      5      2000.07.30D19:03:35.000000000
1      50      5      2000.07.30D18:48:51.000000000
..
```

Since mlens.movie has a single column primary key, the last line of the mlens.q [380] library specifies that the mlens.movie table is the foreign key for the movieId column in the mlens.rating table.

```
q)meta rating
c         | t f           a
----------| ---------------
userId    | i             p
movieId   | i mlens.movie
rating    | f
timestamp | p
```

This allows us to perform queries with "dot notation" to extract movie data without having to first join the tables.

```
q)t:select from rating where movieId.title like "Transformers*"
q)select[>rating] avg rating, count i by movieId.title,movieId.year from t
title                                    year| rating   x
```

## 12.2. CONTENT-BASED FILTERING                                                                265

```
-------------------------------------------| -----------
"Transformers: The Movie"                   1986| 3.357143 7
"Transformers"                              2007| 3.346154 39
"Transformers: Revenge of the Fallen"       2009| 2.425    20
"Transformers: Dark of the Moon"            2011| 2.363636 11
"Transformers: Age of Extinction"           2014| 1.875    4
```

Ignoring how much it pains me, it seems that the viewing public believes the Transformers movies have progressively gotten worse over time.

The `links.csv` file includes numeric identifiers to map the movie with different online movie databases and the `tags.csv` file includes user-provided tags to describe each movie. We will run our analysis without using these two files.

## 12.2 Content-Based Filtering

The first recommendation algorithm we will review uses our own preferences in combination with item (in our case movie) similarities. It does not require the use of other user's ratings. It does require, however, the movies to have distinguishing features. Our movie data set has genres for each movie. The more detailed the genres are, the better the recommendations can be. The MovieLens data set only has 19 genres, but we've added 12 more representing the decade the movie was released.

Without providing our own movie ratings, content-based filtering can only recommend the most popular movies. To achieve relevant recommendations we need to identify a few movies that we liked and others that we disliked. Recommendation algorithms work better when there is a wide range between the lowest and highest rating in our list. Said another way, if all our ratings were the same value, we haven't actually identified which movies we like. We've merely identified which movies we've watched.

Let's identify a few movies we've liked and disliked. No hurt feelings if you disagree with my ratings, feel free to create your own.

```
q)r:1!select `mlens.movie$movieId,rating:0n from movie
q)r,:([]movieId:173 208 260 435 1197 2005 1968i;rating:.5 .5 4 .5 4 4 4f)
q)r,:([]movieId:2918 4006 53996 69526 87520 112370i;rating:5 5 4 4 5 5f)
q)select movieId,rating,movieId.title from r where not null rating
movieId rating title
-------------------------------------------------------
```

| | | |
|---|---|---|
| 173 | 0.5 | "Judge Dredd" |
| 208 | 0.5 | "Waterworld" |
| 260 | 4 | "Star Wars: Episode IV - A New Hope" |
| 435 | 0.5 | "Coneheads" |
| 1197 | 4 | "Princess Bride, The" |
| 1968 | 4 | "Breakfast Club, The" |
| 2005 | 4 | "Goonies, The" |
| 2918 | 5 | "Ferris Bueller's Day Off" |
| 4006 | 5 | "Transformers: The Movie" |
| 53996 | 4 | "Transformers" |
| 69526 | 4 | "Transformers: Revenge of the Fallen" |
| 87520 | 5 | "Transformers: Dark of the Moon" |
| 112370 | 5 | "Transformers: Age of Extinction" |

Our goal is to find a set of coefficients that describes our preferences for each genre. We can then multiply these coefficients by the existence of each movie's genres to find a total predicted rating for the movie.

The problem is strikingly similar to linear regression, except for the fact that many of the values are null. We are unable to invert a matrix with null values, but because q's sum operator ignores null values, we can use gradient descent to find the set of coefficients that minimize the difference between the predicted scores and our ratings. The algorithm will ignore the null values where we have no rating but will generate scores for all movies. It is these scores that give us the recommendations for the movies we have not rated.

We start by creating the Y matrix for our regression.

```
q)Y:value[r]1#`rating
```

Our X matrix will have one row for each genre (where the order matches genres position in the genre enumeration) and one column for each movie in the MovieLens data set.

```
q)show X:"f"$flip genre in/: value[movie]`genres
1 1 0 0 0 0 0 1 0 1 0 0 1 0 1 0 0 0 0 0 0 0 0 0 0 0 0 1 0 0 0 0 0 0 0 0..
1 0 0 0 0 0 0 0 0 0 0 1 0 0 0 0 0 0 0 0 0 0 0 0 0 0 0 0 0 0 0 0 0 0 0 0..
1 1 0 0 0 0 0 1 0 0 0 0 1 0 0 0 0 0 0 0 0 0 0 0 0 1 0 0 0 0 0 1 0 1 0 0..
1 0 1 1 1 0 1 0 0 0 1 1 0 0 0 0 0 1 1 1 1 0 0 0 0 0 0 0 0 0 0 0 0 0 1 1 0..
1 1 0 0 0 0 0 0 0 0 0 0 0 0 0 0 0 0 0 0 0 0 0 0 0 0 0 0 1 0 0 0 0 0 0 0..
1 1 1 1 1 1 1 1 1 1 1 1 1 1 1 1 1 1 1 1 1 1 1 1 1 1 1 1 1 1 1 1 1 1 1 1..
0 0 1 1 0 0 1 0 0 0 1 0 0 0 1 0 1 0 0 0 0 0 0 1 0 0 1 0 0 0 0 0 0 0 1 0..
..
```

## 12.2. CONTENT-BASED FILTERING

Initializing our THETA matrix to zeros starts the gradient descent process in neutral territory. Some values will end up positive (because we like some genres), and some values will end up negative (because we dislike some genres). We will add an extra element to account for the bias term common in all our regressions.

```
q)theta:raze 0N!THETA:(1;1+count X)#0f
,0 0 0 0 0 0 0 0 0 0 0 0 0 0 0 0 0 0 0 0 0 0 0 0 0 0 0 0 0 0f
```

We then declare a regularization function and run a few rounds of gradient descent.

```
q)rf:.ml.l1[.1]
q)theta:first .fmincg.fmincg[20;.ml.lincostgrad[rf;Y;X];theta]
Iteration 20 | cost: 0.0001099164
```

Mapping the THETA coefficients back to the genres shows which ones we like, and which we dislike. It seems I liked the movies of my youth (before the industrious and penniless days of high school and college) and then again after I graduated. Were the movies of the 1990s really that bad or was I too busy to appreciate them?

```
q){(5#x),-5#x}desc genre!1_theta
1980     | 1.815592
2010     | 1.520157
1970     | 0.5677416
Sci-Fi   | 0.4898451
2000     | 0.2898831
Romance  | -0.05405762
Children | -0.06177756
Drama    | -0.5253188
Fantasy  | -0.7428669
1990     | -2.799961
```

Let's see how closely the derived scores match our provided ratings.

```
q)THETA:(count[Y];0N)#theta
q)r:update score:first .ml.plin[X;THETA] from r
q)select[>score] rating,score,movieId.title from r where not null rating
rating score      title
-----------------------------------------------------------
5      5.043186   "Transformers: Dark of the Moon"
5      4.964268   "Transformers: The Movie"
5      4.806975   "Transformers: Age of Extinction"
5      4.572733   "Ferris Bueller's Day Off"
4      4.139418   "Breakfast Club, The"
4      4.028458   "Goonies, The"
```

```
4       4.018918   "Transformers"
4       4.011642   "Princess Bride, The"
4       3.954092   "Star Wars: Episode IV - A New Hope"
4       3.940458   "Transformers: Revenge of the Fallen"
0.5     0.6792367  "Waterworld"
0.5     0.6215067  "Coneheads"
0.5     0.4810754  "Judge Dredd"
```

We can get closer with more rounds of gradient descent, but this is already pretty good. Now it is time to reveal the recommendations!

```
q)select[10;>score] movieId,score,movieId.title from r
movieId score     title
-----------------------------------------------
85261   5.680565  "Mars Needs Moms"
92681   5.521147  "Journey 2: The Mysterious Island"
81564   5.442022  "Megamind"
4121    5.441443  "Innerspace"
8633    5.441443  "Last Starfighter, The"
77561   5.429446  "Iron Man 2"
101076  5.429446  "G.I. Joe: Retaliation"
610     5.400777  "Heavy Metal"
1274    5.400777  "Akira"
157865  5.375096  "Ratchet & Clank"
```

*Innerspace* deeply disturbed me as a child and *The Last Starfighter* was awesome. But why is "Mars Needs Moms" at the top of my list?

```
q)select genres from movie where movieId = 85261
genres
-----------------------------------------------
Action Adventure Animation Children Comedy Sci-Fi IMAX 2010
```

Because it is loaded with all the genres I showed a preference for. It checks all the boxes—as do all the movies at the top of the list. Movies with a single genre will be hard-pressed to make it to the top of anyone's recommendation list. These ratings were performed without using other user's rating information. Let's review the rating data before we demonstrate a few ways we can use it to generate recommendations.

## 12.3 Rating Data Summary

We first look at the breadth of our rating data. It has approximately 600 distinct users 10,000 movies and 100,000 ratings.

```
q)(count distinct@) each exec nu:userId, nm:movieId, nr:i from rating
nu| 610
nm| 9724
nr| 100836
```

We should also review the distribution of the ratings. It seems that only users who have submitted ratings for more than 20 movies have been included. The hope is that we can demean each user and end up with an unbiased rating for the movies they rated. If the users only rated a few movies, the ratings could be suspect.

```
q)t:select nr:count rating by userId from rating
q)select nu:count userId by 10 xbar nr from t
nr | nu
---| ---
20 | 109
30 | 73
40 | 43
50 | 49
60 | 29
70 | 21
80 | 21
90 | 17
100| 16
110| 19
..
```

Many of the movies received less than 10 ratings. This leads us to consider the possibility of throwing away the movies with only a few ratings—knowing that we are also throwing away a large percentage of our data.

```
q)t:select nr:count rating by movieId from rating
q)select nm:count movieId by 10 xbar nr from t
nr| nm
--| ----
0 | 7455
10| 972
20| 415
```

```
30| 244
40| 188
50| 115
60| 76
70| 49
80| 39
90| 33
..
```

Looking at the distribution of the ratings, we can see that there is a consistent upward bias. Given a range of values between .5 and 5, we would expect the average to be around 2.75. We see, however, that the median and average are around 3.5—with the mode at 4.

```
q)`min`med`avg`mode`max!(min;med;avg;.ml.mode;max)@\:rating`rating
min  | 0.5
med  | 3.5
avg  | 3.501557
mode | 4
max  | 5
```

Viewed another way, we can see that a majority of the movies have a rating of 3.5 and a majority of the users rate movies a 3.5. There is only a single user that has an average rating between 0.5 and 1.5.

```
q)t:select avg rating by movieId from rating
q)t:select nm:count i by .5 xbar rating from t
q)s:select avg rating by userId from rating
q)t lj select nu:count i by .5 xbar rating from s
rating| nm     nu
------| --------
0.5   | 108
1     | 188    1
1.5   | 340
2     | 840    9
2.5   | 1282   39
3     | 2286   163
3.5   | 2410   245
4     | 1551   139
4.5   | 423    13
5     | 296    1
```

## 12.4 Null-Aware Aggregations

Thus far, we have not encountered null values in our data. Though the .ml.dt decision-tree function was capable of propagating null values down the tree, we rarely found the need to use it. Most popular machine-learning data sets are complete because it is hard to handle missing values. Rating data, however, is rife with null values. It is thus important to take a step back and review a few functions specifically designed to augment q's native operators to handle null values in matrix aggregations.

Although q's operators handle null values for vector aggregating functions such as avg and sdev, they do not have special handling for matrices. For example, we can compute the average of a simple vector that has nulls.

```
q)avg 1 2 3 0N
2f
```

But if we extend this to a matrix, the avg operator propagates the null values.

```
q)avg (1 2 3 0N;1 2 3 4)
1 2 3 0n
```

If these were movie ratings, we would have hoped that the last rating was the number 4 instead of a null value.

The funq project includes null-aware variants of many of the native mathematical operators. Let's begin with the basics, and work our way up to the .ml.nwavg null-aware-weighted-average function used in .ml.waom.

The null-aware functions begin with simple counting. The .ml.ncount function returns the number of non-null values. For a simple vector, it subtracts the number of null values from the total number of elements. In principle, this approach could be taken for matrices as well. A more memory-efficient approach is used, however. Instead of transforming the whole matrix to a list of boolean vectors and then summing the result, .ml.ncount accumulates the number of null values one row at a time. The effect for small data sets is minimal, but the memory saved for large data sets can be quite substantial.

**.ml.ncount**

```
ncount:{count[x]-$[type x;sum null x;0i {x+null y}/ x]}
```

The `.ml.nsum` function uses the same iterative approach to zero-fill and accumulate the summation—one row at a time. If the supplied value is a vector, the native `sum` operator is used instead.

**.ml.nsum**

```
nsum:{$[type x;sum x;0i {x+0i^y}/ x]}
```

With these two functions as a foundation, we can begin to compute more null-aware aggregations. The `.ml.navg` function combines them to compute a null-aware average.

**.ml.navg**

```
navg:{$[type x;avg x;nsum[x]%ncount x]}
```

Returning to our pseudo rating-vectors, we can see how the `.ml.navg` null-aware-average function returns the value we expect.

```
q).ml.navg (1 2 3 0N;1 2 3 4)
1 2 3 4f
```

Truth be told, we can actually use the native `avg` operator to compute the average over a matrix of data, but it requires us to first transpose the data.

```
q)avg each flip (1 2 3 0N;1 2 3 4)
1 2 3 4f
```

This method has two drawbacks. The first, as mentioned in Section 2.8 [28], is that transposing a matrix allocates a lot of memory. We should, therefore, avoid this if possible. The second drawback is that we need to pepper our code with conditional statements checking whether the data is a vector or matrix before attempting to take the average. The `.ml.navg` function avoids both of these.

Moving on, we can use the `.ml.navg` function two times to compute a null-aware variance.

**.ml.nvar**

```
nvar:{$[type x;var x;navg[x*x]-m*m:navg x]}
```

We can then re-scale the results of a population variance `.ml.nvar` to compute a sample variance `.ml.nsvar`.

**.ml.nsvar**

## 12.5. USER-USER COLLABORATIVE FILTERING

```
nsvar:{$[type x;svar x;(n*nvar x)%-1+n:ncount x]}
```

The population deviation .ml.ndev and sample deviation .ml.nsdev are simple transformations of their respective variance computations.

**.ml.ndev**

```
ndev:sqrt nvar::
```

**.ml.nsdev**

```
nsdev:sqrt nsvar::
```

Calculating the average of a matrix is common, but as with most functions in the funq project, it is the *weighted* variant that is actually used more often. In the case of the .ml.knn k-nearest-neighbors function, the final result is computed by calling the .ml.waom function, which computes the weighted average or mode—depending on the type of the data. And since the data we are averaging is a list of movie recommendations, we need the ability to compute a weighted average that ignores null values.

**.ml.nwavg**

```
nwavg:{[w;x]$[type x;w wavg x;(%/){x+y*(0f^z;not null z)}/[0 0f;w;x]]}
```

Similar to the .ml.navg function, the .ml.nwavg function uses the native variant of the operator if the x argument is an atom or list. If the argument is a matrix, however, the function iterates over the rows keeping track of the cumulative weighted sum and the weighted count. The weighted sum is then divided by the weighted count to produce a list of weighted averages.

## 12.5 User-User Collaborative Filtering

The concept behind user-user collaborative filtering is to recommend movies that like-minded users liked. We can, for example, use a distance metric to compute the distance between our ratings and every other user's ratings. Averaging the top n users generates suggested scores for our own recommendations. This is, in fact, k-nearest neighbors with a twist. When we first used .ml.knn in Chapter 2 [11], we never had null values in our data. Here, however, our data is dominated by null values. With our portfolio of null-aware functions, we are well-equipped to make recommendations with the MovieLens rating data.

To analyze the rating data, we must first transform the data from a table into a matrix. As we saw, many movies had less than 10 ratings. These movies are susceptible to having very high or low average ratings due their low representation in the data set. It is also possible that these movies have highly biased ratings because they don't have the support of many reviewers making their averages statistically significant.

The MovieLens data set was specifically designed to include users who have rated at least 10 movies. We can also exclude any movie that has fewer than 10 ratings. This dramatically drops the number of movies in our data set. It also reduces the chance that we will get recommended a niche movie, which may or may not be what we want. We will declare a variable n, which defines the minimum number of ratings per movie we require to be included in our analysis. You can then change this to see how it affects the recommendations.

We start by generating a vector of movie ids, which will be used to generate our rating matrix.

```
q)n:10
q)m:exec distinct movieId from rating where n<(count;i) fby movieId
q)m
`mlens.movie$1 3 6 47 50 70 101 110 151 157 163 216 223 231 235 260 296 ..
```

Then, with a technique reminiscent of pivoting, we can generate a rating matrix R that has a different user in every row and the movies corresponding to m in every column.

```
q)R:value exec (movieId!rating) m by userId from rating where movieId in m
q)R
4   4 4 5 5    3 4 5 3 5 4 5 3 3 4 4 4 5 4 3 5    4 5 4 4 4 5 5 3 3 4 3 3  ..
                                                                            ..
                                       0.5                                  ..
        2                 2 5 1          5               2    5   5 3       ..
4       4       4         5 2 3    4 4       5           5 3      5 3       ..
    5 4 4 1   5 3    3    2 5 5 4 5 5 5 3    3 5 5 3 4 3 3              5 5 ..
4.5       4.5             5       5   5                  3 5        4     4.5..
  ..
```

We then add our own ratings to the end of the matrix as an additional user.

```
q)R,:r[([]movieId:m);`rating]
```

## 12.5. USER-USER COLLABORATIVE FILTERING

Since we are searching for the most similar users, we can consider each user as a feature and each movie a different sample. As with other data sets, the features in our data set may have different average values. Since each user's bias is different, let's record, and remove, each of these biases from the full R matrix—saving the average user values in the au vector and the centered user ratings in the U matrix.

```
q)U:R-au:avg each R
```

We can now pass this matrix to the .ml.fknn fit-k-nearest-neighbors function to obtain a vector of movie ratings. We will average the top 30 most similar users to generate our recommendations.

```
q)k:30
q)p:last[au]+.ml.fknn[0N!1f-;.ml.cordist\:;k;U;U] last U
1 1 1 1 1 1 1 1 1 1 1 1 1 1 1 1 1 1 1 1 0.9707253 0.9707253 0.9682458 0.9..
q)`score xdesc update score:p,movieId.title from ([]movieId:m)#r
movieId| rating score    title                                                 ..
-------| -----------------------------------------------------------------------..
3000   |        5.179525 "Princess Mononoke (Mononoke-hime)"                   ..
81591  |        5.179525 "Black Swan"                                          ..
89864  |        5.179525 "50/50"                                               ..
373    |        4.811273 "Red Rock West"                                       ..
2300   |        4.781935 "Producers, The"                                      ..
1178   |        4.781935 "Paths of Glory"                                      ..
38038  |        4.781818 "Wallace & Gromit in The Curse of the Were-Rabbi..
1215   |        4.781818 "Army of Darkness"                                    ..
6283   |        4.781818 "Cowboy Bebop: The Movie (Cowboy Bebop: Tengoku ..
49286  |        4.679525 "Holiday, The"                                        ..
..
```

### Correlation Distance

This example used the .ml.cordist correlation-distance function, which transforms the cor correlation operator into a distance function by subtracting the results from 1.

**.ml.cordist**

```
cordist:1f-(cor)::                              / correlation distance
```

To transform the correlation distance into a weight to be used for the weighted average of user ratings, we subtracted the distance from 1 again to obtain the original correlation.

Notice how we added the `0N!` operator in front of the weight function `1f-` so the weight vector is printed. We can see that the first several weights are exactly 1. Although it sounds like the resulting recommendations will be highly relevant, the reality is not so rosy. The overlap between the movies I rated and the ratings within the data set is quite small. To compute a correlation, we need at least two points in common. Because the `.ml.cordist` function is null-aware, it removes all samples where either of the values are null. The closest users, in fact, have only ranked two movies exactly like I did and therefore have perfect correlation. Would you value a recommendation where only two movies were agreed upon?

The proposed solution[2] is to fill the null values with 0. Because we removed the average rating from each user, it is possible to fill unrated movies with 0 to give them an average rating. This dampens the correlation between my ratings and other users that have not rated movies in common.

Re-running the analysis after filling the U rating matrix as well as our own rating vector with zeros produces better recommendations. Notice how the intermediate weight values displayed by the `0N!` operator show the highest weight (our own ratings) as 1 followed by a quick drop. This is a more realistic representation of our similarity with other users. To improve the recommendations, by hopefully increasing our similarity with other users, we will have to rate more movies.

```
q)p:last[au]+.ml.fknn[0N!1f-;.ml.cordist\:;k;U;0f^U] 0f^last U
1 0.2838208 0.2359943 0.2300916 0.216486 0.2142453 0.2129929 0.2031045 0...
q)`score xdesc update score:p,movieId.title from ([]movieId:m)#r
movieId| rating score    title                                             ..
-------| ------------------------------------------------------------------..
1967   |        5.507974 "Labyrinth"                                       ..
2723   |        5.507974 "Mystery Men"                                     ..
2968   |        5.507974 "Time Bandits"                                    ..
3681   |        5.016335 "For a Few Dollars More (Per qualche dollaro in ..
87520  | 5      5        "Transformers: Dark of the Moon"                  ..
3543   |        4.972727 "Diner"                                           ..
1233   |        4.85659  "Boot, Das (Boat, The)"                           ..
475    |        4.77668  "In the Name of the Father"                       ..
249    |        4.77668  "Immortal Beloved"                                ..
1303   |        4.73121  "Man Who Would Be King, The"                      ..
```

---

[2] M. D. Ekstrand, J. T. Riedland and J. A. Konstan, "Collaborative Filtering Recommender Systems," *FNT in Human–Computer Interaction*, vol. 4, no. 2, pp. 81-173, 2011, doi: 10.1561/1100000009.

## 12.5. USER-USER COLLABORATIVE FILTERING

We did not fill the U matrix supplied as the target ratings so that our recommendations are only built using actual ratings from other users. Zero-filling the target rating matrix would lower the recommendation for the least rated movies, resulting in a high recommendation for the most rated movies. Leaving the null values present allows the actual user's ratings to filter through.

### Spearman Correlation Distance

We can also choose different distance metrics to see how they effect the recommendations. Instead of using the Pearson correlation coefficient to measure similarity with the cor operator, we can use the Spearman correlation coefficient implemented in .ml.scor.

**.ml.scor**

```
scor:{srank[x i] cor srank y i:wnan(x;y)} / Spearman's rank correlation
```

The .ml.scor Spearman-correlation function is null-aware and therefore removes all samples that are either null in the x or y arguments before computing the correlation of the ranked values. Ranking the values focuses the statistic on the relative ordering between values rather than their actual value.

On first blush, it looks like we could use the rank operator to rank the values, but the Spearman rank specifies that all elements with the same value should be assigned the average rank associated with that value. The Spearman rank .ml.srank function handles this distinction.

**.ml.srank**

```
/ Spearman's rank (tied values get averaged rank)
srank:{@[x;g;:;avg each (x:"f"$rank x) g@:where 1<count each g:group x]}
```

By first grouping the data, the .ml.srank function finds duplicate values and then uses the avg operator to assign the average value for each occurrence. Notice how equivalent values are handled differently between the rank operator and the .ml.srank function.

```
q)rank 1 1 2 2 3 3
0 1 2 3 4 5
q).ml.srank 1 1 2 2 3 3
0.5 0.5 2.5 2.5 4.5 4.5
```

To use the Spearman correlation as a distance metric, we've defined the .ml.scordist Spearman-correlation-distance composition.

**.ml.scordist**

```
scordist:1f-scor::                      / Spearman's rank correlation distance
```

The top results are indeed different.

```
q)p:last[au]+.ml.fknn[0N!1f-;.ml.scordist\:;k;U;0f^U] 0f^last U
1 0.1594521 0.1457522 0.1349354 0.1232368 0.1122949 0.1102498 0.1100127 0..
q)`score xdesc update score:p,movieId.title from ([]movieId:m)#r
movieId| rating score    title
-------| --------------------------------------------------
59315  |        5.256305 "Iron Man"
663    |        5.256305 "Kids in the Hall: Brain Candy"
87520  | 5      5        "Transformers: Dark of the Moon"
60069  |        4.897255 "WALL-E"
33162  |        4.859157 "Kingdom of Heaven"
3148   |        4.859157 "Cider House Rules, The"
3618   |        4.859157 "Small Time Crooks"
491    |        4.839518 "Man Without a Face, The"
188    |        4.839518 "Prophecy, The"
101    |        4.806676 "Bottle Rocket"
..
```

The cosine similarity statistic is a popular metric to use for user-user recommendations, but based on our manipulation of the data, the results are exactly the same as using .ml.cordist.

```
q)p:last[au]+.ml.fknn[0N!1f-;.ml.cosdist\:;k;U;0f^U] 0f^last U
1 0.2838208 0.2359943 0.2300916 0.216486 0.2142453 0.2129929 0.2031045 0...
q)`score xdesc t:update score:p,movieId.title from ([]movieId:m)#r
movieId| rating score    title                                           ..
-------| ---------------------------------------------------------------..
1967   |        5.507974 "Labyrinth"                                      ..
2723   |        5.507974 "Mystery Men"                                    ..
2968   |        5.507974 "Time Bandits"                                   ..
3681   |        5.016335 "For a Few Dollars More (Per qualche dollaro in ..
87520  | 5      5        "Transformers: Dark of the Moon"                 ..
3543   |        4.972727 "Diner"                                          ..
1233   |        4.85659  "Boot, Das (Boat, The)"                          ..
475    |        4.77668  "In the Name of the Father"                      ..
249    |        4.77668  "Immortal Beloved"                               ..
```

1303    |       4.73121   "Man Who Would Be King, The"                  ..
..

This occurred because we first centered the data and then filled all missing values with zero. The cosine similarity statistic is, in fact, the same as Pearson correlation when the data has been centered.

User-based recommendations suffer three problems. As we've seen, a large item set with few ratings results in a low overlap between user's ratings. This is exacerbated when a new user wants recommendations—known as the cold start problem. With virtually no overlap with other users it is impossible to make recommendations. The second problem is relevant to systems that have many more users than items. In these environments, the cost of creating user similarities is very high—compared to item similarities. And finally, user similarities are very sensitive to the rating changes. Generating recommendations using user-based similarities requires frequent recalculations.

## 12.6 Item-Item Collaborative Filtering

An alternative to user-user collaborative filtering is item-item collaborative filtering. Since most rating database (our small data set excluded) have more users than items, it is more convenient to generate item-item similarities offline, and then combine these with user ratings to generate recommendations on-demand. Changes in user ratings have a small impact on item similarities and recommendations built with slightly stale item similarities still produce good results.

Item-based recommendations also offer a solution to the cold start problem. With a single movie rating, it is possible to generate a list of other movies that you would probably enjoy. Amazon first introduced (and patented[3]) item-item similarities in 1998.

To start the item-based recommendation process, we build an item matrix I—this time with the item averages removed and stored in ia.

```
q)I-:ia:avg each I:flip R
```

The user-user recommendations we built for ourselves only required us to find the similarity between our ratings and every other rating. In order to build the item-item recommendation model, however, we need to find the similarity between every

---
[3]G. D. Linden, J. A. Jacobi, and E. A. Benson, "Collaborative recommendations using item-to-item similarity mappings," US6266649B1, 24-Jul-2001.

pair of movies. Although this is expensive, it only needs to be done once, and we can then use the resulting distance matrix to generate recommendations quickly for any user rating vector.

```
q)D:((0^I) .ml.cosdist\:) peach 0^I
```

Again, we filled the item matrix I with zeroes before computing the pairwise cosine similarity distances in parallel. This dampens movies without many ratings and therefore prevents obscure movies with only a single rating in common from having a similarity of 1 (or a distance of 0).

Finally, we pass our rating vector to the .ml.knn k-nearest-neighbors function and add the item averages back.

```
q)p:ia+.ml.knn[1f-;k;last each I] D
q)`score xdesc t:update score:p,movieId.title from ([]movieId:m)#r
movieId| rating score    title
-------| ----------------------------------------
80549  |       6.212963 "Easy A"
98243  |       6.208333 "Rise of the Guardians"
104211 |       6.154762 "We're the Millers"
152077 |       6.095238 "10 Cloverfield Lane"
117590 |       6.05303  "Horrible Bosses 2"
138036 |       5.888889 "The Man from U.N.C.L.E."
135569 |       5.883333 "Star Trek Beyond"
3980   |       5.809524 "Men of Honor"
6595   |       5.738095 "S.W.A.T."
103042 |       5.712121 "Man of Steel"
..
```

In summary, user-user collaborative filtering and item-item collaborative filtering both use personal preferences along with the k-nearest neighbors algorithm to recommend items—the first uses user-neighbors, the second uses item-neighbors. To generate movie recommendations, user-user collaborative filtering averages the movie ratings of the nearest users. It treats each user as an observation and movie ratings as the target y variable of the k-nearest neighbors algorithm. Item-item collaborative filtering, however, treats each movie as an observation, and each user's ratings are treated as the target y variable. The recommended rating for each movie is based on the person's own ratings of that movie's nearest neighbors.

Analyzing movie ratings as similarities between specific users—or movies—misses the opportunity to simplify the analysis by recognizing common patterns between users and similarly between movies. By looking at my ratings it is possible to suggest that the movies I rated highly were mostly science fiction movies. Given this fact, it is likely that I would like other science fiction movies. Similar arguments can be performed for romantic comedies, westerns, etc. We used manually labeled genres at the beginning of the chapter when we demonstrated content-based filtering. But is it possible to allow the data to speak for itself?

## 12.7 Collaborative Filtering

By factoring the rating matrix into a user-matrix and an item-matrix, we obtain two matrices that, when multiplied together, not only return—hopefully to a close approximation—the original ratings, but also inferred ratings for the previously unrated user-movie pairs. This approach, it turns out, is quite powerful and there are multiple ways to approach the problem. The first approach we will implement uses the skills we developed when building neural networks. By defining a cost and gradient function that models the action of multiplying two matrices together and comparing the resulting matrix with our known rating matrix, we can use gradient descent to iteratively approach a good solution.

We start by defining, and implementing, the .ml.pcf predict collaborative filtering function.

**.ml.pcf**

```
/ collaborative filtering predict
pcf:{[X;THETA] mtm[THETA;X]}
```

No surprise, it merely multiplies the X and THETA matrices together. Notice, however, how we did not prepend a vector of ones as we've done for each of the preceding prediction functions. There is no need for a bias term in collaborative filtering. Depending on our use of the algorithm, the X and THETA parameters can refer to either the user or item matrix. In our case, the X parameter will refer to the item matrix and the THETA parameter refers to the user matrix.

To initialize the item and user matrices we must first decide on how many common—also known as *latent*—factors we want to decompose the matrix into. This is, of course, a tunable parameter. If we pick a number that is too low, we will end up with a model that has high bias. Likewise, if we choose too many factors, the model will have high variance. Let's pick 10 factors and randomly initialize an X and THETA matrix with values between -1 and 1.

```
q)nf:10
q)n:(ni:count U 0;nu:count U)
q)xtheta:2 raze/ XTHETA:(X:-1+ni?/:nf#2f;THETA:-1+nu?/:nf#2f)
```

Using the .ml.pcf function we obtain a possible rating matrix.

```
q).ml.pcf[X;THETA]
-0.7208892 1.024562  0.1860672  0.4068872  1.627996   0.2900628 0.2381696..
-0.4796678 0.428767  0.6167455  0.5966718  0.9570856  1.014233  -1.227511..
0.1804408  1.821367  -0.2472533 1.498525   1.951852   0.3116198 0.9475638..
1.288328   2.62753   -1.037841  1.816434   -0.1108183 -1.109695 2.066944 ..
-0.9558165 0.4032054 1.761311   -0.8783708 1.891194   0.8553893 0.1382998..
0.5999857  0.7982246 0.7003919  1.051228   1.744277   1.365974  0.4163143..
-0.7920772 0.131434  0.7699091  -0.4519912 1.046256   1.446477  -2.876881..
..
```

How well did this model the original rating matrix? To know this we must define a cost function.

## 12.8 Collaborative Filtering Cost

The collaborative-filtering cost function (Equation 12.1 [283]) is similar to the linear-regression cost function and is defined as the square of the prediction error. The regularization term, however, is a little different. Instead of just adding terms to regularize the THETA matrix, the collaborative-filtering cost function also adds a term to regularize the X matrix.

### .ml.cfcost

```
/ collaborative filtering cost
cfcost:{[rf;Y;X;THETA]
 J:(.5f%m:count X 0)*revo[sum] E*E:pcf[X;THETA]-Y; / cost
 if[count rf,:();J+:sum rf[;m][;0]@\:(X;THETA)];  / regularization
 J}
```

Because we've factored out of the regression terms as a parameter to the function, the .ml.cfcost collaborative-filtering cost function is short and intuitive. The first line squares the prediction error and averages the values across all samples. The second line computes the regularization cost for X and THETA and adds the results to the total cost. Notice how we did not set the first element of the X and THETA

## 12.8. COLLABORATIVE FILTERING COST

$$J(x,\theta) = \frac{1}{2m} \sum_{(i,j):y^{(i,j)}!=0\text{N}} \left((\theta^{(j)})^T(x^{(i)}) - y^{(i,j)}\right)^2 + \frac{\lambda_1}{m}\sum_{i=1}^{n_i}\sum_{k=1}^{n}\left|x_k^{(i)}\right| + \frac{\lambda_2}{2m}\sum_{i=1}^{n_i}\sum_{k=1}^{n}\left(x_k^{(i)}\right)^2$$
$$+ \frac{\lambda_1}{m}\sum_{j=1}^{n_u}\sum_{k=1}^{n}\left|\theta_k^{(j)}\right| + \frac{\lambda_2}{2m}\sum_{j=1}^{n_u}\sum_{k=1}^{n}\left(\theta_k^{(j)}\right)^2$$

where: $m$ = number of samples
$n$ = number of features
$n_i$ = number of items
$n_u$ = number of users

Equation 12.1: Collaborative Filtering Cost

matrices to 0. The first elements of our parameter matrices are not bias terms, and we should, therefore, keep all the coefficients when computing the regularization cost.

We can now compute the cost—without regularization—of our initial X and THETA parameters.

```
q).ml.cfcost[();U;X;THETA]
37.48993
```

In order to reduce that cost we need to take a few steps of regularized gradient descent. Recall that the .fmincg.fmincg function requires a single vector of coefficients. This was stored in the xtheta variable when we first generated the X and THETA matrices. To compute the cost, therefore, we need to be able to cut the vector back into the X and THETA matrices. The .ml.cfcut collaborative-filtering-cut function accepts the dimensions of the rating matrix: item count followed by user count.

### .ml.cfcut

```
/ collaborative filtering cut where n:(ni;nu)
cfcut:{[n;x]n cut'(0,n[0]*count[x]div sum n) cut x}
```

The function determines the number of latent factors by dividing the vector length by the sum of the item and user counts. This is used to build dimensions for the cut operator so it can split the x vector into two sub-vectors corresponding to the elements of the X and THETA matrices. These sub-vectors are then reshaped into the original X and THETA matrices by another application of cut operator.

The item and user dimensions required by the .ml.cfcut function are stored in the variable n.

```
q)n
2121 611
```

Passing these dimensions and the xtheta vector to the .ml.cfcut function returns our original X and THETA matrices.

```
q)(count first::) each .ml.cfcut[n;xtheta]
2121 611
```

## 12.9 Collaborative Filtering Gradient

The last step before we can perform gradient descent is to derive the gradient and implement the .ml.cfcostgrad collaborative-filtering-cost-gradient function (Equation 12.2 [284]). Our cost is no longer a function of a single variable $\theta$. It is also a function of the variable $x$. There are, therefore, two gradients—one for each parameter. Taking the partial derivative with respect to each variable gives us these two gradient functions.

$$G(x_k^{(i)}) = \frac{\partial J(x,\theta)}{\partial x_k^{(i)}} = \frac{1}{m} \sum_{j:y^{(i,j)}!=0N} \left((\theta^{(j)})^T(x^{(i)}) - y^{(i,j)}\right) \theta_k^{(j)} + \frac{\lambda_1}{m}\text{sign}(x_k^{(i)}) + \frac{\lambda_2}{m}x_k^{(i)}$$

$$G(\theta_k^{(j)}) = \frac{\partial J(x,\theta)}{\partial \theta_k^{(j)}} = \frac{1}{m} \sum_{i:y^{(i,j)}!=0N} \left((\theta^{(j)})^T(x^{(i)}) - y^{(i,j)}\right) x_k^{(i)} + \frac{\lambda_1}{m}\text{sign}(\theta_k^{(j)}) + \frac{\lambda_2}{m}\theta_k^{(j)}$$

Equation 12.2: Collaborative Filtering Gradient

Written concisely, and taking advantage of the q's ability to overload operators, our .ml.cfgrad collaborative-filtering-gradient function is marginally different from the linear regression gradient function. The differences begin with zero-filling the E error term. We only accumulate errors when the predicted rating differs from actual rating. When the actual rating is missing, we should not attribute an error. The null rating in the Y variable causes the resulting element in the error term E to

## 12.9. COLLABORATIVE FILTERING GRADIENT

be null as well. We did not have to zero-fill the E variable in the .ml.cfcost function because q's sum operator automatically handles the null values. To compute the gradient, however, we took advantage of matrix operators to both multiply and sum over the results. Matrix operators cannot handle null values, so we must zero-fill the argument. The effect of zero-filling the E variable does exactly what we want—it drops the element from the cost and sets the gradient to 0. The remaining differences are the inclusion of both X and THETA regularization terms as well as the absence of special handling for the bias term.

**.ml.cfgrad**

```
/ collaborative filtering gradient
cfgrad:{[rf;Y;X;THETA]
  G:(1f%m:count X 0)*(mm[THETA;E];mmt[X]E:0f^pcf[X;THETA]-Y); / gradient
  if[count rf,:();G+:sum rf[;m][;1]@\:(X;THETA)]; / regularization
  G}
```

Passing the matrices to the .ml.cfgrad function allows us to see the partial derivatives of both the X and THETA variables.

```
q).ml.cfgrad[();U;X;THETA]
-0.006553207  -0.006641072  -0.01787628   0.0003285256 -0.01225925  0.00033..
-0.007660023  -0.0008102865 -0.002562815  -0.01449283  -0.005853858 -0.01..
```

Combining the cost and the gradient terms together, we have a function .ml.cfcostgrad that can be used with the .fmincg.fmincg function-minimization-conjugate-gradient function.

**.ml.cfcostgrad**

```
/ collaborative filtering cost & gradient
cfcostgrad:{[rf;n;Y;xtheta]
  THETA:last X:cfcut[n] xtheta;X@:0; / unroll theta
  J:(.5%m:count X 0)*revo[sum] E*E:0f^pcf[X;THETA]-Y; / cost
  G:(1f%m)*(mm[THETA;E];mmt[X;E]);                    / gradient
  if[count rf,:();JG:rf[;m][;;(X;THETA)];J+:sum JG@'0;G+:sum JG@'1];
  (J;2 raze/ G)}
```

We can use L2 regularization by defining the rf regularization function and then run 300 rounds of gradient descent.

```
q)rf:.ml.l2[1f]
q)xtheta:first .fmincg.fmincg[300;.ml.cfcostgrad[rf;n;U];xtheta]
Iteration 300 | cost: 7.933628
```

The total regularized cost was reduced to 8, and we can now generate recommendations for all users and movies.

```
q)P:au+.ml.pcf . XTHETA:.ml.cfcut[n] xtheta
```

The last element of P has our own predictions.

```
q)show t:`score xdesc update score:last P,movieId.title from ([]movieId:m)#r
movieId| rating score     title
-------| -------------------------------------------------------------------
102903 |        4.816849  "Now You See Me"
8368   |        4.659156  "Harry Potter and the Prisoner of Azkaban"
88125  |        4.563624  "Harry Potter and the Deathly Hallows: Part 2"
69757  |        4.493222  "(500) Days of Summer"
527    |        4.410929  "Schindler's List"
81834  |        4.39508   "Harry Potter and the Deathly Hallows: Part 1"
1262   |        4.374126  "Great Escape, The"
59315  |        4.359956  "Iron Man"
96821  |        4.35581   "Perks of Being a Wallflower, The"
1197   | 4      4.341298  "Princess Bride, The"
87520  | 5      4.291138  "Transformers: Dark of the Moon"
67255  |        4.286396  "Girl with the Dragon Tattoo, The (Man som hatar kvinn..
58559  |        4.282767  "Dark Knight, The"
2135   |        4.279154  "Doctor Dolittle"
40815  |        4.277921  "Harry Potter and the Goblet of Fire"
..
```

Reviewing how the model scored the movies we already rated shows many deviations.

```
q)select from t where not null rating
movieId| rating score     title
-------| -------------------------------------------------------
87520  | 5      4.240333  "Transformers: Dark of the Moon"
1197   | 4      4.236887  "Princess Bride, The"
260    | 4      4.07051   "Star Wars: Episode IV - A New Hope"
2918   | 5      3.687183  "Ferris Bueller's Day Off"
53996  | 4      3.681714  "Transformers"
69526  | 4      3.598175  "Transformers: Revenge of the Fallen"
1968   | 4      3.499976  "Breakfast Club, The"
2005   | 4      3.461538  "Goonies, The"
208    | 0.5    1.635517  "Waterworld"
435    | 0.5    1.190442  "Coneheads"
173    | 0.5    0.9763219 "Judge Dredd"
```

# 12.10 Stochastic Gradient Descent

We can address this in a few ways. One option is to perform more iterations of regularized gradient descent. This has marginal benefit, however, if decreases in the cost function have already plateaued. The other option is to make the model more flexible. We can achieve this by reducing the regularization parameter or increasing the number of latent factors.

## 12.10 Stochastic Gradient Descent

We originally discussed stochastic gradient descent in Section 9.13 [204]. Its benefits included the ability to limit the size of matrix multiplications and therefore increased speed for extremely large data sets. It also adds a bit of randomness, which increases the odds of finding a global minimum for problems that have local minima that can distract the gradient descent algorithm.

Our goal is to factor the rating matrix into user and item matrices. The problem, by construction, is a non-convex problem. This results in the possibility of finding solutions that are not globally optimal. Using stochastic gradient descent is, therefore, a popular algorithm. Rewriting the collaborative-filtering cost function as a matrix-factorization problem with L2 regularization (Equation 12.3 [287]) demonstrates the similarities.

$$\min_{x,\theta} \sum_{(i,j):y^{(i,j)}!=0\text{N}} \left((\theta^{(j)})^T(x^{(i)}) - y^{(i,j)}\right)^2 + \lambda_2 \left(\sum_i \|x^{(i)}\|^2 + \sum_j \|\theta^{(j)}\|^2\right)$$

Equation 12.3: Matrix-Factorization Optimization

By iterating across each non-null value in the Y matrix, we can adjust the X and THETA values to more precisely generate ratings. Each iteration has three steps. The first step is to compute the prediction error for that rating. Next, the THETA values are adjusted using the regularized gradient. The final step in the iteration is to update the corresponding X values as well. These steps are defined in Equation 12.4 [288].

Since we are attempting to fit both the X and THETA matrix simultaneously, we cannot reuse the .ml.sgd stochastic-gradient-descent function. The setup is unique, and common, enough that we've built a specific stochastic-gradient-descent-matrix-factorization function .ml.sgdmf.

$$e^{(i,j)} \leftarrow (\theta^{(j)})^T(x^{(i)}) - y^{(i,j)}$$
$$\theta^{(j)} \leftarrow \theta^{(j)} + \alpha\left(e^{(i,j)}x^{(i)} - \lambda_2\theta^{(j)}\right)$$
$$x^{(i)} \leftarrow x^{(i)} + \alpha\left(e^{(i,j)}\theta^{(j)} - \lambda_2 x^{(i)}\right)$$

where $\alpha$ = the learning rate

Equation 12.4: Matrix-Factorization Updates

Similar to the .ml.sgd function, the .ml.sgdmf function accepts the learning rate alpha and the sampling function, which allows us to choose how the random sampling will occur. The function also requires an L2 regularization parameter l2, the rating matrix Y and the initial X and THETA matrices as the pair XTHETA. An xy argument that specifies which element from the rating matrix Y we are fitting is passed as the final argument.

### .ml.sgdmf

```
/ using learning rate (a)lpha, and (l2) regularization parameter, factorize
/ matrix Y using stochastic gradient descent by solving for each non null
/ value one at a time. (s)ampling (f)unction: til = no shuffle, 0N? =
/ shuffle, {x?x} = bootstrap. pass (::) for xy to initiate sgd.
sgdmf:{[a;l2;sf;Y;XTHETA;xy] / sgd matrix factorization
 if[(::)~xy;:XTHETA .z.s[a;l2;sf;Y]/ I sf count I:flip twhere not null Y];
 e:(Y . xy)-dot . xt:XTHETA .'I:flip(::;xy 1 0); / error
 XTHETA:./[XTHETA;0 1,'I;+;a*(e*xt 1 0)-l2*xt]; / adjust X and THETA
 XTHETA}
```

The first line of the .ml.sgdmf function detects that the null value :: has been passed in as the xy argument. This indicates that this is the first call to the function and the algorithm should recursively call itself for each non-null rating. The indices of the non-null ratings are obtained with the .ml.twhere tensor-where function. Although the use of the where operator is limited to one-dimensional tensors, the .ml.twhere function can be used with tensors of any dimension. Instead of returning a single list of indices, the .ml.twhere function returns a list of lists—one for each dimension. A full discussion on its implementation is delayed until Section 13.7 [303]. Nevertheless, we provide a quick demonstration of how applying .ml.twhere to a matrix of booleans returns the row and column indices, which can then be used to index back into the matrix to obtain the desired values.

## 12.10. STOCHASTIC GRADIENT DESCENT 289

```
q).ml.twhere  (10101010b;01010101b)
0 0 0 0 1 1 1 1
0 2 4 6 1 3 5 7
```

The second line of the function computes the error between the predicted rating using the current X and THETA values and the actual rating in Y. This error is then used on the third line to compute the gradient. After calculating the L2 gradient regularization term, the X and THETA values are updated for the row and column associated with the single rating found using the xy coordinates. Each non-null rating is *fit* in-turn until one full round of stochastic gradient descent has been performed.

Running one round of stochastic gradient descent with a learning rate of .1 and an L2 regularization coefficient of .01 gives us new X and THETA matrices.

```
q)XTHETA:(X:-1+ni?/:nf#1f;THETA:-1+nu?/:nf#2f)
q).ml.sgdmf[.1;.01;0N?;U;(X;THETA);::]
-0.003227587 -0.6764047 0.2050813 0.4731565  0.6626243  -0.346361   -0..
 0.1999661    0.426763  0.3328475 0.01620137 -0.1522201 -0.09352175 -0.0..
```

By using the .ml.iter iteration utility along with a cf cost function and mf minimization function, we can iterate until the cost reduction tapers off.

```
q)cf:.ml.cfcost[rf;U] .
q)mf:.ml.sgdmf[.1;.01;0N?;U;;::]
q)XTHETA:first .ml.iter[-1;.001;cf;mf] XTHETA
iter: 1 | cost: 12.80589 | pct: 0w
iter: 2 | cost: 10.82125 | pct: 0.1549786
iter: 3 | cost: 9.607452 | pct: 0.1121682
iter: 4 | cost: 9.16514  | pct: 0.0460385
iter: 5 | cost: 8.997055 | pct: 0.01833955
iter: 6 | cost: 8.885109 | pct: 0.01244259
iter: 7 | cost: 8.810266 | pct: 0.008423353
iter: 8 | cost: 8.697529 | pct: 0.01279616
iter: 9 | cost: 8.694172 | pct: 0.0003858986
```

Reviewing our own ratings shows that the algorithm has made some progress.

```
q)P:au+.ml.pcf . XTHETA
q)t:`score xdesc update score:last P,movieId.title from ([]movieId:m)#r
q)select from t where not null rating
movieId| rating score    title
-------| -------------------------------------------
```

```
87520  | 5    4.894698 "Transformers: Dark of the Moon"
2918   | 5    4.583587 "Ferris Bueller's Day Off"
1197   | 4    4.510925 "Princess Bride, The"
1968   | 4    4.419653 "Breakfast Club, The"
260    | 4    4.328439 "Star Wars: Episode IV - A New Hope"
2005   | 4    4.029706 "Goonies, The"
53996  | 4    3.847088 "Transformers"
69526  | 4    3.648373 "Transformers: Revenge of the Fallen"
208    | 0.5  0.9584068 "Waterworld"
173    | 0.5  0.7640596 "Judge Dredd"
435    | 0.5  0.6458871 "Coneheads"
```

## 12.11 Alternating Least Squares

There is no closed-form solution for factoring the rating matrix into a user and item matrix. Gradient descent is the hammer that allows us to solve many such problems, but factoring the rating matrix is a non-convex problem that results in slow convergence. There are many matrix factorization techniques, but one in particular is quite elegant. By first assuming the user matrix is correct, and solving for the item matrix, we've transformed the structure into a quadratic optimization problem that can be solved with linear regression. We can then assume the resulting item matrix is correct and use the same technique to solve for the user matrix. By alternately solving for the user and item matrix—each time assuming the other matrix is correct—we iteratively approach an optimal solution for each matrix. This algorithm is called alternating least squares.

We are again faced by the problem of null values littering our matrix. Linear regression will not produce a solution if any of the values are null. We therefore must implement a slight variant on the standard linear regression. Although we were able to use both L1 and L2 regularization when using gradient descent, a closed form solution for linear regression only exists for L2 regularization. This was introduced in the section called "L2 Regularization" [210] and is called ridge regression. This limits our alternating-least-squares-with-weighted-regularization function .ml.alswr to only support L2 regularization.

**.ml.alswr**

```
/ ALS-WR (a)lternating (l)east (s)quares with (w)eighted (r)egularization
alswr:{[l2;Y;XTHETA]
  X:flip f2nd[wridge[l2;;XTHETA 1]] Y; / hold THETA constant, solve for X
```

## 12.11. ALTERNATING LEAST SQUARES

```
  THETA:flip wridge[l2;;X] peach Y;    / hold X constant, solve for THETA
  (X;THETA)}
```

As the name implies, the algorithm alternates between performing least squares across one dimension of the rating matrix followed by performing least squares across the other dimension. To handle null values, the algorithm calls the .ml.wridge weighted-ridge-regression function instead of the .ml.ridge ridge-regression function.

**.ml.wridge**

```
/ given (l2) regularization parameter, target vector y and data matri(X),
/ return theta vector resulting from performing weighted ridge regression by
/ scaling the regularization parameter by the count of non-null values
wridge:{[l2;y;X]first ridge[l2*count i;enlist y i;X[;i:where not null y]]}
```

The .ml.wridge function ultimately calls the .ml.ridge function but first finds—and drops—all rows that have null values. Each row (or column) of the rating matrix may have a different number of null values. Determining a method of scaling the regularization is critical for generating accurate predictions. The funq project follows the recommendation by Y. Zhou, D. Wilkinson, R. Schreiber and R. Pan[4] and multiplies the L2 regularization term by the number of non-null items within the record.

Our next step is to reinitialize our X and THETA values and use the .ml.alswr alternating-least-squares-with-weighted-regularization function to find optimal user and item matrices.

```
q)XTHETA:(X:-1+ni?/:nf#1f;THETA:-1+nu?/:nf#2f)
```

We can define a cost and minimization function and see how a few rounds of alternating least squares quickly reduces the cost.

```
q)cf:.ml.cfcost[();U] .
q)mf:.ml.alswr[.01;U]
q)XTHETA:first .ml.iter[1;.0001;cf;mf] XTHETA
iter: 153 | cost: 5.332245 | pct: 9.749835e-05
```

We can then check our top ranked recommendations,

---

[4]Y. Zhou, D. Wilkinson, R. Schreiber, and R. Pan, "Large-Scale Parallel Collaborative Filtering for the Netflix Prize," in *Proc. 4th Int'l Conf. Algorithmic Aspects in Information and Management*, LNCS 5034, 2008, pp. 337–348.

```
q)P:au+.ml.pcf . XTHETA
q)show t:`score xdesc update score:last P,movieId.title from ([]movieId:m)#r
movieId| rating score     title                                              ..
-------| ----------------------------------------------------------------------..
4041   |        9.896469 "Officer and a Gentleman, An"                       ..
6620   |        8.359824 "American Splendor"                                 ..
52435  |        8.108858 "How the Grinch Stole Christmas!"                   ..
2110   |        7.913437 "Dead Men Don't Wear Plaid"                         ..
111364 |        7.611533 "Godzilla"                                          ..
28     |        7.477486 "Persuasion"                                        ..
5151   |        7.44557  "40 Days and 40 Nights"                             ..
112175 |        7.297408 "How to Train Your Dragon 2"                        ..
7318   |        7.249879 "Passion of the Christ, The"                        ..
1289   |        7.223914 "Koyaanisqatsi (a.k.a. Koyaanisqatsi: Life Out o..
..
```

and confirm the resulting score is close to our original ratings.

```
q)show s:select from t where not null rating
movieId| rating score     title
-------| ----------------------------------------------------------
87520  | 5      5.096276 "Transformers: Dark of the Moon"
2918   | 5      4.424326 "Ferris Bueller's Day Off"
260    | 4      4.310197 "Star Wars: Episode IV - A New Hope"
1197   | 4      4.287267 "Princess Bride, The"
1968   | 4      3.9999   "Breakfast Club, The"
69526  | 4      3.997378 "Transformers: Revenge of the Fallen"
53996  | 4      3.911313 "Transformers"
2005   | 4      3.77456  "Goonies, The"
435    | 0.5    0.7810836 "Coneheads"
208    | 0.5    0.7383508 "Waterworld"
173    | 0.5    0.3256579 "Judge Dredd"
```

The stochastic gradient descent and alternating least squares algorithms are the most popular methods for factorizing very large matrices. While stochastic gradient descent is preferable because it only requires one row and one column to be loaded into memory for each operation, it typically requires more epochs of stochastic gradient descent than alternating least squares. And while many computations in alternating least squares can be run in parallel, stochastic gradient descent is fundamentally a serial algorithm. There have been many papers written attempting to find the holy grail of minimizing memory requirements and maximizing parallel computations. A promising approach is called CCD++ and uses a

## 12.11. ALTERNATING LEAST SQUARES

technique called coordinated descent.[5] As our data sets get bigger, there is much to be gained by finding better parallel matrix-factorization algorithms.

In the next chapter we take a step away from fitting models on training data sets and introduce an algorithm that transformed the internet and the world: PageRank.

---

[5]H.-F. Yu, C.-J. Hsieh, S. Si, and I. Dhillon, "Scalable Coordinate Descent Approaches to Parallel Matrix Factorization for Recommender Systems," *in 2012 IEEE 12th International Conference on Data Mining*, 2012, pp. 765–774, doi: 10.1109/ICDM.2012.168.

# Chapter 13

# PageRank

> The importance of a Web page is an inherently subjective matter, which depends on the readers interests, knowledge and attitudes. But there is still much that can be said objectively about the relative importance of Web pages.
>
> — Lawrence Page and Sergey Brin and Rajeev Motwani and Terry Winograd *The PageRank Citation Ranking: Bringing Order to the Web (1998)*

The IEEE International Conference on Data Mining (ICDM) in December 2006 listed Google's PageRank algorithm among the top 10 machine-learning algorithms.[1] While its ranking has since fallen out of the top 10, its impact on our lives remains. The algorithm is cleverly named after one of its authors, Larry Page, and the fact that it ranks web pages. Before the invention of the PageRank algorithm, search engines listed web pages based on their content, the number of links directed to the page and an overlay of human subjectivity. It was, therefore, possible to increase a web page's rank by repeating keywords within the hidden HTML and creating other web pages with back-pointing links. Using the PageRank algorithm has made it much harder to game search engines to increase a web pages chances of appearing at the top of a search result—a process known as Search Engine Optimization (SEO).

---

[1] X. Wu et al., "Top 10 algorithms in data mining," *Knowl Inf Syst*, vol. 14, no. 1, pp. 1–37, Jan. 2008, doi: 10.1007/s10115-007-0114-2.

We intuitively understand that the importance of an academic journal article increases when an influential article cites it. It was this same intuition that led to the creation of the PageRank algorithm. The rank a web page obtains from the PageRank algorithm also depends on the rank of the pages that link to it. Viewed from the opposite angle, a page distributes (a fraction of) its own rank equally among each of the pages it links to. This recursive relationship, where a page's rank depends on the rank of its referring pages, which in-turn depends on the rank of its referring pages is what makes the algorithm so innovative, and also so hard to trick. No matter how many pages you create with links to your favorite web page, its ranking will not increase unless those new pages are linked to by higher ranked pages themselves.

The algorithm makes the naive assumption that the order of a page's links are irrelevant and that the content of the page and the linked page have no relationship to the link's importance. Even though you may believe that the first few links on a page are clicked on more often than the last few links, the PageRank algorithm does not treat the links differently. You may also believe that a web surfer is more likely to click a link about kdb+ when they are visiting a page about kdb+, but there is no specific way to handle this with the PageRank algorithm. Finally, the algorithm also assumes that web surfers randomly pick a starting page to begin surfing, while in practice, many surfers start their online experience with a visit to a few favorite sites. Even with these deficiencies, the PageRank algorithm does a very good job assigning a value of relative importance among web pages. Its power is enhanced when combined with an orthogonal algorithm like rankings obtained by content filters.

To understand the underlying mathematics of the PageRank algorithm, we must first describe a random surfer. Imagine a web surfer arriving at a random web page who then randomly clicks on links. Sometimes this surfer decides there is nothing interesting on the page, is bored with the current topic, or there are no links on the page and jumps to another random page. This is known as the random surfer model. This was probably more relevant in the early days of the internet—when we didn't just *Google* exactly the information we wanted. Google's search algorithm has obviously been improved over time, but the PageRank algorithm is still an important component.

We will cover three different implementations of the PageRank algorithm and discuss the computational challenges encountered when attempting to create a ranking of all the pages on the internet.

## 13.1 Adjacency Matrix

A mathematical solution to ranking pages begins by first describing the links between pages as an adjacency matrix. For example, suppose page A has links to pages B and C, page B has links to pages C and D, page C only has a link to page D, and finally, page D has links back to pages A, B, C and E, which has no further links. This network is displayed in Figure 13.1 [297].

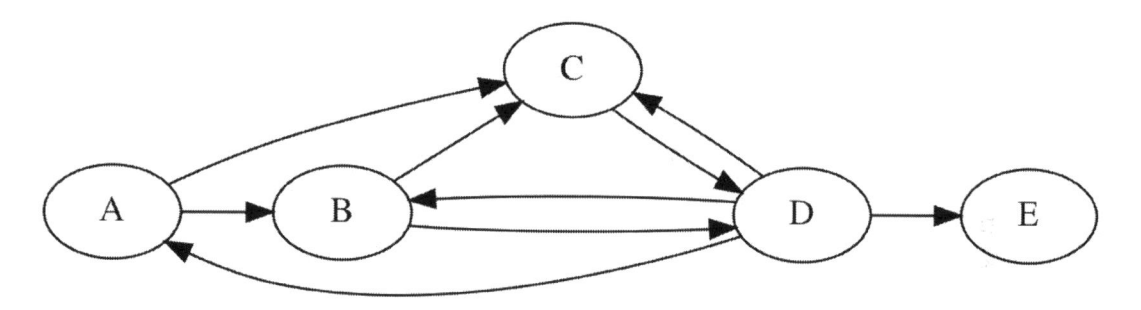

Figure 13.1: Example Web Page Links

We can model such a network with the following table.

```
q)show t:([page:`A`B`C`D`E]A:01100b;B:00110b;C:00010b;D:11101b;E:00000b)
page| A B C D E
----| ---------
A   | 0 0 0 1 0
B   | 1 0 0 1 0
C   | 1 1 0 1 0
D   | 0 1 1 0 0
E   | 0 0 0 1 0
```

The adjacency matrix A can then be extracted.

```
q)show A:"f"$value flip value t
0 1 1 0 0
0 0 1 1 0
0 0 0 1 0
1 1 1 0 1
0 0 0 0 0
```

## 13.2 Markov Matrix

A Markov matrix (also known as a stochastic matrix) has rows and/or columns that sum to 1. It can also be thought of as a probability or transition matrix because it can be used to transform a vector from one state to the next by a single matrix multiplication. Let's first transform our adjacency matrix into a Markov matrix by dividing each row by the total number of links.

```
q)A%sum each A
0    0.5  0.5  0    0
0    0    0.5  0.5  0
0    0    0    1    0
0.25 0.25 0.25 0    0.25
```

Notice that the last row has become null. The problem here is that page E has no links and was therefore divided by 0. If you recall, the PageRank algorithm assumes the web surfer will randomly travel to a new web page in this case. We can represent this by adding links to all other pages in the network (including itself) and adjust the Markov matrix M accordingly.

```
q)show M:((s=0)%n:count A)+A%1|s:sum each A
0    0.5  0.5  0    0
0    0    0.5  0.5  0
0    0    0    1    0
0.25 0.25 0.25 0    0.25
0.2  0.2  0.2  0.2  0.2
```

If we assume, now, that we started on page A with probability 1, we can use the Markov matrix M to transition the probabilities from page A to each of the pages that page A links to with equal probability.

```
q)1 0 0 0 0f $ M
0 0.5 0.5 0 0
```

We see that a surfer starting on page A clicks to page B with 50% probability and page C with the remaining 50% probability. We can take another step by multiplying the initial vector by M two times. Since page C only has a single link to page D and page B will split its probability between pages C and D, we should expect the new state vector to have 25% weight on page C and 75% on page D.

```
q)2 $[;M]/ 1 0 0 0 0f
0 0 0.25 0.75 0
```

## 13.3. GOOGLE MATRIX

Letting the surfer continue this process until a steady state is reached, we can find the probability a surfer will be on each of the pages in the network.

```
q)$[;M] over 1 0 0 0 0f
0.1117318 0.1675978 0.2513966 0.3575419 0.1117318
```

Page D is clearly the winner here, and we would declare that it has the highest rank.

## 13.3 Google Matrix

Before proceeding, let's consider the fact that we allowed the surfer to randomly travel to a new page when there were no links on the current page. That seems quite reasonable. But is it reasonable for a person to follow the one and only link on a page? The PageRank algorithm does not think so. It allows for the web surfer to give up following links and randomly choose a new page. This is considered the damping factor--because its effect is to smooth out the differences between the highest and lowest values.

This damping factor is commonly taken as .85 (which corresponds to a probability of random surfing of .15). If we dampen the Markov matrix M by this damping factor, we arrive at the Google matrix G. Note that damping has no effect on pages with no links because the surfer will be visiting a random page anyway.

```
q)d:.85
q)(d*M)+(1f-d)%n
0.03   0.455  0.455  0.03   0.03
0.03   0.03   0.455  0.455  0.03
0.03   0.03   0.03   0.88   0.03
0.2425 0.2425 0.2425 0.03   0.2425
0.2    0.2    0.2    0.2    0.2
```

The transformation from the adjacency matrix to the Google matrix is encapsulated in the .ml.google function.

### .ml.google

```
/ given a (d)amping factor (1 - the probability of random surfing) and the
/ (A)djacency matrix, create the Markov Google matrix
google:{[d;A]
  M:A%1f|s:sum each A;            / convert to Markov matrix
```

```
  M+:(0f=s)%n:count M;         / add links to dangling pages
  M:(d*M)+(1f-d)%n;            / dampen
  M}
```

We can get a more intuitive understanding of how the Google Matrix behaves by varying the damping factor d. At one extreme, setting the damping factor to 1 represents no random surfing unless a page with no links is encountered.

```
q)\l funq.q
q).ml.google[1;A]
0    0.5  0.5  0    0
0    0    0.5  0.5  0
0    0    0    1    0
0.25 0.25 0.25 0    0.25
0.2  0.2  0.2  0.2  0.2
```

This is the same as our original example. At the other extreme, setting the damping factor to 0 assumes every new page a surfer visits has no relationship to the links on the pages.

```
q).ml.google[0;A]
0.2 0.2 0.2 0.2 0.2
0.2 0.2 0.2 0.2 0.2
0.2 0.2 0.2 0.2 0.2
0.2 0.2 0.2 0.2 0.2
0.2 0.2 0.2 0.2 0.2
```

All transition probabilities are equal and the resulting ranks are also equal.

```
q)$[;.ml.google[0;A]] over n#1f%n
0.2 0.2 0.2 0.2 0.2
```

## 13.4 Power Method

Using the Google matrix to derive each page's rank is known as the power method. It is elegant and converges quickly. The closer our initial vector is to the optimal solution the fewer iterations are required. It is therefore common to start with an equal-weighted initial vector. We can see how many iterations are required for convergence by counting the results of using the scan operator (instead of over).

## 13.5. ALGEBRAIC PAGERANK

```
q)G:.ml.google[.85;A]
q)$[;G] over 1 0 0 0 0f
0.1219009 0.1737088 0.2475351 0.3349542 0.1219009
q)count $[;G] scan 1 0 0 0 0f
37
q)count $[;G] scan n#1%n
34
```

## 13.5 Algebraic PageRank

Given the damping factor and the adjacency matrix, it is also possible to compute the page ranks algebraically. As we iterate through power method, the PageRank algorithm converges to a value that satisfies the following equation.

$$R = dRM + \frac{1-d}{n}I$$

Where d is the damping parameter, M is the Markov matrix, R is the PageRank vector, n is the rank of the matrix, 1 is a vector of ones and I is the identity matrix with ones along the diagonal. In summary, it states that the PageRank vector is the rank vector that remains unchanged when multiplied by the transition matrix and then dampened.

If we subtract the dMR term to the left-hand side and factor out the rank vector R, we obtain an equation that can be solved by least squares regression.

$$R(I - dM) = \frac{1-d}{n}I$$

The .ml.pageranka function uses least squares to solve for the rank vector R. The implementation calls .ml.mlsq, which defaults to the native q linear least squares operator lsq that is implemented as a matrix inversion of the normal equations. The .ml.mlsq function can be overwritten if a faster (and/or more robust) implementation is available.[2]

**.ml.pageranka**

```
/ given a (d)amping factor (1 - the probability of random surfing) and the
/ (A)djacency matrix, obtain the pagerank algebraically
```

---

[2]The QML math library developed by Andrey Zholos provides interfaces to fast and robust implementations of linear least squares, which can use QR, LQ or SVD factorization.

```
pageranka:{[d;A]
  M:A%1f|s:sum each A;          / convert to Markov matrix
  M+:(0f=s)%n:count M;          / add links to dangling pages
  r:prb first mlsq[(1;n)#(1f-d)%n] eye[n]-d*M;  / compute rankings
  r}
```

In one shot, we can compute the PageRank vector.

```
q).ml.pageranka[d;A]
0.1219009 0.1737088 0.2475351 0.3349542 0.1219009
```

It may seem that this approach is clearly better than the iterative algorithm, but as with most choices—it depends. If you have no prior knowledge about the approximate page rankings, the iterative approach may take a long time to converge. On the other hand, if you have rankings stored from a previous run of the PageRank algorithm, it may only take a few iterations to converge a slightly changed adjacency matrix. The network of page links on an intranet—not to mention the internet—doesn't change drastically from day to day. Given the large size of the adjacency matrix, it would be preferable to perform a few iterations, rather than a full linear least squares.

The power method, too, has its own problems. When we scale the adjacency matrix up to the full size of a typical network, we realize that most of the values are 0 and the matrix is very sparse. Taking advantage of this fact drastically reduces the amount of computation we need to perform. Before we tackle the sparse matrix implementation of the PageRank algorithm, let's first review an iterative approach that does not destroy the sparsity of the adjacency matrix.

## 13.6 Iterative PageRank

The .ml.pageranki function accepts the damping factor d, the adjacency matrix A and a vector of initial page ranks r.

### .ml.pageranki

```
/ given a (d)amping factor (1 - the probability of random surfing), the
/ (A)djacency matrix and an initial (r)ank vector, obtain a better ranking
/ (iterative model)
pageranki:{[d;A;r]
  w:sum r*0f=s:sum each A;          / compute dangling weight
  r:sum[A*r%1f|s]+w%n:count A;      / compute rankings
```

```
r:(d*r)+(1f-d)%n;            / dampen
r}
```

This time, instead of manipulating the adjacency matrix to fill in dangling links and perform damping, we perform these modifications on the incoming and outgoing rank vectors respectively. This vastly reduces the number of operations needed because the rank vector grows linearly with the number of pages while the adjacency matrix grows quadratically. The function first computes the total weight that will be lost due to dangling links. Knowing that we are going to multiply the adjacency matrix by the supplied rank vector, we can convert the adjacency matrix into a Markov matrix by adjusting the rank vector directly. And finally, the function dampens the resulting ranks.

We can compute the page ranks by first initializing the rank vector r with equal weights, and then applying the `.ml.pageranki` iterative-page-rank algorithm until convergence.

```
q)0N!r:n#1f%n:count A
0.2 0.2 0.2 0.2 0.2
q).ml.pageranki[d;A] over r
0.1219009 0.1737088 0.2475351 0.3349542 0.1219009
```

The solution converges just as quickly as the power method but doesn't require the generation of a dense matrix. This will be useful as we take the next step to implement a sparse matrix version of the PageRank algorithm.

## 13.7  Sparse Matrices

The adjacency matrix describing links between pages across the internet is filled with zeros. Web pages typically only link to a few other pages—not every other page on the internet. Having to build a full matrix for all the possible links between pages is a waste of memory. The alternative is to store the data in a sparse matrix. Matlab has native handling of sparse matrices: transposition, multiplication, inversion, etc. To do this in q, however, we must implement our own sparse matrix functions.

### Tensor Shape

The first order of business is to decide on a storage format. There is no canonical sparse matrix format. Formats range from intuitive and convenient to efficient.

Regardless of the storage format, we need to record the dimensions of the matrix. Without this separate record, we would have no way of knowing the actual dimensions of the matrix if any of the last rows or columns had all zeros. By only listing the non-zero values, a sparse matrix representation would completely lose all evidence of these dimensions. To obtain the matrix dimensions we enlist the help of the .ml.shape function, which accepts an atom, vector, matrix, or even a nested matrix whose values are themselves vectors (in other words, a tensor).

**.ml.shape**

```
shape:{$[0h>t:type x;0#0;n:count x;n,.z.s x 0;1#0]}
```

The result of the function is a list of integers indicating the size of each of the tensor's dimensions. A three-element vector, for example, has a shape of 3.

```
q).ml.shape 1 2 3
,3
```

A 3 x 4 matrix has a shape of:

```
q).ml.shape n # til prd n:3 4
3 4
```

This is sufficient for our purposes, but .ml.shape works equally well for higher rank tensors.

```
q).ml.shape n # til prd n:3 4 5
3 4 5
```

And if you are wondering, an empty list has a shape of 0,

```
q).ml.shape ()
,0
```

and an atom doesn't have a shape:

```
q).ml.shape 0
`long$()
```

## Tensor Where

Generating the sparse matrix also requires us to find the indices of the non-zero matrix values. This sounds similar to the where operator, which finds the indices of the non-zero elements of a vector.

## 13.7. SPARSE MATRICES

```
q)where 010101011101b
1 3 5 7 8 9 11
```

In our case, we need it to work for matrices. The `.ml.twhere` function extends the `where` operator's functionality for tensors (of any rank).

**.ml.twhere**

```
/ tensor variant of where
twhere:{
 if[type x;:enlist where x];
 x:(,'/) til[count x] {((1;count y 0)#x),y}' .z.s each x;
 x}
```

For a vector, the results are the same.

```
q).ml.twhere 010101011101b
1 3 5 7 8 9 11
```

For a matrix, however, the function returns two vectors—one element each for the non-zero elements. The first vector contains the row indices of the non-zero elements and the second vector contains the column indices of the non-zero elements.

```
q).ml.twhere enlist 010101011101b
0 0 0 0 0 0 0
1 3 5 7 8 9 11
```

And if we reshape the value into a three-dimensional tensor, we get one vector for each of the three dimensions.

```
q).ml.twhere 2 2 3 # 010101011101b
0 0 0 1 1 1 1
0 1 1 0 0 1 1
1 0 2 1 2 0 2
```

Returning to our adjacency matrix, we can obtain the coordinates of the non-zero values.

```
q).ml.twhere "b"$A
0 0 1 1 2 3 3 3 3
1 2 2 3 3 0 1 2 4
```

## Indexing at Depth

Using these coordinates, we can index back into the matrix to obtain the non-zero values. The q operator `'` is often used as "each-both". When the operator is applied to a tensor instead of a function, however, it can be thought of as "apply at depth". For example, we can extract the first two non-zero elements.

```
q)0 0 A' 1 2
1 1f
q)A'[0 0;1 2]
1 1f
```

Combined with the "dot-index" operator `.`, we can retrieve all the non-zero elements of the adjacency matrix.

```
q)(A') . .ml.twhere "b"$A
1 1 1 1 1 1 1 1f
```

## Sparse Tensors

Combining these techniques allows us to store all the relevant data of a sparse tensor: the dimensions, the non-zero values and then the indices of the non-zero values.

### .ml.sparse

```
/ sparse from tensor
sparse:{(shape x;(x') . I),I:twhere "b"$x}
```

If passed a matrix, the function returns a four-element list. The first element indicates the dimensions of the original matrix. The second element is the vector of non-zero values, and the third and fourth elements are the i and j indices corresponding to the non-zero values stored at (i;j).

This is how our test adjacency matrix would be stored as a sparse matrix.

```
q).ml.sparse A
5 5
1 1 1 1 1 1 1 1f
0 0 1 1 2 3 3 3
1 2 2 3 3 0 1 2 4
```

## 13.7. SPARSE MATRICES

Notice how the sparse matrix representation is actually larger than our original matrix. The matrix is not sparse enough and the specification of each of the i and j indices generates a lot of repetition. For larger matrices that have a higher percentage of zero values, however, the savings can be substantial.

We first observe that it is also possible to convert a sparse tensor back into a full tensor with the .ml.full function.

**.ml.full**

```
/ tensor from sparse
full:{./[x[0]#0f;flip 2_x;:;x 1]}

q).ml.full .ml.sparse A
0 1 1 0 0
0 0 1 1 0
0 0 0 1 0
1 1 1 0 1
0 0 0 0 0
```

Before moving on to computing page ranks on this sparse matrix representation of the adjacency matrix, we quickly note that this representation of sparse matrices is by no means authoritative. The actual use-case dictates which format is preferred. Some, like the Dictionary of Keys (DOK) format, store the data as a dictionary of the indices mapped to their values:

```
q){flip[i]!(x') . i:.ml.twhere "b"$ x} A
0 1| 1
0 2| 1
1 2| 1
1 3| 1
2 3| 1
3 0| 1
3 1| 1
3 2| 1
3 4| 1
```

Other formats, such as the List of List (LIL), drop the need to store the row index by including it implicitly in the data structure. Because there is one list for each row, we only need to store the column and its corresponding matrix value.

```
q){i,''(x@')i:where each "b"$ x} A
((1;1f);(2;1f))
((2;1f);(3;1f))
```

```
,(3;1f)
((0;1f);(1;1f);(2;1f);(4;1f))
()
```

Finally, we are using a variant of the Coordinate list (COO) format that stores tuples containing the row index, column index and matrix value. Because q stores dictionaries as lists, this format is visually similar to the DOK format.

```
q)flip {i,enlist (x') . i:.ml.twhere "b"$ x}   A
0 1 1f
0 2 1f
1 2 1f
1 3 1f
2 3 1f
3 0 1f
3 1 1f
3 2 1f
3 4 1f
```

You may have noticed that there is a lot of repetition when multiple values appear in the same row or column. For more storage compression, other formats, such as Compressed Sparse Row (CSR) or Compressed Sparse Column (CSC), can be used that only store changes in the row or column index. This compression comes at the expense of algorithmic complexity. We will retain each of the indices to take advantage of q's vector operators.

## 13.8 Sparse Matrix Iterative PageRank

Just having the .ml.sparse and .ml.full functions is not enough to implement a sparse matrix iterative version of the PageRank algorithm. In a perfect world, we would pass the sparse matrix to the original .ml.pageranki function and q would know how to handle the basic matrix operations just like Matlab. The k struct underlying all q objects has just enough room to hold flags for the existing four attributes (`s, `u, `p, `g). Having more flags to identify matrices and sparse matrices could speed up matrix manipulation and allow native handling of sparse matrices. Alas, this is not currently possible, and we must write our own function to perform sparse matrix multiplication: .ml.smm.

**.ml.smm**

## 13.8. SPARSE MATRIX ITERATIVE PAGERANK

```
/ sparse matrix multiplication
smm:{
 t:ej[`;flip `v``c!1_y;flip`w`r`!1_x];
 t:0!select sum w*v by c,r from t;
 m:enlist[(x[0;0];y[0;1])],reverse value flip t;
 m}
```

Using .ml.smm we can now implement a sparse version of the iterative PageRank algorithm .ml.pageranks as well.

### .ml.pageranks

```
/ (S)parse adjacency matrix and an initial (r)ank vector, obtain a better
/ ranking (iterative model)
pageranks:{[d;S;r]
 w:sum r*0f=s:0f^sum'[S[1] group S 2]til n:S[0;0];   / compute dangling weight
 r:first full[smm[sparse enlist r%1f|s;S]]+w%n;      / compute rankings
 r:(d*r)+(1f-d)%n;                                   / dampen
 r}
```

Pulling everything together, we can generate the page ranks using sparse matrices.

```
q).ml.pageranks[d;.ml.sparse A] over r
0.1219009 0.1737088 0.2475351 0.3349542 0.1219009
```

Having to create a sparse matrix by first creating a full matrix and then calling .ml.sparse defeats the memory-saving advantages of the sparse matrix. We are in luck because network diagrams are typically stored as a list of node pairs. Let's take a look at some rather large network graphs to test our algorithm. The Stanford Analysis Project site hosts downloadable network graphs for analysis. We will download the Berkeley and Stanford directed web graph[3] using the berkstan.q [379] library. There are 685,230 distinct pages (or nodes) and 7,600,595 links (or edges) between pages. The graph consists of two vectors: the first vector is a list of the "from" nodes and the second vector is a list of the "to" nodes.

```
q)\l berkstan.q
[down]loading berkstan network graph
q)berkstan.l
1 1 1 1 1  1  1       1      254913 254913 254913 254913 254913 254913 254..
2 5 7 8 9 11 17 254913 438238 255378 255379 255383 255384 255392 255393 255..
```

---
[3] J. Leskovec, K. J. Lang, A. Dasgupta, and M. W. Mahoney, "Community Structure in Large Networks: Natural Cluster Sizes and the Absence of Large Well-Defined Clusters," *Internet Mathematics*, 6(1), 29-123, 2009.

The Stanford Berkeley data set has ensured that the nodes are compactly represented and range from 1 to 685,230. If we used the nodes directly as matrix indices we would build a matrix with one dimension too big. This is not a problem because we are building a sparse matrix. The resulting page rank vector will be as long as the largest matrix index. There are other data sets, however, that are not as cleanly presented. Sometimes the nodes skip values and introduce many unused values with very large node value ranges. Other times the nodes are represented as symbols and not integers. In both of these cases, we need to map each of the nodes to a list of contiguous integers starting at 0 so that the network can be mapped to a compact matrix.

Regardless of the data type, the method is the same. Create a list of all the unique node values and map each one to it's associated index. After computing the page ranks on these indices, we can then map the indices back to their original node values.

This technique may sound familiar to you. It is exactly how enumerations are generated and used. We are in fact enumerating the nodes. The first step is to generate a list of unique nodes—sorting them so mapping from value to index is quicker.

```
q)node:asc distinct raze berkstan.l
```

We then map from the original node value to the new index.

```
q)l:node?berkstan.l
```

By prefixing the two vectors stored in l with the matrix dimensions and a list of ones, we can now generate a compact sparse adjacency matrix.

```
q)show S:(1 2#1+max over l), .ml.prepend[1f] l
685230 685230
1 1 1 1 1 1 1 1 1 1 1 1 1 1 1 1 1 1 1 1 1 1 1 1 1 1 1 1 1 1 1 1..
0 0 0 0 0 0 0 0 0 254912 254912 254912 254912 254912 254912 254912 254912..
1 4 6 7 8 10 16 254912 438237 255377 255378 255382 255383 255391 255392 2..
```

Attempting to convert this sparse matrix to a full matrix will fail on the 32-bit free version of kdb+. The size is larger than the 4 GB limit (don't say I didn't warn you). Our sparse matrix implementation of the PageRank algorithm allows us to easily manipulate this network. Even though complete convergence of such a large matrix takes many iterations, the top ranks quickly become apparent. We will run 10 iterations to highlight these pages.

```
q)show r:10 .ml.pageranks[d;S]/ n#1f%n:S[0;0]
1.983984e-05 4.488031e-06 5.791966e-07 5.280395e-07 3.00803e-06 5.280395e..
```

## 13.8. SPARSE MATRIX ITERATIVE PAGERANK

Then we map the sorted (descending) page ranks back to their original node values.

```
q)node[i]!r i:idesc r
272919| 0.009701693
438238| 0.007590779
210376| 0.005189093
210305| 0.005103315
601656| 0.003726667
571448| 0.003548818
316792| 0.002754501
..
```

With this iterative approach we can see if the ranks change much after one more iteration. It seems not.

```
q)node[i]!r i:idesc .ml.pageranks[d;S] r
272919| 0.009701693
438238| 0.007590779
210376| 0.005189093
210305| 0.005103315
601656| 0.003726667
571448| 0.003548818
316792| 0.002754501
..
```

Using this approach, we can use the stored page ranks and periodically re-apply the iterative algorithm to reflect any changes in the ranking that network changes may cause.

We now take a step away from machine-learning algorithms to review the .ut.plot function which has helped us visualize data sets, algorithm parameters and evaluation metrics. To motivate our analysis of text graphics, we will generate the Mandelbrot set and the requisite complex arithmetic functions. Before turning your nose up at the thought of more math, take solace in the knowledge that the chapter ends with a lighthearted demonstration of how financial time series charts can be displayed in a single line of text. Join me, let's have some fun.

# Chapter 14

# Graphics

> Above all else show the data.
> — Edward R. Tufte *The Visual Display of Quantitative Information*

Visually inspecting data—with a proper chart—often reveals structure that is difficult to extract by numerical analysis alone. We first encountered the .ut.plt projection in Chapter 3 [45] when we demonstrated how the centroids moved and converged towards the center of each cluster as we iterated over the k-means algorithm. Then we saw how the optimal number of k-means centroids could be picked by visual inspection of the elbow plot in Section 3.6 [61]. Section 4.7 [78] showed how we can choose the optimal number of clusters used in hierarchical agglomerative clustering by visually inspecting a silhouette plot. Our understanding of how the expectation-maximization algorithm learned the essence of each handwritten digit from the MNIST data set in Chapter 5 [83] was enhanced by our ability to view each digit. Similarly, we saw how the neural networks generated in Chapter 11 [237] sometimes incorrectly classified images—even though I assume you were able to identify them correctly.

We introduced four different impurity functions in Section 7.1 [132], and although they are each mathematically different, their plots reveal how similar they actually are. Section 8.4 [169] used .ut.plt to demonstrate how adding more trees to the random forest always increases accuracy within the training data. Similarly, Section 8.5 [173] used a plot to show how increasing the number of stumps in an ensemble also increases its accuracy. And finally, Section 9.7 [190] plotted the sin function to explain gradient descent and Section 10.3 [220] plotted the sigmoid function to demonstrate logistic regression's activation function.

Edward R. Tufte is famous for promoting graphical representations of data that maximize the information content while minimizing the amount of ink drawn on the page. Although kdb+ does not come with a built-in graphics package, a fixed-width font and q's ability to pretty print matrices with aligned columns allow us to create a function that can plot one, two or three-dimensional data sets. With our limited canvas, we are forced to focus on showing the data.

## 14.1 ASCII plots

Generating an ASCII plot requires the user to make three choices. The user must first select how many rows and columns the plot should cover. The palette of ASCII characters must be selected and the method of data aggregation for overlapping data points must be chosen.

### Plot Dimensions

Fixed-width (terminal) fonts are twice as high as they are wide. We should therefore specify approximately twice as many columns as rows in order to create a square plot. Note that some pictures look better when we use one less than twice as many rows. The default implementation of the .ut.plt projection, uses an odd number of columns.

**.ut.plt**

```
plt:plot[19;10;c10;avg]          / default plot function
```

This allows the plot to be visually centered—rather than have a gap in the middle.

### Character Selection

After picking the number of columns and rows, we must then choose how to associate grayscale values with different ASCII characters. ASCII characters vary in density between the space character " ", which has no visual *ink*, and the "@" character, which has the most *ink*. In addition to binning the x and y coordinates

# 14.1. ASCII PLOTS

into the specified width and height, the z coordinate must also be binned into the number of characters we chose.

For small images—or for images with little variability on intensity value, we can choose a small list of 10 characters.

**.ut.c10**

```
c10:" .-:=+x#%@"                          / 10 characters
```

For a slightly more detailed view, 16 characters can be used.

**.ut.c16**

```
c16:" .-:=+*xoX0#$&%@"                    / 16 characters
```

Paul Bourke suggests a 70 character "continuous" gradation.[1] Q escapes the backslash and quote characters by preceding them with an extra backslash. These characters are printed as two characters and are therefore inappropriate for displaying a single *pixel*. We drop these two characters from the list and provide a 68 character *palette*.

**.ut.c68**

```
c68:" .'`^,:;Il!i><~+_-?][}{1)(|/tfjrxn"  / 68 characters
c68,:"uvczXYUJCLQ00Zmwqpdbkhao*#MW&8%B@$"
```

Note that some characters such as "(" and ")" are mirror images of each other and don't actually add extra shades of gray. In addition, the amount of *ink* used to print a character depends on the font.

## Aggregation Function

The final choice we need to make is how to aggregate samples that fall within the same bin. There are times when we want to use the avg operator to average across all the values in a bin. This provides the average density. We used this configuration for displaying MNIST digits. At other times, we want to use the sum operator to sum the values in each bin. This gives us the ability to see how densely the data is plotted when each of our Z-values are equal. And finally, when the Z-values represent a categorical value, it is most appropriate to use the .ml.mode operator to see the most represented class within the bin.

---

[1] P. Bourke, "Character representation of grey scale images," Feb-1997. [Online]. Available: http://paulbourke.net/dataformats/asciiart/. [Accessed: 20-Dec-2019].

After making these choices, the last parameter to the .ut.plot utility is the actual data, which can be a single vector of x values, a pair of vectors representing x and y coordinates or even a triplet of vectors representing x, y and z coordinates.

**.ut.plot**

```
/ using (a)ggregation (f)unction, plot (X) using (c)haracters limited to
/ (w)idth and (h)eight. X can be x, (x;y), or (x;y;z)
plot:{[w;h;c;af;X]
 if[type X;X:enlist X];                 / promote vector to matrix
 if[1=count X;X:(til count X 0;X 0)];   / turn ,x into (x;y)
 if[2=count X;X,:count[X 0]#1];         / turn (x;y) into (x;y;z)
 if[not `s=attr X 0;c:1_c];             / remove space unless heatmap
 l:heckbert[h div 2].(min;max)@\:X 1;   / generate labels
 x:-1_nseq[w] . (min;max)@\:X 0;        / compute x axis
 y:-1_nseq[h] . (first;last)@\:l;       / compute y axis
 Z:(y;x) bin' "f"$X 1 0;                / allocate (x;y) to (w;h) bins
 Z:af each X[2]group flip Z;            / aggregating overlapping z
 Z:c nbin[count c;0f^Z];                / map values to characters
 p:./[(h;w)#" ";key Z;:;value Z];       / plot points
 k:@[count[y]#0n;0|y bin l;:;l];        / generate key
 p:reverse k!p;                         / generate plot
 p}
```

## Heat Maps

The first three lines of the .ut.plot utility massage the X parameter into x, y and z vectors. If only x values are supplied, they are treated as the y vector and an evenly spaced x vector is provided. Similarly, if no z values are supplied, a vector of ones is generated. Before moving into the data manipulation, the 4th line of the function checks for an `s attribute on the x vector of the X parameter. This was a tricky way of flagging the X parameter as a being a heat map and that we should therefore not remove the space character from the c parameter. The `s attribute is applied in .ut.hmap after converting a matrix of data into a triplet of x, y and z vectors.

**.ut.hmap**

```
/ cut m x n matrix X into (x;y;z) where x and y are the indices for X
/ and z is the value stored in X[x;y] - result used to plot heatmaps
hmap:{[X]@[;0;`s#]tcross[til count X;reverse til count X 0],enlist raze X}
```

## 14.1. ASCII PLOTS

As an example, given a diagonal matrix with the values 1, 2 and 3,

```
q)\l funq.q
q).ml.diag 1+til 3
1 0 0
0 2 0
0 0 3
```

the .ut.hmap function converts the matrix to coordinate vectors.

```
q).ut.hmap .ml.diag 1+til 3
0 0 0 1 1 1 2 2 2
2 1 0 2 1 0 2 1 0
1 0 0 0 2 0 0 0 3
```

As Example 14.1 [317] demonstrates, these coordinate vectors can then be passed to the .ut.plt projection to visualize the data.

**Example 14.1** Heat Map

```
q)  .ut.plt .ut.hmap .ml.diag 1+til 3
2.5| "                    "
2  | ":                   "
   | "                    "
1.5| "                    "
   | "                    "
1  | "          x         "
   | "                    "
0.5| "                    "
   | "                    "
0  | "                  @"
```

A value of 0 within a heat map means that the value should receive the minimum *ink* and should therefore not be printed. In this case, the space character " " is preserved. In other plotting scenarios, any (x;y;z) triplet is intended to be plotted, so we do not remove the space character.

## Table Cross

The .ml.hmap heat map function uses the .ut.tcross table cross utility to efficiently cross two vectors of coordinates. The native cross operator generates a long list of paired values. Generating many small vectors is a good way to fragment q's memory.

```
q)til[10] cross til 10
0 0
0 1
0 2
0 3
0 4
0 5
0 6
..
```

Given that we want to flip this result, it is better to use a more efficient algorithm that returns two long vectors. Crossing two tables generates what looks like the same long list of paired coordinates.

```
q)([]x:til 10) cross ([]y:til 10)
x y
---
0 0
0 1
0 2
0 3
0 4
..
```

Recall, however, that kdb+ is a columnar database and that the x and y columns are themselves vectors. We can, therefore, extract the columns without reallocating memory.

```
q)value flip ([]x:til 10) cross ([]y:til 10)
0 0 0 0 0 0 0 0 0 0 1 1 1 1 1 1 1 1 1 1 2 2 2 2 2 2 2 2 2 2 3 3 3 3 3 3..
0 1 2 3 4 5 6 7 8 9 0 1 2 3 4 5 6 7 8 9 0 1 2 3 4 5 6 7 8 9 0 1 2 3 4 5 6..
```

The .ut.tcross table-cross function uses q's ability to efficiently cross tables to return a pair of long vectors instead of a long vector of pairs.

**.ut.tcross**

```
/ table x cross y
tcross:{value flip ([]x) cross ([]y)}
```

## Axis Labels

After the space character is removed for all plots other than heat maps, the next line of the .ut.plot utility uses Paul Heckbert's "nice numbers for graph labels" algorithm[2] to generate labels for the y axes.

We have two goals when generating axes labels. The first is to round the min (max) value down (up) to reasonably *nice* numbers. The second goal is to find a few evenly spaced labels between the min and max labels that are also *nice* numbers. A poor way of generating labels would be to divide the min and max values into evenly spaced values. If, for example, we wanted to divide the range from $-.01\pi$ to $.01\pi$ into 5 bins, we would have very wide labels with a level of detail that is irrelevant.

```
q)enlist each reverse .ut.nseq[5] . -1 1*.01*.ml.pi
0.03141593
0.01884956
0.006283185
-0.006283185
-0.01884956
-0.03141593
```

One option is to round the numbers to an appropriately close order of magnitude.

```
q)enlist each reverse .ut.nseq[5] . .ut.rnd[.01] -1 1*.01*.ml.pi
0.03
0.018
0.006
-0.006
-0.018
-0.03
```

## Nice Numbers

We are left with a few challenges. How can we automatically determine that order of magnitude? How can we make these numbers look less *ugly*? The Heckbert algorithm accomplishes these goals by first observing the fact that we use a base-10 numeral system and the only numbers that can evenly divide 10 are 1, 2, 5 and 10—these are referred to as nice numbers. The .ut.nicenum function is designed to round a number to a scaled nice number.

---

[2] P. S. Heckbert, "NICE NUMBERS FOR GRAPH LABELS," in *Graphics Gems*, A. S. Glassner, Ed. San Diego: Morgan Kaufmann, 1990, pp. 61–63.

### .ut.nicenum

```
/ use Heckbert's values to (r)ou(nd) or floor (x) to the nearest nice number
nicenum:{[rnd;x]
  s:`s#$[rnd;0 1.5 3 7;0f,1e-15+1 2 5f]!1 2 5 10f;
  x:f * s x%f:10 xexp floor 10 xlog x;
  x}
```

It can be run in two modes. While the first mode rounds the supplied values up to the next nice number,

```
q)(x;.ut.nicenum[0b] x:1+til 10)
1 2 3 4 5 6 7 8 9 10
1 2 5 5 5 10 10 10 10 10
```

the second mode rounds the number to the nearest nice number.[3]

```
q)(x;.ut.nicenum[1b] x:1+til 10)
1 2 3 4 5 6 7 8 9 10
1 2 5 5 5 5 10 10 10 10
```

The first line of .ut.nicenum function distinguishes between these two modes by creating a different step function depending on the supplied rnd parameter. Step functions in q are similar to dictionaries. They have a domain and a range. But instead of returning a null value when the values used to index into the dictionary don't match a specific key, a step function returns the value corresponding to the last key that is smaller than, or equal to, the supplied value. The key of a step function must obviously be in ascending order, but it is the existence of the `s attribute on the dictionary itself—not just the key—that turns it into a step function.

```
q)0N!`s#0 1.5 3 7!1 2 5 10;
`s#`s#0 1.5 3 7!1 2 5 10
```

## Heckbert Algorithm

The Heckbert algorithm starts by rounding the range of values *up* to the nearest nice number.

### .ut.heckbert

---

[3]Heckbert's original nice number implementation does, in fact, define 7 as being closer to 10 than 5.

## 14.1. ASCII PLOTS

```
/ given suggested (n)umber of labels and the (m)i(n) and (m)a(x) values, use
/ Heckbert's algorithm to generate a series of nice numbers
heckbert:{[n;mn;mx]
  r:nicenum[0b] mx-mn;        / range of values
  s:nicenum[1b] r%n-1;        / step size
  mn:s*floor mn%s;            / new min
  mx:s*ceiling mx%s;          / new max
  l:sseq[s;mn;mx];            / labels
  l}
```

It then computes a nice step size by rounding the raw step size to the nearest nice number. New nice min and max values are generated by taking the floor and ceiling of the step-scaled raw min and max values. The final stage of the .ut.heckbert function generates a range of values using the nice min, nice max and nice step size—how nice. Here are a few examples.

```
q).ut.heckbert[5;.01;.08]
0 0.02 0.04 0.06 0.08 0.1
q).ut.heckbert[5;12;51]
10 20 30 40 50 60f
q).ut.heckbert[5;80;121]
70 80 90 100 110 120 130f
```

## Binning Numbers

With the min and max y-labels determined, the .ut.plot utility proceeds to use the .ut.nseq sequence function to generate the x and y bins in which the data points will be placed. The function then allocates each of the data points—identified by their x and y coordinates—into the bins. These coordinates, which are stored in the Z variable, are grouped and aggregated with the provided aggregating function af. The new Z values must then be mapped to characters specified in c. The .ut.nbin binning function divides the range of the x argument into n evenly-spaced bins.

### .ut.nbin

```
/ allocate x into n bins
nbin:{[n;x](n-1)&floor n*.5^x%max x-:min x}
```

We've determined the character set, identified the labels, binned the x and y axes, and aggregated and binned the z values. It is finally time to generate the ASCII plot

p. By iteratively using the . apply function, *paint* is applied to an empty canvas, which is generated by reshaping the null character.

```
q)(5;10)#" "
" "    " "
" "    " "
" "    " "
" "    " "
" "    " "
```

The coordinates of each point are pulled from the key of the grouped Z values while the character destined for each *pixel* is found in the dictionary's values.

## Assigning Axis Labels

A bit of hand waving needs to be performed in order to determine the row for each label. When we used the .ut.heckbert function to generate labels, we only requested labels for half of the rows. This was only a *suggestion* for the algorithm because the Heckbert algorithm is allowed to generate more or less labels in order to ensure they are nice. Asking half as many labels as there are rows gives us enough room for a few extra labels. Ultimately, however, there are a different number of labels as there are rows in our grid. We may therefore be forced to place evenly-spaced labels unevenly on the grid. This is accomplished by starting with a vector of null labels and then using the bin operator to find the exact row that corresponds to the predefined labels. Example 14.2 [322] shows how these evenly-spaced labels are unevenly-placed.

---

**Example 14.2** Axis Labels

```
q).ut.plt til 5
4| "              +"
 | "               "
3| "         +     "
 | "               "
2| "     +         "
 | "               "
 | "               "
1| "   +           "
 | "               "
0| "+              "
```

---

## 14.2. MANDELBROT SET

Notice how there is an extra row between the 1 and 2.

The function completes by generating a dictionary where the key is the label vector and the value is the matrix of characters. When displayed in the terminal, q adds a vertical axes-line between the labels and data. Note that the dictionary is reversed to meet our expectation that small numbers appear at the bottom of a chart and rise as we move to the top.

## 14.2 Mandelbrot Set

An interesting (and fun) picture to render with ASCII art is the Mandelbrot set. The Mandelbrot set is defined as the set of complex numbers for which the function $f_c(z) = z^2 + c$ remains bounded when iterated, beginning with $z = 0$. For example, the complex number 0 is in the Mandelbrot set because the absolute value of the series $f_0(0), f_0(f_0(0)), ...$ remains below 2.

### Complex Multiplication

Q does not have complex numbers as native types, so we must implement complex multiplication ourselves. We will represent a complex number as a pair of values: the real component and the imaginary component. Addition of two complex numbers in this notation is simply the addition of the real and imaginary components respectively. Multiplication, however, is a bit more, ahem, complex. If we denote two complex numbers as $x + yi$ and $u + vi$, the rule for multiplication is defined in Equation 14.1 [323].

$$(x + yi)(u + vi) = (xu - yv) + (xv + yu)i$$

Equation 14.1: Complex Multiplication

The funq project provides this as the .ml.cmul complex-multiplication function.

**.ml.cmul**

```
cmul:{((-/)x*y;(+/)x*(|)y)}        / complex multiplication
```

Notice how we used the (-/) notation instead of an anonymous function {x[0]-x[1]} to subtract the two values stored in the result of x*y. The notation

(-/) starts with the first element of the list and subsequently subtracts each of the remaining elements. In this case, there are only two elements, so the result is the same as subtraction.

Unlike +/, which is a common operation defined in q as sum, -/ is quite uncommon, and is not defined. Beyond 2 elements, subtraction is not typically a useful operation. The .ml.cmul function uses the k notation for sum and reverse for symmetry: +/ and | respectively.

## Complex Square

The Mandelbrot function requires us to square z. Instead of calling .ml.cmul with the same argument twice, we can optimize the code and create a new .ml.csqr complex square function that takes a single argument.

**.ml.csqr**

```
csqr:{((-/)x*x;2f*(*/)x)}          / complex square
```

## Black and White Mandelbrot

To generate a black and white Mandelbrot plot we must start with a grid of complex coordinates. An interesting range turns out to be between -2 and .5 in the real domain (x-axis), and symmetrically between -1.25 and 1.25 in the imaginary domain (y-axis). Using the .ut.nseq function in combination with the .ut.tcross function, we can generate all the points for a 1,000 x 1,000 grid.

```
q)w:1000
q)c:.ut.tcross . (.ut.nseq .) each flip (-1+w;-2 -1.25;.5 1.25)
q)c
-2    -2        -2        -2        -2       -2        -2        -2       ..
-1.25 -1.247497 -1.244995 -1.242492 -1.23999 -1.237487 -1.234985 -1.23248..
```

The .ml.mbrotf Mandelbrot function applies one iteration of the Mandelbrot equation.

**.ml.mbrotf**

```
mbrotf:{[c;x]c+csqr x}                      / Mandelbrot function
```

## 14.2. MANDELBROT SET

Running multiple iterations will cause some points on the grid to grow without bound in absolute value. Other points will remain below 2. After 11 iterations, we can see some values are reaching the limits of double floating-point precision.

```
q)11 .ml.mbrotf[c]/0f
-3.60838e+307  -3.157932e+307 -1.164717e+307 -1.231343e+306 1.259006e+306..
-7.206195e+307 -9.438187e+306 6.77516e+306   5.367006e+306  1.864063e+306..
```

In fact, one more iteration renders some values null, and others infinite.

```
q)12 .ml.mbrotf[c]/0f
0w 0w -0w -0w 0w 0w -0w -0w 0w 0w -0w 0w 0w -0w -0w 0w 0w -0w -0w 0w 0w -..
```

Although the absolute value of a complex number can be computed by using the Euclidean norm function .ml.enorm,

```
q).ml.enorm c
2.358495 2.35717 2.355846 2.354525 2.353205 2.351888 2.350572 2.349258 2...
```

we can use the more efficient .ml.enorm2 function as long as we compare the result to 4 instead of 2.

```
q).ml.enorm2 c
5.5625 5.55625 5.550013 5.543788 5.537575 5.531375 5.525188 5.519013 5.51..
```

The .ml.mbrotp Mandelbrot predicate returns a vector of booleans indicating if each element is in the Mandelbrot set.

**.ml.mbrotp**

```
mbrotp:{not 4f<0w^enorm2 x}              / Mandelbrot predicate
```

It is important that we fill any null values with positive infinity 0w to prevent them from being incorrectly flagged as belonging in the Mandelbrot set.

Example 14.3 [326] shows how we can use the plotting function .ut.plot to obtain a glimpse of the Mandelbrot set after 15 rounds.

## Grayscale Mandelbrot

This is not, however, the image we are most familiar with. We typically see a color version where each color represents how many iterations of the Mandelbrot function a given point remains in the Mandelbrot set. To compute these values, we define the .ml.mbrota Mandelbrot-accumulator function.

**Example 14.3** Black and White Mandelbrot Set

```
q)x:w cut .ml.mbrotp 15 .ml.mbrotf[c]/0f
q)-1 value .ut.plot[59;30;.ut.c10;avg] .ut.hmap x;
```

```
                                                       -
                                                      =-.
                                                  .:.#@#  .
                                                  #@@@@=
                                            .    . +@@@@.
                                          .x@x:+@%@@@@@@@@#@-  :.=.
                                          :@@@@@@@@@@@@@@@@%@@#.
                                        .##@@@@@@@@@@@@@@@@@@%-
                      -     .          =#@@@@@@@@@@@@@@@@@@@@%+=
                      .#x:+%=x-        %@@@@@@@@@@@@@@@@@@@@@@x.
                         .=@@@@@@@#:x@@@@@@@@@@@@@@@@@@@@@@@@@#-
                         ...+@@@@@@@@@@@@@@@@@@@@@@@@@@@@@@@@@=
           .             .-#@@@@@@@@@@@@@@@@@@@@@@@@@@@@@@@@@#-
           -             -:#@@@@@@@@@@@@@@@@@@@@@@@@@@@@@@@@@x-
                         -..+@@@@@@@@@@@@@@@@@@@@@@@@@@@@@@@@=
                         .=@@@@@@@#:x@@@@@@@@@@@@@@@@@@@@@@@@#-
                       -##:+@+x-       %@@@@@@@@@@@@@@@@@@@@@@x.
                      -     .         =#@@@@@@@@@@@@@@@@@@@@%+=
                                        .##@@@@@@@@@@@@@@@@@@%-
                                          :@@@@@@@@@@@@@@@@%@@x.
                                          x@x:+@%@@@@@@@@#@-  :-+.
                                            .    .  x@@@@.   .
                                                  #@@@@=
                                                  .:-#@#   .
                                                     +-.
                                                      -
```

#### .ml.mbrota

```
mbrota:{[c;x;n](x;n+mbrotp x:mbrotf[c;x])} / Mandelbrot accumulator
```

The final parameter, n, of the .ml.mbrota Mandelbrot-accumulator function is incremented by 1 if the parameter x passes the .ml.mbrot Mandelbrot predicate. By using the // adverb, we can iterate over both the x and n parameters and generate a grayscale plot in Example 14.4 [328].

## 14.3 Portable Image Formats

Suppose now that we want to store our Mandelbrot image to a file and view it with a standard graphics program. Do we need to write code to export the data to binary formats such as .tiff or .png? There is, in fact, a simpler approach. We can store the data in the .pbm, .pgm and .ppm file formats, which correspond to Portable BitMap, Portable GrayMap and Portable PixMap respectively.

### Portable BitMap

The .pbm Portable BitMap format is the simplest, and easiest to understand. All we need to do is store the text "P1" to identify the format, the dimensions of our image—in this case 1,000 x 1,000—and then a long list of 0s and 1s representing black and white. The .ut.pbm function implements this format.

#### .ut.pbm

```
/ create netpbm bitmap using ascii (or (b)inary) characters for matrix x
pbm:{[b;X]
 s:($[b;"P4";"P1"];-3!count'[(X;X 0)]);
 s,:$[b;enlist"c"$raze((0b sv 8#)each 8 cut raze::)each flip X;" "0:"b"$X];
 s}
```

The first argument of the function is a boolean allowing us to indicate if a more compact binary format P4 should be used. Using the ASCII implementation results in the following text.

```
q)x:w cut .ml.mbrotp 15 .ml.mbrotf[c]/0f
q).ut.pbm[0b] x
"P1"
"1000 1000"
```

**Example 14.4** Gray Scale Mandelbrot Set

```
q)x:w cut last 15 .ml.mbrota[c]// (0f;0)
q)-1 value   .ut.plot[59;30;.ut.c10;avg] .ut.hmap x;
                          ...........................
                          .....................--:!---......
                          .................------:=#=:=----......
                          ...............---------:=x%#x:-----....
                          .............----------:+##@@@x+:------....
                          ...........----------::::=x@@@@@%=::-------..
                          .........----------==+===++x@@@@@@#+=+::::=:-.
                          ........---------::x@@@#%@@@@@@@@@@@@#+#x%x:-
                          ......-----------:::=+%@@@@@@@@@@@@@@@@@@@+:-
                          ......-::::-----::::=x@@@@@@@@@@@@@@@@@@@@#=:-
                          .....----:=#+===x+=====+%@@@@@@@@@@@@@@@@@%%=
                          ....--------:=+#@@%@@%%#++#@@@@@@@@@@@@@@@@@x:
                          ..---------::==#%@@@@@@@%@@@@@@@@@@@@@@@@@@@x:
                          ..------::::+#x#@@@@@@@@@@@@@@@@@@@@@@@@@@@#:-
                          --:::+=====+x#@@@@@@@@@@@@@@@@@@@@@@@@@@@x=:-
                          -:::=x==++++##@@@@@@@@@@@@@@@@@@@@@@@@@@@x=:-
                          ..------::::+#x#@@@@@@@@@@@@@@@@@@@@@@@@@@@#:-
                          ..---------::==#%@@@@@@@@%@@@@@@@@@@@@@@@@@@x:
                          ....--------:=+#@@%@@%@#+x#@@@@@@@@@@@@@@@@@x:
                          .....----:=#+===x+=====+%@@@@@@@@@@@@@@@@@%%=
                          ......-::::-----::::=x@@@@@@@@@@@@@@@@@@@@#=:-
                          ......-----------:::=+%@@@@@@@@@@@@@@@@@@@+:-
                          ........---------:::+@@@%%@@@@@@@@@@@@#+#x%x:-
                          .........----------==+===++x@@@@@@#+++::::=:-.
                          ...........----------::::=x@@@@@@%=::-------..
                          .............----------:+##@@@xx:-------....
                          ...............---------::=x%#+:-----......
                          .................------:=#=:=----......
                          ...................--=:---......
                          .......................
```

## 14.3. PORTABLE IMAGE FORMATS

```
"0 0 0 0 0 0 0 0 0 0 0 0 0 0 0 0 0 0 0 0 0 0 0 0 0 0 0 0 0 0 0 0 ..
"0 0 0 0 0 0 0 0 0 0 0 0 0 0 0 0 0 0 0 0 0 0 0 0 0 0 0 0 0 0 0 0 ..
"0 0 0 0 0 0 0 0 0 0 0 0 0 0 0 0 0 0 0 0 0 0 0 0 0 0 0 0 0 0 0 0 ..
"0 0 0 0 0 0 0 0 0 0 0 0 0 0 0 0 0 0 0 0 0 0 0 0 0 0 0 0 0 0 0 0 ..
"0 0 0 0 0 0 0 0 0 0 0 0 0 0 0 0 0 0 0 0 0 0 0 0 0 0 0 0 0 0 0 0 ..
..
```

The binary implementation stores the format and dimensions in ASCII, but the 0 and 1 values are stored as single bits—and 8 can therefore be stored in a single byte.

```
q).ut.pbm[1b] x
"P4"
"1000 1000"
"\000\000\000\000\000\000\000\000\000\000\000\000\000\000\000\000\000\000..
```

Storing the data in a file allows us to view the resulting image shown in Figure 14.1 [330].

```
q)`:mandel.pbm 0: .ut.pbm[0b] x
`:mandel.pbm
```

Using the hcount handle-count operator we can see that storing a binary version of the PBM format achieves a compression ratio of 16:1.

```
q)hcount `:mandel.pbm 0: .ut.pbm[0b] x
2000013
q)hcount `:mandel.pbm 0: .ut.pbm[1b] x
125014
```

This results from the fact that each ASCII *pixel* is represented by two bytes: a 0 or 1 character followed by a space character. Since these pixels can be represented as a single bit, 8 such *pixels* and 8 such spaces—16 bytes—can be stored in a single byte.

### Portable GrayMap

The P2 and P5 .pgm Portable GrayMap formats are ASCII and binary extensions to the Portable BitMap format. Although the P2 ASCII format has no upper limit to each *pixel* value, the P5 binary format stores each *pixel* in a single byte and thus limits the values to the range 0 through 255.

**.ut.pgm**

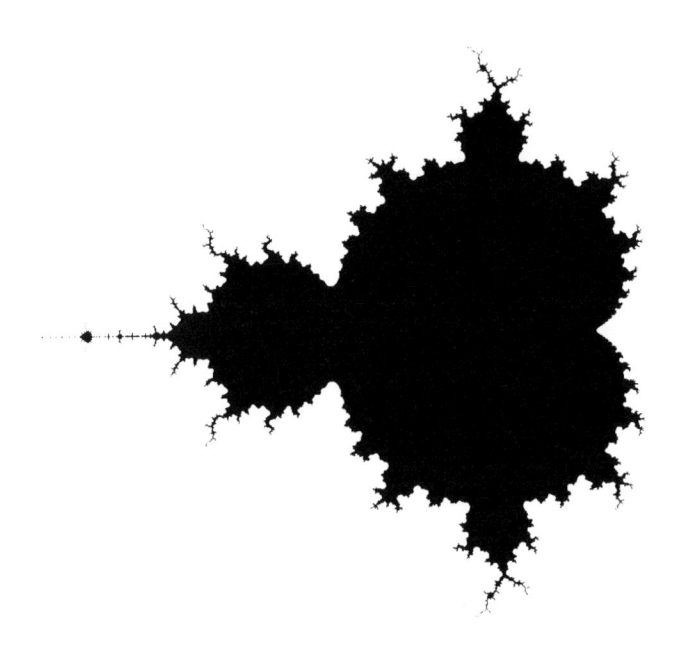

Figure 14.1: Black and White Mandelbrot Set

## 14.3. PORTABLE IMAGE FORMATS

```
/ create netpbm graymap using ascii (or (b)inary) characters for matrix x
pgm:{[b;mx;X]
 if[b;if[255<mx|max (max') X;'`limit]]; / binary version has 255 max
 s:($[b;"P5";"P2"];-3!count'[(X;X 0)];string mx);
 s,:$[b;enlist "c"$raze flip X;" "0:"h"$X];
 s}
```

Given the flexible range of permissible values, it would not be obvious how to scale the values from white to black. Would an image whose values were limited to 0 and 1 be a black and white image, or would it be an image with two very close shades of black? To remove this ambiguity, the format requires us to provide the maximum value, which represents full color saturation, as the parameter mx. This permits the rendering application to scale the gray values appropriately. In this example, 0 is the darkest value and 15 is the lightest value. To make the image comparable with the black and white image, we invert the colors by subtracting the values from 15.

```
q).ut.pgm[0b;15] 15-x
"P2"
"1000 1000"
"15"
"15 15 15 15 15 15 15 15 15 15 15 15 15 15 15 15 15 15 15 15 15 15 15 ..
"15 15 15 15 15 15 15 15 15 15 15 15 15 15 15 15 15 15 15 15 15 15 15 ..
"15 15 15 15 15 15 15 15 15 15 15 15 15 15 15 15 15 15 15 15 15 15 15 ..
"15 15 15 15 15 15 15 15 15 15 15 15 15 15 15 15 15 15 15 15 15 15 15 ..
..
```

The binary format header is the same but encodes one *pixel* integer per byte.

```
q).ut.pgm[1b;15] 15-x
"P5"
"1000 1000"
"15"
"\017\017\017\017\017\017\017\017\017\017\017\017\017\017\017\017\017\017..
```

Figure 14.2 [332] shows each iteration of the Mandelbrot set in a different shade of gray.

In this example, we achieved a compression ratio of approximately 2.5:1 because the values were either a single or double digit followed by a space.

```
q)hcount `:mandel.pgm 0: .ut.pgm[0b;15] 15-x
2597424
q)hcount `:mandel.pgm 0: .ut.pgm[1b;15] 15-x
```

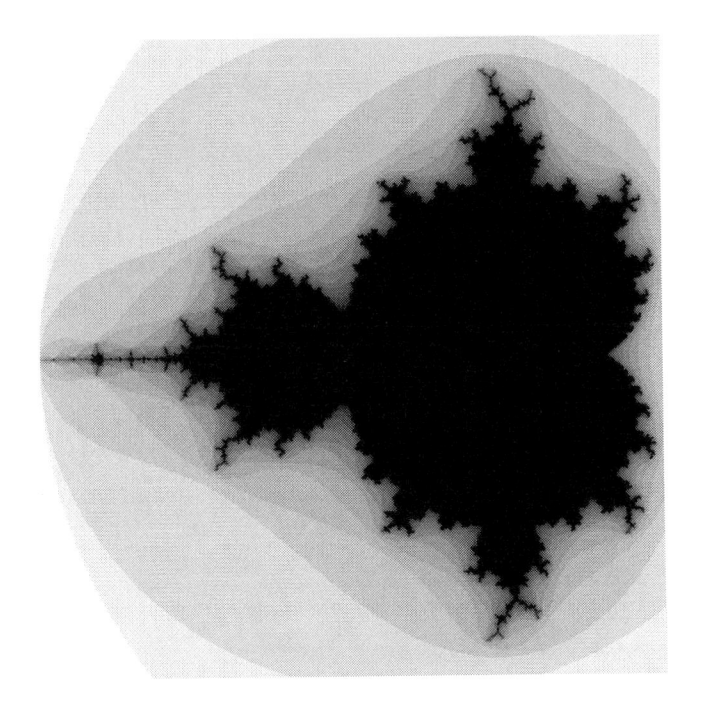

Figure 14.2: Grayscale Mandelbrot Set

## 14.3. PORTABLE IMAGE FORMATS 333

```
1000017
```

The maximum compression ratio that can be achieved is 4:1. This corresponds to the case where each pixel is a three-digit number followed by a space.

## Portable PixMap

The .ppm Portable PixMap format is the most complex because it records a single integer for each of the red, green and blue (RGB) primary colors per *pixel*.

**.ut.ppm**

```
/ create netpbm pixmap using ascii (or (b)inary) characters for matrix x
ppm:{[b;mx;X]
 if[b;if[255<mx|max (max') (max'') X;'`limit]]; / binary version has 255 max
 s:($[b;"P6";"P3"];-3!count'[(X;X 0)];string mx);
 s,:$[b;enlist "c"$2 raze/flip X;" "0:raze flip each "h"$X];
 s}
```

Unlike the .pbm and .pgm formats, which store a matrix of values, the .ppm format stores a three-dimensional tensor. The first two dimensions still represent the x and y coordinates of the *pixel*. The values of this outer matrix, however, are no longer individual integers, but are themselves RGB triplets.

```
q)0N!flip[(0;0;til 1+20)] x;
((0 0 0;0 0 0;0 0 0;0 0 0;0 0 0;0 0 0;0 0 0;0 0 0;0 0 0;0 0 0;0 0 0..
```

Though there is no natural way to represent the Mandelbrot set in color, we can choose two hard-coded values for the red and green colors, and let the blue color vary just like the grayscale image did.

The resulting tensor can be stored in either the P3 ASCII format or the P6 binary format. We can see that, once again, the binary version can achieve a maximum compression ratio of 4:1. This optimal scenario occurs when each of the RGB integers have three characters each followed by the required space character.

```
q)hcount `mandel.ppm 0: .ut.ppm[0b;255] flip[(100;100;100+10*til 1+15)] x
12000017
q)hcount `mandel.ppm 0: .ut.ppm[1b;255] flip[(100;100;100+10*til 1+15)] x
3000018
```

This is a low compression ratio—especially since this is the best case scenario. Converting this binary .ppm format to a .png format, which takes advantage of the fact that there are only 15 colors repeated in large blocks of contiguous *pixels*, reduces the size even further: from 3,000,018 to 34,523 bytes. The PBM, PGM and PPM formats are useful for converting between other formats, but are not optimal for permanent storage.

## 14.4 Sparklines

To end the chapter, the book, the journey and the fun, I'd like to return to Edward R. Tufte's quote "Above all show the data." ASCII plots, due to a lack of resolution, are forced to have a high data to ink ratio. In his book "The Visual Display of Quantitative Information", he defines the data to ink ratio as the portion of a graphic's ink devoted to the non-redundant display of data information.[4]

Sparklines are wonderful examples of visualizations that have a high data to ink ratio. In fact, sparklines have a data to ink ration of 1.0 because they are all data. They are very small line charts that can be displayed anywhere text or numbers can be found and typically reflect changes in values over time.

### Representing Unicode Characters

Though our palette is still limited, we can generate simple sparklines by expanding the character encoding from ASCII to UTF-8. Q has no special knowledge of Unicode characters, it merely stores the bytes. Given that each Unicode character can be represented by using from one to four bytes, the count of a Unicode string will not necessarily be the same as the number of visual characters.

We can use 8 specific Unicode characters to build a sparkline. First we generate 8 integer triplets that represent the Unicode bytes.

```
q)226 150,/:129+til 8
226 150 129
226 150 130
226 150 131
226 150 132
226 150 133
226 150 134
```

---

[4] E. R. Tufte, The Visual Display of Quantitative Information. Graphics Press, 1983.

## 14.4. SPARKLINES

```
226 150 135
226 150 136
```

We can then cast these triplets to characters.

```
q)"c"$226 150,/:129+til 8
"\342\226\201"
"\342\226\202"
"\342\226\203"
"\342\226\204"
"\342\226\205"
"\342\226\206"
"\342\226\207"
"\342\226\210"
```

## Displaying Unicode Characters

Then, to display these Unicode characters we need to pass them to the STDOUT handle 1 or STDERR handle 2. Using a negative handle will automatically append a newline.

```
q)-1 raze "c"$226 150,/:129+til 8;
```

By reusing the .ut.nbin binning function we can map any list of numbers to the first 8 non-negative integers.

```
q).ut.nbin[8] til 32
0 0 0 0 1 1 1 1 2 2 2 2 3 3 3 3 4 4 4 4 5 5 5 5 6 6 6 6 7 7 7 7
```

The .ut.spark utility combines these two steps in a single projection.

**.ut.spark**

```
/ generate unicode sparkline
spark:raze("c"$226 150,/:129+til 8)nbin[8]::
```

## Generating Sparklines

We can use the .ut.spark utility to plot any vector of numbers. The sin and cos functions can be easily recognized.

```
q)-1 .ut.spark sin til 25;
▃▁▂▅▆▁▁▃▇▅▁▁▂▆▆▁▁▄▇▄▁▁▃▇
q)-1 .ut.spark cos til 25;
█▃▁▁▄█▅▁▁▃▇▆▁▁▄█▄▁▁▃▇▅▁▁▃
```

## 14.5 Charting Stock Prices

Financial time-series data sets are often represented with sparklines.

The UCI machine-learning data archive has a "Dow Jones Index" data set[5] that includes weekly high, low, open, close and volume data for each of the Dow Jones Industrial Average (DJIA) index during the first two quarters of 2011.

### Dow Jones Industrial Average

To plot the price path of each of the 30 DJIA components, we start by loading the data with the dji.q [379] library.

```
q)\l dji.q
[down]loading dji data set
"unzip -n dow_jones_index.zip"
```

Instead of using the select operator to query the closing price, we can use the exec operator, which returns a dictionary instead of a keyed table when used with a by clause. Using Q-SQL provides us with the convenience of accessing the stock and close variables without having to scope them separately to the dji.t table. In addition, the exec operator permits us to use the by clause to group the data.

```
q)6#exec close by stock from dji.t
AA  | 16.42 15.97 15.79 16.13 17.14 17.37  17.28  16.68 16.58  16.03  16...
AXP | 44.36 46.25 46    43.86 43.82 46.75  45.53  43.53 43.72  44.28  44...
BA  | 69.38 70.07 71.68 69.23 71.38 72.14  73.04  72.3  71.8   71.64  69...
BAC | 14.25 15.25 14.25 13.6  14.29 14.77  14.75  14.2  14.12  14.38  14...
CAT | 93.73 94.01 92.75 95.68 99.59 103.54 105.86 102   103.04 100.02 105..
CSCO| 20.97 21.21 20.72 20.93 22.05 18.7   18.85  18.64 18.4   17.95  17...
```

---

[5]M. Brown, Pelosi, and H. Dirska, "Dynamic-Radius Species-Conserving Genetic Algorithm for the Financial Forecasting of Dow Jones Index Stocks," presented at the *Machine Learning and Data Mining in Pattern Recognition Lecture Notes in Computer Science*, 2013, vol. 7988, doi: 10.1007/978-3-642-39712-7_3.

## 14.5. CHARTING STOCK PRICES

### Price Paths

With the dictionary of price paths, we can apply the `.ut.spark` utility to each price vector.

```
q)-1@'6#exec .ut.spark close by stock from dji.t;
```

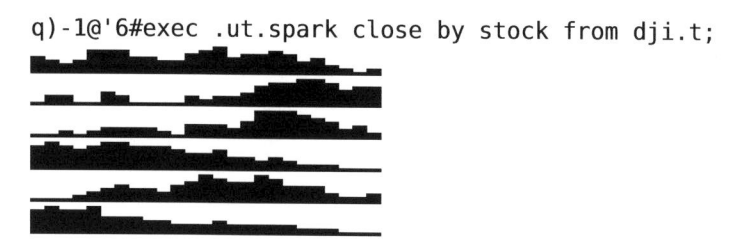

To include the stock name along with each sparkline, we need to concatenate the strings together. Note that Q-SQL treats the "," character as a term separator. We need to surround the commands with parentheses in order to use it as the join operator we are familiar with.

```
q)-1@'6#exec (string[stock 0],": ",.ut.spark close) by stock from dji.t;
AA:
AXP:
BA:
BAC:
CAT:
CSCO:
```

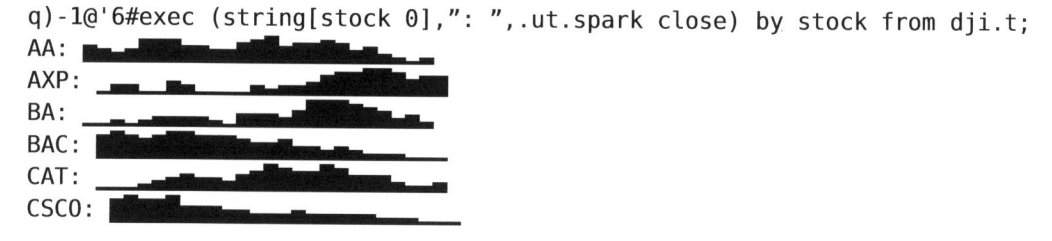

### Padding Strings

Notice, however, that each line is a different length because the number of letters in each stock ticker varies. To improve this plot, we can pad each ticker with spaces. Supplying a positive (negative) integer as the left operand to the $ operator left- (right-) aligns the string to the specified length.

```
q)-1@'6#exec ((4$string stock 0),": ",.ut.spark close) by stock from dji.t;
AA  :
AXP :
BA  :
BAC :
CAT :
CSCO:
```

And here we complete our functional introduction to machine learning in q. Perhaps you came with a machine-learning background and found the algorithm implementations in q stunningly elegant. Or maybe you were already familiar with q and have come away with an appreciation for how machine-learning algorithms can find patterns in big data sets. The q language was designed to be expressive, fast, and functional. When used to build composable utilities and algorithms, this combination often results in powerful solutions. I hope the inclusion of terminal plots, interesting data sets, flexible interfaces and intuitive explanations made the journey fun.

# Appendix A

# Source Code

## A.1 Utilities

**funq.q**

```
\l ut.q
\l ml.q
\l fmincg.q
\l porter.q

/ attempt to load c libraries
(.ut.loadf ` sv hsym[`$getenv`QHOME],) each`qml.q`svm.q`linear.q;
if[`qml in key `;system "l qmlmm.q"] / use qml matrix operators
```

**ut.q**

```
\d .ut

/ assert minimum required version of q

/ throw verbose exception if x <> y
assert:{if[not x~y;'`$"expecting '",(-3!x),"' but found '",(-3!y),"'"]}

assert[2016.05.12] 2016.05.12&.z.k / supports random permutation 0N?
assert[3.4] 3.4&.z.K  / supports reshape for an arbitrary list of dimensions
```

```
/ data loading utilities

/ load (f)ile if it exists and return success boolean
loadf:{[f]if[()~key f;:0b];system "l ",1_string f;1b}

unzip:$["w"=first string .z.o;"7z.exe x -y -aos";"unzip -n"]
gunzip:$["w"=first string .z.o;"7z.exe x -y -aos";"gunzip -f -N -v"]
untar:"tar -xzvf"                   / tar is now in windows 10 system32

/ (b)ase url, (f)ile, (e)xtension, (u)ncompress (f)unction
download:{[b;f;e;uf]
 if[0h=type f;:..z.s[b;;e;uf] each f];
 if[l~key l:`$":",f;:l];                        / local file exists
 if[()~key z:`$":",f,e;z 1: .Q.hg`$":",0N!b,f,e]; / download
 if[count uf;system 0N!uf," ",f,e];              / uncompress
 l}

/ load http://yann.lecun.com/exdb/mnist/ dataset
mnist:{
 d:first (1#4;1#"i") 1: 4_(h:4*1+x 3)#x;
 x:d#$[0>i:x[2]-0x0b;:::;first ((2 4 4 8;"hief")@\:i,()) 1:] h _x;
 x}

/ load http://etlcdb.db.aist.go.jp/etlcdb/data/ETL9B dataset
etl9b:{(2 1 1 4 504, 64#1;"hxxs*",64#" ") 1: x}

/ general utilities

/ generate a sequence of (s)-sized steps between (b)egin and (e)nd
sseq:{[s;b;e]b+s*til 1+floor 1e-14+(e-b)%s}

/ generate a sequence of (n) steps between (b)egin and (e)nd
nseq:{[n;b;e]b+til[1+n]*(e-b)%n}

/ round y to nearest x
rnd:{x*"j"$y%x}

/ allocate x into n bins
nbin:{[n;x](n-1)&floor n*.5^x%max x-:min x}

/ table x cross y
tcross:{value flip ([]x) cross ([]y)}
```

## A.1. UTILITIES 341

```
/ return memory (used;allocated;max)
/ returned in units specified by x (0:B;1:KB;2:MB;3:GB;...)
mem:{(3#system"w")%x (1024*)/ 1}

/ given a dictionary mirroring the group operator return value, reconstruct
/ the original ungrouped list.  generate the dictionary key if none provided
ugrp:{
 if[not type x;x:til[count x]!x];
 x:@[sum[count each x]#k;value x;:;k:key x];
 x}

/ append a total row and (c)olumn to (t)able
totals:{[c;t]
 t[key[t]0N]:sum value t;
 t:t,'flip (1#c)!enlist sum flip value t;
 t}

/ surround a (s)tring or list of stings with a box of (c)haracters
box:{[c;s]
 if[type s;s:enlist s];
 m:max count each s;
 h:enlist (m+2*1+count c)#c;
 s:(c," "),/:(m$/:s),\:(" ",c);
 s:h,s,h;
 s}

/ use (w)eight vector or dictionary to partition (x). (s)ampling (f)unction:
/ til = no shuffle, 0N? = shuffle, list or table = stratify
part:{[w;sf;x]
 if[99h=type w;:key[w]!.z.s[value w;sf;x]];
 if[99h<type sf;:x (floor sums n*prev[0f;w%sum w]) _ sf n:count x];
 x@:raze each flip value .z.s[w;0N?] each group sf; / stratify
 x}

/ one-hot encode vector, (symbol columns of) table or (non-key symbol
/ columns of) keyed table x.
onehot:{
 if[98h>t:type x;:u!x=/:u:distinct x];      / vector
 if[99h=t;:key[x]!.z.s value x];            / keyed table
 D:.z.s each x c:where 11h=type each flip x; / list of dictionaries
 D:string[c] {(`$(x,"_"),/:string key y)!value y}' D; / rename uniquely
 x:c _ x,' flip raze D;                      / append to table
 x}
```

```
/ Heckbert's axis label algorithm

/ use Heckbert's values to (r)ou(nd) or floor (x) to the nearest nice number
nicenum:{[rnd;x]
 s:`s#$[rnd;0 1.5 3 7;0f,1e-15+1 2 5f]!1 2 5 10f;
 x:f * s x%f:10 xexp floor 10 xlog x;
 x}

/ given suggested (n)umber of labels and the (m)i(n) and (m)a(x) values, use
/ Heckbert's algorithm to generate a series of nice numbers
heckbert:{[n;mn;mx]
 r:nicenum[0b] mx-mn;              / range of values
 s:nicenum[1b] r%n-1;              / step size
 mn:s*floor mn%s;                  / new min
 mx:s*ceiling mx%s;                / new max
 l:sseq[s;mn;mx];                  / labels
 l}

/ plotting utilities

/ cut m x n matrix X into (x;y;z) where x and y are the indices for X
/ and z is the value stored in X[x;y] - result used to plot heatmaps
hmap:{[X]@[;0;`s#]tcross[til count X;reverse til count X 0],enlist raze X}

/ using (a)ggregation (f)unction, plot (X) using (c)haracters limited to
/ (w)idth and (h)eight. X can be x, (x;y), or (x;y;z)
plot:{[w;h;c;af;X]
 if[type X;X:enlist X];                   / promote vector to matrix
 if[1=count X;X:(til count X 0;X 0)];     / turn ,x into (x;y)
 if[2=count X;X,:count[X 0]#1];           / turn (x;y) into (x;y;z)
 if[not `s=attr X 0;c:1_c];               / remove space unless heatmap
 l:heckbert[h div 2].(min;max)@\:X 1;     / generate labels
 x:-1_nseq[w] . (min;max)@\:X 0;          / compute x axis
 y:-1_nseq[h] . (first;last)@\:l;         / compute y axis
 Z:(y;x) bin' "f"$X 1 0;                  / allocate (x;y) to (w;h) bins
 Z:af each X[2]group flip Z;              / aggregating overlapping z
 Z:c nbin[count c;0f^Z];                  / map values to characters
 p:./[(h;w)#" ";key Z;:;value Z];         / plot points
 k:@[count[y]#0n;0|y bin l;:;l];          / generate key
 p:reverse k!p;                           / generate plot
 p}
```

## A.1. UTILITIES

```
c10:" .-:=+x#%@"                            / 10 characters
c16:" .-:=+*xoX0#$&%@"                      / 16 characters
c68:" .'`^,:;Il!i><~+_-?][}{1)(|/tfjrxn"    / 68 characters
c68,:"uvczXYUJCLQ0OZmwqpdbkhao*#MW&8%B@$"

plt:plot[19;10;c10;avg]                     / default plot function

/ generate unicode sparkline
spark:raze("c"$226 150,/:129+til 8)nbin[8]::

/ image manipulation utilities

/ remove gamma compression
gexpand:{?[x>0.0405;((.055+x)%1.055) xexp 2.4;x%12.92]}
/ add gamma compression
gcompress:{?[x>.0031308;-.055+1.055*x xexp 1%2.4;x*12.92]}

/ convert rgb to grayscale
grayscale:.2126 .7152 .0722 wsum

/ create netpbm bitmap using ascii (or (b)inary) characters for matrix x
pbm:{[b;X]
 s:($[b;"P4";"P1"];-3!count'[(X;X 0)]);
 s,:$[b;enlist"c"$raze((0b sv 8#)each 8 cut raze::)each flip X;" "0:"b"$X];
 s}

/ create netpbm graymap using ascii (or (b)inary) characters for matrix x
pgm:{[b;mx;X]
 if[b;if[255<mx|max (max') X;'`limit]]; / binary version has 255 max
 s:($[b;"P5";"P2"];-3!count'[(X;X 0)];string mx);
 s,:$[b;enlist "c"$raze flip X;" "0:"h"$X];
 s}

/ create netpbm pixmap using ascii (or (b)inary) characters for matrix x
ppm:{[b;mx;X]
 if[b;if[255<mx|max (max') (max'') X;'`limit]]; / binary version has 255 max
 s:($[b;"P6";"P3"];-3!count'[(X;X 0)];string mx);
 s,:$[b;enlist "c"$2 raze/flip X;" "0:raze flip each "h"$X];
 s}

/ text utilities

/ map (u)nicode characters to their (a)scii equivalents
```

```
ua:(!/) 2 1 0#""
ua["\342\200\223"]:"--"                    / endash
ua["\342\200\224"]:"---"                   / emdash
ua["\342\200[\231\230]"]:"'"               / single quotes
ua["\342\200[\234\235]"]:"\""              / double quotes
ua["\342\200\246"]:"..."                   / ellipses
ua["\302\222"]:"'"                         / single quotes
ua["\302\241"]:"!"                         / !
ua["\302\243"]:"$"                         / pound symbol
ua["\302\260"]:"o"                         / o
ua["\302\262"]:"^2"                        / ^2
ua["\302\263"]:"^3"                        / ^3
ua["\302\267"]:"-"                         / -
ua["\302\274"]:"1/4"                       / 1/4
ua["\302\275"]:"1/2"                       / 1/2
ua["\302\276"]:"3/4"                       / 3/4
ua["\302\277"]:"?"                         / ?
ua["\303[\200\201\202\203\204\205]"]:"A"   / A
ua["\303\206"]:"AE"                        / AE
ua["\303\207"]:"C"                         / C
ua["\303[\210\211\212\213]"]:"E"           / E
ua["\303[\214\215\216\217]"]:"I"           / I
ua["\303\220"]:"D"                         / D
ua["\303\221"]:"N"                         / N
ua["\303[\222\223\224\225\226\230]"]:"O"   / O
ua["\303[\231\232\233\234]"]:"U"           / U
ua["\303\235"]:"Y"                         / y
ua["\303\237"]:"s"                         / s
ua["\303[\240\241\242\243\244\245]"]:"a"   / a
ua["\303\246"]:"ae"                        / ae
ua["\303\247"]:"c"                         / c
ua["\303[\250\251\252\253]"]:"e"           / e
ua["\303[\254\255\256\257]"]:"i"           / i
ua["\303\260"]:"d"                         / d
ua["\303\261"]:"n"                         / n
ua["\303[\262\263\264\265\266\270]"]:"o"   / o
ua["\303[\271\272\273\274]"]:"u"           / u
ua["\303\275"]:"y"                         / y
ua:1_ua

/ map (h)tml entities to their (a)scii equivalents
ha:(!/) 2 1 0#""
ha["&lt;"]:"<"                             / <
```

```
ha["&gt;"]:">"                              / >
ha["&amp;"]:"&"                             / &
ha["&apos;"]:"'"                            / '
ha["&quot;"]:"\""                           / "
ha[" "]:" "                            /
ha:1_ha

/ map (p)unctuation characters to their (w)hitespace replacements
pw:(!/) 2 1 0#""
pw["[][\n\\/()<>@#$%^&*=_+.,;:!?-]"]:" "    / replace with whitespace
pw["['\"0-9]"]:""                           / delete
pw:1_pw

/ search (s)tring for all instances of key[d] and replace with value[d]
sr:{[d;s] ssr/[s;key d;value d]}
```

## A.2 Machine-Learning Algorithms

**ml.q**

```
\d .ml

/ returns boolean indicating preference not to flip matrices
noflip:{system"g"}              / redefine to customize behavior

/ apply (f)unction (in parallel) to the 2nd dimension of (X)
f2nd:{[f;X]$[noflip[];(f value::) peach flip (count[X]#`)!X;f peach flip X]}

/ matrix primitives

mm:{$[;y] peach x}              / X * Y
mmt:{(y$) peach x}              / X * Y'
mtm:{f2nd[$[;y];x]}             / X' * Y
minv:inv                        / X**-1
mlsq:lsq                        / least squares
dot:$                           / dot product
diag:{$[0h>t:type x;x;@[n#t$0;;:;]'[til n:count x;x]]}
eye:{diag x#1f}
mdet:{[X]                       / determinant
 if[2>n:count X;:X];
 if[2=n;:(X[0;0]*X[1;1])-X[0;1]*X[1;0]];
```

```
   d:dot[X 0;(n#1 -1)*(.z.s (X _ 0)_\:) each til n];
   d}
 mchol:{[X]                          / Cholesky decomposition
  m:count X;
  L:(m;m)#0f;
  i:-1;
  while[m>i+:1;
   L[i;i]:sqrt X[i;i]-dot[L i;L i];
   j:i;
   while[m>j+:1;
    L[j;i]:(X[j;i]-dot[L i;L j])%L[i;i];
    ];
   ];
  L}

 / tensor variant of where
 twhere:{
  if[type x;:enlist where x];
  x:(,'/) til[count x] {(((1;count y 0)#x),y}' .z.s each x;
  x}

 / returns true if all values are exactly equal
 identical:{min first[x]~':x}

 / returns true if x is a matrix as defined by q
 ismatrix:{
  if[type x;:0b];
  if[not all 9h=type each x;:0b];
  b:identical count each x;
  b}

 / basic utilities

 / find row indices of each atom/vec y in matrix/flipped table x
 mfind:{{[x;i;j;y]?[y=x;i&j;i]}[y]/[count[first x]#n;til n:count x;x]}

 / return first index of atom/vec y in vec/dict/matrix/flipped table x
 find:{$[0h>type first x;?;type x;key[x]mfind::;mfind][x;y]}
 imax:{find[x;max x]}            / index of max element
 imin:{find[x;min x]}            / index of min element

 / (pre|ap)pend n rows of repeated x to matri(X)
 pend:{[n;x;X]$[n>0;,[;X];X,](abs n;count X 0)#x}
```

## A.2. MACHINE-LEARNING ALGORITHMS

```
prepend:pend[1]                    / prepend 1 row of repeated x to matri(X)
append:pend[-1]                    / append  1 row of repeated x to matri(X)
/ where not any null
wnan:{$[all type each x;where not any null x;::]}

/ norm primitives

mnorm:sum abs::                    / Manhattan (taxicab) norm
enorm2:{x wsum x}                  / Euclidean norm squared
enorm:sqrt enorm2::                / Euclidean norm
pnorm:{[p;x]sum[abs[x] xexp p] xexp 1f%p} / parameterized norm

/ distance primitives

hdist:sum (<>)::                   / Hamming distance
mdist:mnorm (-)::                  / Manhattan (taxicab) distance
edist2:enorm2 (-)::                / Euclidean distance squared
edist:enorm (-)::                  / Euclidean distance
pedist2:{enorm2[x]+/:enorm2[y]+-2f*mtm["f"$y;"f"$x]} / pairwise edist2
mkdist:{[p;x;y]pnorm[p] x-y}                 / Minkowski distance
hmean:1f%avg 1f%                             / harmonic mean
cossim:{sum[x*y]%enorm[x i]*enorm y i:wnan(x;y)} / cosine similarity
cosdist:1f-cossim::                          / cosine distance
cordist:1f-(cor)::                           / correlation distance
/ Spearman's rank (tied values get averaged rank)
srank:{@[x;g;:;avg each (x:"f"$rank x) g@:where 1<count each g:group x]}
scor:{srank[x i] cor srank y i:wnan(x;y)}    / Spearman's rank correlation
scordist:1f-scor::                 / Spearman's rank correlation distance

/ null-aware primitives (account for nulls in matrices)

ncount:{count[x]-$[type x;sum null x;0i {x+null y}/ x]}
nsum:{$[type x;sum x;0i {x+0i^y}/ x]}
navg:{$[type x;avg x;nsum[x]%ncount x]}
nwavg:{[w;x]$[type x;w wavg x;(%/){x+y*(0f^z;not null z)}/[0 0f;w;x]]}
nvar:{$[type x;var x;navg[x*x]-m*m:navg x]}
ndev:sqrt nvar::
nsvar:{$[type x;svar x;(n*nvar x)%-1+n:ncount x]}
nsdev:sqrt nsvar::

/ normalization primitives

/ return a function that applies (d)yadic function to the result of
```

```
/ (a)ggregating vector/matrix/dictionary/table x
daxf:{[d;a;x]$[0h>type first x; d[;a x]; d[;a x] peach]}
/ apply (d)yadic function to the result of (a)ggregating
/ vector/matrix/dictionary/table x
dax:{[d;a;x]daxf[d;a;x] x}

/ apply the result of f[x] to x
fxx:{[f;x]f[x] x}

/ normalize each vector to unit length
normalize:dax[%;enorm]
/ centered
demean:fxx demeanf:daxf[-;navg]
/ feature normalization (centered/unit variance)
zscore:fxx zscoref:{daxf[%;nsdev;x] demeanf[x]::}
/ feature normalization (scale values to [0,1])
minmax:fxx minmaxf:{daxf[%;{max[x]-min x};x] daxf[-;min;x]::}
/ convert densities into probabilities
prb:dax[%;sum]

/ given (g)rouped dictionary, compute the odds
odds:{[g]prb count each g}
/ given (w)eight vector and (g)rouped dictionary, compute the weighted odds
wodds:{[w;g]prb sum each w g}

/ frequency and mode primitives

/ given a (w)eight atom or vector and data (x), return a dictionary (sorted
/ by key) mapping the distinct items to their weighted count
wfreq:{[w;x]@[x!count[x:asc distinct x]#0*first w;x;+;w]}
freq:wfreq[1]

/ given a (w)eight atom or vector and data (x), return x with maximum
/ weighted frequency
wmode:imax wfreq::          / weighted mode
mode:wmode[1]               / standard mode

/ weighted average or mode
isord:{type[x] in 0 8 9h}                  / is ordered
aom:{$[isord x;avg;mode]x}                 / average or mode
waom:{[w;x]$[isord x;nwavg;wmode][w;x]}    / weighted average or mode

/ binary classification evaluation metrics (summary statistics)
```

## A.2. MACHINE-LEARNING ALGORITHMS

```
/ given actual values (y) and (p)redicted values, compute (tp;tn;fp;fn)
tptnfpfn:{[y;p]tp,(("i"$count y)-tp+sum f),f:(sum p;sum y)-/:tp:sum p&y}

/ aka Rand measure (William M. Rand 1971)
accuracy:{[tp;tn;fp;fn](tp+tn)%tp+tn+fp+fn}
precision:{[tp;tn;fp;fn]tp%tp+fp}
recall:sensitivity:hitrate:tpr:{[tp;tn;fp;fn]tp%tp+fn}  / true positive rate
selectivity:specificity:tnr:{[tp;tn;fp;fn]tn%tn+fp}     / true negative rate
fallout:fpr:{[tp;tn;fp;fn]fp%fp+tn}                     / false positive rate
missrate:fnr:{[tp;tn;fp;fn]fn%fn+tp}                    / false negative rate

/ receiver operating characteristic
roc:{[y;p]
 r:(til[count s]-s;s:0f,sums y i:idesc p); / (fp;tp)
 r:(r%last each r),enlist 0w,p i;          / (fpr;tpr;threshold)
 r:r@\:where reverse differ reverse r 2;   / filter duplicate thresholds
 r}

auc:{[x;y] .5*sum (x-prev x)*y+prev y} / area under the curve

/ f measure: given (b)eta and tp,tn,fp,fn compute the harmonic mean of
/ precision and recall
f:{[b;tp;tn;fp;fn]
 f:1+b2:b*b;
 f*:r:recall[tp;tn;fp;fn];
 f*:p:precision[tp;tn;fp;fn];
 f%:r+p*b2;
 f}
f1:f[1]

/ Fowlkes–Mallows index (E. B. Fowlkes & C. L. Mallows 1983)
/ geometric mean of precision and recall
fmi:{[tp;tn;fp;fn]tp%sqrt(tp+fp)*tp+fn}

/ returns a number between 0 and 1 indicating the similarity of two datasets
jaccard:{[tp;tn;fp;fn]tp%tp+fp+fn}

/ Matthews correlation coefficient
/ correlation coefficient between the observed and predicted
/ -1 0 1 (none right, same as random prediction, all right)
mcc:{[tp;tn;fp;fn]((tp*tn)-fp*fn)%prd sqrt(tp;tp;tn;tn)+(fp;fn;fp;fn)}
```

```
/ given true labels y and predicted labels p, return a confusion matrix
cm:{[y;p]
 n:count u:asc distinct y,p;
 m:./[(n;n)#0;flip (u?p;u?y);1+];
 t:([]y:u)!flip (`$string u)!m;
 t}

/ use all (f)old(s) (except the (i)th) to fit a model using the (f)itting
/ (f)unction and then use (p)rediction (f)unction on fs[i]. fs can be a list
/ of tables or (y;X) pairs -- corresponding to ff arguments.
xv:{[ff;pf;fs;i]                / cross validate
 v:fs i;fs _: i;                / split training and validation sets
 a:$[type v;enlist raze fs;[v@:1;(raze;,'/)@'flip fs]]; / build ff arguments
 m:ff . a;                      / fit model on training set
 p:pf[m] v;                     / make predictions on validation set
 p}

/ k nearest neighbors

/ find (k) smallest values from (d)istance vector (or matrix) and use
/ (w)eighting (f)unction to return the best estimate of y
knn:{[wf;k;y;d]
 if[not type d;:.z.s[wf;k;y] peach d];   / recurse for matrix d
 if[any n:null d;d@:i:where not n; y@:i]; / filter null distances
 p:(waom . (wf d:::;y)@\:#[;iasc d]::) peach k&count d; / make predictions
 p}

/ given (w)eighting (f)unction, (d)istance (f)unction, atom or vector of (k)
/ values, a (y) vector and matri(X), 'fit' a knn 'model'
fknn:{[wf;df;k;y;X] knn[wf;k;y] df[X]::}
pknn:@                  / predict knn by applying model returned from fknn to X

/ partitional clustering initialization methods

/ generate (k) centroids by randomly choosing (k) samples from matri(X)
forgy:{[k;X]neg[k]?/:X}         / Forgy method
/ generate (k) centroids by applying (c)entroid (f)unction to (k) random
/ partitions of matri(X)
rpart:{[cf;k;X](cf'') X@\:value group count[X 0]?k} / random partition

/ return the index of n (w)eighted samples
iwrand:{[n;w]s binr n?last s:sums w}
/ find n (w)eighted samples of x
```

## A.2. MACHINE-LEARNING ALGORITHMS

```
wrand:{[n;w;x]x iwrand[n] w}

/ k-means++ initialization algorithm
/ using (d)istance (f)unction and matri(X), append the next centroid to the
/ min centroid (d)istance and all (C)entroids
kpp:{[df;X;d;C]
 if[not count C;:(0w;X@\:1?count X 0)];   / first centroid
 if[count[X 0]=n:count C 0;:(d;C)];       / no more centroids
 d&:df[X] C[;n-1];                         / update distance vector
 C:C,'X@\: first iwrand[1] d;              / pick next centroid
 (d;C)}
kmeanspp:kpp[edist2]            / k-means++ initialization
kmedianspp:kpp[mdist]           / k-medians++ initialization

/ partitional clustering algorithms

/ using the (d)istance (f)unction, group matri(X) based on the closest
/ (C)entroid and return the cluster indices
cgroup:{[df;X;C]value group imin f2nd[df X] C}

/ Stuart Lloyd's algorithm. uses (d)istance (f)unction to assign the
/ matri(X) to the nearest (C)entroid and then uses the (c)entroid (f)unction
/ to update the centroid location.
lloyd:{[df;cf;X;C]cf X@\: cgroup[df;X;C]}

kmeans:lloyd[edist2;avg'']              / k-means
kmedians:lloyd[mdist;med'']             / k-medians
khmeans:lloyd[edist2;hmean'']           / k harmonic means
skmeans:lloyd[cosdist;normalize (avg'')::] / spherical k-means

/ using (d)istance (f)unction, find the medoid in matri(X)
medoid:{[df;X]X@\:imin f2nd[sum df[X]::] X}
/ given a (d)istance (f)unction, return a new function that finds a medoid
/ during the "update" step of lloyd's algorithm
pam:{[df]lloyd[df;flip f2nd[medoid df]::]} / partitioning around medoids

/ cluster purity primitives

/ given matri(X) compute the sum of squared errors (distortion)
sse:{[X]sum edist2[X] avg each X}
/ given matri(X) and cluster (I)ndices, compute within-cluster sse
ssw:{[X;I]sum (sse X@\:) peach I}
/ given matri(X) and cluster (I)ndices, compute between-cluster sse
```

```
ssb:{[X;I]count'[I] wsum edist2[(avg '')G] (avg raze::) each G:X@\:I}
/ using (d)istance (f)unction, matri(X) and (C)entroids, compute total
/ cluster distortion
distortion:{[X;C]ssw[X] cgroup[edist2;X] C}

/ given (d)istance (f)unction, matri(X), and cluster (I)ndices, compute the
/ silhouette statistic. group I if not already grouped
silhouette:{[df;X;I]
 if[type I;s:.z.s[df;X]I:value group I;:raze[s] iasc raze I];
 if[1=n:count I;:count[I 0]#0f]; / special case a single cluster
 a:{[df;X](1f%-1+count X 0)*sum f2nd[df X] X}[df] peach G:X@\:/:I;
 b:{[df;G;i]min{f2nd[avg x[z]::]y}[df;G i]'[G _ i]}[df;G] peach til n;
 s:0f^(b-a)%a|b;          / 0 fill to handle single point clusters
 s}

/ hierarchical agglomerative clustering

/ Lance-Williams algorithm linkage functions. can be either a vector of four
/ floats or a function that accepts the cluster counts of i, j and list of
/ all cluster counts
lw.single:.5 .5 0 -.5
lw.complete:.5 .5 0 .5
lw.average:{(x%sum x _:2),0 0f}
lw.weighted:.5 .5 0 0
lw.centroid:{(((x,neg prd[x]%s)%s:sum x _:2),0f}
lw.median:.5 .5 -.25 0
lw.ward:{((k+/:x 0 1),(neg k:x 2;0f))%\:sum x}

/ implementation of Lance-Williams algorithm for performing hierarchical
/ agglomerative clustering. given (l)inkage (f)unction to determine distance
/ between new and remaining clusters, (D)issimilarity matrix, cluster
/ (a)ssignments and (L)inkage stats: (j;i). returns updated (D;a;L)
lancewilliams:{[lf;D;a;L]
 n:count D;
 d:D@'di:imin peach D;                  / find closest distances
 if[null d@:i:imin d;:(D;a;L)]; j:di i; / find closest clusters
 c:$[9h=type lf;lf;lf(freq a)@/:(i;j;til n)]; / determine coefficients
 nd:sum c*nd,(d;abs(-/)nd:D (i;j));     / calc new distances
 D[;i]:D[i]:nd;                          / update distances
 D[;j]:D[j]:n#0n;                        / erase j
 a[where j=a]:i;              / all elements in cluster j are now in i
 L:L,'(j;i);                  / append linkage stats
 (D;a;L)}
```

## A.2. MACHINE-LEARNING ALGORITHMS

```
/ given a (l)inkage (f)unction and (D)issimilarity matrix, run the
/ Lance-Williams linkage algorithm for hierarchical agglomerative clustering
/ and return the linkage stats: (from index j;to index i)
link:{[lf;D]
 D:@'[D;a:til count D;;;0n];    / define cluster assignments and ignore loops
 if[-11h=type lf;lf:get lf];    / dereference lf
 L:last .[lancewilliams[lf]] over (D;a;2#()); / obtain linkage stats
 L}

/ use (L)inkage stats to create (k) clusters
clust:{[L;k]
 if[0h>type k;:first .z.s[L] k,()]; / special case atoms
 c:1 cut til 1+count L 0;            / initial clusters
 k@:i:idesc k;                       / sort k descending
 fl:(1-mk:last k)_ flip L;           / drop unwanted links
 fls:(0,-1_count[c]-k) cut fl;       / list of flipped link stats
 c:{[c;fl]{x[y 1],:x y 0;x[y 0]:();x}/[c;fl]}\[c;fls]; / link into k clusters
 c:c except\: enlist ();             / remove empty clusters
 c:c iasc i;                         / reorder based on original k
 c}

/ random variate primitives

pi:acos -1f
twopi:2f*pi
logtwopi:log twopi

/ Box-Muller
bm:{
 if[count[x] mod 2;:-1_.z.s x,rand 1f];
 x:raze (sqrt -2f*log first x)*/:(cos;sin)@\:twopi*last x:2 0N#x;
 x}

/ random number generators
/ generate (n) uniform distribution variates
runif:{[n]n?1f}
/ generate (n) Bernoulli distribution variates with (p)robability of success
rbern:{[n;p]p>runif n}
/ generate (n) binomial distribution (sum of Bernoulli) variates with (k)
/ trials and (p)robability
rbinom:{[n;k;p](sum rbern[k]::) each n#p}
/ generate (n) multinomial distribution variate-vectors with (k) trials and
```

```
/ (p)robability vector defined for each class
rmultinom:{[n;k;p](sum til[count p]=/:sums[p] binr runif::) each n#k}
/ generate (n) normal distribution variates with mean (mu) and standard
/ deviation (sigma)
rnorm:{[n;mu;sigma]mu+sigma*bm runif n}

/ C(n,k) or n choose k
choose:{[n;k](%). prd each(n-k;0)+\:1f+til k&:n-k}
/ P(n,k) or n permute k
permute:{[n;k]prd(1f+n-k)+til k}

/ [log]likelihood and maximum likelihood estimator (mle)

/ binomial likelihood (without the binomial coefficient nCk)
binl:{[n;p;k](p xexp k)*(1f-p) xexp n-k}
/ binomial log likelihood
binll:{[n;p;k](k*log p)+(n-k)*log 1f-p}
/binl:exp binll::              / more numerically stable
/ binomial mle with Dirichlet smoothing (a)
binmle:{[n;a;x]enlist avg a+x%n}
/ weighted binomial mle with Dirichlet smoothing (a)
wbinmle:{[n;a;w;x]enlist w wavg a+x%n}

/ binomial density
bind:{[n;p;k] choose[n;k]*binl[n;p;k]}

/ binomial mixture model likelihood
bmml:prd binl::
/ binomial mixture model log likelihood
bmmll:sum binll::
/bmml:exp bmmll::              / more numerically stable
/ binomial mixture model mle with Dirichlet smoothing (a)
bmmmle:{[n;a;x]enlist avg each a+x%n}
/ weighted binomial mixture model mle with Dirichlet smoothing (a)
wbmmmle:{[n;a;w;x]enlist w wavg/: a+x%n}

/ multinomial likelihood approximation (without the multinomial coefficient)
multil:{[p;k]p xexp k}
/ multinomial log likelihood
multill:{[p;k]k*log p}
/ multinomial mle with (a)dditive smoothing
multimle:{[a;x]enlist each prb a+sum each x}
/ weighted multinomial mle with (a)dditive smoothing
```

## A.2. MACHINE-LEARNING ALGORITHMS

```
wmultimle:{[a;w;x]enlist each prb a+w wsum/: x}

/ multinomial mixture model likelihood
mmml:prd multil::
/ multinomial mixture model log likelihood
mmmll:sum multill::
/mmml:exp mmmll::              / more numerically stable
/ multinomial mixture model mle with Dirichlet smoothing (a)
mmmmle:{[n;a;x]enlist avg each a+x%n}
/ weighted multinomial mixture model mle with Dirichlet smoothing (a)
wmmmmle:{[n;a;w;x]enlist w wavg/: a+x%n}

/ Gaussian kernel
gaussk:{[mu;sigma;x] exp (enorm2 x-mu)%-2f*sigma}

/ Gaussian likelihood
gaussl:{[mu;sigma;x] exp[(x*x-:mu)%-2f*sigma]%sqrt sigma*twopi}
/ Gaussian log likelihood
gaussll:{[mu;sigma;x] -.5*logtwopi+log[sigma]+(x*x-:mu)%sigma}
/ Gaussian mle
gaussmle:{[x](mu;avg x*x-:mu:avg x)}
/ weighted Gaussian mle
wgaussmle:{[w;x](mu;w wavg x*x-:mu:w wavg x)}

/ Gaussian multivariate
gaussmvl:{[mu;SIGMA;X]
 if[type SIGMA;SIGMA:diag count[X]#SIGMA];
 p:exp -.5*sum X*mm[minv SIGMA;X-:mu];
 p%:sqrt mdet[SIGMA]*twopi xexp count X;
 p}
/ Gaussian multivariate log likelihood
gaussmvll:{[mu;SIGMA;X]
 if[type SIGMA;SIGMA:diag count[X]#SIGMA];
 p:sum X*mm[minv SIGMA;X-:mu];
 p+:log[mdet SIGMA]+logtwopi*count X;
 p*:-.5;
 p}
/ Gaussian multivariate mle
gaussmvmle:{[X](mu;avg X (*\:/:)' X:flip X-mu:avg each X)}
/ weighted Gaussian multivariate mle
wgaussmvmle:{[w;X](mu;w wavg X (*\:/:)' X:flip X-mu:w wavg/: X)}
```

```
/ expectation maximization

likelihood:{[l;lf;X;phi;THETA]
 p:(@[;X]lf .) peach THETA;    / compute [log] probability densities
 p:$[l;p+log phi;p*phi];        / apply prior probabilities
 p}

/ using (l)ikelihood (f)unction, (w)eighted (m)aximum likelihood estimator
/ (f)unction with prior probabilities (p)hi and distribution parameters
/ (THETA), optionally (f)it (p)hi and perform expectation maximization
em:{[fp;lf;wmf;X;phi;THETA]
 W:prb likelihood[0b;lf;X;phi;THETA];  / weights (responsibilities)
 if[fp;phi:avg each W];         / new phi estimates
 THETA:wmf[;X] peach W;          / new THETA estimates
 (phi;THETA)}

/ term frequency primitives

/ term document matrix built from (c)orpus and (v)ocabulary
tdm:{[c;v](-1_@[(1+count v)#0;;+;1]::) each v?c}

lntf:log 1f+                    / log normalized term frequency
dntf:{[k;x]k+(1f-k)*x%max each x} / double normalized term frequency

idf: {log count[x]%sum 0<x}      / inverse document frequency
idfs:{log 1f+count[x]%sum 0<x}   / inverse document frequency smooth
idfm:{log 1f+max[x]%x:sum 0<x}   / inverse document frequency max
pidf:{log (max[x]-x)%x:sum 0<x}  / probabilistic inverse document frequency
tfidf:{[tff;idff;x]tff[x]*\:idff x}

/ naive Bayes

/ fit parameters given (w)eighted (m)aximization (f)unction returns a
/ dictionary with prior and conditional likelihoods
fnb:{[wmf;w;y;X]
 if[(::)~w;w:count[y]#1f];      / handle unassigned weight
 pT:(odds g; (wmf . (w;X@\:) @\:) peach g:group y);
 pT}

/ using a [log](l)ikelihood (f)unction and prior probabilities (p)hi and
/ distribution parameters (T)HETA, perform naive Bayes classification
pnb:{[l;lf;pT;X]
 d:{(x . z) y}[lf]'[X] peach pT[1]; / compute probability densities
```

## A.2. MACHINE-LEARNING ALGORITHMS

```
  c:imax $[l;log[pT 0]+sum flip d;pT[0]*prd flip d];
  c}

/ decision trees

/ classification impurity functions
misc:{1f-avg x=mode x}                    / misclassification
wmisc:{[w;x]1f-avg x=wmode[w;x]}          / weighted misclassification
gini:{1f-enorm2 odds group x}             / Gini
wgini:{[w;x]1f-enorm2 wodds[w] group x}   / weighted Gini
entropy:{neg sum x*log x:odds group x}    / entropy
wentropy:{[w;x]neg sum x*log x:wodds[w] group x} / weighted entropy

/ regression impurity functions
mse:{enorm2[x-avg x]%count x}             / mean squared error
wmse:{[w;x]enorm2[x-w wavg x]%count x}    / weighted mean squared error
mae:{avg abs x-avg x}                     / mean absolute error
wmae:{[w;x]avg abs x-w wavg x}            / weighted mean absolute error

rms:{sqrt avg x*x}                        / root mean square error

/ combinations of length x (or all lengths if null x) from count (or list) y
cmb:{
 if[not 0>type y;:y .z.s[x] count y];     / list y
 if[null x;:raze .z.s[;y] each 1+til y];  / null x = all lengths
 c:flip enlist flip enlist til y-:x-:1;
 c:raze c {(x+z){raze x,''y}'x#\:y}[1+til y]/til x;
 c}

/ use (i)m(p)urity (f)unction to compute the (w)eighted information gain of
/ x after splitting on y
ig:{[ipf;w;x;y]                           / information gain
 g:ipf[w] x;
 g-:sum wodds[w;gy]*(not null key gy)*w[gy] ipf' x gy:group y;
 (g;:::;gy)}

/ use (i)m(p)urity (f)unction to compute the (w)eighted gain ratio of x
/ after splitting on y
gr:{[ipf;w;x;y]                           / gain ratio
 g:ig[ipf;w;x;y];                         / first compute information gain
 g:@[g;0;%[;ipf[w;y]]];                   / then divide by splitinfo
 g}
```

```
/ use (i)m(p)urity (f)unction to pick the maximum (w)eighted information
/ gain of x after splitting across all sets of distinct y
sig:{[ipf;w;x;y]                    / set information gain
 c:raze cmb[;u] peach 1+til 1|count[u:distinct y] div 2; / combinations of y
 g:(ig[ipf;w;x] y in) peach c;      / all gains
 g@:i:imax g[;0];                   / highest gain
 g[1]:in[;c i];                     / replace split func
 g}

/ use (i)m(p)urity (f)unction to pick the maximum (w)eighted information
/ gain of x after splitting across all values of y
oig:{[ipf;w;x;y]                    / ordered information gain
 g:(ig[ipf;w;x] y >) peach u:asc distinct y; / all gains
 g@:i:imax g[;0];                   / highest gain (not gain ratio)
 g[1]:>[;avg u i+0 1];              / replace split func
 g}

/ use (i)m(p)urity (f)unction to pick the maximum (w)eighted gain ratio of x
/ after splitting across all values of y
ogr:{[ipf;w;x;y]                    / ordered gain ratio
 g:oig[ipf;w;x;y];                  / first compute information gain
 g:@[g;0;%[;ipf[w;g[1] y]]];        / then divide by splitinfo
 g}

/ given a vector of (w)eights (or ::) and a (t)able of features where the
/ first column is the target attribute, create a decision tree using the
/ (c)ategorical (g)ain (f)unction and (o)rdered (g)ain (f)unction. the
/ (i)m(p)urity (f)unction determines which statistic to minimize. a dict of
/ (opt)ions specify the (max) (d)epth, (min)imum # of (s)amples required to
/ (s)plit, (min)imum # of (s)amples at each (l)eaf, (min)imum (g)ain and the
/ (max)imum (f)eature (f)unction used to sub sample features for random
/ forests.  defaults are: opt:`maxd`minss`minsl`ming`maxff!(0N;2;1;0;::)
dt:{[cgf;ogf;ipf;opt;w;t]
 if[(::)~w;w:n#1f%n:count t];       / compute default weight vector
 if[1=count d:flip t;:(w;first d)]; / no features to test
 opt:(`maxd`minss`minsl`ming`maxff!(0N;2;1;0;::)),opt; / default options
 if[0=opt`maxd;:(w;first d)];       / check if we've reached max depth
 if[identical a:first d;:(w;a)];    / check if all values are equal
 if[opt[`minss]>count a;:(w;a)];    / check if insufficient samples
 d:((neg floor opt[`maxff] count d)?key d)#d:1 _d;  / sub-select features
 d:{.[x isord z;y] z}[(cgf;ogf);(ipf;w;a)] peach d;  / compute gains
 d:(where (any opt[`minsl]>count each last::) each d) _ d; / filter on minsl
 if[0=count d;:(w;a)];              / check if all leaves have < minsl samples
```

## A.2. MACHINE-LEARNING ALGORITHMS

```
 if[opt[`ming]>=first b:d bf:imax d[;0];;:(w;a)];  / check gain of best feature
 c:count k:key g:last b;              / grab subtrees, feature names and count
 / distribute nulls down each branch with reduced weight
 if[c>ni:null[k]?1b;w:@[w;n:g nk:k ni;%;c-1];g:(nk _g),\:n];
 if[(::)~b 1;t:(1#bf)_t];             / don't reuse exhausted features
 b[2]:.z.s[cgf;ogf;ipf;@[opt;`maxd;-;1]]'[w g;t g]; / split sub-trees
 bf,1_b}

/ use decision (tr)ee to make predictions for (d)ictionary
pdt:{[tr;d]
 if[98h=type d;:.z.s[tr] peach d];  / iterate on a table
 p:waom . pdtr[tr;d];
 p}
/ use decision (tr)ee to recursively find leaf/leaves for (d)ictionary
pdtr:{[tr;d]
 if[2=count tr;:tr];              / (w;a)
 if[not null k:d tr 0;if[(a:tr[1][k]) in key tr[2];:.z.s[tr[2] a;d]]];
 v:(,'/) tr[2] .z.s\: d;    / dig deeper for null values
 v}


/ decision tree pruning primitives

/ Wilson score - binary confidence interval (Edwin Bidwell Wilson)
wscore:{[z;f;n](f+(.5*z2n)+-1 1f*z*sqrt((.25*z2n)+f-f*f)%n)%1f+z2n:z*z%n}
/ pessimistic error
perr:{[z;w;x]last wscore[z;wmisc[w;x];count x]}

/ use (e)rror (f)unction to post-prune (tr)ee
prune:{[ef;tr]
 if[2=count tr;:tr];                / (w;a)
 b:value tr[2]:.z.s[ef] each tr 2;  / prune subtree
 if[any 3=count each b;:tr];        / can't prune
 e:ef . wa:(,'/) b;                 / pruned error
 if[e<((sum first::) each b) wavg (ef .) each b;:wa];
 tr}

/ return the leaves of (tr)ee
leaves:{[tr]$[2=count tr;enlist tr;raze .z.s each last tr]}

/ using (e)rror (f)unction, return the decision (tr)ee's risk R(T) and
/ number of terminal nodes |T|
dtriskn:{[ef;tr](sum'[l[;0]] wsum ef ./: l;count l:leaves tr)}
```

```
/ using (e)rror (f)unction and regularization coefficient a, compute cost
/ complexity for (tr)ee
dtcc:{[ef;a;tr](1f;a) wsum dtriskn[ef;tr]}

/ given a decision (tr)ee, return all the subtrees sharing the same root
subtrees:{[tr]
 if[2=count tr;:enlist tr];
 str:tr 2; / subtree
 if[all l:2=count each str;:enlist (,'/) str]; / prune
 strs:(@[str;;:;].) each raze flip each flip (i;.z.s each str i:where not l);
 trs:@[tr;2;:;] each strs;
 trs,:enlist (,'/) leaves tr; / collapse this node too
 trs}

/ given an (i)m(p)urity function and the pair of values (a;tr), return the
/ minimum (a)lpha and its associated sub(tr)ee.
dtmina:{[ipf;atr]
 if[2=count tr:last atr;:atr];
 en:dtriskn[ipf;tr];
 ens:dtriskn[ipf] peach trs:subtrees tr;
 a:neg (%) . en - flip ens;
 atr:(a;trs)@\:i imin a i:idesc ens[;1]; / sort descending # nodes
 atr}

/ given an (e)rror function, a cost parameter (a)lpha and decision (tr)ee,
/ return the subtree that minimizes the cost complexity
dtmincc:{[ef;tr;a]
 if[2=count tr;:tr];
 strs:subtrees tr;
 strs@:iasc (count leaves::) each strs; / prefer smaller trees
 str:strs imin dtcc[ef;a] each strs;
 str}

/ k-fold cross validate (i)th table in (t)able(s) using (d)ecision (t)ree
/ (f)unction, (a)lphas and misclassification (e)rror (f)unction
dtxv:{[dtf;ef;a;ts]xv[dtmincc[ef]\[;a]dtf::;pdt\:/:;ts]}

/ decision tree utilities

/ print leaf: prediction followed by classification error% or regression sse
pleaf:{[w;x]
 v:waom[w;x];                    / value
 e:$[isord x;string sum e*e:v-x;string[.1*"i"$1e3*1f-avg x = v],"%"];
```

## A.2. MACHINE-LEARNING ALGORITHMS

```
  s:string[v]," (n = ",string[count x],", err = ",e,")";
  s}

/ print (tr)ee with i(n)dent
ptree:{[n;tr]
  if[not n;:(pleaf . first xs),last xs:.z.s[n+1;tr]];
  if[2=count tr;:(tr;"")];
  s:1#"\n";
  s,:raze[(n)#enlist "|   "],raze string[tr 0 1],\:" ";
  s:s,/:string k:asc key tr 2;
  c:.z.s[n+1] each tr[2]k;          / child
  x:first each c;
  s:s,'": ",/:(pleaf .) each x;
  s:raze s,'last each c;
  x:(,'/) x;
  (x;s)}

/ given (p)arent id, (n)ode id, label and (tr)ee print Graphviz node
pnode:{[p;n;l;tr]
  s:n," [label = \"";                                     / label
  st:$[b:2=count tr;();tr 2];                             / sub tree
  cn:n,/:"0"^(neg max count each cn)$ cn:string til count st; / child node ids
  c:$[b;enlist (tr;st);.z.s[n]'[cn;key st;value st]];     / children
  s,:pleaf . x:(,'/) first each c;                        / error stats
  if[not b;s,:"\\n",raze string[2#tr],\: " "];            / node title
  s:enlist s,"\"]";
  if[count p;s,:enlist p," -> ",n," [label = \"",string[l],"\"]"]; / edge
  s,:raze last each c;
  (x;s)}

/ print graph text for use with the 'dot' Graphviz command, graph-easy or
/ http://webgraphviz.com
pgraph:{[tr]
  s:enlist "digraph Tree {";
  s,:enlist "node [shape = box]";
  s,:last pnode["";"0";`;tr];
  s,:1#"}";
  s}

/ decision tree projections

/ given a (t)able of classifiers and labels where the first column is target
/ attribute, create a decision tree
```

```
aid:dt[sig;oig;wmse]            / automatic interaction detection
thaid:dt[sig;oig;wmisc]         / theta automatic interaction detection
id3:dt[ig;ig;wentropy]          / iterative dichotomizer 3
q45:dt[gr;ogr;wentropy]         / like c4.5
ct:dt[oig;oig;wgini]            / classification tree
rt:dt[oig;oig;wmse]             / regression tree

/ random forest

/ generate (n) decision trees by applying (f) to a resampled (with
/ replacement) (t)able
bag:{[n;f;t](f ?[;t]::) peach n#count t} / (b)ootstrap (ag)gregating

/ given an atom or list (k), and bootstrap aggregating (m)odel, make
/ prediction on (d)ictionary
pbag:{[k;m;d]
 if[count[m]<max k;'`length];
 if[98h=type d;:.z.s[k;m] peach d]; / iterate on a table
 p:k {aom x#y}\: pdt[;d] peach m;
 p}

/ discrete adaptive boosting

/ given (t)rain (f)unction, discrete (c)lassifier (f)unction, initial
/ (w)eights, and (t)able with -1 1 discrete target class values in first
/ column, return ((m)odel;(a)lpha;new (w)eights)
adaboost:{[tf;cf;w;t]
 if[(::)~w;w:n#1f%n:count t];     / initialize weights
 m:tf[w] t;                       / train model
 p:cf[m] t;                       / make predictions
 e:sum w*not p=y:first flip t;    / compute weighted error
 a:.5*log (c:1f-e)%e;             / compute alpha (minimize exponential loss)
 / w*:exp neg a*y*p;                / increase/decrease weights
 / w%:sum w;                        / normalize weights
 w%:2f*?[y=p;c;e];                / increase/decrease and normalize weights
 (m;a;w)}

/ given an atom or list (k), (t)rain (f)unction, discrete (c)lassifier
/ (f)unction, and (t)able perform max(k) iterations of adaboost
fab:{[k;tf;cf;t] 1_max[k] (adaboost[tf;cf;;t] last::)\ (::)}

/ given an atom or list (k), discrete (c)lassifier function, adaboost
/ (m)odel, make prediction on (d)ictionary
```

## A.2. MACHINE-LEARNING ALGORITHMS

```
pab:{[k;cf;m;d]
 if[count[m]<mx:max k;'`length];
 if[98h=type d;:.z.s[k;cf;m] peach d]; / iterate on a table
 p:m[;1] * cf[;d] peach m[;0];
 p:signum $[0h>type k;sum k#p;sums[mx#p] k-1];
 p}

/ regularization primitives

/ reverse of over (start deep and end shallow)
revo:{[f;x]$[type x;f x;type first x;f f peach x;f .z.s[f] peach x]}

/ given l1 regularization (l)ambda and size of dimension (m), return two
/ function compositions that compute the cost and gradient
l1:{[l;m]((l%m)*revo[sum] abs::;(l%m)*signum::)}

/ given l2 regularization (l)ambda and size of dimension (m), return two
/ function compositions that compute the cost and gradient
l2:{[l;m]((.5*l%m)*revo[sum] {x*x}::;(l%m)*)}

/ given (a)lpha and (l)ambda (r)atio elastic net parameters, convert them
/ into l1 and l2 units and return a pair of l1 and l2 projections
enet:{[a;lr](l1 a*lr;l2 a*1f-lr)}

/ gradient descent utilities

/ accumulate cost by calling (c)ost (f)unction on the result of applying
/ (m)inimization (f)unction to THETA.  return (THETA;new cost vector)
acccost:{[cf;mf;THETA;c] (THETA;c,cf THETA:mf THETA)}

/ print # of iterations, current (c)ost and % decrease to (h)andle, return a
/ continuation boolean: % decrease > float (p) or iterations < integer (p)
continue:{[h;p;c]
 pct:$[2>n:count c;0w;1f-(%/)c n-1 2];
 b:$[-8h<type p;p>n;p<pct];
 s:" | " sv ("iter: ";"cost: ";"pct: ") ,' string (n;last c;pct);
 if[not null h; h s,"\n\r" b];
 b}

/ keep calling (m)inimization (f)unction on (THETA) and logging status to
/ (h)andle until the % decrease in the (c)ost (f)unction is less than
/ (p). return (cost vector;THETA)
iter:{[h;p;cf;mf;THETA](continue[h;p]last::)acccost[cf;mf]//(::;cf)@\:THETA}
```

```
/ (a)lpha: learning rate, gf: gradient function
gd:{[a;gf;THETA] THETA-a*gf THETA}  / gradient descent

/ optimize (THETA) by using gradient descent with learning rate (a) and
/ (g)radient (f)unction over (n) subsamples of (X) and (Y) generated with
/ (s)ampling (f)unction: til = no shuffle, 0N? = shuffle, {x?x} = bootstrap
sgd:{[a;gf;sf;n;Y;X;THETA]         / stochastic gradient descent
 I:(n;0N)#sf count X 0;
 THETA:THETA (gd[a] . (gf .;:::)@'{(x[;;z];y)}[(Y;X)]::)/ I;
 THETA}

/ linear regression

/ given target matrix Y and data matri(X), return the THETA matrix resulting
/ from minimizing sum of squared residuals
normeq:{[Y;X]mm[mmt[Y;X]] minv mmt[X;X]} / normal equations ols

/ given (l2) regularization parameter, target matrix Y and data matri(X),
/ return the THETA matrix resulting from performing ridge regression
ridge:{[l2;Y;X]mm[mmt[Y;X]] minv mmt[X;X]+diag count[X]#l2}

/ given (l2) regularization parameter, target vector y and data matri(X),
/ return theta vector resulting from performing weighted ridge regression by
/ scaling the regularization parameter by the count of non-null values
wridge:{[l2;y;X]first ridge[l2*count i;enlist y i;X[;i:where not null y]]}

/ linearly predict Y values by prepending matri(X) with a vector of 1s and
/ multiplying the result to (THETA) coefficients
plin:{[X;THETA]mm[THETA] prepend[1f] X}

/ linear regression cost
lincost:{[rf;Y;X;THETA]
 J:(.5%m:count X 0)*revo[sum] E*E:plin[X;THETA]-Y;         / cost
 if[count rf,:();THETA[;0]:0f; J+:sum rf[;m][;0][;THETA]]; / regularization
 J}

/ linear regression gradient
lingrad:{[rf;Y;X;THETA]
 G:(1f%m:count X 0)*mmt[0f^mm[THETA;X]-Y] X:prepend[1f] X; / gradient
 if[count rf,:();THETA[;0]:0f; G+:sum rf[;m][;1][;THETA]]; / regularization
 G}
```

## A.2. MACHINE-LEARNING ALGORITHMS

```q
/ linear cost & gradient
lincostgrad:{[rf;Y;X;theta]
 THETA:(count Y;0N)#theta; X:prepend[1f] X;          / unroll theta
 J:(.5%m:count X 0)*revo[sum] E*E:0f^mm[THETA;X]-Y;  / cost
 G:(1f%m)*mmt[E] X;                                  / gradient
 if[count rf,:();THETA[;0]:0f;JG:rf[;m][;;THETA];J+:sum JG@'0;G+:sum JG@'1];
 (J;raze G)}

/ activation primitives (derivatives optionally accept `z`a!(z;a) dict)

linear:(::)                                 / linear
dlinear:{1f+0f*$[99h=type x;x`z;x]}         / linear gradient
sigmoid:1f%1f+exp neg::                     / sigmoid
dsigmoid:{x*1f-x:$[99h=type x;x`a;sigmoid x]} / sigmoid gradient
tanh:1f-2f%1f+exp 2f*                       / hyperbolic tangent
dtanh:{1f-x*x:$[99h=type x;x`a;tanh x]}     / hyperbolic tangent gradient
relu:0f|                                    / rectified linear unit
drelu:{"f"$0f<=$[99h=type x;x`z;x]}         / rectified linear unit gradient
lrelu:{x*1 .01@0f>x}                        / leaky rectified linear unit
dlrelu:{1 .01@0f>$[99h=type x;x`z;x]}       / leaky rectified linear unit gradient

softmax:prb exp::                   / softmax
ssoftmax:softmax dax[-;max]::       / stable softmax
dsoftmax:{diag[x] - x*\:/:x:softmax x} / softmax gradient

/ loss primitives

/ given true (y) and (p)redicted values return the log loss
logloss:{[y;p]neg (y*log 1e-15|p)+(1f-y)*log 1e-15|1f-p}
/ given true (y) and (p)redicted values return the cross entropy loss
celoss:{[y;p]neg sum y*log 1e-15|p}
/ given true (y) and (p)redicted values return the mean squared error loss
mseloss:{[y;p].5*y*y-:p}

/ logistic regression

/ logistic regression predict
plog:sigmoid plin::

/ logistic regression cost
logcost:{[rf;Y;X;THETA]
 J:(1f%m:count X 0)*revo[sum] logloss[Y] plog[X;THETA];  / cost
 if[count rf,:();THETA[;0]:0f; J+:sum rf[;m][;0][;THETA]]; / regularization
```

```
 J}

/ logistic regression gradient
loggrad:{[rf;Y;X;THETA]
 G:(1f%m:count X 0)*mmt[sigmoid[mm[THETA;X]]-Y] X:prepend[1f] X; / gradient
 if[count rf,:();THETA[;0]:0f; G+:sum rf[;m][;1][;THETA]]; / regularization
 G}

logcostgrad:{[rf;Y;X;theta]
 THETA:(count Y;0N)#theta; X:prepend[1f] X; / unroll theta
 J:(1f%m:count X 0)*revo[sum] logloss[Y] P:sigmoid mm[THETA] X; / cost
 G:(1f%m)*mmt[P-Y] X;                                          / gradient
 if[count rf,:();THETA[;0]:0f;JG:rf[;m][;;THETA];J+:sum JG@'0;G+:sum JG@'1];
 (J;raze G)}

logcostgradf:{[rf;Y;X]
 Jf:logcost[rf;Y;X]enlist::;
 Gf:loggrad[rf;Y;X]enlist::;
 (Jf;Gf)}

/ one vs all

/ given binary classification fitting (f)unction, fit a one-vs.-all model
/ against Y for each unique (lbls)
fova:{[f;Y;lbls] (f "f"$Y=) peach lbls}

/ neural network matrix initialization primitives

/ Xavier Glorot and Yoshua Bengio (2010) initialization
/ given the number of (i)nput and (o)utput nodes, initialize THETA matrix
glorotu:{[i;o]sqrt[6f%i+o]*-1f+i?/:o#2f}  / uniform
glorotn:{[i;o]rnorm'[o#i;0f;sqrt 2f%i+o]} / normal

/ Kaiming He, Xiangyu Zhang, Shaoqing Ren, Jian Sun (2015) initialization
/ given the number of (i)nput and (o)utput nodes, initialize THETA matrix
heu:{[i;o]sqrt[6f%i]*-1f+i?/:o#2f}   / uniform
hen:{[i;o]rnorm'[o#i;0f;sqrt 2f%i]}  / normal

/ neural network primitives

/ use (h)idden and (o)utput layer functions to predict neural network Y
pnn:{[hof;X;THETA]
 X:X (hof[`h] plin::)/ -1_THETA;
```

## A.2. MACHINE-LEARNING ALGORITHMS

```
 Y:hof[`o] plin[X] last THETA;
 Y}

/ (r)egularization (f)unction, holf: (h)idden (o)utput (l)oss functions
nncost:{[rf;holf;Y;X;THETA]
 J:(1f%m:count X 0)*revo[sum] holf[`l][Y] pnn[holf;X] THETA; / cost
 if[count rf,:();THETA[;;0]:0f;J+:sum rf[;m][;0][;THETA]]; / regularization
 J}

/ (r)egularization (f)unction, hgof: (h)idden (g)radient (o)utput functions
nngrad:{[rf;hgof;Y;X;THETA]
 ZA:enlist[(X;X)],(X;X) {(z;x z:plin[y 1;z])}[hgof`h]\ -1_THETA;
 P:hgof[`o] plin[last[ZA]1;last THETA]; / prediction
 G:hgof[`g]@'`z`a!/:1_ZA;               / activation gradient
 D:reverse{[D;THETA;G]G*1_mtm[THETA;D]}\[E:P-Y;reverse 1_THETA;reverse G];
 G:(1%m:count X 0)*(D,enlist E) mmt' prepend[1f] each ZA[;1]; / full grad
 if[count rf,:();THETA[;;0]:0f; G+:sum rf[;m][;1][;THETA]]; / regularization
 G}

/ neural network cut
nncut:{[n;x]n cut' sums[prev[n+:1]*n:-1_n] cut x}

/ (r)egularization (f)unction, (n)etwork topology dimensions, hgolf:
/ (h)idden (g)radient (o)utput (l)oss functions
nncostgrad:{[rf;n;hgolf;Y;X;theta]
 THETA:nncut[n] theta;                  / unroll theta
 ZA:enlist[(X;X)],(X;X) {(z;x z:plin[y 1;z])}[hgolf`h]\ -1_THETA;
 P:hgolf[`o] plin[last[ZA]1;last THETA];    / prediction
 J:(1f%m:count X 0)*revo[sum] hgolf[`l][Y;P]; / cost
 G:hgolf[`g]@'`z`a!/:1_ZA;                  / activation gradient
 D:reverse{[D;THETA;G]G*1_mtm[THETA;D]}\[E:P-Y;reverse 1_THETA;reverse G];
 G:(1f%m)*(D,enlist E) mmt' prepend[1f] each ZA[;1]; / full gradient
 if[count rf,:();THETA[;;0]:0f;JG:rf[;m][;;THETA];J+:sum JG@'0;G+:sum JG@'1];
 (J;2 raze/ G)}

/ collaborative filtering

/ collaborative filtering predict
pcf:{[X;THETA] mtm[THETA;X]}

/ collaborative filtering cost
cfcost:{[rf;Y;X;THETA]
 J:(.5f%m:count X 0)*revo[sum] E*E:pcf[X;THETA]-Y; / cost
```

```
  if[count rf,:();J+:sum rf[;m][;0]@\:(X;THETA)];   / regularization
  J}

/ collaborative filtering gradient
cfgrad:{[rf;Y;X;THETA]
  G:(1f%m:count X 0)*(mm[THETA;E];mmt[X]E:0f^pcf[X;THETA]-Y); / gradient
  if[count rf,:();G+:sum rf[;m][;1]@\:(X;THETA)]; / regularization
  G}

/ collaborative filtering cut where n:(ni;nu)
cfcut:{[n;x]n cut'(0,n[0]*count[x]div sum n) cut x}

/ collaborative filtering cost & gradient
cfcostgrad:{[rf;n;Y;xtheta]
  THETA:last X:cfcut[n] xtheta;X@:0; / unroll theta
  J:(.5%m:count X 0)*revo[sum] E*E:0f^pcf[X;THETA]-Y; / cost
  G:(1f%m)*(mm[THETA;E];mmt[X;E]);                    / gradient
  if[count rf,:();JG:rf[;m][;;(X;THETA)];J+:sum JG@'0;G+:sum JG@'1];
  (J;2 raze/ G)}

/ using learning rate (a)lpha, and (l2) regularization parameter, factorize
/ matrix Y using stochastic gradient descent by solving for each non null
/ value one at a time.  (s)ampling (f)unction: til = no shuffle, 0N? =
/ shuffle, {x?x} = bootstrap.  pass (::) for xy to initiate sgd.
sgdmf:{[a;l2;sf;Y;XTHETA;xy] / sgd matrix factorization
  if[(::)~xy;:XTHETA .z.s[a;l2;sf;Y]/ I sf count I:flip twhere not null Y];
  e:(Y . xy)-dot . xt:XTHETA .'I:flip(::;xy 1 0); / error
  XTHETA:./[XTHETA;0 1,'I;+;a*(e*xt 1 0)-l2*xt];   / adjust X and THETA
  XTHETA}

/ ALS-WR (a)lternating (l)east (s)quares with (w)eighted (r)egularization
alswr:{[l2;Y;XTHETA]
  X:flip f2nd[wridge[l2;;XTHETA 1]] Y; / hold THETA constant, solve for X
  THETA:flip wridge[l2;;X] peach Y;    / hold X constant, solve for THETA
  (X;THETA)}

/ top n svd factors
nsvd:{[n;usv]n#''@[usv;1;(n:min n,count each usv 0 2)#]}

/ use svd decomposition to predict missing exposures for new user
/ (ui=0b) or item (ui=1b) (r)ecord
foldin:{[usv;ui;r]@[usv;0 2 ui;;;mm[enlist r] mm[usv 2 0 ui] minv usv 1]}
```

## A.2. MACHINE-LEARNING ALGORITHMS

```
/ gradient checking primitives

/ compute numerical gradient of (f)unction evaluated at x using steps of
/ size (e)psilon. compute partial derivatives if (e)psilon is a list
numgrad:{[f;x;e](.5%e)*{x[y+z]-x[y-z]}[f;x] peach diag e}

/ return analytic gradient using (g)radient (f)unction and numerical
/ gradient by evaluating (c)ost (f)unction on theta perturbed by (e)psilon
checkgrad:{[e;cf;gf;theta]
 ag:gf theta;                         / analytic gradient
 ng:numgrad[cf;theta] count[theta]#e; / numerical gradient
 (ag;ng)}

/ hgolf: (h)idden (g)radient (o)utput (l)oss functions
checknngrad:{[e;rf;n;hgolf]
 theta:2 raze/ glorotu'[1+-1_n;1_n];     / initialize theta
 X:glorotu[n 1;n 0];                     / random X matrix
 y:1+(1+til n 1) mod last n;             / random y vector
 Y:flip eye[last n]"i"$y-1;              / transform into Y matrix
 cgf:nncostgrad[rf;n;hgolf;Y;X];         / cost gradient function
 r:checkgrad[e;first cgf::;last cgf::;theta]; / generate gradients
 r}

checkcfgrad:{[e;rf;n]
 ni:n 0;nu:n 1 ;nf:10;            / (n) (i)tems, (n) (u)sers, (n) (f)eatures
 xtheta:2 raze/ (X:ni?/:nf#1f;THETA:nu?/:nf#1f); / initialize theta
 Y:mm[nf?/:nu#1f]ni?/:nf#1f;             / random recommendations
 Y*:0N 1@.5<ni?/:nu#1f;                  / drop some recommendations
 cgf:cfcostgrad[rf;n;Y];                 / cost gradient function
 r:checkgrad[e;first cgf::;last cgf::;xtheta]; / generate gradients
 r}

/ sparse matrix manipulation

/ shape of a tensor (atom, vector, matrix, etc)
shape:{$[0h>t:type x;0#0;n:count x;n,.z.s x 0;1#0]}
/ rank of a tensor (atom, vector, matrix, etc)
dim:count shape::
/ sparse from tensor
sparse:{(shape x;(x') . I),I:twhere "b"$x}
/ tensor from sparse
full:{./[x[0]#0f;flip 2_x;::;x 1]}
/ sparse matrix transpose
```

```
smt:{(reverse x 0;x 1;x 3;x 2)}
/ sparse matrix multiplication
smm:{
 t:ej[`;flip `v``c!1_y;flip`w`r`!1_x];
 t:0!select sum w*v by c,r from t;
 m:enlist[(x[0;0];y[0;1])],reverse value flip t;
 m}
/ sparse matrix addition
sma:{
 t:flip[`v`r`c!1_y],flip`v`r`c!1_x;
 t:0!select sum v by c,r from t;
 m:enlist[x 0],reverse value flip t;
 m}

/ Google PageRank

/ given a (d)amping factor (1 - the probability of random surfing) and the
/ (A)djacency matrix, create the Markov Google matrix
google:{[d;A]
 M:A%1f|s:sum each A;          / convert to Markov matrix
 M+:(0f=s)%n:count M;          / add links to dangling pages
 M:(d*M)+(1f-d)%n;             / dampen
 M}

/ given a (d)amping factor (1 - the probability of random surfing) and the
/ (A)djacency matrix, obtain the pagerank algebraically
pageranka:{[d;A]
 M:A%1f|s:sum each A;          / convert to Markov matrix
 M+:(0f=s)%n:count M;          / add links to dangling pages
 r:prb first mlsq[(1;n)#(1f-d)%n] eye[n]-d*M; / compute rankings
 r}

/ given a (d)amping factor (1 - the probability of random surfing), the
/ (A)djacency matrix and an initial (r)ank vector, obtain a better ranking
/ (iterative model)
pageranki:{[d;A;r]
 w:sum r*0f=s:sum each A;      / compute dangling weight
 r:sum[A*r%1f|s]+w%n:count A;  / compute rankings
 r:(d*r)+(1f-d)%n;             / dampen
 r}

/ given a (d)amping factor (1 - the probability of random surfing), the
/ (S)parse adjacency matrix and an initial (r)ank vector, obtain a better
```

## A.2. MACHINE-LEARNING ALGORITHMS

```
/ ranking (iterative model)
pageranks:{[d;S;r]
 w:sum r*0f=s:0f^sum'[S[1] group S 2]til n:S[0;0]; / compute dangling weight
 r:first full[smm[sparse enlist r%1f|s;S]]+w%n;    / compute rankings
 r:(d*r)+(1f-d)%n;                                 / dampen
 r}

/ dimensionality reduction

covm:{[X] mmt[X;X]%count X 0}       / covariance matrix
pca:{[X] last .qml.mev covm X}      / eigen vectors of scatter matrix
project:{[V;X] mtm[V] mm[V;X]}      / project X onto subspace V

/ Markov clustering

addloop:{x|diag max peach x|flip x}

expand:{[e;X](e-1)mm[X]/X}

inflate:{[r;p;X]
 X:X xexp r;                              / inflate
 X*:$[-8h<type p;(p>iasc idesc::)';p<] X; / prune
 X%:sum peach X;                          / normalize
 X}

/ if (p)rune is an integer, take p largest, otherwise take everything > p
mcl:{[e;r;p;X] inflate[r;p] expand[e] X}

chaos:{max {max[x]-enorm2 x} peach x}
interpret:{1_asc distinct f2nd[where] 0<x}

/ complex primitives

cmul:{(((-/)x*y;(+/)x*(|)y)}       / complex multiplication
csqr:{(((-/)x*x;2f*(*/)x)}         / complex square

/ Mandelbrot

mbrotf:{[c;x]c+csqr x}                       / Mandelbrot function
mbrotp:{not 4f<0w^enorm2 x}                  / Mandelbrot predicate
mbrota:{[c;x;n](x;n+mbrotp x:mbrotf[c;x])}   / Mandelbrot accumulator
```

## A.3 External Libraries Ported to Q

**fmincg.q**

/ Minimize a continuous differentiable multivariate function. Starting point
/ is given by "X" (D by 1), and the function named in the string "f", must
/ return a function value and a vector of partial derivatives. The Polack-
/ Ribiere flavour of conjugate gradients is used to compute search
/ directions, and a line search using quadratic and cubic polynomial
/ approximations and the Wolfe-Powell stopping criteria is used together with
/ the slope ratio method for guessing initial step sizes. Additionally a
/ bunch of checks are made to make sure that exploration is taking place and
/ that extrapolation will not be unboundedly large. "n" gives the length of
/ the run: if it is positive, it gives the maximum number of line searches,
/ if negative its absolute gives the maximum allowed number of function
/ evaluations. You can (optionally) give "n" a second component, which will
/ indicate the reduction in function value to be expected in the first
/ line-search (defaults to 1.0). The function returns when either its length
/ is up, or if no further progress can be made (ie, we are at a minimum, or
/ so close that due to numerical problems, we cannot get any closer). If the
/ function terminates within a few iterations, it could be an indication that
/ the function value and derivatives are not consistent (ie, there may be a
/ bug in the implementation of your "f" function). The function returns the
/ found solution "X", a vector of function values "fX" indicating the
/ progress made and "i" the number of iterations (line searches or function
/ evaluations, depending on the sign of "n") used.

/ Usage: (X; fX; i) = .fmincg.fmincg[n; f; X]

/ See also: checkgrad

/ Copyright (C) 2001 and 2002 by Carl Edward Rasmussen. Date 2002-02-13

/ (C) Copyright 1999, 2000 & 2001, Carl Edward Rasmussen

/ Permission is granted for anyone to copy, use, or modify these programs and
/ accompanying documents for purposes of research or education, provided this
/ copyright notice is retained, and note is made of any changes that have
/ been made.

/ These programs and documents are distributed without any warranty, express
/ or implied.  As the programs were written for research purposes only, they
/ have not been tested to the degree that would be advisable in any important

## A.3. EXTERNAL LIBRARIES PORTED TO Q

```
/ application.  All use of these programs is entirely at the user's own risk.

/ [ml-class] Changes Made:
/ 1) Function name and argument specifications
/ 2) Output display

/ [nick psaris] changes made:
/ 1) ported to q
/   a) renamed "length" as "n"
/   b) placed within .fmincg namespace
/   c) moved constants out of function and into namespace
/   d) refactored to overcome 'locals and 'branch parse errors
/   e) pass/return variables as dict to overcome 8 function parameter limit
/   f) introduced BREAK variable to overcome q's lack of break statement
/ 2) max length "n" is now mandatory

\d .fmincg / function minimize nonlinear conjugate gradient

RHO:.01        / a bunch of constants for line searches
SIG:.5         / RHO and SIG are the constants in the Wolfe-Powell conditions
INT:.1         / don't reevaluate within 0.1 of the limit of the current bracket
EXT:3f         / extrapolate maximum 3 times the current bracket
MAX:20         / max 20 function evaluations per line search
RATIO:100      / maximum allowed slope ratio
REALMIN:2.2251e-308

dot:$                         / override for performance

wolfepowell:{[d1;d2;f1;f2;z1]$[d2>d1*neg SIG;1b;f2>f1+d1*RHO*z1]}
polackribiere:{[df1;df2;s](s*((dot[df2]df2)-dot[df1]df2)%dot[df1]df1)-df2}
quadfit:{[f2;f3;d2;d3;z3]z3-(.5*d3*z3*z3)%(f2-f3)+d3*z3}
cubicfit:{[f2;f3;d2;d3;z3]
 A:(6f*(f2-f3)%z3)+3f*d2+d3;
 B:(3f*f3-f2)-z3*d3+2f*d2;
 z2:(sqrt[(B*B)-A*d2*z3*z3]-B)%A; / numerical error possible-ok!
 z2}
cubicextrapolation:{[f2;f3;d2;d3;z3]
 A:(6f*(f2-f3)%z3)+3f*d2+d3;
 B:(3f*f3-f2)-z3*d3+2f*d2;
 z2:(z3*z3*neg d2)%(B+sqrt[(B*B)-A*d2*z3*z3]); / numerical error possible-ok!
 z2}

minimize:{[F;v]
```

```
     v[`z2]:$[v[`f2]>v`f1;quadfit;cubicfit] . v`f2`f3`d2`d3`z3;
     if[v[`z2] in 0n -0w 0w;v[`z2]:.5*v`z3];     / if numerical problem then bisect
     v[`z2]:(v[`z3]*1f-INT)|v[`z2]&INT*v`z3;     / don't accept too close to limits
     v[`z1]+:v`z2;
     v[`X]+:v[`z2]*v`s;
     v[`f2`df2]:F v`X;
     v[`d2]:dot . v`df2`s;
     v[`z3]-:v`z2;                    / z3 is now relative to the location of z2
     v}

extrapolate:{[F;v]
     v[`z2]:cubicextrapolation . v`f2`f3`d2`d3`z3;
     v[`z2]:$[$[0>v`z2;1b;0w=v`z2];$[.5>=v`limit;v[`z1]*EXT-1;.5*v[`limit]-v`z1];
     / extrapolation beyond max? -> bisect
     $[-.5<v`limit;v[`limit]<v[`z2]+v`z1;0b];.5*v[`limit]-v`z1;
     / extrapolation beyond limit? -> set to limit
     $[-.5>v`limit;(EXT*v`z1)<v[`z2]+v`z1;0b];v[`z1]*EXT-1;
     v[`z2]<v[`z3]*neg INT;v[`z3]*neg INT;
     / too close to limit?
     $[-.5<v`limit;v[`z2]<(v[`limit]-v`z1)*1f-INT;0b];(v[`limit]-v`z1)*1f-INT;
     v[`z2]];
     v[`f3]:v`f2;v[`d3]:v`d2;v[`z3]:neg v`z2;    / set pt 3 = pt 2
     v[`z1]+:v`z2;v[`X]+:v[`z2]*v`s;             / update current estimates
     v[`f2`df2]:F v`X;
     v[`d2]:dot . v`df2`s;
     v}

loop:{[n;F;v]
     v[`i]+:n>0;                      / count iterations?!
     v[`X]+:v[`z1]*v`s;               / begin line search
     v[`f2`df2]:F v`X;
     v[`i]+:n<0;                      / count epochs?!
     v[`d2]:dot . v`df2`s;
     v[`f3]:v`f1;v[`d3]:v`d1;v[`z3]:neg v`z1; / initialize pt 3 = pt 1
     v[`M]:$[n>0;MAX;MAX&neg n-v`i];
     v[`success]:0b;v[`limit]:-1;     / initialize quantities
     BREAK:0b;
     while[not BREAK;
      while[$[0<v`M;wolfepowell . v`d1`d2`f1`f2`z1;0b];
       v[`limit]:v`z1;                / tighten the bracket
       v:minimize[F;v];
       v[`M]-:1;v[`i]+:n<0;           / count epochs?!
       ];
```

## A.3. EXTERNAL LIBRARIES PORTED TO Q

```
   if[wolfepowell . v`d1`d2`f1`f2`z1;BREAK:1b];   / failure
   if[v[`d2]>SIG*v`d1;v[`success]:1b;BREAK:1b];   / success
   if[v[`M]=0;BREAK:1b];                          / failure
   if[not BREAK;
    v:extrapolate[F;v];
    v[`M]-:1;v[`i]+:n<0;           / count epochs?!
    ];
   ];
  v}

 onsuccess:{[v]
  v[`f1]:v`f2;
  1"Iteration ",string[v`i]," | cost: ", string[v`f1], "\r";
  v:@[v;`s;polackribiere . v`df1`df2]; / Polack-Ribiere direction
  v[`df2`df1]:v`df1`df2;               / swap derivatives
  v[`d2]:dot . v`df1`s;
  / new slope must be negative, otherwise use steepest direction
  if[v[`d2]>0;v[`s]:neg v`df1;v[`d2]:dot[v`s;neg v`s]];
  v[`z1]*:RATIO&v[`d1]%v[`d2]-REALMIN; / slope ratio but max RATIO
  v[`d1]:v`d2;
  v}

 fmincg:{[n;F;X]
  v:`X`i!(X;0);
  ls_failed:0b;                  / no previous line search has failed
  fX:();
  v[`f1`df1]:F v`X;              / get function value and gradient
  v[`s]:neg v`df1;               / search direction is steepest
  v[`d1]:dot[v`s;neg v`s];       / this is the slope
  v[`z1]:(n:n,1)[1]%1f-v`d1;     / initial step is red/(|s|+1)
  n@:0;                          / n is first element
  v[`i]+:n<0;                    / count epochs?!

  while[v[`i]<abs n;             / while not finished
   X0:v`X`f1`df1;                / make a copy of current values
   v:loop[n;F;v];
   if[v`success;fX,:v`f2;v:onsuccess v];
   if[not v`success;
    v[`X`f1`df1]:X0;      / restore point from before failed line search
    / line search failed twice in a row or we ran out of time, so we give up
    if[$[ls_failed;1b;v[`i]>abs n];-1"";:(v`X;fX;v`i)];
    v[`df2`df1]:v`df1`df2;                         / swap derivatives
    v[`z1]:1f%1f-v[`d1]:dot[v[`s]]neg v`s]:neg v`df1; / try steepest
```

```
  ];
  ls_failed:not v`success;       / line search failure
  ];
 -1"";(v`X;fX;v`i)}
```

**porter.q**

```
/ this is the porter stemmer algorithm ported to q.  it follows the
/ algorithm presented in:

/ Porter, 1980, An algorithm for suffix stripping, Program, Vol. 14,
/ no. 3, pp 130-137

/ https://tartarus.org/martin/PorterStemmer/def.txt

/ this implementation includes the three points of departure from the
/ original paper introduced here:

/ https://www.tartarus.org/~martin/PorterStemmer

/ note that this implementation stems single words - not full text.
/ this obviates global variables and .porter.stem, therefore, can be
/ 'peach'ed.  instead of run-time computations and function calls,
/ hard-coded offsets and $[;;] operators are used for performance.
/ implementation accuracy can be verified by running the trailing code

/ nick psaris
/ release 1: august 2018

\d .porter

/ are the letters in x vowels
vowel:{
  v:x in "aeiou";  / aeiou are vowels
 / y is a vowel if the preceding letter is a consonant
  v[i where not (1b,v) i:where x="y"]:1b;
  v}

/ are the letters in x consonants
cons:not vowel::

/ returns true if x contains a vowel
hasvowel:any vowel::
```

## A.3. EXTERNAL LIBRARIES PORTED TO Q

```
/ returns true if x ends in a double consonant
doublec:{$[2>count x;0b;(=) . -2#x;last cons x;0b]}

/ return true if last three letters are consonant - vowel -
/ consonant and last letter is not in "wxy"
cvc:{$[3>count x;0b;101b~-3#cons x;not last[x] in "wxy";0b]}

/ if a<m replace n characters with (r)eplacement suffix
r:{[a;n;r;x]$[a<m n:n _ x;n,r;x]}

/ compute m where m in c?(vc){m}v? and c and v are consecutive lists
/ of consonants and vowels
m:{sum[x] - first x:x where differ x:cons x}

/ remove plurals and -ed or -ing
step1ab:{
 x:$[not x like "*s";x;x like "*sses";-2_x;
  x like "*ies";-2_x;x like "*ss";x;-1_x];
 if[x like "*eed";:$[0<m -3_x;-1_x;x]];
 if[not x like o:"*ed";if[not x like o:"*ing";:x]];
 if[not hasvowel n:(1+neg count o)_x;:x];x:n;
 if[x like "*at";:x,"e"];
 if[x like "*bl";:x,"e"];
 if[x like "*iz";:x,"e"];
 if[doublec x;:$[last[x] in "lsz";x;-1_x]];
 if[1=m x;if[cvc x;:x,"e"]];
 x}

/ replace y with i when there exist other vowels
step1c:{if[x like "*y";if[hasvowel -1_x;x[-1+count x]:"i"]];x}

/ map double suffices to single ones
step2:{
 c:x -2+count x;
 if[c="a";:$[x like "*ational";r[0;-7;"ate";x];
   x like "*tional";r[0;-6;"tion";x];x]];
 if[c="c";:$[x like "*enci";r[0;-4;"ence";x];
   x like "*anci";r[0;-4;"ance";x];x]];
 if[c="e";:$[x like "*izer";r[0;-4;"ize";x];x]];
 if[c="l";:$[x like "*bli";r[0;-3;"ble";x];x like "*alli";r[0;-4;"al";x];
   x like "*entli";r[0;-5;"ent";x];x like "*eli";r[0;-3;"e";x];
   x like "*ousli";r[0;-5;"ous";x];x]];
```

```
  if[c="o";;$[x like "*ization";r[0;-7;"ize";x];
    x like "*ation";r[0;-5;"ate";x];x like "*ator";r[0;-4;"ate";x];x]];
  if[c="s";;$[x like "*alism";r[0;-5;"al";x];
    x like "*iveness";r[0;-7;"ive";x];x like "*fulness";r[0;-7;"ful";x];
    x like "*ousness";r[0;-7;"ous";x];x]];
  if[c="t";;$[x like "*aliti";r[0;-5;"al";x];x like "*iviti";r[0;-5;"ive";x];
    x like "*biliti";r[0;-6;"ble";x];x]];
  if[c="g";;$[x like "*logi";r[0;-4;"log";x];x]];
  x}

/ handle -ic-, -full, -ness etc
step3:{
  c:x -1+count x;
  if[c="e";;$[x like "*icate";r[0;-5;"ic";x];x like "*ative";r[0;-5;"";x];
    x like "*alize";r[0;-5;"al";x];x]];
  if[c="i";;$[x like "*iciti";r[0;-5;"ic";x];x]];
  if[c="l";;$[x like "*ical";r[0;-4;"ic";x];x like "*ful";r[0;-3;"";x];x]];
  if[c="s";;$[x like "*ness";r[0;-4;"";x];x]];
  x}

/ remove -ant, -ence etc, in context <c>vcvc<v>
step4:{
  c:x -2+count x;
  if[c="a";;$[x like "*al";r[1;-2;"";x];x]];
  if[c="c";;$[x like "*ance";r[1;-4;"";x];x like "*ence";r[1;-4;"";x];x]];
  if[c="e";;$[x like "*er";r[1;-2;"";x];x]];
  if[c="i";;$[x like "*ic";r[1;-2;"";x];x]];
  if[c="l";;$[x like "*able";r[1;-4;"";x];x like "*ible";r[1;-4;"";x];x]];
  if[c="n";;$[x like "*ant";r[1;-3;"";x];x like "*ement";r[1;-5;"";x];
    x like "*ment";r[1;-4;"";x];x like "*ent";r[1;-3;"";x];x]];
  if[c="o";;$[x like "*ion";$[x[-4+count x] in "st";r[1;-3;"";x];x];
    x like "*ou";r[1;-2;"";x];x]];
  if[c="s";;$[x like "*ism";r[1;-3;"";x];x]];
  if[c="t";;$[x like "*ate";r[1;-3;"";x];x like "*iti";r[1;-3;"";x];x]];
  if[c="u";;$[x like "*ous";r[1;-3;"";x];x]];
  if[c="v";;$[x like "*ive";r[1;-3;"";x];x]];
  if[c="z";;$[x like "*ize";r[1;-3;"";x];x]];
  x}

/ remove final e if m>1, change -ll to -l if m>1
step5:{
  if["e"=last x;x:$[0=a:m x;x;1<a;-1_x;not cvc -1_x;-1_x]];
  if["l"=last x;if[doublec x;if[1<m x;:-1_x]]];
```

## A.4. DATA LIBRARIES

```
 x}

stem:{
 if[3>count x;:x];
 x:step1ab x;
 x:step1c x;
 x:step2 x;
 x:step3 x;
 x:step4 x;
 x:step5 x;
 x}
```

# A.4  Data Libraries

### berkstan.q

```
berkstan.f:"web-BerkStan.txt"
berkstan.b:"http://snap.stanford.edu/data/"
-1"[down]loading berkstan network graph";
.ut.download[berkstan.b;;".gz";.ut.gunzip] berkstan.f;
berkstan.l:("II";"\t") 0:  4_read0 `$berkstan.f
```

### dji.q

```
 dji.f:"dow_jones_index"
 dji.b:"http://archive.ics.uci.edu/ml/machine-learning-databases/"
 dji.b,:"00312/"
-1"[down]loading dji data set";
.ut.download[dji.b;;".zip";.ut.unzip] dji.f;
 dji.t:("HSDEEEEJFFJEEFHF";1#",")0: ssr[;"$";""] each read0 `$dji.f,".data"
```

### emma.q

```
/ emma
emma.f:"158.txt"
emma.b:"http://www.gutenberg.org/files/158/"
-1"[down]loading emma text";
.ut.download[emma.b;;"";""] emma.f;
emma.txt:{x where not x like "VOLUME*"} read0 `$emma.f
emma.chapters:1_"CHAPTER" vs "\n" sv 39_-373_emma.txt
emma.s:{(3+first x ss"\n\n\n")_x} each emma.chapters
```

## iris.q

```
iris.f:("iris.data";"bezdekIris.data") 1
iris.b:"http://archive.ics.uci.edu/ml/machine-learning-databases/"
iris.b,:"iris/"
-1"[down]loading iris data set";
.ut.download[iris.b;;"";""] iris.f;
iris.XY:150#/:("FFFFS";",") 0: `$iris.f
iris.X:-1_iris.XY
iris.y:first iris.Y:-1#iris.XY
iris.c:`slength`swidth`plength`pwidth`species
iris.t:`species xcols flip iris.c!iris.XY
```

## mansfield.q

```
/ mansfield park
mansfield.f:"141.txt"
mansfield.b:"http://www.gutenberg.org/files/141/"
-1"[down]loading mansfield park text";
.ut.download[mansfield.b;;"";""] mansfield.f;
mansfield.txt:read0 `$mansfield.f
mansfield.chapters:1_"CHAPTER" vs "\n" sv 35_-373_mansfield.txt
mansfield.s:{(2+first x ss"\n\n")_x} each mansfield.chapters
```

## mlens.q

```
mlens.f:("ml-latest";"ml-latest-small") 1 / pick the smaller dataset
mlens.b:"http://files.grouplens.org/datasets/movielens/" / base url
-1"[down]loading latest movielens data set";
.ut.download[mlens.b;;".zip";.ut.unzip] mlens.f;
-1"loading movie definitions: integer movieIds and enumerated genres";
mlens.movie:1!("I**";1#",") 0: `$mlens.f,"/movies.csv"
-1"removing movies without genres";
update 0#'genres from `mlens.movie where genres like "(no genres listed)";
-1"converting unicode in titles to ascii";
update .ut.sr[.ut.ua] peach rtrim title from `mlens.movie;
-1"extracting the movie's year from the title";
update year:"I"$-1_/:-5#/:title from `mlens.movie;
update -7_/:title from `mlens.movie where not null year;
-1"adding `u on movieId and splitting genres";
update `u#movieId,`$"|"vs'genres from `mlens.movie
-1"adding the decade as a genre";
update genres:(genres,'`$string 10 xbar year) from `mlens.movie
-1"enumerating genres";
```

## A.4. DATA LIBRARIES

```
mlens.movie:update `genre?/:genres from mlens.movie
-1"loading movie ratings";
mlens.rating:("IIFP";1#",") 0:`$mlens.f,"/ratings.csv"
-1"adding `p on userId and linking movieId to movie table";
update `p#userId,`mlens.movie$movieId from `mlens.rating;
```

### mnist.q

```
mnist.zf:(
 "train-labels.idx1-ubyte";
 "train-images.idx3-ubyte";
 "t10k-labels.idx1-ubyte";
 "t10k-images.idx3-ubyte")
mnist.f:ssr[;".";"-"] each mnist.zf
mnist.b:"http://yann.lecun.com/exdb/mnist/"
-1"[down]loading handwritten-digit data set";
.ut.download[mnist.b;;".gz";.ut.gunzip] mnist.f;
/ rename unzipped file to match zipped file
mnist.zf {[zf;f]if[zfs~key zfs:`$":",zf;system "r ",zf," ",f]}' mnist.f;

mnist.Y:enlist mnist.y:"i"$.ut.mnist read1 `$mnist.f 0
mnist.X:flip "f"$raze each .ut.mnist read1 `$mnist.f 1

mnist.Yt:enlist mnist.yt:"i"$.ut.mnist read1 `$mnist.f 2
mnist.Xt:flip "f"$raze each .ut.mnist read1 `$mnist.f 3
```

### northanger.q

```
/ northanger abbey
northanger.f:"121.txt"
northanger.b:"http://www.gutenberg.org/files/121/"
-1"[down]loading northanger abbey text";
.ut.download[northanger.b;;"";""] northanger.f;
northanger.txt:read0 `$northanger.f
northanger.chapters:1_"CHAPTER" vs "\n" sv 57_-373_northanger.txt
northanger.s:{(3+first x ss"\n\n\n")_x} each northanger.chapters
```

### pandp.q

```
/ pride and prejudice
pandp.f:"1342-0.txt"
pandp.b:"http://www.gutenberg.org/files/1342/"
-1"[down]loading pride and prejudice text";
.ut.download[pandp.b;;"";""] pandp.f;
```

```
pandp.txt:read0 `$pandp.f
pandp.chapters:1_"Chapter" vs "\n" sv  6_'166_-373_ pandp.txt
pandp.s:{(2+first x ss"\n\n")_x} each .ut.sr[.ut.ua] peach pandp.chapters
```

## persuasion.q

```
/ persuasion
persuasion.f:"105.txt"
persuasion.b:"http://www.gutenberg.org/files/105/"
-1"[down]loading persuasion text";
.ut.download[persuasion.b;;"";""] persuasion.f;
persuasion.txt:read0 `$persuasion.f
persuasion.chapters:1_"Chapter" vs "\n" sv  44_-373_persuasion.txt
persuasion.s:{(3+first x ss"\n\n\n")_x} each persuasion.chapters
```

## sands.q

```
/ sense and sensibility
sands.f:"161.txt"
sands.b:"http://www.gutenberg.org/files/161/"
-1"[down]loading sense and sensibility text";
.ut.download[sands.b;;"";""] sands.f;
sands.txt:read0 `$sands.f
sands.chapters:1_"CHAPTER" vs "\n" sv  43_-373_sands.txt
sands.s:{(3+first x ss"\n\n\n")_x} each sands.chapters
```

## smsspam.q

```
smsspam.f:"smsspamcollection"
smsspam.b:"http://archive.ics.uci.edu/ml/machine-learning-databases/"
smsspam.b,:"00228/"
-1"[down]loading sms-spam data set";
.ut.download[smsspam.b;;".zip";.ut.unzip] smsspam.f;
smsspam.t:flip `class`text!("S*";"\t")0: `:SMSSpamCollection
```

## stopwords.q

```
stopwords.f:"stop-word-list.txt"
stopwords.b:"http://xpo6.com/wp-content/uploads/2015/01/"
-1"[down]loading xpo6 stop words";
.ut.download[stopwords.b;;"";""] stopwords.f;
stopwords.xpo6:asc enlist[""],read0 `$":",stopwords.f

stopwords.f:"stop.txt"
```

## A.4. DATA LIBRARIES

```
stopwords.b:"http://snowball.tartarus.org/algorithms/english/"
-1"[down]loading snowball stop words";
.ut.download[stopwords.b;;"";""] stopwords.f;
stopwords.snowball:asc distinct trim {(x?"|")#x} each read0 `$":",stopwords.f
```

### uef.q

```
uef.s:("s1.txt";"s2.txt";"s3.txt";"s4.txt")
uef.a:("a1.txt";"a2.txt";"a3.txt")
uef.d:("dim032.txt";"dim064.txt";"dim128.txt")
uef.d,:("dim256.txt";"dim512.txt";"dim1024.txt");
uef.b:"http://www.cs.uef.fi/sipu/datasets/"
-1"[down]loading uef data sets";
.ut.download[uef.b;;"";""] uef.s,uef.a,uef.d;

uef,:`s1`s2`s3`s4!("JJ";10 10) 0:/: `$uef.s
uef,:`a1`a2`a3!("JJ";8 8) 0:/: `$uef.a
uef,:(!) . flip {(`$"d",string x;(x#"J";x#6) 0: y)}'[16*\6#2;`$uef.d]
```

### wdbc.q

```
wdbc.f:"wdbc.data"
wdbc.b:"http://archive.ics.uci.edu/ml/machine-learning-databases/"
wdbc.b,:"breast-cancer-wisconsin/"
-1"[down]loading wisconsin-diagnostic-breast-cancer data set";
.ut.download[wdbc.b;;"";""] wdbc.f;
wdbc.XY:(" C",30#"E";",") 0: `$wdbc.f
wdbc.X:1_wdbc.XY
wdbc.y:first wdbc.Y:1#wdbc.XY
wdbc.c:`radius`texture`perimeter`area`smoothness`compactness`concavity
wdbc.c,:`concave_points`symmetry`fractal_dimension
wdbc.c:raze `$"_" sv'string raze wdbc.c,\:/: `mean`se`worst
wdbc.t:flip (`diagnosis,wdbc.c)!wdbc.XY
```

### weather.q

```
weather.f:"weather.csv"
weather.t:`Play xcols (" SSSSS";1#",") 0: `$weather.f
```

### winequality.q

```
winequality.f:`red`white!("winequality-red.csv";"winequality-white.csv")
winequality.b:"http://archive.ics.uci.edu/ml/machine-learning-databases/"
winequality.b,:"wine-quality/"
```

```
 -1"[down]loading wine-quality data set";
 .ut.download[winequality.b;;"";""] each winequality.f;
 .winequality.load:{[f]
  YX:value flip t:`quality xcols .Q.id (12#"F";1#";")0:f;
  d:`X`Y`y`t!(1_YX;1#YX;YX 0;t);
  d}
 winequality,:.winequality.load each `$winequality.f
```

# Index

,'/, 42
-, 23
-16!, 20
., 42, 56, 57, 306, 322
.Q.hg, 15, 16
.fmincg.fmincg, 200, 201, 213, 224, 233, 245, 252, 283, 285
.ml, 187, 188
.ml.acccost, 202
.ml.adaboost, 173, 174, 176
.ml.alswr, 290, 291
.ml.append, 185
.ml.bag, 167, 170, 171
.ml.binl, 88
.ml.bmml, 101
.ml.celoss, 255, 256
.ml.cfcost, 282, 285
.ml.cfcostgrad, 284, 285
.ml.cfcut, 283, 284
.ml.cfgrad, 284, 285
.ml.cgroup, 36, 53, 58–60
.ml.clust, 68, 76, 77, 80
.ml.cm, 91, 92
.ml.cmb, 149
.ml.cmul, 323, 324
.ml.continue, 202
.ml.cordist, 275, 276, 278
.ml.cossim, 27
.ml.csqr, 324
.ml.ct, 151, 152, 159, 162, 164, 171

.ml.dax, 96, 97, 255
.ml.daxf, 97, 196, 199
.ml.demeanf, 199
.ml.distortion, 53, 61
.ml.dlrelu, 252
.ml.dot, 188
.ml.drelu, 252, 253
.ml.dsigmoid, 249, 252, 253
.ml.dt, 138, 143–147, 159, 169, 174, 271
.ml.dtanh, 252
.ml.dtcc, 153
.ml.dtmina, 155
.ml.dtmincc, 157
.ml.dtriskn, 153
.ml.dtxv, 158
.ml.edist, 23, 28, 39
.ml.edist2, 39, 40, 63
.ml.em, 92
.ml.enet, 212
.ml.enorm, 24, 25, 325
.ml.enorm2, 25, 325
.ml.entropy, 146, 159
.ml.f2nd, 28–31, 188
.ml.fab, 176, 177
.ml.find, 35, 36
.ml.fknn, 41, 275
.ml.forgy, 50
.ml.fova, 232, 233
.ml.freq, 34, 75
.ml.full, 307, 308

.ml.fxx, 197
.ml.gaussmvl, 105
.ml.gd, 191, 192, 194, 200, 202, 205
.ml.gini, 154, 159
.ml.glorotn, 245
.ml.glorotu, 244
.ml.google, 299
.ml.hdist, 100
.ml.hen, 245
.ml.heu, 245
.ml.hmap, 317
.ml.hmean, 64
.ml.identical, 145
.ml.ig, 146, 148
.ml.imax, 33, 35, 43
.ml.imin, 35, 36, 53
.ml.ismatrix, 182
.ml.isord, 32
.ml.iter, 201–204, 207, 289
.ml.iwrand, 55
.ml.kmeans, 58
.ml.kmeanspp, 57
.ml.kmedianspp, 63
.ml.knn, 32, 39, 273, 280
.ml.kpp, 55–57, 63, 100
.ml.l1, 208, 209, 211, 213
.ml.l2, 211, 213
.ml.lancewilliams, 71, 72, 75
.ml.leaves, 153
.ml.likelihood, 90
.ml.lincost, 193, 194, 202, 212
.ml.lincostgrad, 200, 212, 213, 224, 252
.ml.lingrad, 194
.ml.link, 68, 71, 72, 76
.ml.lloyd, 58, 59, 64, 65
.ml.lntf, 128
.ml.logcost, 222, 223
.ml.logcostgrad, 224, 233, 252

.ml.loggrad, 223
.ml.logloss, 221, 223, 224, 253–255
.ml.lrelu, 247
.ml.lw, 75
.ml.mbrot, 327
.ml.mbrota, 325, 327
.ml.mbrotf, 324
.ml.mbrotp, 325
.ml.mchol, 188
.ml.mdet, 105, 188
.ml.mdist, 23, 63
.ml.mfind, 36, 37
.ml.minmax, 196, 197
.ml.minmaxf, 196–198
.ml.minv, 105, 188
.ml.misc, 134, 154
.ml.mkdist, 23
.ml.mlsq, 188, 301
.ml.mm, 188
.ml.mmml, 95
.ml.mmt, 188
.ml.mnorm, 23–25
.ml.mode, 34, 35, 37, 47, 315
.ml.mse, 159
.ml.mseloss, 258
.ml.mtm, 188
.ml.multil, 94
.ml.multill, 129
.ml.navg, 199, 272, 273
.ml.ncount, 271
.ml.ndev, 273
.ml.nncost, 246–248, 252, 258
.ml.nncostgrad, 243, 244, 252, 257, 258
.ml.nncut, 252
.ml.nngrad, 248, 252
.ml.noflip, 29
.ml.normeq, 189, 212, 215
.ml.nsdev, 199, 273

## A.4. DATA LIBRARIES

.ml.nsum, 272
.ml.nsvar, 272
.ml.nvar, 272
.ml.nwavg, 33, 199, 271, 273
.ml.odds, 110
.ml.oig, 152
.ml.pab, 177, 178
.ml.pageranka, 301
.ml.pageranki, 302, 303, 308
.ml.pageranks, 309
.ml.pam, 64, 65
.ml.pbag, 168
.ml.pcf, 281, 282
.ml.pdt, 142, 168
.ml.pdtr, 142
.ml.pedist2, 40, 70
.ml.pend, 186
.ml.pgraph, 139-141
.ml.pi, 191
.ml.pknn, 43
.ml.pleaf, 139, 140
.ml.plin, 186
.ml.plog, 221
.ml.pnb, 36, 112, 120
.ml.pnn, 246-248
.ml.pnode, 140
.ml.pnorm, 24, 25
.ml.prb, 95-97, 255, 256
.ml.prepend, 185
.ml.ptree, 139
.ml.rbern, 84
.ml.rbinom, 86, 87, 93
.ml.relu, 250, 251, 253, 256
.ml.revo, 193, 209, 210
.ml.ridge, 211, 212, 291
.ml.rms, 162, 187
.ml.rmultinom, 93
.ml.roc, 228
.ml.rpart, 52

.ml.rt, 159, 161, 170
.ml.runif, 84, 85
.ml.scor, 277
.ml.scordist, 278
.ml.sgd, 205-207, 287, 288
.ml.sgdmf, 287, 288
.ml.shape, 304
.ml.sig, 146, 148, 149
.ml.sigmoid, 224, 239, 247, 249, 250, 253, 255
.ml.silhouette, 68, 79, 80
.ml.smm, 308, 309
.ml.softmax, 255, 256
.ml.sparse, 308, 309
.ml.srank, 277
.ml.sse, 53
.ml.ssoftmax, 255
.ml.ssw, 53
.ml.subtrees, 155
.ml.tanh, 247, 250
.ml.tdm, 119
.ml.tptnfpfn, 121, 228
.ml.twhere, 288, 305
.ml.waom, 32, 33, 143, 271, 273
.ml.wbinmle, 88
.ml.wbmmmle, 102
.ml.wentropy, 147, 151
.ml.wfreq, 33-35
.ml.wgaussmvmle, 105
.ml.wgini, 151
.ml.wmmmmle, 94, 95
.ml.wmode, 33-35
.ml.wmse, 161
.ml.wmultimle, 121
.ml.wnan, 27
.ml.wodds, 111
.ml.wridge, 291
.ml.xv, 42, 43, 158
.ml.zscore, 198

.ml.zscoref, 198, 199
.qml.conmin, 200
.qml.min, 200
.ut.download, 13–15
.ut.ha, 115
.ut.heckbert, 321, 322
.ut.hmap, 316, 317
.ut.mnist, 98
.ut.nbin, 321, 335
.ut.nicenum, 319, 320
.ut.nseq, 190, 191, 321, 324
.ut.onehot, 162, 163
.ut.part, 17–19, 42, 156
.ut.pbm, 327
.ut.plot, 21, 47, 311, 316, 319, 321, 325
.ut.plt, 47, 313, 314, 317
.ut.pw, 115
.ut.rnd, 129
.ut.spark, 335, 337
.ut.sr, 115, 116
.ut.sseq, 213
.ut.tcross, 317, 318, 324
.ut.totals, 92
.ut.ua, 114
.ut.ugrp, 47, 59, 60, 68, 78
.z.s, 15, 76
/, 47, 56, 57, 248
::, 23, 24, 27, 32, 177, 202, 233, 257, 288
?, 35–37, 51, 56, 85, 168–170, 206, 229
?[;;], 37
@, 24, 43, 233
#, 206, 210
$, 337
&, 32, 72
_, 18
\, 176, 248

0N!, 15, 30, 276

## A
abs, 23
activation function, 7, 238, 239, 241, 244, 246, 247, 249–251, 253–257, 314
AdaBoost, 7, 173–177
adjacency matrix, 8, 297–299, 301–303, 305–307, 310
alternating least squares, 8, 290–292
AUC, 230
avg, 47, 52, 199, 271, 272, 277, 315

## B
Bernoulli, 84, 99, 101
Bernoulli mixture model, 6, 99, 101
bin, 322
binomial, 6, 86, 87, 90, 101, 254
Binomial mixture model, 102
binr, 56
bootstrap aggregation, 165–167, 172, 173

## C
CART, 6, 136, 151, 162
collaborative-filtering, 282, 287
conjugate gradient, 7
cor, 275, 277
cos, 335
cosine distance, 26, 27
cosine similarity, 26, 27, 278–280
cost function, 7, 192–194, 200, 202, 207, 208, 222, 223, 246, 253–255, 257, 282, 287, 289
cross, 214, 317
cross entropy, 7, 255, 256
cross validation, 5–7, 42, 43, 156, 178, 179
cut, 283, 284

## D

damping factor, 299, 300, 302
decision stump, 7, 166, 176–178
decision tree, 6, 130–132, 134, 137–139, 143, 145, 154, 156, 157, 159, 161, 164, 165, 167–169, 173–179
decision trees, xx, 6, 33, 158, 164–166, 177, 184
dissimilarity matrix, 5, 68, 70–73

## E

each, 32, 36, 96
eager learning, 11, 262
elastic net, 7, 212, 214
elbow method, 5
ensemble, 7, 165–169, 173–175, 177–179, 313
entropy, 134–137, 151
Euclidean distance, 21, 22, 26–28, 39, 46, 57, 59, 63, 65, 70, 73, 79, 80
exec, 336
exp, 38
expectation-maximization, 5, 81, 83–87, 90, 92, 97, 99, 102, 103, 106, 107, 109
expectation-maximization algorithm, 94, 98, 103, 112, 313

## F

fallout, 227
feed-forward, 7, 239, 240, 246, 248, 249
flip, 28
Forgy method, 50, 64
FPR, 227

## G

gain ratio, 150
Gaussian mixture model, 6, 103
get, 23
Gini impurity, 135, 136, 151, 154
Google Matrix, 300
Google matrix, 8, 299, 300
gradient descent, 7, 8, 182, 191, 192, 194, 203–207, 213, 215, 241, 247, 253, 259, 266–268, 281, 283–285, 287, 290
Graphviz, 6
group, 35, 51, 60, 110

## H

Hamming distance, 57
hcount, 329
heat map, 99, 316, 317
Heaviside step function, 238, 239
hierarchical agglomerative clustering, 5, 67, 68, 70, 78, 79, 81, 107, 313
higher-order function, 41, 64, 97, 196, 199
hyperbolic tangent, 7, 250

## I

iasc, 32
ID3, 6, 134, 137, 146–148
impurity function, 6, 134, 135, 137, 144, 146, 147, 153, 154, 159, 313
information gain, 144, 147, 150, 151, 169
information-gain, 6, 146, 148
instance-based algorithm, 12
inv, 183, 190

## K

k-fold cross validation, 42, 156, 158, 161
k-harmonic means, 5, 52, 63–65

k-means, xx, 5, 43, 45–47, 49, 50, 54, 58, 59, 61–65, 81, 83, 84, 103, 107, 109, 313
k-means++, 5, 50, 55, 57, 100
k-medians, 5, 63–65
k-medians++, 63
k-medoids, 5, 51, 64, 65
k-nearest neighbors, 5, 8, 11–13, 20, 28, 31, 33, 41, 43, 45, 59, 70, 273, 280
k-NN, 5, 12, 32, 41
key, 15

**L**

Lance-Williams algorithm, 5, 67, 68, 70–75
LASSO, 7, 209
lazy learning, 11, 262
lemmatization, 117
likelihood, 6, 83–87, 89, 90, 92, 94, 95, 101, 102, 104, 105, 107, 109, 110, 112, 113, 119, 128–130
linear regression, 7, 8, 180, 181, 186, 192, 193, 199, 200, 205, 209, 211, 212, 217, 219, 221–223, 257–259, 266, 284, 290
linear regularization, 8
linear-regression, 194, 282
linkage, 5, 68, 72, 74–77
Lloyd's algorithm, 58, 62
log-loss, 7, 221, 223, 254, 256
logistic, 220
logistic regression, 7, 193, 215, 217–219, 221, 223, 226, 246, 247, 259, 314
logistic-regression, 222, 223
lower, 116
lsq, 183, 184, 190, 215, 301

**M**

Mandelbrot set, 8, 323, 325, 331, 333
Manhattan distance, 21, 22, 27, 63, 65, 80
Markov matrix, 8, 298, 299, 301, 303
matrix factorization, 215, 290
max, 196
min, 72, 196
Minkowski distance, 22
mixture model, 94
mmu, 183, 184, 187
MNIST, 6, 7, 98, 107, 231, 233, 240, 254, 256, 313, 315
mode, 34
model-based algorithm, 12
mtm, 40
multinomial, 6, 92, 94, 95, 113, 119, 128–130, 254
multinomial mixture model, 94, 95

**N**

naive Bayes, 109, 110, 119, 120, 124, 127, 128
naive Bayes algorithm, 6, 109, 110, 113, 119, 127
neural network, 7, 193, 210, 215, 231, 235, 237, 239–245, 250, 252, 254, 255, 257–259, 281, 313
neural-network, 246
normal equations, 7, 189, 190, 215, 301
null-aware, 33, 199, 271, 272, 274, 276, 277

**O**

one-hot encoding, 6, 162, 163
one-of-k encoding, 162
one-vs.-all, 7, 231–233, 235
one-vs.-rest, 231
over, 49, 56, 209, 210

## P

PageRank algorithm, 8, 295, 296, 298, 299, 301–303, 308–310
PageRank vector, 301, 302
peach, 29, 31, 32, 168, 215
perceptron, 7, 237–241
Porter stemmer, 6, 117
power method, 8, 300–303
precision, 122, 123

## R

random forest, 7, 166, 172, 173, 313
random number generator seed, 19
random partition, 50, 64
rank, 277
raze, 42
recall, 122, 123, 227
receiver operating characteristic, 227
recommender system, xx, 8, 193, 259
regularization, 7, 8, 182, 193, 194, 208–215, 222–225, 233, 235, 240, 241, 246–248, 253, 258, 259, 267, 282, 283, 285, 287–291
ridge regression, 7, 211, 258, 290
RMSE, 162, 262
ROC, 227, 229, 230

## S

sdev, 199, 271
select, 336
sigmoid, 7, 220, 223, 235, 239, 246, 249, 250, 254, 255, 314
signum, 178
silhouette, 5, 68, 79–81, 313
sin, 314, 335
softmax, 7, 254, 255
sparkline, 8, 334, 336, 337
sparse matrix, xx, 8, 303, 304, 307–310
sparse tensor, 306, 307
sqrt, 26, 39
SSB, 53
SSE, 53
ssr, 115
SSW, 53
stochastic gradient descent, 7, 205–207, 287, 289, 292
stochastic matrix, 298
sum, 23, 266, 272, 285, 315, 324
supervised learning, 5, 6, 11, 12, 32, 91

## T

Taxicab distance, 21
tensor, 209, 210, 304–307, 333
til, 18, 206, 213
TPR, 123, 227

## U

unsupervised learning, 11, 107

## V

vanishing-gradient problem, 7, 244, 250, 251

## W

wavg, 33
where, 288
wsfull, 28, 187
wsum, 25

# Acknowledgments

First and foremost I thank my family. You have provided endless support and inspiration. And Jasmine, for the late nights spent typing away by your hospital bedside, this book is for you. May your memory live on as your laughter lives within me. You taught me how important it is to have fun.

Thank you, Brett Bond, for suggesting I take the Coursera machine learning course. You started me on an amazing and fulfilling journey. Roy Lowrance, thank you for reading Q Tips and wishing q tables existed in Python. I took this as a challenge to bring machine learning algorithms to q.

A very special acknowledgment is required for Daniel Krizian. Your passion for kdb+ kept me going when I wondered who would want to use machine learning in q. This book has benefited from your steadfast dedication to testing every line of code, criticizing my naming conventions, recommending function refactoring and holding the library to a standard that even I thought was impossible.

Thank you Zhonghua Jiang and Jorge Sawyer. You stuck with me when the book was a jumble of disjointed chapters. Your early suggestions required multiple rewrites, but the end result was well worth the effort. Your machine learning knowledge kept me honest.

Alexandre Beaulne, working with you over the past two books has been an absolute honor. Your nightly page-by-page feedback kept me up late for over two months—thoroughly dedicated to making corrections. Your keen eye for formatting made me fix layout errors that would otherwise have slipped by. If only my automated spell and grammar checker were better, your job would have been much easier.

Years of close collaboration with Attila Vrabecz continued through the final stages of this book. Thank you for your pearls of wisdom, algorithm improvements, comment spell-checking and criticism of images that crossed pages. I spent days trying to fix that problem, and was finally able to extend the AsciiDoc toolchain to permit floating tables, figures, examples and equations.

Stephen Taylor, your typesetting suggestions were spot on. Who knew that French spacing, leading, measure and kerning could be so interesting. And Andrew Wilson, thank you for providing the final reading prior to publication. The book benefited from your collaboration and I look forward to further improvements to q under your machine learning guidance.

Christopher Aycock, Rebecca Kelly, Mark Lefevre, Ryan Sparks and Ye Tian, thank you for providing your support and feedback as the book came to completion.

Lastly, I would like to thank Kx Systems for creating q and their timely responses to all my questions, bug reports, and feature requests.

Of course, any errors that remain are my sole responsibility.

# About the Author

Nick Psaris has been developing trading and risk management platforms for over 20 years. After graduating from Duke University with a degree in Physics and Chinese, he began his career in finance at Morgan Stanley in New York. After obtaining his CFA charter in 2003 and a Masters in Computational Finance from the Tepper School of Business at Carnegie Mellon University in 2006, Nick moved to Hong Kong, where he learned q by building an equity portfolio trading and backtesting system.

Nick became hooked on the language and has been using q to develop systems ever since. After spending three years at Liquid Capital Markets Hong Kong building a high frequency automated market making system, he built an inventory optimization platform at a top tier American investment bank. Nick returned to New York in 2016 and built the data and analytics platform for the Central Risk Book team. He is now combining his love for data and machine learning to build a recommender engine.

Nick is an adjunct professor for Carnegie Mellon University's MSCF program, where he uses q to co-teach the Market Microstructure and Algorithm Trading class. In his spare time, Nick enjoys swimming, running and reading. He is passionate about donating blood and supporting pediatric cancer research to #DFYchildhoodCancers.

Made in the USA
Middletown, DE
29 September 2024